LIBRARY OF NEW TESTAMENT STUDIES

600

Formerly the Journal for the Study of the New Testament Supplement series

Editor
Chris Keith

Editorial Board
Dale C. Allison, John M.G. Barclay, Lynn H. Cohick, R. Alan Culpepper,
Craig A. Evans, Robert Fowler, Simon J. Gathercole, Juan Hernandez Jr.,
John S. Kloppenborg, Michael Labahn, Love L. Sechrest, Robert Wall,
Catrin H. Williams, Britanny Wilson

The New Testament in Comparison

Validity, Method, and Purpose in Comparing Traditions

Edited by John M. G. Barclay and B. G. White

LONDON • NEW YORK • OXFORD • NEW DELHI • SYDNEY

T&T CLARK
Bloomsbury Publishing Plc
50 Bedford Square, London, WC1B 3DP, UK
1385 Broadway, New York, NY 10018, USA
29 Earlsfort Terrace, Dublin 2, Ireland

BLOOMSBURY, T&T CLARK and the T&T Clark logo are trademarks of Bloomsbury Publishing Plc

First published in Great Britain 2020
This paperback edition published in 2021

Volume Editors' Part of the Work © John M. G. Barclay and B. G. White, 2020
Each chapter © of Contributor

John M. G. Barclay and Benjamin G. White have asserted their right under the Copyright, Designs and Patents Act, 1988, to be identified as Editors of this work.

All rights reserved. No part of this publication may be reproduced or transmitted in any form or by any means, electronic or mechanical, including photocopying, recording, or any information storage or retrieval system, without prior permission in writing from the publishers.

Bloomsbury Publishing Plc does not have any control over, or responsibility for, any third-party websites referred to or in this book. All internet addresses given in this book were correct at the time of going to press. The author and publisher regret any inconvenience caused if addresses have changed or sites have ceased to exist, but can accept no responsibility for any such changes.

A catalogue record for this book is available from the British Library.

A catalog record for this book is available from the Library of Congress.

ISBN: HB: 978-0-5676-8478-3
PB: 978-0-5677-0215-9
ePDF: 978-0-5676-8479-0
ePUB: 978-0-5676-8481-3

Series: Library of New Testament Studies, volume 600
ISSN 2513-8790

Typeset by RefineCatch Limited, Bungay, Suffolk

To find out more about our authors and books visit www.bloomsbury.com and sign up for our newsletters.

To Durham postgraduate students in New Testament, past and present

Contents

List of Contributors		viii
Translations		ix
Abbreviations		x
1	Introduction: Posing the Questions *John M. G. Barclay and B. G. White*	1
2	'O wad some Pow'r the giftie gie us, To see oursels as others see us!': Method and Purpose in Comparing the New Testament *John M. G. Barclay*	9
3	Making Friends and Comparing Lives *C. Kavin Rowe*	23
4	The Past is a Foreign Country: On the Shape and Purposes of Comparison in New Testament Scholarship *Troels Engberg-Pedersen*	41
5	The Possibility of Comparison, the Necessity of Anachronism and the Dangers of Purity *Dale B. Martin*	63
6	Beyond Compare, or: Some Recent Strategies for Not Comparing Early Christianity with Other Things *Matthew V. Novenson*	79
7	On Comparing, and Calling the Question *Margaret M. Mitchell*	95
8	A Response to Friend-Critics *C. Kavin Rowe*	125
9	Relational Hermeneutics and Comparison as Conversation *Jonathan A. Linebaugh*	143
10	Comparing Like with Like?: The New Testament in Its Christian Literary Environment *Francis Watson*	159
11	Resemblance and Relation: Comparing the Gospels of Mark, John and Thomas *Simon Gathercole*	173
Bibliography		193
Index of Modern Authors		203
Index of Subjects		206

List of Contributors

John M. G. Barclay is Lightfoot Professor of Divinity at the Department of Theology & Religion, Durham University (Durham, UK).

Troels Engberg-Pedersen is Professor Emeritus of New Testament at the Faculty of Theology, University of Copenhagen (Copenhagen, Denmark).

Simon Gathercole is Reader in New Testament at the Faculty of Divinity, University of Cambridge (Cambridge, UK).

Jonathan A. Linebaugh is Lecturer in New Testament at the Faculty of Divinity, University of Cambridge (Cambridge, UK).

Dale B. Martin is the Woolsey Professor Emeritus of Religious Studies at Yale University (New Haven, CT).

Margaret M. Mitchell is Shailer Mathews Distinguished Service Professor of New Testament and Early Christian Literature at the University of Chicago Divinity School (Chicago, IL).

Matthew V. Novenson is Senior Lecturer in New Testament and Christian Origins at the School of Divinity, University of Edinburgh (Edinburgh, UK).

C. Kavin Rowe is Professor of New Testament at the Duke University Divinity School (Durham, NC).

Francis Watson is Research Chair in Biblical Interpretation at the Department of Theology & Religion, Durham University (Durham, UK).

B. G. White is Assistant Professor of Biblical Studies at the Department of Religious & Theological Studies, The King's College (New York City, NY).

Translations

All translations of non-English texts are the authors', unless otherwise indicated.

The New Testament Greek utilized in this volume is from Barbara Aland et al., *Novum Testamentum Graece* (28th edn) (Stuttgart: Deutsche Bibelgesellschaft, 2012).

Abbreviations

All abbreviations, including those of biblical documents, are consistent with the *SBL Handbook of Style* (2nd edn) (Atlanta: SBL Press, 2014).

1

Introduction

Posing the Questions

John M. G. Barclay and B. G. White

To put ancient texts into comparison is not only a historical but also a *hermeneutical* procedure. Comparison seeks to elucidate the meaning of a text by placing it into a comparative frame with other texts or traditions: that act, and the means by which it is performed, is clearly a scholarly act of *interpretation*. Despite this, and notwithstanding the frequency with which New Testament scholars undertake such comparisons, it is surprising how rarely we have *reflected* on this procedure, its aims, methods and indeed its possibility. There have been surveys of scholarly projects of comparison, and a famous critique of 'parallelomania', but examples of deeper reflection on method and on the intellectual basis of the comparative procedure are few and far between.[1] The most important theoretical interventions on this topic have been provided by Jonathan Z. Smith, whose critical rigour and broad expertise in the comparative study of religion helped to expose weaknesses in some scholarship on the New Testament and early Christianity.[2] In fact, Smith performed a significant role in conceptualizing the task of 'comparative religion' at a time when its methods and, indeed, its legitimacy were brought into question – and with it, the legitimacy of 'Religious Studies' and 'the Anthropology of Religion'. Smith's initial stance was primarily critical of comparisons, questioning their often one-sided search for similarities and the quest for 'universal archetypes' in the work of Mircea Eliade and others. His balancing emphasis on difference, and his insistence that the comparative act is a scholarly *construction*, were soon subsumed within the postmodern storm

---

[1] For a survey of trends and large-scale comparative projects, see L. M. White and J. T. Fitzgerald, 'Quod erat comparandum: The Problem of Parallels', in J. T. Fitzgerald, T. H. Olbricht and L. M. White (eds), *Early Christianity and Classical Culture: Comparative Studies in Honor of Abraham J. Malherbe* (Leiden: Brill, 2003), 13–39. For well-known criticisms, see S. Sandmel, 'Parallelomania', *JBL* 81 (1962): 1–13.

[2] Among Smith's important contributions are the following: *Map is Not Territory: Studies in the History of Religions* (Chicago: University of Chicago Press, 1982); *Imagining Religion: From Babylon to Jonestown* (Chicago: University of Chicago Press, 1982); *To Take Place: Toward Theory in Ritual* (Chicago: University of Chicago Press, 1987); *Drudgery Divine: On the Comparison of Early Christianities and the Religions of Late Antiquity* (Chicago: University of Chicago Press, 1990). One of his last essays in the comparative mode was 'Re: Corinthians', in R. Cameron and M. P. Miller (eds), *Redescribing Paul and the Corinthians* (Atlanta: Society of Biblical Literature, 2011), 17–34.

that challenged the very notion of 'comparative religion' and the whole intellectual structure of anthropology. Within this larger critique, comparison now appeared both intellectually suspect, since it abstracts features of culture from their irreducibly particular context, and politically unacceptable, since it overwrites 'native' cultures by the imposition of Western hegemonic categories. In response, Smith came to soften his critique of comparativism, and to offer some constructive rules for its operation, and he thus became the guru for a chastened 'new comparativism' in the study of religion.[3] In this 'reconstructed' comparativism, both the possibility and the legitimacy of comparison are strongly asserted, though with careful attention to the particularity of each item compared, with full recognition of the scholarly artifice involved, and with openness to self-critical reflection and constant 'rectification'.[4] Moreover, whatever comparisons now take place, they are accompanied by alertness to the 'hybridization' of religious traditions, to the ways that modern selves (both objects and agents of comparison) are 'multiply situated', and to the *moral* significance of comparison at a time when friction between sometimes solipsistic traditions encourages the search for some process that enables communication and mutual understanding.

The exercise whereby New Testament scholars place their texts into comparison with others thus sits within a context of lively intellectual debate, from which we could and should learn much. It seems all too easy to perform comparisons, and alarmingly difficult to perform them well. The mere juxtaposition of texts or traditions can result in little or no illumination. The items to compare can be poorly chosen (being too different to make comparison fruitful), or the comparison can be one-sidedly weighted towards either similarity or difference, in a way that makes the results unbalanced. Comparison can be superficial or trivial, or can abstract individual motifs so far from their context as to render the comparison misleading. It can be conducted without any clear aim (and therefore clear result), or it can be governed by an apologetic or polemical agenda such that the results are determined from the beginning. The categories used in comparison can be culturally over-determined, while loaded claims to 'uniqueness' can mask hidden value judgements about the superiority of the tradition so acclaimed.[5] The potential pitfalls are many. But if there is one theme that has emerged most strongly in the discussion of comparison in the last few decades, it is that any properly disciplined (as opposed to merely instinctive) comparison is, and should be recognized as, *a scholarly construct*, about which we should be highly self-

---

[3] See, for instance, the central role of his essay 'In Comparison a Magic Dwells' in K. C. Patton and B. C. Ray (eds), *A Magic Still Dwells: Comparative Religion in the Postmodern World* (Berkeley: University of California Press, 2000), 23–44. In an epilogue in that volume ('The "End" of Comparison: Redescription and Rectification', 237–41), Smith speaks of 'subsequent re-evaluations in my own work' (237), and acknowledges the influence of an essay by F. J. P. Poole ('the most suggestive article on comparison of the past two decades'): 'Metaphors and Maps: Towards Comparison in the Anthropology of Religion', *JAAR* 54 (1986): 411–57. Smith has not been without his critics, who include R. Segal in 'Classification and Comparison in the Study of Religion: The Work of Jonathan Z. Smith', *JAAR* 73 (2005): 1175–88.

[4] See, e.g., W. E. Paden, 'Elements of a New Comparativism', in Patton and Ray, *A Magic Still Dwells*, 182–92, a revised version of an essay under the same title published in *MTSR* 8 (1996): 5–14.

[5] This last is one of the points famously articulated in Smith's chapter 'On Comparison' in *Drudgery Divine* (36–53). It is not by accident that that chapter will be cited by most of the authors in this present volume.

conscious. In the much-cited words of Jonathan Smith: 'In the study of religion, as in any disciplined inquiry, comparison, in its strongest form, brings differences together within the space of the scholar's mind for the scholar's own intellectual reasons.'[6]

In this creative act, which Smith calls elsewhere 'a methodical manipulation of difference',[7] at least the following five challenges face the scholar at the outset of the enterprise:[8]

1. *Choosing what to compare.* The two (or more) phenomena placed into comparison clearly have to be similar enough to make comparison possible, and different enough to make it interesting, but it is not always easy to judge how these two criteria should be measured, and how they should be balanced. Comparisons that seem over-weighted by similarity *or* by difference are generally less satisfactory than those that give full weight to both. Comparisons that search for *genealogy* (e.g. the sources of ideas) obviously need to establish a historical relationship between the two phenomena, but it is widely recognized that an *analogical* comparison is equally valid, and is not bound by this historical criterion. Thus, for instance, one may usefully compare the letters of Paul with texts with which Paul has no genealogical relation and which post-date his life, provided that these texts have enough in common to justify their comparison.

2. *Selecting for the purpose of comparison.* Any comparison is partial: it is hardly possible or even useful to compare complete wholes with complete wholes. As Poole writes, 'Comparison does not deal with phenomena *in toto* or in the round, but only with an aspectual characteristic of them. Analytical control over the framework of comparison involves theoretically focused selection of significant aspects of the phenomena.'[9] But there are clearly dangers here: one may select something relatively trivial, or only superficially similar in the two phenomena, or far more important in one of them than in the other. The necessary selection is in itself a dangerous exercise, if it leaves the larger contexts out of consideration: there is, it seems, an important dialectic between focused selection and the larger, contextual horizon of the items selected.

3. *Categorizing the items compared.* To put two items into comparison requires placing them *together* within a common category or frame, and this *third action* is necessarily an intellectual, scholarly construct. Baptism and circumcision might be analysed and compared as 'initiation rites', but whence comes that scholarly category 'rites', and what intellectual baggage does it bring? Some categories are so familiar that we hardly notice that they are loaded with historical and philosophical assumptions: culture, gender, person, politics, art and, of course, religion. Within 'religion', we have created all kinds of categories that might, or might not, mislead: mysticism, sacrifice, rite, myth, magic, the numinous, the sacred and, not least, 'God/god'. It is impossible to operate without some such analytical tools; the danger is that their intellectual heritage might

---

[6] Smith, 'On Comparison', 51.
[7] Smith, 'In Comparison a Magic Dwells', 40, as reprinted in Patton and Ray (eds), *A Magic Still Dwells*.
[8] See also the 12 Propositions advanced by Margaret M. Mitchell in Chapter 7.
[9] Poole, 'Metaphors and Maps', 414.

obscure or alter the meaning of the phenomena being considered.[10] The fraught relationship between Western rationalism and religion makes this danger particularly acute, but the problem is inescapable. Anachronistic labels can be helpful, or hugely problematic, but deciding which is which is a judgement call.[11] The use of a category that is not native to the item being discussed is a sign of our scholarly *control* over the discussion, and no analysis can avoid the use of such power. To decide where this power enables the text to speak well, and where it *overpowers* or distorts the text will always be a matter of scholarly judgement.

4. *Determining the purpose of the comparison.* Every comparison has an agenda, and openness and self-consciousness about that agenda is always better than the opposite. Some comparisons are designed to illuminate only one of the *comparanda*, others to illuminate both, but in either case it is best to articulate the purpose of the illumination and to be self-critical in that articulation, lest the whole exercise be determined by an anticipated result. Implicit bias can take many forms – cultural, moral and religious – and it is always worth asking how one's own interests might shape the results.

5. *Measuring degrees of similarity or difference.* If no two cultural or religious items are completely similar, some may certainly be more similar than others. It is difficult, however, to give a generalized, 'overall' measure of such things, and it may be misleading to do so. X may be more like Y than it is like Z in certain respects, but there may well be other respects in which it is more like Z. Similarity and difference is always 'in respect of' something, and bringing a third phenomenon into the picture helps to show where similarities and differences are most striking. It is, however, another matter to judge how to weight the significance of the varying points of similarity and difference. Luke may be more like Mark than it is like John in many respects, but not in respect of their resurrection narratives. Is that significant? Significant to whom or for what purpose? In historical terms? In theological terms? The more we are clear about how and why we make such judgements the better. Blanket statements about the 'distinctiveness' of a collection of texts are generally based on a judgement that *weighs* what they have in common with one another as more significant than what differentiates them, and then places their differences from other texts above their points of similarity with them. It is good to be aware of that, and to be ready to defend decisions of this kind.

At all of these points there are scholarly choices to be made, scholarly purposes to be examined and explained, and scholarly constructions at play. Comparison, we might say, is a hermeneutical art, at least as much an 'invention' as a 'discovery'. Of course, none of this attention given to this hermeneutical act should lessen, at all, the closest

---

[10] See the remarks by Smith, 'The "End" of Comparison', 239: 'The second task of description is that of reception-history, a careful account of how *our* second-order scholarly tradition has intersected with the exemplum. That is to say, we need to describe how the datum has become accepted as significant for the purpose of argument.'

[11] See, for instance, the discussion of this topic by Dale B. Martin in Chapter 5.

and most profound attention to the texts (or other cultural items) being examined. Nothing can be substituted for the hard work of getting deep into the material being compared, understanding it, as far as possible, on its own terms. But when we come to comparison, we are not simply discerning what is 'in' the text; we are creating a connection with another text in which we dictate the terms of the comparison. Some comparative procedures may, no doubt, seem more 'intrusive' than others, but it would be naïve to ignore our agency in this task, which operates in all of the five areas outlined earlier.

All of the above judgement calls receive discussion in the course of this volume, but many of these essays also press beyond these procedural questions to consider the philosophical foundations undergirding the hermeneutical act of comparison, foundations that are, in fact, basic to the humanities and social sciences in the modern world. Indeed, because comparison is a hermeneutical act, all the questions posed earlier open up to, or expose, a set of deeper questions about knowledge, reason and the role of the interpreter. These questions were common, especially in relation to 'religion', from the start of the Enlightenment, as Jonathan A. Linebaugh's essay makes clear in his reading of Johann Georg Hamann. They were central to the twentieth-century debate about hermeneutics between Gadamer and Habermas, as elucidated here by Troels Engberg-Pedersen. And they have surfaced in a distinctive post-modern (or post-liberal) form, inspired by Wittgenstein and MacIntyre, as evidenced here in C. Kavin Rowe's essays, and in the essays of some of his critics. These debates run right through the humanities and social sciences, but it is rare to find them articulated and explored (as they deserve to be) among New Testament scholars. It is not accidental that it is the topic of comparison that brings them to the surface, because here, as we have seen, the hermeneutical issues are clear and the stakes are high.

The philosophical issues cluster around the question: to what degree is comparison possible? That is, can one *understand* more than the tradition one inhabits oneself? Or, to the contrary, can one understand one's own tradition and beliefs *only* by stepping, to some degree, outside of them? To pose these provocative questions is to ask what it means to 'understand'. Is this a matter of exercising and developing a universally available reason, common to all at least in its procedures, or is even *that* form of reason culturally and historically specific? Or does understanding in its full form require particular and therefore non-universal 'participation'? Since we stand at a historical and cultural distance from the New Testament, however much we may claim to belong to its 'tradition', some measure of 'detachment' in historical terms may seem inevitable and, on some reckonings, desirable. Or is 'detachment' in fact both an illusion and a loss? Is the reader always in some kind of relationship to the text, and is that dialogical relationship actually what makes a reading both interesting and good? The philosophical opinions that swirl around these questions in the course of this volume touch on many significant and urgent issues. Is the Enlightenment goal of cultivating a universal reason still intact, or are there deep cultural and religious incompatibilities among human beings ('multiverses', as some would say) that render it illusory? How radical is the incommensurability between 'worlds' that some would assert? Would the claim that lived traditions are, at the deepest level, simply incomparable or untranslatable render invalid the 'humanistic' project of mutual understanding, and would that have dire results, intellectually, politically and morally? Is religion particularly recalcitrant with regard to modern notions of reason, because of its strong claims to revelation or transcendence? Can we make 'progress' in the study of religion, or is every step forward in one respect a step backwards in another? And does the scholarly study of religion (including comparative religion) perform an important political and cultural task in our current world context, or does it represent an attempt to overpower religions by framing them in its own, alien, terms? More generally, how can we negotiate cultural and religious difference well in the contemporary world, and does the use of comparison help or hinder, clarify or obscure this delicate task?

The purpose of this volume is to reflect deeply on the exercise of comparison in relation to New Testament studies, and in so doing not to reach a consensus, but at least to expose some critical questions. The essays collected here mostly began as papers presented at a conference in Durham, UK, in June 2017. The initiative for the conference arose from discussion among postgraduate students at Durham University about the comparative exercises they were undertaking in their doctoral theses, and it owes much to the focusing of those questions by Tavis Bohlinger, in conversation with our former colleague, Dr T. J. Lang (now at St Andrews). Justin Allison and Ben White helped greatly in developing the agenda and setting up the conference, and the latter has had a special role in the editing of this volume.[12] The intellectual passion of these postgraduate students has sustained this project from its inception through the practicalities of the conference to the creation of this book, its published product. As the conference questions became sharper, C. Kavin Rowe's book *One True Life*[13] supplied a particular stimulus, both throughout the conference and in these essays, although these are shaped by a wider range of questions about comparison: they include responses to his usefully provocative work but are not limited by that remit. The conference proved to be a site of intense discussion and strong disagreement, amid mutual and collegial respect, and all the essays initially presented at the conference have been developed in the light of those conversations. Three essays (by Simon Gathercole, Jonathan A. Linebaugh, and Matthew V. Novenson) were commissioned after the conference, adding to the spectrum of perspectives.

The ten essays in this volume have been arranged in clusters, but are not divided into sections, as there is too much interconnection in theme and substance to allow for neat divisions. John M. G. Barclay's essay opens the conversation by exploring the value of comparison in helping us to see the familiar (including ourselves) from a different angle. C. Kavin Rowe then highlights a set of issues (developed from his *One True Life*) concerning comparisons of traditions that involve truth claims for their way of being in the world: narrative, the significance of incommensurable forms of life, understanding and opacity, and friendship. This is followed by Troels Engberg-Pedersen, who explores how comparison in New Testament studies is best described and justified, and its purposes defined; in the process, he identifies some of the key philosophical and

---

[12] Ben would like to note his gratitude to his diligent faculty assistant at The King's College, Aspen Scafa, who assisted with several features of this book, especially the bibliography.
[13] C. Kavin Rowe, *One True Life: The Stoics and Early Christians as Rival Traditions* (New Haven: Yale University Press, 2016).

hermeneutical issues that underlie this exercise. Dale B. Martin defends the possibility of comparison, and the necessity of (some forms of) anachronism, and Matthew V. Novenson challenges the claims to 'distinctiveness' that often arise in comparative exercises. Margaret Mitchell emphasises the significance of comparison as an intellectual and rhetorical exercise in early Christianity, and gives a careful analysis of one of its developed literary forms, the *Protrepticus* of Clement of Alexandria. She then offers twelve important propositions about academic comparison in the study of the New Testament and ancient Christianity, and finishes with a robust critique of Kavin Rowe's *One True Life*. C. Kavin Rowe then replies to his critics in this volume, and develops further his own views. At this point, the conversation is taken in a new direction by Jonathan A. Linebaugh, who draws on the work of Johann Georg Hamann to expound a 'relational hermeneutics', using the image of a 'conversation' to figure comparison as less a method than a mode of relating that properly involves the person who facilitates the conversation. Francis Watson makes the case for comparing New Testament texts with early Christian texts outside the canon, regardless of their date, while Simon Gathercole rounds out the volume with a discussion of method and goal in comparison, worked through in an outline comparison between the gospels of Mark, John and Thomas.

Between them, these essays pass to and fro between particular examples of comparison and the wider discussion of method and theory, weaving a tapestry of scholarly conversation that is broad ranging but also closely focused. We hope that others will find these discussions as stimulating as we have ourselves, and that this volume will provide a catalyst for continuing reflection on comparisons in New Testament and early Christian studies (and in other fields besides): what comparisons are, what they are for, to what extent they are possible, and how to perform them best. Thus the volume circles back to its genesis in the questions of postgraduate students, whose research often works at the 'coalface' of comparison creation. May they – and all of us – find in this volume both inspiration and wisdom for probing the foundational issues of the comparative enterprise.

2

'O wad some Pow'r the giftie gie us, To see oursels as others see us!'[1]

Method and Purpose in Comparing the New Testament

John M. G. Barclay

What is the use of comparisons? It is clear that everyday life and very many conceptual operations entail processes of comparison, but these can be put to many different uses, and it is incumbent on scholars to be clear why they are conducting this mental operation. With the purpose comes the method: there is no one comparative method, but a variety of possible procedures that can serve a range of ends. In some of his most important and most suggestive comments on this topic, Jonathan Z. Smith has noted that: 'In the case of the study of religion, as in any disciplined inquiry, comparison, in its strongest form, brings differences together within the space of the scholar's mind for the scholar's own intellectual reasons.'[2] Referring in this context to 'the scholar's interest, be this expressed in a question, a theory, or a model', he concludes:

> A comparison is a disciplined exaggeration in the service of knowledge. It lifts out and strongly marks certain features within difference as being of possible intellectual significance, expressed in their being 'like' in some stipulated fashion. Comparison provides the means by which *we* 'revision' phenomena as *our* data in order to solve *our* theoretical problems.[3]

As the italics indicate, the stress here is on scholarly comparison as a created, strategic phenomenon, with an intellectual purpose. But Smith is right to leave open what that purpose might be, since there are many different ends to which this procedure can be put. My purpose in this essay is to hold up for consideration *one* possible purpose for comparison, which is to see the familiar in a new light ('to see ourselves as others see

---

[1] Robert Burns, 'To a Louse', in Robert Burns, *Poems and Songs*, ed. J. Kinsley (Oxford: Oxford University Press, 1969), 157.
[2] J. Z. Smith, *Drudgery Divine: On the Comparison of Early Christianities and the Religions of Late Antiquity* (Chicago: University of Chicago Press, 1990), 51.
[3] Smith, *Drudgery Divine*, 53, italics original.

us') and thereby to generate the possibility of new understandings, including better understandings of ourselves as the people conducting the comparison and of the frames and tools by which we conduct that comparison. It is this reflexive procedure, both in defamiliarizing our own assumptions, and in unsettling the very concepts by which we compare, that has made one anthropologist relabel comparison as a kind of 'controlled equivocation',[4] and that may prove to be, at many different levels, one of the most beneficial effects of the whole comparative exercise.

I will start with an analysis of one example of comparison from antiquity (Josephus' *Against Apion*), in order to identify three key moves in comparison (selection, generalization and redescription), to assess Josephus' purpose, and to ask whether anything new was learned by this procedure (and if not, why not). I will then explore how comparison, better conducted, might give us the opportunity to see the familiar (one's self, or a well-known tradition) from a new perspective – that is, not necessarily a *better* perspective, but a different one, from which one may choose to learn. With a brief illustration from my own research on Paul and gift, I will finish by summarizing and evaluating the benefits of the comparative procedure.

Josephus and the procedures and goals of comparison

The ancient Greeks loved comparisons. The different city states compared themselves to each other, in their practices and beliefs; they compared their (imagined) past with their present; and as they traded and colonized all over the Mediterranean world, they compared themselves with the others they encountered. Herodotus is the most famous of the ancient comparativists, with his nuanced and even self-critical comparisons of Greeks and Egyptians (*Histories* book 2), but elements of this comparative urge are found all over the Greek (and then Roman) intellectual map.[5] I will focus here on just one example of this comparative activity as adapted by the Jewish historian, Josephus – a good reminder, if we needed it, that ancient Judaism was by no means hermetically sealed as a cultural tradition, even when describing itself.

In the course of his presentation of the Jewish/Judaean people in his *Contra Apionem*, Josephus presents their cultural configuration as a *politeuma*, and compares it in various respects with the *politeumata* of the Athenians and Spartans (*Contra Apionem* 2.145–286).[6] The comparison is pursued in multiple aspects: Moses is a founding figure of the Jewish constitution, like Lycurgus in Sparta or Solon in Athens, only more ancient and of impeccable character (2.151–63); in their styles of government, other constitutions operate by monarchy, aristocracy, or democracy, but Jews use a

---

[4] Eduardo Viveiros de Castro, 'Perspectival Anthropology and the Method of Controlled Equivocation', *Tipiti: Journal for the Society for the Anthropology of Lowland South America* 2 (2004): 3–22.

[5] For a recent overview, challenging notions that the ancients were always derogatory about 'others', see E. S. Gruen, *Rethinking the Other in Antiquity* (Princeton: Princeton University Press, 2011).

[6] For detail, see my *Flavius Josephus: Translation and Commentary Volume 10: Against Apion* (Leiden: Brill, 2007) (hereafter: *Josephus Against Apion*). On the near-synonyms *politeuma* and *politeia* in this context, see *Josephus Against Apion*, 249, note 534.

different system, the rule of God, with a specially coined label, 'theocracy' (2.164–71);[7] the Spartan constitution operates by practices, the Athenian by words (laws), while the Jewish is a combination of the two (2.171–74); other constitutions place *eusebeia* as one of the virtues, but the Jewish constitution makes all virtues a subset of *eusebeia* (2.170–1, 181). The most developed point of comparison concerns the boundaries of religious toleration (2.258–70), where the infamous Spartan practice of 'foreigner deportation' is rehearsed, and where several famous cases of Athenian intolerance are described (e.g. the trial of Socrates), in order to show that it is not unreasonable for Jews to have some religious boundaries, in beliefs and practices, and that, by comparison, the Jewish attitudes to others and their beliefs are a lot more measured.

Josephus professes himself forced into these comparisons by the vicious accusations levelled against Jews by Apollonius Molon (2.147, 255–7). This was not the first time he had portrayed the Jewish laws as a constitution (cf. *Antiquities* book 4), but it was the first time he had made such extensive use of the Greek tradition of comparison. We will return later to his apologetic purpose, and how this has affected his comparisons, but it will be helpful first to identify some of the key features of the comparative method and its results.

First, setting up the comparison requires Josephus to *select* certain characteristics of the Jewish tradition out of its mass of details and traditions. 'Constitutional' analysis allows him to cover a large cultural terrain, but there is nothing said in this context about (for instance) such core Jewish practices as Scripture interpretation, because *for these comparative purposes* such features were not strictly relevant. Many elements of the law (e.g. male circumcision) are also left to one side: it is simply impossible to compare everything at once, and even such a broad-brush comparison as this requires strategic selectivity.

Second, in order to make the comparison work, Josephus has to *generalize* certain features of the Jewish tradition: Moses is not just Moses (unique and singular) but a 'legislator' (*nomothetēs*), comparable to Lycurgus, Solon and Zaleukos, similar even in their claims to divine authorship of their laws (2.153–63); Jewish devotion to God is a form of 'piety' (*eusebeia*) comparable to that of others, and their social legislation a form of 'benevolence' (*philanthrōpia*, 2.146). Categories have to be chosen or created, and labels applied, that provide the shared basis, the *tertium quid* in respect of which two or more things can be compared.

Third, the comparison requires a form of *redescription*. The terms *politeuma* or *politeia* are not 'native' to the Jewish tradition, and constitute a novel way of structuring and describing its contents, but they derive from an intellectual tradition of political theory that was the nearest equivalent to social-scientific theory in the ancient world. Of course, that tradition was not culturally 'neutral', a perspective gained 'from nowhere': it arose from the Greek tradition and had various inbuilt Greek assumptions. All redescriptions have their own intellectual heritage. Nonetheless, through such comparison, with its angles of perception different from those native to Jewish tradition, Josephus is able to identify certain features of that tradition that might not

---

[7] For discussion of what Josephus means by this self-conscious neologism, see Josephus, *Against Apion*, 262–63, note 638.

have been seen in any other way: the role of God, Temple and priests in the Jewish political order, for instance, and the social significance of the Jewish limits of association in marriage, meals and the home.

All of this is slanted, of course, by Josephus to indicate Jewish superiority. His comparison has, in this text, an explicitly *apologetic* purpose, which entails both praise of Jewish virtue and polemical attacks on the inadequacies of others.[8] The distinction of the Jewish constitution from others, in its unique form of 'theocracy', is intended to show its higher value, with all the loaded and biased claims that can be hidden, as J. Z. Smith has shown, in claims to 'uniqueness'.[9] By trading on generalities without rigour or precision (e.g. the antithesis between 'words' and 'deeds'), Josephus can make sweeping claims that trade on ancient stereotypes but have no basis in history or social reality. The comparison between Jewish attitudes to non-Jews and the Spartan 'foreigner-deportation' is far-fetched, and not a comparison of like-for-like: the basis of comparison is here too imprecise to reveal much about either society. And so on. Even so, despite these gross deficiencies in the comparative method, one might say that *some* fresh light is here shone on the Jewish tradition by, for instance, forcing Josephus to clarify exactly where (and to some extent why) Jews did traditionally put limits on certain kinds of interaction with non-Jews (e.g. in marriage). From a modern, scholarly, perspective, the comparison is disappointing, but if it does nothing else, it points out the potential for a comparison to require an insider to reframe his/her tradition and to identify and analyse in new ways what makes it what it is. And in Josephus' case, the purpose of all this was to build bridges of mutual understanding between Jews and other residents in Rome; his representation of Judaism serves to both honour and explain the beliefs and commitments of his fellow Jews at a time and in a place of extreme sensitivity and tension.[10] That communicative benefit in comparison is not to be derided, and is a feature to which we will return at the end.

What I have picked out here – selection, generalization and redescription – are the core methods recognized by contemporary theorists of the scholarly procedure of comparison, although there is no standard terminology in such matters. It is generally agreed that comparison as analogy should be distinguished from genealogy. Although phenomena that are related by historical connection (derivation, influence or borrowing) can be compared, comparison itself does not depend on genealogical connection and should be theoretically distinguished from it. In other words, comparison is not answering the question of *origins*, tracing the sources or history of ideas: it is to be distinguished from tradition-history, although in New Testament scholarship these have often been confused.[11] Two things can be compared even if they are separated by time

---

[8] For the apologetic genre of the whole work (explicit in 2.147), see *Josephus Against Apion*, xxx–xxxvi.
[9] Smith, *Drudgery Divine*, 36–53.
[10] On the context and purpose of this work, see *Josephus Against Apion*, xxxvi–liii.
[11] In the long discussion about early Christianity and the 'mystery religions', the comparison was entangled with the question of 'borrowing' and 'connection' – such that the comparison could be prematurely dismissed if it were proved that the mystery religions were *later* phenomena. As Smith comments, 'It is as if the only choices the comparativist has are to assert either identity or uniqueness, and that the only possibilities for utilizing comparisons are to make assertions regarding dependence' (*Drudgery Divine*, 47). In fact, chronological connection or contemporaneity are not strictly relevant to comparison, even if the comparison is likely to be thicker and more multi-faceted if the *comparanda* are drawn from similar cultural and historical contexts.

and context. It might, in fact, be illuminating to put New Testament texts into comparison with *later* phenomena (Mithraism, for instance, or other early Christian texts, or rabbinic texts); they do not have to be contemporary.¹² Similarly, one does not have to establish some genealogical connection between, say, early Christian thought and Epicurean philosophy to be able to offer a worthwhile comparison between them. It is also now agreed that comparison is not just juxtaposition – the placing of two or more phenomena side by side. One needs to perform some scholarly operation on the phenomena other than just describe them in their own terms and place them alongside each other. And it is increasingly recognized (not least following the work of Smith) that an interesting comparison requires both similarity and difference, and not just one or the other. As Poole put it, 'Difference makes a comparative analysis interesting; similarity makes it possible.'¹³ Where Smith challenged the modernist tendency to focus only on similarity (especially the search for universal archetypes in the work of Mircea Eliade and others), the 'new comparativism' challenges postmodern claims for incommensurable particularity (cultural difference that 'goes all the way down'): recognizing both similarity and difference, and giving due weight to each, seems now an essential component of any worthwhile comparative enterprise.¹⁴

What, then, are these three ingredients of the comparative enterprise, as an intellectual operation? We may consider each in turn:

1. *Selection.* 'Comparison does not deal with phenomena *in toto* or in the round, but only with an aspectual characteristic of them.'¹⁵ Selection is part of what Smith calls 'the methodical manipulation of difference',¹⁶ and it is both a necessary and a potentially distorting procedure. It is necessary not only because nothing can be described *in toto*, let alone two things compared in that form, but also (more positively) because selection allows a focused attention where, within similarity, a specific form of difference can be shown to be particularly significant. It would neither be possible nor (for comparative purposes) interesting to describe *every dimension* of the life of Jews in the first century (for instance, whether or not they wore sandals).¹⁷ It *is* interesting, however, to examine their social boundaries, and the extent to which these were, or were not, identical to those of other ethnic groups. But selection is also, of course, potentially hazardous if one abstracts, in

---

¹² On comparisons among early Christian texts, whatever their date, see Chapter 10 by Francis Watson and Chapter 11 by Simon Gathercole in this volume.
¹³ F. J. P. Poole, 'Metaphors and Maps: Towards Comparison in the Anthropology of Religion', *JAAR* 54 (1986): 411–57, at 417. This essay was a significant influence on Smith, as the latter acknowledges, and is properly alive to the philosophical issues underlying questions of identity, similarity and difference.
¹⁴ On the interaction between anthropology and postmodernism in this connection, see Kimberly C. Patton and Benjamin C. Ray (eds), *A Magic Still Dwells: Comparative Religion in the Postmodern Age* (Berkeley: University of California Press, 2000).
¹⁵ Poole, 'Metaphors and Maps', 414.
¹⁶ Smith, 'In Comparison a Magic Dwells', 40. I cite from the republication of this essay in Patton and Ray (eds), *A Magic Still Dwells*, 23–44.
¹⁷ Perhaps someone will identify a way in which sandal-wearing *is* significant; I simply mean that, to my knowledge, there is no current frame of analysis which makes the selection of this practice intellectually interesting.

the sense of *isolates*, the selected feature from its larger cultural matrix. As Poole puts it, any religious phenomena we might be interested in (and 'religious' is of course a controversial classification) are 'intricately suspended in broader webs of cultural significance and subtly embedded in wider arrays of social institutions'.[18] New Testament scholarship is replete with examples of motif comparison which have isolated particular concepts (or words) from their cultural and social context and thereby produced thin, and sometimes misleading, comparisons that fail to understand the wider cultural significance of the items compared. Thus any (necessary) selection should sooner or later *open up to* a much broader contextual analysis, textual or social (or both). In textual terms, this means examining whole texts (or textual corpora); in social terms, examining the social location and function of the *comparanda* in a wider perspective, from which apparently similar things may look more different than one had originally thought, and apparently different things surprisingly similar. And that cultures are not just structures of thought but of life (practices embedded in social and existential realities) is something of which we need to be constantly reminded.[19] Nonetheless, selection is necessary and valuable as a strategic element of comparison; but it does not have to result in 'abstraction' or 'extraction', if the analysis properly keeps returning to a wider frame.

2. *Generalization.* Even within a single tradition we manage the mass of data by grouping them under fewer, more generalized, categories. Paul, famously, groups many different phenomena under the category 'flesh' (in a way his interlocutors probably did not recognize or like), just as he (and other Jews) lumped all the various non-Jewish peoples together under the label 'the nations'. There is, therefore, nothing inherently odd or suspicious in the use of 'second-order' categories, and these prove to be essential tools for bringing out (or, rather, constructing) the shared basis on which two things can be compared. Catholics (and others) go to the shrine of St Iago de Compostela, just as Muslims go to Mecca. To describe these both as forms of 'pilgrimage' is to provide a basis for comparison, which may bring out some illuminating structural similarities between them, while also showing that they are in important respects very different. In the study of religion, we necessarily deal in such generalizations all the time: symbol, sacrifice, ritual, gender, ethnicity, asceticism, sacred space, myth, deity, and so on, not to mention religion itself. That some of these categories come under critical scrutiny themselves is part of the self-reflective process of scholarship, and in the course of time some generalizations become too problematic for further use (e.g. 'race' or 'magic'). But that some classificatory generalizations are both necessary and valuable for comparison is clear.[20] Even

---

[18] Poole, 'Metaphors and Maps', 411.

[19] This is a major, and helpful, emphasis (in relation to Stoicism and early Christianity) of C. Kavin Rowe, *One True Life: The Stoics and Early Christians as Rival Traditions* (New Haven: Yale University Press, 2016).

[20] Cf. Poole again: 'both indigene and analyst *create* contexts (of different kinds and for different purposes) that reduce some of the singularity of events for pragmatic or philosophical ends and by analytic, classificatory means', 'Metaphors and Maps', 417.

Rowe, who stresses the incommensurability and 'untranslatability' of lived traditions, eventually places Stoicism and early Christianity into a common comparative structure by referring to the 'narratives', 'commitments' and 'existential barriers' (256) operative in their 'total way of life' or 'pattern of life'; these constitute, in his *constructed* system, points at which they really *can* be compared, even if only to bring out their difference.[21] Of course, such generalizations (usually in the form of abstract nouns) name only categories or classifications, not social or cultural realia themselves, in their irreducible differences. They refer, we should remind ourselves, to phenomena that are always embedded in social practice and specific cultural traditions, but that does not render them illegitimate as intellectual tools for the purpose of comparison.[22]

3. *Redescription*. This is the most controversial aspect of comparison, but also, at least for certain purposes (and here purpose and method intertwine), one of the most valuable. It is possible, of course, to stay within the generalized categories or classifications of one tradition, but that would lead to placing both *comparanda* on the template of only one, with the risk of skewing the interpretation of the other. Moreover, as Poole puts it, 'to encapsulate an analysis within a single religious system – and thus within the semantic networks of the religion's own terms, categories, and understandings – entangles the analysis with the very discourse it seeks to interpret and explain'.[23] To stay within the terms of one tradition (i.e. to resist redescription) is sometimes described by comparativists, in derogatory terms, as succumbing to the 'myopia' or 'tunnel vision' of that tradition.[24] That suggests that a perspective from outside is somehow superior just by being external, and the case for redescription does not need to be loaded in this way. An internal perspective, perfectly valid in its own right and even 'analytical' in its own way, is necessary singular; what happens when we use categories different to those

---

[21] E.g. Rowe, *One True Life*, 235: 'They agree that living is the way that one comes to know the truth of the world; and they agree that one cannot come to know this truth apart from living in the pattern of life in which this truth is learned.' Here and elsewhere Rowe notably eschews categories derived from the social sciences or other scholarly apparatus used in the contemporary study of religion, but he employs categories of his own (with echoes from the Christian tradition) that remain relatively unexamined and undefined: what, for example, is 'the truth of the world' or 'the pattern of life'? Apart from being relatively undefined and imprecise, these may operate at too high a level of generalization as to be useful as tools for analysis and comparison.

[22] Rowe finds fault with the category 'morality' by asking, 'What is morality itself, or morality in general? And where is it to be found? Can anyone live the moral life in general? What would such a life look like? ... Morality as such is an abstraction that modern linguistic habits present to us as a possibility for thought; upon inspection, however it turns out to be impossible to conceive. Try all you'd like; you'll only be able to come up with particular exemplifications of the thing you think you seek' (*One True Life*, 192–3). The same could be said, of course, for 'pattern of life' (Rowe's category): can one conceive it without giving a particular exemplification of it? The fact that 'morality' is a modern intellectual construct, and an abstract noun, does not at all disqualify it from being intellectually useful. Of course, no one could live 'morality in general', but it could still be a useful category by which to group and compare particular ways of living. Whether one prefers to call this 'morality' or 'practice' or 'pattern of life' is a different matter; the point is that abstractions are both necessary and valuable for organizing thought (which is all they can properly claim to do).

[23] Poole, 'Metaphors and Maps', 413.

[24] See, e.g., William E. Paden, who speaks of 'liberation from the myopia of single-culture analysis': 'Elements of a New Comparativism', in Patton and Ray (eds), *A Magic Still Dwells*, 182–92 (at 189).

indigenous to a tradition is not a privileged discovery of its 'real' meaning, but the addition of *another* perspective, with multiple potential benefits. Max Müller (1823–1900), one of the founders of 'comparative religion', is famous for having said, 'He who knows one (religion), knows none.'[25] This is misleading (and typically modernist) if it implies that a religion's own knowledge of itself somehow does not count as 'knowledge'. It would be more accurate to say that whoever knows only one religion, knows only one way of knowing it. What the academic procedure of comparison offers, when it uses comparative categories that come from outside any single tradition, is a supplementary form of knowledge, not 'better' or 'deeper' or 'truer', simply different – and for that very reason, potentially advantageous (depending on one's purpose). To participate in 'the Lord's Supper' is to share in a meal in memory of, and participation with, Christ (on its own internal understanding). It is *also* (from a scholarly, outsider perspective) to participate in a social ritual, which can be compared with other identity-defining rituals in other religious traditions. That is not a truer or more adequate description of the Lord's Supper; it is simply different, and in its difference it allows us to see, and to understand, the same thing from a fresh angle.

On the understanding that all knowledge is situated, what scholarly comparison offers is (at its best) carefully theorized and precise tools for the redescription of both familiar and unfamiliar phenomena. These do not (or at least, should not) claim to 'discover' an underlying reality, but to reconstruct the phenomena intellectually, in a form different from their own already existent constructions of themselves.[26] It is his perception of comparison as purposeful *construct* that makes Smith's work so important in this field, and it is worth citing him again: 'comparison, in its strongest form, brings differences together within the space of the scholar's mind for the scholar's own intellectual reasons. It is the scholar who makes their cohabitation – their "sameness" – possible, not "natural" affinities or processes of history.'[27]

Because these scholarly tools are our invention for our purposes, they cannot claim to be timelessly or comprehensively adequate: there is no claim here to universal transparency or ultimate truth. In fact, it is best to regard such analytic tools as 'sensitizing concepts', start-up categories that launch a fresh way of approaching a phenomenon but that are always themselves open to modification, correction, or abandonment.[28] Knowing

---

[25] The formula was adapted from Goethe's statement about language: 'He who knows one language knows none.'

[26] Smith's emphasis on comparison as construct (see the following citation) made him look suspiciously 'postmodern' in the eyes of some. See, for instance, the criticism of Smith, with emphasis on 'discovery', by Robert A. Segal, 'Classification and Comparison in the Study of Religion: The Work of Jonathan Z. Smith', *JAAR* 73 (2005): 1175–88.

[27] *Drudgery Divine*, 51. As Aaron Hughes remarks, 'while the comparative act may be natural, specific comparisons are not' (*Comparison: A Critical Primer* (Sheffield: Equinox, 2017), 11).

[28] Smith describes the work of comparison as having four 'moments': thick description of two or more phenomena, and of their reception-history in relation to our second-order scholarly tradition; comparison of the exempla, 'with respect to some category, question, theory, or model of interest to us'; 'redescription of the exempla (each in light of the other)'; and finally, 'a rectification of the academic categories in relation to which they have been imagined', 'The "End" of Comparison: Redescription and Rectification', in Patton and Ray (eds), *A Magic Still Dwells*, 237–41 (at 239).

where they have come from, in the history of scholarship, is already to relativize them, and recognizing their fuzzy boundaries and inherent ambiguities is to render them malleable and open to adjustment in relation to the phenomena and with regard to the purpose of the comparison. Thus the redescription envisaged here, by means of a comparative analysis, is not a matter of unmasking the 'false consciousness' of the traditions compared, of providing a 'better' account of their meaning, or substituting for their own self-description something more veridical. But it is to create a new angle of perception, creating new aspects, and even new modes, of understanding.

It is worth repeating that these three elements of comparison are not properly viewed as overwriting, or invalidating, the ethno-concepts of the insider (emic) perspective. It is true that the study of religion has sometimes been conducted in that fashion, not least in functionalist (or other potentially reductionist) forms. And it is true that some concepts, such as 'myth' or 'magic', are popularly conceived as denying, or at least denigrating, the truth claims of the religion under analysis. But this is neither necessary nor helpful. One can properly believe in the truth of one's own 'myths' (sacred, explanatory narratives) and, for an insider, the Lord's Supper is no less significant for being labelled a 'ritual'. As Joachim Wach once asked, 'Does a ruby or an emerald sparkle less if called a jewel?'[29] What comparison, with its necessary use of etic concepts, helpfully provides is a second frame, and an alternative language, which equips us better to be, what we all now necessarily are, that is multiply situated selves (speaking in various voices, to various audiences, for various reasons). In other words, while a comparison that redescribes something very familiar, and perhaps existentially important, can be initially unnerving and destabilizing, it can also enable us to widen and diversify our understanding of the traditions we inhabit.

Coming back to ourselves from a different direction

We have noted how often Smith, following Poole, draws attention to the interests or purposes of scholars when he describes what goes on in comparison. He speaks of 'the scholar's own intellectual reasons' or 'the scholar's interest', and refers to a model for comparison being 'useful'; as we have seen, he speaks of revisioning phenomena 'in order to solve *our* theoretical problems'. Indeed, he finishes his most significant discussion of comparison with a paragraph on 'the scholar's intellectual purpose', closing in these terms: 'Lacking a clear articulation of purpose, one may derive arresting anecdotal juxtapositions or self-serving differentiations, but the disciplined constructive work of the academy will not have been advanced, nor will the study of religion have come of age.'[30]

One may wonder here what constitutes 'advance' and what model of maturity or evolution is implied by 'coming of age', but both of those depend on how one conceives, in general, the purpose of comparison. Smith himself leaves the matter wide open

---

[29] Cited by G. Weckman, 'Questions of Judgment in Comparative Religious Studies', in T. A. Idinopulos, B. C. Wilson and J. C. Hanges (eds), *Comparing Religions* (Leiden: Brill, 2006), 17–25 (at 21).

[30] *Drudgery Divine*, 51–3; last sentence from 53.

('whether explanatory or interpretative, whether generic or specific'), and in truth there are many possible uses to which comparison can be put. One could create comparative schemata in order to systematize, and thereby control, all the 'exotic' forms of religion one encounters – hence the critique of Western comparative religion as an inherently 'imperialist' discourse, based on the 'white mythology' of Western reason. Or one could use it to understand the other, making the unfamiliar less threatening and thereby less liable to prejudice or ignorant hostility – one thinks of the urgent need for secular and Christian Westerners to understand Islam by taking it out of boxes labelled 'irrational' or 'primitive'. But, as my title indicates, I want to focus here on another possible purpose of comparison, which is to provide an opportunity for those familiar with a tradition to become self-reflective, self-aware and even self-critical through the defamiliarizing techniques that result from the comparative method just described. Not all, of course, who study the New Testament or early Christianity inhabit that tradition, but most here enter ground with which they are, at least, already somewhat familiar. To study it historically (even without any comparative element) is already to appreciate one's distance from a phenomenon which one cannot truly inhabit 'just as it was'. To take just one example, the early Christian 'pattern of life' included slavery (that is, Christians owning slaves), which we now not only do not practise, but ideologically repudiate.[31] But to enter deeply into a comparative exercise, placing the historically situated early Christian sources into comparison with another sympathetically researched tradition from the ancient world (or, for that matter, with another form of their own tradition), will involve a redescription of both, adding another layer of defamiliarization. As Fernand Braudel (the French historian) once said, if you live in a foreign country for a year, you may not learn a great deal about that country, but when you return home you will be surprised by your increased comprehension of some of the most profound characteristics of your own homeland.[32] You did not understand these before as you do now, because you were too close to them, and knew them, in a sense, too well. Historical comparisons double this 'reverse culture-shock': they take us to the past (itself a 'foreign country'), and then to parts of the past with which we were quite unfamiliar, using redescriptive forms of analysis so as to place what we previously knew in a significantly new light. The journey never leaves us where we were before, either in our understanding of the other or in our comprehension of ourselves.

For an example of this defamiliarizing process, let me use, briefly, an example from my own research. The notion of 'grace' has been for so long familiar in the Christian tradition, and for Protestants at least so over-determined by Reformation interpretations of this theme, that it is difficult to escape a set of historically determined assumptions about its meaning in Paul. In loaded comparison with Judaism, where Christian 'grace' has been contrasted with Jewish 'works-righteousness', the theme has served Christian apologetics (and Protestant polemics against the Catholic tradition) in a way that has been both intellectually dubious and socially damaging. Arguably, even Sanders' effort

---

[31] For another example of our necessary dislocation from earliest Christianity (in regard to eschatology), see Chapter 4 in this volume by Troels Engberg-Pedersen.

[32] F. Braudel, 'History and the Social Sciences', in P. Burke (ed.), *Economy and Society in Early Modern Europe* (New York: Harper & Row, 1972), 11–42 (at 24).

to escape this legacy, in his comparative project, *Paul and Palestinian Judaism*, did not fully solve this problem, since his understanding of grace tended to fall back into Protestant assumptions, with 'grace' (thus defined) operative both in Judaism and in Paul.[33] A new frame was needed, and could be supplied relatively simply, by placing all this discourse into the anthropological category of 'gift'. By analysing, with the aid of anthropology and social history, the variety of ways in which gifts could be practised and conceptualized, it was possible to defamiliarize our modern, Western assumptions about gift and grace, and to put Paul's letters into comparison with other Second Temple Jewish texts in a way that was self-consciously *not* positioned within just one historical strand of interpretation. Although Paul, of course, has a genealogical relation to his Jewish heritage, the study analysed Jewish texts written both before and after his lifetime, since the issue was not what Paul drew from those texts, but how he stood in analogy to them. The selection of this one theme did not require 'abstraction', because it served only as a door into the analysis of whole texts. Some generalization was required (as different texts use different terms for relations anthropologists generalize as 'gift'), but this could be performed at a level not far 'above' the specific terms of each text. The resulting 'redescription' involved the identification of six possible 'perfections' of grace which, even if they are incomplete, have enabled readers to see Paul (and the history of his reception), together with his Jewish contemporaries, in a different light.[34]

How did this comparison, conducted on these terms, shed light on the familiar? It indicated, for instance, that to figure the prime gifts of God as incongruous in relation to the worth of their recipients was not 'natural' or necessary, but in fact somewhat atypical and problematic from a moral and theological point of view, raising deep questions about cosmic justice and the exercise of divine power. What sort of rationale could Paul provide, and what sort of answers could that have provided to those who considered an incongruous mercy a dangerous misreading of their shared Jewish tradition?[35] Further, by what process did Paul's particular construction of grace (as unconditioned gift) become taken for granted as the essential or necessary meaning of the term, such that, in the history of interpretation of Paul (or of Christianity influenced by him), texts that use the same 'grace' terminology to describe God's giving to *fitting* recipients have come to appear mistaken or bizarre? And what problematics did Paul's configuration of grace (and its accompanying rhetoric) create for his interpreters, not so much because of its ambiguities as because it seemed to create, even invite (Romans 9), awkward questions about divine justice, human agency and the moral ordering of the cosmos? In raising these and other questions, the familiar (the Protestant Paul) becomes something of a stranger, helping us to understand and to scrutinize what we thought we knew in significantly different ways.

---

[33] E. P. Sanders, *Paul and Palestinian Judaism: A Comparison of Patterns of Religion* (London: SCM Press, 1977); for a critique on this point, see my *Paul and the Gift* (Grand Rapids: Eerdmans, 2015), 151–8.

[34] For helpful, critical reviews, see, e.g., those by Margaret Mitchell and Joel Marcus in *JSNT* 39 (2017) 304–30 (with my response, 331–44).

[35] For some of the questions and challenges that might arise in relation to Paul once put into dialogue (comparison) with 4 Ezra, see John M. G. Barclay, 'Constructing a Dialogue: 4 Ezra and Paul on the Mercy of God', in M. Konradt and E. Schläpfer (eds), *Anthropologie und Ethik im Frühjudentum und im Neuen Testament* (Tübingen: Mohr Siebeck, 2014), 3–22 (at 17–20).

But what, we may ask, is the larger point in seeing the familiar differently and in raising new questions about it? The first thing to say is that to undertake a procedure of defamiliarization is not necessarily to *substitute* a new way of seeing for the old: it may have this effect (intentionally or otherwise), but its proper aim is not to overwrite but to supplement the knowledge regime inherent within the tradition itself.[36] Comparison conducted in these terms does not claim to understand things with an objective transparency, as if by stepping outside the tradition's own terms of reference it has acquired some more satisfactory viewpoint, a 'better' understanding that is more comprehensively 'true'. Since comparison involves a measure of generalization, and since it is common to describe this manoeuvre in spatial terms as moving up to a 'higher' level of analysis, it is easy to get the impression that one gains thereby a 'superior' vision of reality.[37] But traditions have their own generalizations, and an alternative viewpoint is equally situated, just different. The aim, then, is to give an *additional*, supplementary perspective that, precisely by being significantly different, enables participants in a tradition to be self-conscious and self-reflective, able to see themselves from more than one angle, and therefore to keep honest and flexible in their modes of thought. Mental flexibility and multi-perspectival adaptability is an important virtue in a context where religious traditions rub up against one another, with evident potential both for enormous benefit and for terrible harm.

Even within the same religious tradition, which often contains considerable diversity of viewpoint and life-pattern, the ability to both understand oneself and (simultaneously) relativize one's position is of enormous social benefit. Paul himself may be an example. Addressing Roman churches which were deeply divided over the observance of Jewish kosher and Sabbath laws, Paul was able both to articulate his own position and to make the mental leap to understand that, from another person's perspective, things might look very different: 'I know and am persuaded in the Lord Jesus that nothing is unclean in itself, but for someone who thinks that it is unclean, for him it is unclean' (Rom 14.14). The fact that Paul can shift between two modes of perception in this case is probably due to the fact that he himself used to think in terms of one, but now thinks in line with the other. It is his memory of his own past that enables him to treat it with seriousness and sympathy, in a way that he does not (and apparently cannot) do with regard to Greek or Roman perceptions of religion. It is that mental flexibility that enables Paul to see a way for believers of different cultural traditions to live together, without condemnation or scorn, and to recognize that people might genuinely honour Christ in a way different from his own. Paul was not a

---

[36] Contrast the claim advanced by Aaron W. Hughes, *Comparison: A Critical Primer* (Sheffield: Equinox, 2017), 53: 'the goal of comparison ought to be to undermine or destabilize identity, not further reinscribe it'. On my reading, identity may be enhanced or made more complex, but need not be undermined.

[37] Kimberley Patton rightly objects to the 'methodological condescension, which seeks to "overwrite" the claims about reality made by those who were or are themselves directly involved in the religious phenomena being considered', and rejects the interpretation of religious conflict as concerning nothing but the struggle for power as an attempt to 'silence those directly involved as effectively as any colonizing overlay' ('Juggling Torches: Why We Still Need Comparative Religion', in Patton and Ray (eds), *A Magic Still Dwells*, 153–71 (at 164–5).

proto-comparativist, but his (admittedly limited) capacity to think in more than one frame is a small indication of what the exercise of comparison can deliver. It adds another way of seeing others and ourselves besides the ways internal to our own tradition, and in a world where traditions continually intertwine and interact, often with friction, that is no small benefit in itself.

Further than this, the humility induced by (comparison-induced) self-refection can be an important motor in the development and enhancement of a tradition. The lines from Robbie Burns that form the title of this essay are from the last stanza of his famous poem 'To a Louse', in which he watches in fascination as a louse, normally associated with the squalor of the poor, crawls over the bonnet of a well-dressed lady in church. In a dig at the snobbery and hypocrisy that he associates with Presbyterian piety, Burns wishes for the gift to see ourselves as others see us, and continues,

> It wad frae monie a blunder free us
>   An' foolish notion;
> What airs in dress an' gait wad lea'e us,
>   An' ev'n Devotion![38]

One does not have to leave 'devotion' (in the sense of continuing commitment to a tradition) to recognize that the capacity for self-reflection, enabled by comparison, creates the capacity for self-criticism, and thus the ability for a tradition to change, develop and adapt. Since no tradition can, in fact, remain fixed, but can be inhabited and continued only through continual processes of change, the capacity to see the limitations of one's own tradition, even its 'blunders and foolish notions', is essential to its development and adaptation to new cultural and historical contexts. By returning to ourselves from a different direction we are able to identify the peculiar shapes of our own tradition: the comparative perspective shows us both where it is peculiar and (on one account) why.[39] In the recursive exchanges that take place across traditions in the act of comparison, 'hidden premises sometimes come to light, making it possible for new ideas and practices to emerge as taken-for-granted forms of order are challenged. The element of surprise in such meetings was (and still is) at once disruptive, and creative.'[40]

To accept the validity and value of the comparative method is by no means to require the full translatability of every cultural feature into the terms of another, or the substitution of the redescribed reality for its native equivalent.[41] It is simply to expect

---

[38] Burns, 'To a Louse', 157.
[39] It is by no means necessary to dismiss this as the operation of 'cosmopolitan liberal theory' (Rowe, *One True Life*, 262). In theological terms, it could just as well be a means for the critical promptings of the Spirit.
[40] Anne Salmond, *The Tears of Rangi: Experiments across Worlds* (Auckland: Auckland University Press, 2017), 17. She here exegetes an evocative Māori haka (war chant): *He iwi kē, he iwi kē* (One strange people, and another); *Titiro atu, titiro mai* (One looking at the other, the other looking back).
[41] If redescription is, of course, a form of translation, it (like all translations) is always performed best when conscious of its own inadequacy and the inevitability that it will 'betray' its source. And, as Viverios de Castro remarks in this connection, 'a good translation is one that allows the alien concepts to deform and subvert the translator's conceptual toolbox so that the *intentio* of the original language can be expressed within the new one' ('Perspectival Anthropology', 5).

that at some levels, and in certain respects, there is sufficient similarity to make a similarity-with-difference comparison possible, and to hope that the new angle of vision, partial and ideologically situated as it is, will enable us to see new things in a familiar tradition, or old things differently. There is no claim here to ultimate adequacy of perspective, or even of greater approximation to such a chimera. Like the historian, the comparativist submits to a lifelong sentence of provisionality, knowing that today's fresh angles of vision will tomorrow be revised, and possibly ridiculed. But what comparison does provide, among other gifts, is the capacity for self-awareness and reflexivity, an ability to shift perspectives, a greater facility in communication to those outside the tradition, and a nimbleness of mind that is schooled to imagine things differently. And those, we may judge, are important survival skills for any religious tradition.

3

Making Friends and Comparing Lives

C. Kavin Rowe

What he sees of the human condition, what unseats his reason, is converted into and treated as an intellectual difficulty...[1]

Can rivals over truth be friends? Paul and Seneca, so it was once imagined, became friends.[2] But at least on that imagining they did not see eye to eye and did not resolve their differences. The short letters are replete with personal affection, but looking for philosophical agreement or even substantive exchange will produce only disappointment. Evidently, the author of their correspondence did not think theoretical agreement or even discussion were necessary for friendship. Friendship has affective possibilities, a set of virtues, fruit to bear – and all this in a way that does not finally depend on the dissolution of difference.[3]

I begin with the imagined friendship between Seneca and Paul because I think we too easily forget that comparison between strong traditions of life asks us what we make of the truth claims of others. It requires us, therefore, to specify what posture of reasoning we take towards them and what the consequences are of our rejection/acceptance. Comparison is finally a question of truth, of relationships, of politics, and thus of practical reason. Which is to say that comparison questions the shape of our existence, both what we've been and what we will become.

The trouble is that the very phenomena that give rise to our projects of comparison can in fact be our undoing. As Cora Diamond puts it in an essay on the 'otherness' of

---

[1] Cora Diamond, 'The Difficult of Reality and the Difficulty of Philosophy', *Partial Answers: Journal of Literature and the History of Ideas* 1 (2003): 1–26 (19). She is discussing Stanley Cavell's notion of 'deflection'. Diamond's topic in this essay is not comparison, but her sense of the world's otherness and the corresponding opacity that is part of human knowing/speaking is germane to the questions I raise in this chapter. The essay as a whole has to do with Cavell, his notion of deflection, the novelist J. M. Coetzee, the ability of ordinary language to render (or not) the strangeness and hardness of the world, and how this (im)possibility is connected to our ability to stand and take what frightens us, what shames us, what turns us away, what horrifies us as a species, and so forth.

[2] The correspondence is not taken as authentic by any modern scholar. And, in fact, it reads neither like Paul nor like Seneca. But before we are too quick to think the ancients so clumsy, we should remember that it was taken as authentic by no less a textual scholar than Jerome.

[3] On the Paul/Seneca correspondence, see Alfons Fürst, Therese Fuhrer, Folker Siegert and Peter Walter, *Der apokryphe Briefwechsel zwischen Seneca und Paulus – Zusammen mit dem Brief des Mordechai an Alexander und dem Brief des Annaeus Seneca über Hochmut und Götterbilder* (SAPERE 11; Tübingen: Mohr Siebeck, 2006).

reality (quoted earlier), 'What [we] see of the human condition, what unseats [our] reason, is converted into and treated as an intellectual difficulty.' As we ourselves know, and as the history of scholarship shows, it is all too easy to take claims about existence – this is how to be truly in the world as a human being – and turn them into thoughts about thoughts (this is what to think if you are interested in questions that interest intellectuals). Our reason shows that it has been unseated not because we cease to think about comparison but because we deflect the questioning of philosophy and cease to think about the truth of our lives.

What follows is a theory-light version of what I take to be essential points in any comparative project that deals with traditions of life that claim truth for their way of being in the world. I obviously do not say everything that could be said; indeed, I do not even try. I focus instead on four things you must think about if you are to think well about comparison between traditions that rule each other out in one human life. These four things are: the narrative determination of texts, traditions, and the meaning of words; the significance of incommensurable and non-compossible forms of life; the relation between understanding and opacity; and the posture of reasoning we call friendship and the virtue learned through scholarly study that makes friendship possible through time.[4] The ensuing sections unfold logically in order, but they should be thought dialogically in relation to one another or, in fact, all at once. It is only by taking them whole that one can see why comparison is a problem of practical reason and why this matters for what we make of comparative enquiry.[5]

Narrative

In what is arguably one of the great books in twentieth-century ethics, Alasdair MacIntyre enjoins his readers to imagine the following situation:

> I am standing waiting for a bus and the young man standing next to me suddenly says, 'The name of the common wild duck is *Histrionicus histrionicus histrionicus*.' There is no problem as to the meaning of the sentence he uttered: the problem is, how to answer the question, what was he doing in uttering it? Suppose he just uttered such sentences at random intervals; this would be one possible form of madness. We would render his action of utterance intelligible if one of the following turned out to be true. He has mistaken me for someone who yesterday had approached him in the library and asked: 'Do you by any chance know the Latin name of the common wild duck?' *Or* he has just come from a session with his psychotherapist who has urged him to break down his shyness by talking to strangers. 'But what shall I say?' 'Oh, anything at all.' *Or* he is a Soviet spy waiting at a prearranged rendez-vous and uttering the ill-chosen code sentence which will

---

[4] Perhaps it goes without saying: you do not necessarily have to think what I think about these points, but if you are interested in 'comparison' you will in fact have positions on them and would thus do well to think about them.

[5] A part of what I will say has strong resonance with the larger argument of *One True Life*, and the rest is either presupposed by that book or follows from it.

identify him to his contact. In each case the act of utterance becomes intelligible by finding its place in a narrative.[6]

There are, of course, virtually countless other situations one could imagine that would make the man's *histrionicus* utterance make sense. The crucial point for all of them is this: every possible sense-making scenario presupposes a narrative.

To the objection that the action (say) of a man throwing clear liquid on a fire is intelligible without a narrative as the discrete action 'putting out fire', MacIntyre could reply with a series of questions that would unearth the narrative(s) we took for granted in reading the action as intelligible: How do you know that the liquid is water? How do you know that he is putting it out rather than simply controlling the rate of its burn? Answering these and other like questions would immediately show that the action's interpretation depended upon a sequence that gave the action its intelligibility. 'I know it's water because I saw the man run to the garden hose and fill his bucket'; 'I know he's putting it out because he yelled, "I have got to put this fire out before it spreads to the dry grass!"' *Or* 'I know he's actually not putting the fire out because he told me just now that he wants only to reduce its heat so he can roast some hotdogs for his children . . .' In each case (and others like them), the justification for the intelligibility of the action involves telling a story about how one knows what sort of action the action is. The intelligibility-delivering sequence is inescapably a narrative. Try all we like to find the action's intelligibility elsewhere – in this or that isolated context – and we still will wind up with story.[7] As MacIntyre states, 'An action is a moment in a possible or actual history or in a number of such histories.'[8]

What MacIntyre's example also shows is that the meaning of the words uttered is tied to the history (and therefore narrative[9]) that makes them make a particular sense. On the face of it, the simple meaning of 'the common name . . . *histrionicus*' is clear. But on closer inspection the clarity is only because we have a sense of how to talk that way at all. It may be that we now talk that way for X or Y purpose (if we speak as, e.g., a spy or an ornithologist), but utter that sentence prior to the development of modern scientific classification, and the priority of 'meaning-in-light-of-a-particular-history' to 'meaning' is immediately evident. Insert it into a first-century text, and the point is even clearer. *Histrionicus histrionicus histrionicus* means no more and no less than what it means in the narrative(s) that tells one what it means.[10]

---

[6] *After Virtue* (3rd edn; South Bend, IN: University of Notre Dame Press, 2009), 210.
[7] Another way to put this point is to say that one cannot refer back behind story to some other more basic unit of intelligibility. The story just is the thing in itself. '[T]he characterization of actions allegedly prior to any narrative form being imposed upon them will always turn out to be the presentation of what are plainly the disjointed parts of some possible narrative' (215). This has been recognized in other disciplines as well. See, e.g., the discussion in Lee Hester and Jim Cheney, 'Truth and Native American Epistemology', *Social Epistemology* 15 (2001): 319–34. They conclude, 'The narrative is as close to the truth as you can get' (332).
[8] MacIntyre, *After Virtue*, 214.
[9] Recounting the history of scientific classification is narrating, i.e., giving the story of its origins, use, etc.
[10] MacIntyre says that there is no problem in the meaning of the sentence; I disagree: there is all the problem in the world with the meaning. Intelligible action and the meaning of the word(s) cannot be divorced. They go together. If while lighting a fire someone says, 'I'm putting out a fire', the

Why does this discussion about actions and words matter for thinking about comparison? There are three chief reasons that, when taken together, point towards a crucial feature of all comparative projects.

First, attending carefully to the conceptual order MacIntyre elucidates helps us to understand something crucial about reading (e.g.) Christian and Stoic texts, viz., the very identification of these texts (or fragments thereof) as Christian or Stoic presupposes a narrative that makes a text intelligible as *this* kind of text rather than *that* kind or *that* kind. We use the description 'Christian' etc. because we find the text intelligible in terms of the history/narrative that is the way we think about Christian/Stoic, etc. Treating the Gospel of Luke or 1 Corinthians as instances of Christian literature means precisely that we take them to exemplify the Christian narrative that we use to name them as 'Christian' in the first place. Arguments about what sort of text an ancient text is – what exactly the Gospel of Philip is, for example – are arguments about the extent to which a text exemplifies the conceptually prior narrative of what it is that we seek instances of. Of course, the narrative we presuppose in locating a text or texts is itself partly dependent on the texts that we try to identify; but just to the extent that we find any particular text to contribute to or be an instance of a tradition of life we read it in light of the narrative that locates it in that tradition.

What this means for comparison is all but obvious: the fact that the identification of this text as a Christian text precedes our comparison – indeed, our interest in comparison rests on this prior identification – means that what is already presumed in the comparison is the narratives that make the comparison make sense as something to do in the first place. At a more comprehensive hermeneutical level, then, when we compare texts, we are not simply comparing Christian text A with Stoic text B (or C, D, etc.) but comparing in light of the narrative that makes text A show up to us as 'this specific sort of thing to be compared' with the narrative that makes text B appear to us as 'this specific sort of thing to be compared'. And what *this* means is that we cannot get to actual comparison without dealing with the narratives that make this particular comparative project or that particular comparative project make sense in the first place.[11]

It is critical to understand that the foregoing discussion about narrative should not be confused with an assumption that traditions are 'pure'.[12] I do not deny and do not think we should deny that human beings who live in roughly the same time and place share all sorts of things in common, can work together against this or for that or on this

---

understanding is either that the person doesn't know the meaning of 'putting out' and wants 'lighting' instead or that the action is unintelligible *as* the action 'putting out a fire'. I think his comment that we 'allocate *conversations* to *genres*, just as we do literary narratives' actually speaks for my point (211, emphasis added). This problem applies to 'propositions' of every sort (see Chapter 4 by Troels Engberg-Pedersen's in this volume and my comment in n.30 in my response).

[11] This is quite a different thing from the comparison of 'motifs' or 'myths' that Jonathan Smith works with in the 'On Comparing Stories' chapter in his *Drudgery Divine*. Smith's 'stories' are really more like extractions and abstractions, the creation of connections that make a story that occurs in the 'space of the scholar's mind' (115). They are not the elucidation of the narrative(s) that makes the words make the sense they do in a text under discussion or the narrative that allows us to locate a text in a particular tradition.

[12] See, e.g., Elizabeth Agnew Cochran's reply to my criticism of her use of Stoicism, 'Bricolage and the Purity of Traditions: Engaging the Stoics for Contemporary Christian Ethics', *JRE* 40 (2012): 720–9.

and on that, can assent to similar claims (we should render unto Caesar what is his), can read the same books, can play music together, can understand each other in a regular and important way at the bank or supermarket or pagan festival, and so on. As Bernard Williams observes, 'Cultures, subcultures, fragments of cultures, constantly meet one another and exchange and modify practices and attitudes. Social practices could never come forward with a certificate saying that they belonged to a genuinely different culture, so that they were guaranteed immunity to alien judgements and reactions.'[13] The point is simply that no matter how diverse a tradition, no matter how rich and deep the contestation over what the tradition entails and does not, no matter how much any tradition has in common with the wider culture in which it is embedded, to name a text (e.g.) Christian is to presuppose a narrative about a tradition of which this text is an exemplar. One may, as some scholars were once wont to do, speak of Christianities as an attempt to avoid notions of pure traditions (or 'orthodoxy'). But this only reinforces the point: at least as the grammar – and therefore thought – runs, Christianities are diverse instances of some larger and presupposed tradition called Christianity. If this were not so, you would not know what to call them or would call them something else. Speaking of Christianities means that you evaluate them in light of a narrative that tells you what to call them. Without the narrative, you would not have the language to use that you actually use.[14] The question of purity is a distraction; nothing human is pure. The question is whether there is a tradition or not. If there is, you have a narrative.[15]

Second, and relatedly, understanding the narrative conditions for intelligible actions and sentence meaning means that focusing on what we might call weight-bearing words – words that are meant to be productive points of thought in comparative projects – is but another way of asking what narrative it is that enables us to know how to understand them and relate them to their occurrence in other texts. The occurrence of *pneuma, sōma, psychē, sarx, theos, autarkē, prohairesis* and so forth in multiple texts from different traditions tells us nothing about either similarity or difference but only that we need to think about the way the words figure in the narrative that gives their sense within the tradition to which the text belongs. Professional biblical scholars, of

---

[13] Williams, *Ethics and the Limits of Philosophy* (Cambridge, MA: Harvard University Press, 1985), 158. From a Christian theological perspective, there are some significant qualifications to at least one part of Williams's point, viz., the church does claim that it is in some way a genuinely new 'culture'. Obviously, its newness takes shape in time and space and is therefore bound up with the social realities of which it was and is a part. But the claim is that its inception – as with the election of the people of Israel – is based on God's prior, founding act.

[14] Of course, this does not mean that any given scholar is aware of the narrative presupposition of the classification of texts. The point, rather, is that it is there whether one is aware of it or not. Another way to put it is this: the singular is conceptually prior to the plural (this would be true also for those who wish to speak of multiple narratives rather than a singular story).

[15] There will always be the question of the boundaries of a tradition – when, e.g., a text or group ceases to be or never was a part of a specific tradition. My assumption about this question is rather simple: by and large, this sort of thing is a matter of ongoing dispute, disagreement, and discovery. But none of the fuzziness about boundaries erases the basic fact that a tradition itself can be seen. Wittgenstein puts the point in relation to the elasticity of word meaning. It is not a defect, he says, that many words don't have a strict meaning. To 'think it is would be like saying that the light of my reading lamp is no real light at all because it has no sharp boundary' (*The Blue and Brown Books* (New York: Harper & Row, 1958), 27). On tradition as a 'singular' thing, see my comments in my response in this volume.

course, have known at least since James Barr's withering critique of Kittel's *Wörterbuch* that words do not mean anything in themselves but mean only in the context of other words.[16] The point at this juncture goes well beyond Barr: 'context' is not simply an immediate textual phenomenon – though it is doubtless that – but is finally the narrative we presuppose in understanding a word's history and use. Words, no less than actions, are moments in a narrative or a history. When we say things such as 'this is a Stoic word' or 'that is a specifically Christian word' we mean that 'this word finds its meaning in the Stoic/Christian narrative or history'. And when we discern similarity and/or difference what we discern is not most fundamentally similarity/difference in the 'concepts' that go with the words but similarity/difference in the way the stories tell what the words mean.

Third, precisely because of the connection between intelligible actions and the sense that words make, the meaning of words is finally a lived meaning. Which is to say (for this volume) something like this: it is one thing to say that 4 is the answer to 2 + 2 for each and every human being who adds 2 to 2;[17] it quite another to say that your life will be transformed if you live certain words. 'If you confess with your mouth and believe in your heart that Jesus is Lord' *sōtēria* will be yours (Rom. 10.9). 'Practise the truth', says Seneca, and 'despise death' (Ep. 98.17; 78.5). Words such as these are intelligible not in abstraction from the actions that show forth what they mean but in the context of a human life whose actions make these words intelligible in human existence. 'Knowledge' of the meaning of words is finally, then, a 'narrative of a life lived in the world'.[18]

In sum, attending to the role that narrative plays in the connection between actions, words and human life leads to the rather pedestrian but crucial insight that projects of comparison are simply swimming in narrative. Comparative work that attempts to get away from or ignores the narrative structure of its work is always self-deceived. When we engage in comparing ancient texts, we engage in narrative reasoning. Indeed, as MacIntyre puts it, 'Narrative is not the work of poets, dramatists and novelists reflecting upon events which had no narrative order before one was imposed by the singer or the writer.' He continues: 'Narrative form is neither disguise nor decoration. Barbara Hardy has written that "we dream in narrative, day-dream in narrative, remember, anticipate, hope, despair, believe, doubt, plan, revise, criticize, construct, gossip, learn, hate and love by narrative".[19] If MacIntyre and Hardy are right – and they are – the question for comparative projects whose *modus operandi* is the discernment of similarity/difference is: How do we agree and/or disagree in narrative? What is (dis)agreement?

---

[16] *The Semantics of Biblical Language* (Oxford: Oxford University Press, 1961).
[17] Although this truth does not tell us why anyone would be counting in particular. For that, we need a narrative; i.e., to understand the action 'counting' or 'adding' we need the same sort of thick narrative understanding as we do to understand *histrionicus histrionicus histrionicus*.
[18] Hester and Cheney, 'Truth and Native American Epistemology', 331. Many writers have long known this, of course, even in the 'bestseller' genre. Among recent ones from that class, see James Rebanks's remarkable book about life as a shepherd in the valleys of the Lake District, *The Shepherd's Life: Modern Dispatches from an Ancient Landscape* (New York: Flatiron Books, 2015): 'We are, I guess, all of us, built out of stories' (80).
[19] MacIntyre, *After Virtue*, 211. Cf. Bernard Williams, 'Life as Narrative', *European Journal of Philosophy* 17 (2007): 305–14.

Disagreement and difference

One of the more obvious features of comparative projects is the focus on the potential agreement/disagreement and on similarity/difference between the things being compared. What is less obvious is the way in which we might actually know agreement/disagreement and similarity/difference when we see it. What is it to agree/disagree? What is it to differ?

For our purposes, we shall focus on only three of the many dimensions of this question. First, as Donald Davidson, Jeffrey Stout and others argued, there are the sorts of disagreements that presuppose a set of shared agreements. It is these agreements that form the background against which the disagreements make sense. When in US government Democrats and Republicans bitterly disagree over the precise political meaning of democracy, they nevertheless share a complex cluster of agreements that make their disagreements intelligible as disagreements (e.g., a non-violent transfer of the presidency every four to eight years, the right to vote members of Congress in or out every few years, the electoral system as a whole, the bicameral nature of Congress, the process for appointing Supreme Court justices and so on). Or when Paul and the apostles and elders in Jerusalem attempted to work out a way for Christian Jews and Christian Gentiles to worship and eat together, Paul may well have differed from Peter, James, and others on many things, but their disagreements were disagreements within a shared commitment to Jesus of Nazareth as God's Messiah, to the authoritative role of Israel's scriptures, to the rejection of pagan idolatry, to the importance of public witness, and to many other things besides.

In short, there is a sort of disagreement where something(s) must be shared in order for *disagreement* to characterize what it is that is occurring. Having an argument, on this view, is actually a remarkable achievement. An argument means that you share enough to recognize on similar or the same terms as your disputant what the disagreement entails. One may or may not be able to resolve the disagreement to each party's satisfaction, but in principle the disagreement is grounded in a deeper (set of) agreement(s). Without such agreements, there is no disagreement; you are simply talking about something else.

Of course, sometimes one actually *is* talking about something else. So, second, there is a sort of difference that on the face of it appears to be a disagreement but on closer inspection requires a more nuanced and difficult description. Such differences are commonly characterized as incommensurable. There is no shared agreement or standard of evaluation such that the difference could be dissolved or resolved as it (in principle) could be with a straightforward disagreement. There are many ways to illustrate incommensurability. The most helpful for thinking about comparison for the thrust of this essay, however, is the sort that Bernard Williams calls incommensurable 'forms of life' (or 'cultures').[20]

To get at the incommensurability of different forms of life, Williams draws an analogy with scientific theories.

---

[20] The immediate connection between Williams's language of form of life or culture to the term tradition of life should be self-evident.

> Some philosophers of science hold that scientific theories may be incommensurable with one another because they differ in the concepts they use, the reference they give to various terms, and what they count as evidence. These theories will not straightforwardly contradict one another. Yet they do exclude one another. If they did not, there would be no difficulty in combining them, as one can combine the topography of separate places. They cannot be combined. ... Some radical philosophers of science will say that you cannot combine the two theories merely because you cannot combine accepting both theories: the research activities characteristic of each theory, the direction of attention appropriate to each, and so on, cannot be combined. You cannot work within both of them.[21]

Williams actually thinks this is a 'wild exaggeration' when it comes to the history of science, but 'a story of this kind may be appropriate to what really are different cultures or forms of life'.[22] The outlook and lived possibilities of one 'society might to an important extent be incommensurable with that of another, but they would still exclude one another. The conflict would lie in what was involved in living within them.'[23] The different forms of life, as he puts it earlier, would each 'track the truth' but in different and incommensurable ways.[24] But how, we might wonder, could different, incommensurable forms of life each track the truth?

Truth here for Williams does not mean what an analytical observer would find true according to the standards of his philosophical investigations. It is, rather, tied directly to the form of life that determines how enquiry is conducted and what the thick concepts are that enable people to 'find their way around in a social world'. 'Granted the way that the people [in a certain form of life] have gone about their inquiries, it must be no accident that the belief they have acquired is a true one, and if the truth on the subject had been otherwise, they would have acquired a different belief, true in those different circumstances.'[25] Assuming one has the cultural and numerical sense relative to the example, a rolled die that comes up 6 would be taken as a 6 and not something else, a 4 as a 4 and not something else, a 2 as a 2 and not something else, and so on.[26] To track the truth is thus to think and live what is true within the form of life whose patterns make truth what it is and comes to be for those who live it.[27]

---

[21] Williams, 'Limits of Philosophy', 157.
[22] Ibid.
[23] Ibid., 158–9.
[24] Ibid., 143.
[25] Ibid., 142–3.
[26] The assumption this sentence names is indispensable to this 'rough' illustration, as Williams notes: 'Perhaps I cannot read four dots as 4, though I can read six dots as 6. What if I can only read six dots as 6, and everything else as not 6?' (218, n. 10). One could, moreover, think a die any number of things other than an object whose rolls turn up numbers. The point is that tracking the truth in this example depends not only on an accurate reading of the number that comes up but also on the whole complex cluster of things that goes into interpreting the roll of a die as a roll of a die at all. One tracks the truth of the number but only because one knows how the whole thing works, as it were.
[27] Williams' description of tracking the truth bears striking resemblance to Lee Hester and Jim Cheney's conception of 'responsible truth' as the sort of truth that *just is* truth in some Native American epistemology. See their 'Truth and Native American Epistemology'.

If, then, there are forms of life that are incommensurable – and there were and are – and there is difference over what truth is – and there was and is – that difference is irresolvable. One cannot decide what is really true. There is no shared standard of measurement, as it were, that would enable each form of life's truth to be measured, evaluated, decided upon.[28] (The notion that one could stand outside a form of life and judge its truth is simply a *reductio*: the standard of truth by which you judge the other's truth is the truth of your own form of life – and so on *ad infinitum* ...) As Williams explains with reference to particular actions, however, for confrontation, collision, and even rejection to occur between incommensurable forms of life it is not necessary that the 'parties conceptualize in the same way the actions in question ... [indeed] they will not do so'. One culture's religious truth takes it, say, that human sacrifice is a necessary part of maintaining the balance of cosmic power and practices accordingly; another culture has no such truth and sees this practice as a 'deliberate killing of a captive'.[29] There is no way to debate or negotiate the meaning of the action on culturally independent grounds. To understand the meaning of the action is to understand the culture; to change the meaning of the action is to change the culture. And yet, they conflict.

Williams's example characterizes well this central feature of incommensurable ways of being true: confrontation, collision, clash. Note, too, the way in which Williams's example illustrates MacIntyre's point about intelligible action: there is no such thing as human 'sacrifice' per se; for one, this is the practice that tracks religious truth; for another, it is murder. The practice itself is the enactment of a religious/ethical narrative that goes with a form of life, a culture, a tradition. Reading Williams and MacIntyre together, that is, helps us to see how incommensurability in the living of life is inseparably tied to the stories that make sense of the lives that we live.[30]

Taking seriously confrontation and collision as a way to describe the encounter of incommensurable difference(s) leads to the third important feature of difference or disagreement, viz., whether the collision is primarily notional or lived. Williams once again: a lived confrontation between two outlooks 'occurs at a given time if there is a group of people for whom each of the outlooks is a real option'. By real option Williams means primarily a socially dense possibility whereby one could 'go over' to the confronting outlook and 'live inside it in their actual historical circumstances and retain their hold on reality, not engage in extensive self-deception, and so on'.[31] A 'notional confrontation, by contrast, occurs when some people know about two divergent outlooks, but at least one of those outlooks does not present a real option' (160). The life, for example, of a 'Bronze Age chief or a medieval samurai are not real

---

[28] This obviously raises all kinds of difficult questions about knowledge vis-à-vis scientific truth, etc. Williams deals with these matters fairly well. Most thinkers would see some sort of significant difference between scientific knowledge and strong traditions that claim truth for their way of life. It's true, e.g., that the sun is a giant ball of hydrogen gas (more or less) whether a certain group of 'traditional' people think this or not. It may equally be true that the sun is an integral part of God's way of creating a life-sustaining planet in our solar system. But this second truth is of a different sort than the first. It does not, e.g., entail a particular position on the sun's chemical composition.
[29] Williams, 'Limits of Philosophy', 158.
[30] Incommensurability is not reducible to story but is tied inseparably to it.
[31] Williams, 'Limits of Philosophy', 160–1.

options for us: there is no way of living them' (ibid.). A notionally divergent outlook may call into question all sorts of current commitments, practices, arguments and so forth, but the result of such questioning could never be to inhabit the outlook that produced the questioning.

Taking note of the difference between notional and lived confrontation helps underline the difficult and dramatic nature of a confrontation that demands a decision about the truth of the sort of life that can and will be lived from the point of confrontation.[32] When this sort of confrontation is rooted in disagreement, the decision can in principle be made on the basis of the resolution of disagreement. When, however, the confrontation over a true life is rooted in incommensurable difference, the decision cannot be made on the basis of resolution. There is no ground on which the resolution could happen. Roman Stoicism and early Christianity, for example, do rule each other out as life options, but they do not straightforwardly contradict each as they would if they shared enough agreements about the words *theos*, *cosmos*, etc. to differ only in their explication. Their difference over the true life is incommensurable difference. It is the difference of different stories by which life is lived – or, in reverse – it is the difference of the lives by which the stories are existentially told.[33]

Irresolvable existential confrontations over truth – those confrontations that simply by posing the question demand a judgement one way or the other with the life you live – are in my view the sort that are the most interesting for the question of 'comparison'. This is precisely because it is unclear how you could really compare them. How, then, might we understand existentially confrontational difference?

Opacity and understanding

'Understanding' has of course been a subject of perennial philosophical interest. I cannot claim to understand the history of understanding or of understanding understanding. Nevertheless, there is a critical point about understanding irresolvable confrontations over true lives that bears directly on our thinking about comparison.

At first glance, of course, understanding does not appear all that difficult: if you understand this sentence, you know what understanding is even if you do not have a rich theory of human understanding in general. Reading ancient texts, in this simplified sense, is not much different from reading this sentence. If there is enough of a context, and if you have some general working knowledge of the assumptions that the text makes use of, you can, if the words are clear enough, understand it. Pick up and read. Or at least: study, pick up, and read.

But what if upon studying, picking up, and reading one discovers that one does not understand what one is reading? This experience, too, presumes some understanding: you understand that you do not understand. But what exactly is it that you understand that you do not understand?

---

[32] For MacInytre, this sort of confrontation has the possibility of an 'epistemological crisis'. For a description and evaluation of his notion, see Rowe, *One True Life*, pp. 249–58.
[33] There isn't a way to join the two stories or to go behind them to tell one story that encompasses them both.

There are of course multiple and often interpenetrating answers to such questions (e.g., you do not know the original language of the text you're reading and therefore cannot see how the words run; or you are unfamiliar with the key weight-bearing terms of the text). But the principal scholarly answer we tend to give today is rooted in what is 'implicit in the work of all scholars in the humanities', viz., the correlation between the belief in the translucifying power of universal reason and the practice of study. The 'faith that such understanding is, in principle, possible is a normative assumption as well as a hopeful one'. The scholar's 'daily business is to make strange goings-on – the historically or culturally distant traces of human activities – more familiar'.[34] Which is to say that we don't understand because we don't yet know enough to understand. Understanding is what we increase by acquiring knowledge. Learn a little more, and we understand a little more. Understanding, in this way of looking at things, is not an either/or but a more and a less, a spectrum along which one is positioned relative to the knowledge one has acquired through training and study. More and less, well and poorly; this is the grammar of scholarly understanding.[35]

The problem with this way of thinking about understanding is not that it does not apply to many things we seek to understand; indeed, it clearly and demonstrably does. The problem is that it leaves out a whole range of the experience of being human.

Gadamer once wrote that the 'finite nature of one's own understanding is the manner in which reality, resistance, the absurd, and the unintelligible assert themselves. If one takes this finitude seriously, one must take the reality of history seriously as well.'[36] Hermeneutics was for Gadamer the science not only of understanding but of opacity, particularly as opacity was rooted in the pre-reflective condition that is the human being's finitude and in the unconquerable otherness of life.[37] It seems to me that much that is assumed in the premise of the humanist understanding is in the nature of the thing committed to denying what Gadamer asserts. But it is Gadamer who makes the deeper and better point. Finitude, historicity, opacity: these are the necessary experience of human thought and understanding. There is no rule – metaphysical, logical, hermeneutical or otherwise – that entails or implies the intelligibility of all forms or traditions of human life. By contrast, finitude is a fact. In at least one utterly stunning and profoundly significant way, it offers permanent, recalcitrant resistance to humanist claims about the translucifying power of universal reason: where we encounter

---

[34] These citations are from Jeffrey Stout, 'Commitments and Traditions in the Study of Religious Ethics', *JRE* 25 (1997): 23–56. In Chapter 6 in this volume, Matthew V. Novenson borrows this citation to agree with Stout, but Novenson's actual argument does not make clear why he does, nor does he appear to recognize that Stout's position here is taken in relation to his pragmatic sense of what we're up to (not because it must be metaphysically the case that understanding works like this).

[35] One could perhaps speak of 'the comparative enterprise in modes appropriate to the academy's self-understanding', though in truth there is no such thing as the academy's self-understanding, as if the academy is a thinking thing with a self or as if there is an intellectual-employment-context whose rules are known and accepted by all who work there. There are only academicians, and these have a wide range of different understandings of their comparative work. The cited phrase is from Jonathan Z. Smith, *Drudgery Divine: On the Comparison of Early Christianities and the Religions of Late Antiquity* (Chicago: University of Chicago Press, 1990), vii.

[36] *Truth and Method*, xxxv.

[37] Hermeneutics thus names not so much a 'methodology but a theory of the real experience that thinking is' (*Truth and Method*, xxxvi).

traditions or forms of life that claim 'living' is necessary to 'understanding' we at once discover the boundary – and concomitant opacity – placed on reason and study by time and death. To understand we must live; to live we must have time; but we cannot live different 'understanding lives' at the same time.[38] In Diamond's way of putting it, reality resists and exceeds our ability to think it; we cannot get our lives across and over into another life to think it without taking ourselves with us.[39] Or, to make this same point differently, we could say that our bodies are necessary to understanding. The understanding intellect *qua* intellect is an abstraction; there is only the I that reasons as long as it is bodily alive. Denying the limits that time and death place on reason involves a corresponding denial of bodily life.[40] In short, the historicity of understanding is connected most deeply to the humanity of understanding: not only to when and where we live but also and always to the time it takes to live from birth to death.[41]

If the premise of understanding in the humanities is 'study something long enough and you will understand it', my question in light of the humanity of understanding is thus: What if the longer you study something the more you understand that you do not understand it because you discover that it is calling you to live in a certain way of life, to become a different sort of person – that understanding in this deeper sense would mean becoming what you are being summoned to become – and you say *no*? The door to that becoming is then closed, and you are shut out. How do you take people seriously who live on the other side of a door that is closed to you? If you're shut out, why read their texts? If you nevertheless do read, what are you doing when you try to read what they have written?[42]

---

[38] We do not have the time before we die to live more than one life. Indeed, you might say that at least one of the most important things death does is to call you to account for, or at least provide closure-like commentary on, the one life you've lived.

[39] See her 'The Difficulty of Reality and the Difficulty of Philosophy'. An example: one of the participants at the conference (I cannot now recall which one) said that the Stoics have 'God' as their companion. For this, I can think of Seneca's 'God in/with you' language or Epictetus's pious language (prayer, etc.) or Cleanthes' hymn – or many other statements – and 'understand' what is meant. But when I read Epictetus and think that I understand what he, too, means, I then realize that I don't know what he really means by 'pray to God', for example, because I cannot pray like he can. The way he uses *theos* is closest to what I think of with *kosmos* or *ktisis*, and, in my understanding, this makes no sense to pray to. I have not ever prayed to the world/creation and do not believe in its inherent sublimity or the divine grain of nature (etc.); so I finally think that I do not really 'understand' in a thick sense what 'pray to God' means in a thick sense for Epictetus. Does pray mean think hard about? Concentrate on the idea of? Talk to? To what? Expect an answer from? From what? and so on and on. In my view, this sort of dynamic is often left out of scholarly discourse, but it is critically important for how we think about understanding other traditions, about the ancient world, and about the use of words in texts.

[40] See also Stanley Hauerwas, 'Bearing Reality: A Christian Meditation', *JSCE* 33 (2013): 3–20, esp. 6–10.

[41] The attempt to transcend existential unintelligibility (we cannot understand with our lives, *in* our lives, another strong tradition of life that claims understanding is a sort of becoming, or inextricably bound with a becoming) is an attempt to transcend finitude, or to transcend reflection's inevitable and inexpungable historicity. I think, to say it slightly differently, that the hermeneutic assumptions of certain modes of scholarly discourse entail a denial of a significant part of the experience of being human, a denial of the limits of animated dust.

[42] The language of summoning, of becoming, of saying no or yes, of being shut out, and so on raises the question of 'conversion'. The wager – in the Pascalian and Kierkegaardian sense – of the convert is the existential correlate of human finitude. Try as you might, you cannot find criteria 'outside' your life or 'before' your living of it that can or will justify your life as the right, rational – indeed, true – one to live (especially vis-à-vis the remarkably wide range, diverse, and different sets of criteria that allegedly exist). MacIntyre et al. worry about this as a 'criterionless choice' in the face of reason's

A scholarly work: friendship and patience

What are we doing if we are reading things that require for their 'understanding' a life that we will not or cannot live – if the kind of conflict or incommensurability between traditions of life is existentially thick? My argument is that we are not doing what we typically think but something much more important, and, further, that to treat comparative enquiry as a predominantly theoretical question is to make a fundamental mistake, that of thinking of comparison as something other than the work of practical reason.

In a generous review of *One True Life*, Professor Teresa Morgan notes that the limitations placed on our knowledge of strong traditions by the fact that we do not or will not live them raise serious questions:

> [Rowe's] conclusion, that the possibilities of comparative scholarship are severely limited, articulates one of the central paradoxes of research in the humanities and social sciences. He might have gone further and shown why, given the inevitable limits of empathy, researchers (including himself) continue to investigate cultures and systems of thought not their own.... No scholarly account of another culture is perfect, but there is no reason to think that reaching an understanding of other world views is impossible. One might argue that it is essential. If we cannot at least try to understand other philosophies, societies or religions, what point is there in research? What hope is there for the world?[43]

The connection between research and hope for the world is explicit in Prof. Morgan's questions. The unarticulated assumption, I think, is that understanding other cultures or 'world views' will somehow lead to a better world. The full thought, then, is something like this: academics contribute to a better world through their research because such research enables us to understand others better and such understanding, in turn, leads to – or is a condition of, or productive of – more harmonious relations between people (presumably in the sense of less violence, less bigotry, less barbaric treatment of people

---

workings. But his worry, rather than his argument against it, is the right position: there is no reason or pattern of reasoning that can justify your life from your thought. Of the various conversions that have been written about, one of the more interesting ones for my purpose here is that of Georg Lukács to Marxism (see the treatment in Alasdair MacIntyre, *Edith Stein: A Philosophical Prologue 1913-1922* (New York: Rowman & Littlefield, 2006), esp. 153–61). Lukács was initially persuaded that Weber's account of the modern world as 'disenchanted' was right and the consequences for work and life inescapable (the severing of soul and work, the reduction of 'value' to the smallness of private life, and so on). When he began to wonder if Weber's account was of things only as they seem but not as they truly are, Lukács discovered that he could not actually answer this question without becoming a different type of person. He, like other inhabitants of modernity, was imprisoned within Weber's picture and could not think his way out. So he became something else, a Marxist (of a particular type). It was only from a different existential vantage point that he could understand how Weber was wrong. On the case for Marxism as a 'religion' – or at least what we moderns usually mean by this term – see Paul Griffiths, *Problems of Religious Diversity* (Oxford: Blackwell, 2001).

[43] Review in *The Tablet*, September 2016.

whom we now understand to be something other than barbarians and thus worthy of humane treatment, conversation, and so forth).

Prof. Morgan's commitment to the human good of research gets to the heart of what comparison of religious traditions might be *for* – the wider purpose of scholarly work within the human lives that even the most absent-minded scholars actually have to live. For this she is to be commended and her thought welcomed. In contrast to Prof. Morgan, however, I see no *essential* connection between academic study of other traditions (or anything else) and more humane relations. Indeed, there is no reason in principle to rule out the possibility that the more you study another form of life the more you may come to *dislike* it, find it completely odious, wish it had never existed, and want it to go away.[44] More and better research does not intrinsically mean more and better human sympathies and consequent action. Research on others may, of course, play some role in a much wider ethical stance towards those others, but it may not, and it may even deepen or increase the problems of alienation it allegedly addresses. Grasping this point is critical because it helps to expose the enormous hope we academics place in the work of understanding itself.[45] If we can understand, we have hope.

Alas, the work of understanding cannot bear this hope. Indeed, as I argued earlier, when it comes to lived traditions of truth, the work of understanding is better described as a becoming, and we cannot become something we will not or cannot become or do not have time to become. I thus think of the purpose of comparative enquiry quite differently.

Charles Taylor's view that 'The great challenge of this century [twenty-first] is understanding the other' sounds about right.[46] But it is not. The greatest challenge is how to understand our lack of understanding another – since this lack will not go away, since we cannot simply overcome it with more and more and more understanding – and, further, how in the face of such lack we can allow others to remain truly other, others whose lives of truth we challenge or reject simply by the fact that we go another, quite different way in the world and locate our lives by stories that are not theirs. What practices and habits do we need, say, to take the pagan as the pagan and not, say, as an implicit Christian or anonymous liberal democrat who just does not yet know his true desire to live in light of the common good or to protect the inalienable rights he has yet

---

[44] Examples where academic study is said to lead to more humane relations are exactly and only cases where this is alleged to have happened. The actual causal link between study and behaviour is impossible to demonstrate. It could easily be rather that the scholar(s) was really nice and the adherents of the tradition being studied happened to have among their current number some very kind and generous people – and the two sides, as it were, were able to get along in the plain human sense of getting along well together. Had the academic and the tradition's representatives been of different temperaments, it could have gone otherwise. But let us grant that somehow we could establish a causal relation between research and hope for the world in the form of better human action in any (or, in fact, every) case: simply because it has gone this way one time, or multiple times, or even always in the past does not mean it would go that way tomorrow or the next day or, indeed, ever again. It is always possible for things to go differently.

[45] Reading Prof. Morgan's statement suggests the thought that without being able to place our hope for more humane relations in the work of understanding, it is pointless to do research on other traditions at all. This kind of 'hope in or don't do it' is understandable but also unnecessary.

[46] 'Understanding the Other: A Gadamerian View of Conceptual Schemes', in *Dilemmas and Connections* (Cambridge, MA: Belknap Press of Harvard University Press, 2011), 24–38.

to discover exist – or whatever set of character traits we would most like to assign to the people we would most like to have in the world with us?[47]

Rather than continuing to hope that we can escape the barriers placed on understanding by our bodily existence in time and death, I suggest that friendship is the best reasonable answer to hermeneutical and existential opacity.[48] In his book on the role and importance of practical reason for public dispute and common life, Eugene Garver notes, with Aristotle, that treating a practical problem as a purely technical one can be an ethical error.[49] Virtues and vices are at work in our understanding of and judgements about others' reasoning. To neglect the ethics of reasoning is not, so Garver argues, to attain clearer or purer reasoning about others' reasoning but is instead to neglect the basic way we reason at all – thus essentially distorting not only what is going on in the reasoning of those whom we seek to understand but also our own. By contrast, paying attention to the habits and dispositions that form part of what reasoning is requires us to specify what we need to become in order to engage richly with those with whom we do not or cannot agree or those whose lives we do not or will not live. What we need to become, says Garver, is friends. Friendship is the human relational pattern of sustained, intellectually productive conflict – especially, one might say, when the conflict is rationally irresolvable.[50]

Friendship, after all, does not require theoretical understanding for its practice. Moreover, it aims at truth[51] – not the sort of shared truth that is a product of agreement about 'content-full morality' or anything so grand, but the sort of relational, friendly truth that emerges from truth-telling about the conditions that make our lives. We might speak here of a kind of understanding: we understand one another as friends do, even if the grammars of our traditions remain grammars of conflict and summons. Paul and Seneca could, after all, write letters to each other, or so someone who understood friendship across traditions knew how to imagine.

---

[47] I am very suspicious of attempts at dialogue, etc. that wind up meaning that other people are not as serious about their lives – and the claim to truth that goes with their lives – as they seem to believe that they are. And so I am interested to think as well as possible about questions of otherness in ways that preserve a certain amount of opacity or resistance to cosmopolitan understanding.

[48] The word 'reasonable' in the sentence to which this note is attached is meant literally: friendship is a posture of practical reason.

[49] Eugene Garver, *For the Sake of Argument: Practical Reasoning, Character, and the Ethics of Belief* (Chicago: University of Chicago Press, 2004), 10ff.

[50] Garver argues that modern democracies are insufficiently 'ambitious' in their attempt to make the right sort of space for human flourishing precisely because they too easily abandon friendship for justice (passim). Aiming for justice does not ipso facto require the virtues and practices that go with friendship – trust, for example, and truth telling. But, according to Garver, it is precisely these kinds of things that politics needs for human beings to flourish. Attention to virtues and vices is what is missing in Prof. Barclay's suggestion that comparison of the sort he outlines might just be the critical prompting of the Spirit. It is true that it might work that way. After all, as Barth famously said, God can speak even through a dead dog (CD I/1, 55: 'Russian Communism, a flute concerto, a blossoming shrub, or a dead dog'). But the point is that it *might* or might *not*. How would we know? Situating comparative work within a wider context of virtue/vice makes clear that the effort to put scholarly comparison to work in certain ways – prompting self-criticism, ameliorating hostility between religious traditions, etc. – is often merely *assertion* or wishful thinking about its good. It certainly does not ipso facto 'create the capacity for self-criticism, and thus the ability for a tradition to change' (Barclay, Chapter 2, p. 37 emphasis mine). I take comparison to be a good, but I'm able to specify it as a good only within a wider context of virtue and vice, viz., as a way practical reason deals with human difference (friendship).

[51] Garver, *For the Sake of Argument*, 43 et passim.

As the reference to Paul and Seneca should remind us, friendship was of course a topic of extensive discussion in the ancient world, too.[52] What is missing from the discussion as a whole is an emphasis on patience as a (the?) central practice that makes friendship possible through time.[53] Indeed, patience is the requisite virtue for becoming and being friends with those who are and will remain opaque to you precisely because it is what enables you to take the time it requires to become friends with strangers.[54] You can, I think, learn to be friends with people who have different schemes of life – and when the conflict between you is existential and irresolvable – but to be true friends with them you have to learn to be patient. How can you learn patience if you are an academic? You take the time and effort it requires to study extensively a strong tradition of truth that you do not understand and cannot or will not live, and you grant to that concomitant existential opacity a certain kind of integrity; that is, that lives that are not yours are still as serious about their lives as you are about yours.[55]

[52] For an excellent study that traces 'friendship' from Homeric Greece to the Christians in the fourth and fifth centuries and argues that ancient friendships were much more like modern ones than has been thought in recent scholarship, see David Konstan, *Friendship in the Classical World* (Cambridge: Cambridge University Press, 1997). For studies that relate friendship to NT texts, see the essays in John Fitzgerald (ed.), *Friendship, Flattery, and Frankness of Speech: Studies in the New Testament World* (Leiden: Brill, 1996); and idem (ed.), *Greco-Roman Perspectives on Friendship* (Atlanta: Scholars Press, 1997).

[53] From the world of late antiquity, St Augustine is the outstanding exception. See his remarkable little work *On Patience*.

[54] And, for Christians, to love your enemies. Of course, we need a whole lot more than patience to love our enemies. For example, a commitment not to kill them. If we are patient and if we refuse to kill when things would suggest killing is the best (or even least bad) option, then we have all the time we need to work on being friends – even in and through times of great antipathy. Friendship then turns out to resist and substitute for violence. In her essay in this volume, Mitchell faults me for not saying enough in *One True Life* about Christian violence (n. 109). I did deal with this question in much more detail in *World Upside Down*, but one cannot cover everything satisfactorily in each book. Here is the main suggestion for Christians to realize their vocation not to kill: become nonviolent. A second suggestion: embrace just war. In my view, there is no other Christian option than these two. To the extent that we have practised otherwise, we have betrayed Jesus and our vocation. Mitchell's implicit suggestion – that there is a traceable connection between the commitment to traditioned reason and military action and its cousins – is a common feature, of course, of a certain modern narrative about politics and religion, and it often goes with an appeal to the purported *pax*-making capacities of liberal democracies. That narrative, however, is best understood not as a demonstrable truth about the political effect of serious religious commitment but as the legitimation of modern nation-states and their 'right' to use force to ensure that no one outside their sphere of justified force can legitimately use force. For a helpful introduction to the larger question of narratives about politics and religion in modernity and the way in which they bear on this particular point, see William T. Cavanaugh, *The Myth of Religious Violence* (New York: Oxford University Press, 2009). For sophisticated arguments that include robust religious commitments within the practices of liberal democracy – rather than pitting them against one another, as Rorty did, for example – see Jeffrey Stout's *Democracy and Tradition* (Princeton: Princeton University Press, 2004) and *Blessed are the Organized: Grassroots Democracy in America* (Princeton: Princeton University Press, 2010). Stout himself is not religious, of course, but he recognizes, among many other crucial things, the indispensability of tradition for thought/practice and sees clearly that religious sensibilities often work to counter the oppression and violence that are endemic to political life within even the best of liberal democracies.

[55] One of the more difficult dangers of scholarly work is the temptation to study other human beings or their artefacts (texts, etc.) in a way that denies them the seriousness with which they take their own lives, their own traditions, their own claims to truth – as if scholarly seriousness is somehow a higher, better, truer or more comprehensive seriousness than that of the adherents of the traditions we study. Cf. Garver, 45: 'ultimate orientations or modes of thinking are ways of looking and acting; they are not objects to look at, and so judging between them makes them into something they are not. To judge between incommensurable modes of thought is not a good way to make friends.'

'Textual friendships', as we might call them in our particular area of enquiry, with people/texts who think the human story runs another way are thus a 'spiritual exercise' (as the ancient philosophers would have said), or a means 'to work on oneself' (as Wittgenstein would have said), an academic's manner of developing the patience needed to be(come) a friend.[56] Textual friendships is the name of a hermeneutics that refuses to deflect the truth of reason's rootedness in the life of the reasoner.

Lest someone object that developing patience is an underwhelming product of comparative academic work, it should be rejoined that without patience friendship is impossible. Lest someone object that friendship is not really an academic enough way to think about comparison, it should be rejoined that friendship *is* a posture of reasoning – and a posture of reasoning about the reasoning of others and how best to engage it. Reason that reasons apart from postures of this or that sort is an abstraction; there is no such reason. Friendship names the posture of reasoning that best befits irresolvable existential conflict.[57]

To put this personally: I do not know how much I understand Seneca, but I do now think of him as a friend. Of course, inasmuch as Seneca is long dead, my friendship is 'imagined' or 'textual'. But that in a sense is exactly the point of the study: I hope that I have practised patience in trying to be friends with Seneca through his texts.[58] If so, I will have learned something of what is required to be friends with someone who thinks the human story goes another way. My reason will have acquired something of the posture it needs to be in a world with people whose lives imply that mine is false (and vice-versa) and who may remain opaque to me, and I to them, until we die.

This is a practical suggestion for a practical problem, which is to say that it is practical reason's answer to the questions it cannot escape when faced with incompatible and incommensurable claims to existential truth and the ineliminable fact that we can live only one true life. As should now be obvious, this way of thinking is an overall attempt to reframe comparison of traditions of truth/life as a practical problem. Insofar as comparison is repeatedly conceived as a theoretical problem, we should expect only more theories, some of which will be clearer than others, some of which will have more promise than others, some of which will raise better questions than others, but none of

---

[56] Anthropologists who conduct field work are being trained in patience, too, but in a different, perhaps more direct, way than those scholars who study ancient texts.

[57] One may wish to argue for a different posture, but in so arguing the point about postured reasoning would simply be reinforced. Though it has now been over a quarter of a century since publication, I continue to think Charles Taylor's essay on the types of argument that can be made via practical reason and Martha Nussbaum's reply stand out among concise treatments for their insight into the argumentative power of *ad hominem* reasoning, biography, passion/emotion, and human relationships. See Taylor, 'Explanation and Practical Reason' and Nussbaum's reply in Martha Nussbaum and Amartya Sen (eds), *The Quality of Life* (New York: Oxford University Press, 1993).

[58] I found it harder to become friends with Epictetus. Whether this is because of his rough pedagogy, his particular expressions, the subjects Arrian selected to publish from his notes or something else altogether, I'm not sure. But I know I have to be more patient in becoming friends with him than with Seneca (or Marcus, for that matter). The challenge, then, is to continue reading Arrian's records with the understanding that I am learning how to be a friend.

which will get down to the real business of comparing lives.[59] That is what comparison of traditions has always been and still is – the attempt to see why other people live the lives that they do.

Conclusion

Looking back through the sections of this chapter, the logic is this: irresolvable existential conflict (of which there is plenty in the world) is entangled in the narratives that make sense of the truths that we claim for our lives, the words we use to claim them, the texts we use to inscribe them; the way to be intellectually productive in the face of such conflicts is to become friends. To be friends with those with whom you conflict over truth requires you to be patient. To study alternative traditions as an academic is to learn patience. As a whole, this is what it is to treat comparison of strong traditions of life/truth – what looks on first glance like a theoretical problem – as a problem of practical reason.

---

[59] For an attempt to think of the 'other' in comparison as an explicitly theoretical question, see Jonathan Z. Smith, 'What a Difference a Difference Makes', in Jacob Neusner and Ernest Frerichs (eds), *To See Ourselves as Others See Us: Christians, Jews, 'Others' in Late Antiquity* (Chico, CA: Scholars Press, 1985), 3–48. Smith's essay is of considerable interest because, on the one hand, he recognizes that the question of 'otherness' or 'others' is an inescapably relational and therefore political question, and, on the other, he continues to talk as if theorizing otherness is the way to come to terms with it. Smith also recognizes that opacity is a necessary part of any thinking about the other, but only up to a point. The otherness of a housefly, e.g., is impenetrable and thus 'of no theoretical interest' (47). I would rather say that the interest in the housefly lies precisely in the fact that it is impenetrable.

4

The Past Is a Foreign Country

On the Shape and Purposes of Comparison in New Testament Scholarship

Troels Engberg-Pedersen

This essay addresses three different issues in relation to the exercise of comparison in New Testament scholarship.[1] I first provide a philosophically informed, but basically empirical description of the way comparison has been and is done in historical-critical scholarship. Next, I discuss the underlying justification for this way of doing it. This section addresses more directly the philosophical issues underlying the empirical practice. Finally, I articulate a number of different purposes with engaging in comparison, which do not necessarily exclude one another, but should be formally distinguished. So: description, justification and purposes.

As part of the analysis, I will employ a number of concepts that should at least be vaguely defined. A 'worldview' consists of a more or less coherent set of beliefs about time, place, gods, human beings, agency, the physics and ethics of everyday life and much more. A 'conceptual scheme' abstracts the basic features of a given worldview as understood by the human beings living within it. A 'social practice' is to be distinguished from the 'ideas' that human beings may employ to describe the practice, but the social practice will always be informed by *some* ideas in the minds of its agents. The concepts of 'understanding', 'imagining', 'believing', 'asserting', 'models' and more will be addressed later.

Description

From Wettstein onwards

In 'Quod est comparandum: The Problem of Parallels',[2] L. Michael White and John T. Fitzgerald provide a helpful overview of the historical practice of adducing 'parallels' in

---

[1] The title of the essay of course refers to the first sentence in L. P. Hartley's 1953 novel *The Go-Between*: 'The past is a foreign country; they do things differently there.'
[2] In *Early Christianity and Classical Culture: Comparative Studies in Honor of Abraham J. Malherbe* (ed. J. T. Fitzgerald, T. H. Olbricht and L. M. White; Supplements to Novum Testamentum CX; Leiden: Brill, 2003), 13–39.

New Testament scholarship since the Reformation. They show that the search for parallels began as part of a new, philologically oriented approach to early Christian literature focused on textual criticism, but that it was quickly extended to serve much more broadly the best possible understanding of 'the meaning of words and sentences'. I quote here from White and Fitzgerald two splendid statements made by Johann Jacob Wettstein in his *Novum Testamentum Graecum* (the italics are mine):

> We get to know the meaning of words and sentences in the first instance from other passages by the same author, then from the rest of the sacred writings, as well as from the version of the seventy translators, then from the authors who lived about the same time in the same region, *and finally from common usage*. . . . And, since *the sacred writers invented no new language*, but made use of the one they had learned from their contemporaries, the same judgement is also required of their writings. By 'common usage' I understand the common speech of the apostolic age, but not the usage of medieval writers, and much less that of the scholastic and modern theologians.

> If you wish to get a thorough and complete understanding of the books of the New Testament, *put yourself in the place of* those to whom they were first delivered by the apostles as a legacy. *Transfer yourself in thought to* that time and that area where they first were read. Endeavor, *so far as possible*, to acquaint yourself with the customs, practices, habits, opinions, accepted ways of thought, proverbs, symbolic language, and everyday expressions of these men, and with the ways and means by which they attempt to persuade others or to furnish a foundation for faith. Above all, keep in mind, when you turn to a passage, that *you can make no progress by means of any modern system*, whether of theology or logic, or by means of opinions current today.[3]

Note the following features of this description. (1) Wettstein is quite clear that there is a huge gap between the meanings of words and sentences in the ancient world and in later ages. In other words, he had a clear grasp of what we may call 'the historical difference'. (2) In his historical turn, he called for study not only of the same author, the rest of the New Testament and the LXX, but also of common Greek usage, which he later specifies as 'the customs, practices, habits, opinions, accepted ways of thought, proverbs, symbolic language, and everyday expressions of these men'. (2a) Here it is noteworthy that while he does begin from so-called 'sacred' literature, he in no way hesitates to extend his search into non-sacred culture. '[T]he sacred writers invented no new language', and Wettstein's interest lies in 'the common speech of the apostolic age.' (2b) Also highly noteworthy is the fact that while he does not exclude 'higher' literature, he specifically mentions both more everyday literature and also 'customs, practices, habits' and the like. What he is after is in fact the whole 'way of life'. (3) Note further that in order to overcome the gap between the past and the present, he invoked what we

---

[3] White and Fitzgerald, 'Quod est comparandum', 16. The original statements are found in 2 vols, 1751–2, 2: 876 and 878, respectively.

may call the faculty of the imagination ('put yourself in the place of those ...'). However, he did this in a manner that will appear somewhat deficient to us. He rightly says that in order to get 'a thorough and complete understanding of the books of the New Testament' (a wonderfully optimistic, but also quite illusory endeavour) one cannot make use of 'any modern system' or the 'opinions current today'. Instead, one must acquaint oneself *as far as possible* with all the ancient ways of speaking. The qualification 'as far as possible' shows that Wettstein understood the actual *im*possibility of the task. But he did not pay sufficient attention to this point. Seen from a twentieth- and twenty-first-century perspective, we need to register a deficiency in his picture. Wettstein did not sufficiently recognize the self-reflective insight that has been formulated, not least in the twentieth-century hermeneutics of both the Frankfurter School and Hans-Georg Gadamer, to the effect that as modern readers we too have a worldview and a conceptual scheme that we can never leave completely behind. Even though we can (and should) become aware of that scheme, we can never altogether forget it so as to make the complete leap back in history that Wettstein was in principle calling for.

Historical, contextual comparison

In the light of these insights, we may describe *historical comparison* as *a contextualizing practice* with the following shape. (1) As students of the New Testament, we *come to* that study with a conceptual scheme of our own. (2) We then study as broadly as possible the ancient world that we intuitively see as the 'context' for the New Testament writings and practices. This world is defined by the Greek language – but of course also by Jewish and Latin texts and practices that belong before, during and after the New Testament. In this study, we are constantly open towards recognizing cases of some kind of friction between our own conceptual scheme and what we find in the sources. Since our aim is to understand *them*, we will constantly adjust the conceptual scheme (our own) that we bring to the study so as imaginatively to end up with a conceptual scheme (theirs) that is as close to their own understanding as we can possibly get. Here the criterion is one of maximal coherence, not just based on our own premises, but also on theirs to the extent that we can imaginatively envisage them. But we must also always recognize that Wettstein's '*complete* understanding' will forever remain outside our grasp. We cannot leave completely behind our own conceptual schemes, and these do differ in quite radical ways from those of the ancient world. (3) Once we have acquainted ourselves in this way with the comprehensive context of the New Testament writings, we may turn to those writings themselves and study them in Greek *in the light of* our grasp of their context in the manner proposed by Wettstein. This is where we will bring in *parallels* from the wider context to what we find in the New Testament writings themselves. And this, then, is where we may engage in more extensive comparison, with the shape and purposes to be discussed later.

There are two important features to this whole approach. One lies in its direction. We do not just begin from any New Testament writing in its Greek form. We begin from the outside. This is not just because we need to know the language before any black dots on the white page will make any sense to us. So, we will have to have learned Greek beforehand. It is also because we empirically do have a much broader knowledge of the ancient world before we even open the Greek New Testament. We know a great deal of the historical, social and literary context of the New Testament writings. Nor is this something that either can or should be forgotten when we finally open our New Testament text. On the contrary, we will constantly seek to sharpen our knowledge and understanding of all elements in the wider context that may be relevant to our understanding of the New Testament writings themselves. Only then will the similarities *and* differences that we may discover be sufficiently precise for us to obtain the best possible understanding of our New Testament writing *through* the comparison. The crucial notion here is that of 'context', which insists that no intelligible text is uniquely different from all others. They may differ (even widely) in this or the other clearly identifiable respect. But they are never uniquely different from everything else. And the very fact that the differences can be clearly identified shows that they all belong together in a broader context.[4]

The other feature of the whole approach concerns the kind of historical knowledge of the Greek–Jewish–Roman context that we possess at the outset. Such knowledge – haphazard and accidental as it may be – always has elements of a 'model' in it, that is, it contains features that are already generalized. For instance, were we to study Virgil's *Aeneid* in Latin, we would already have *some* knowledge of Virgil's time and place, his earlier poems, the genre, including the Homeric poems, the difference between Homer and Virgil (and their social situation and cultural impact down through the ages), the social and political situation in which Virgil composed his poem, and much more. Though such knowledge may be intuitive and unarticulated, it will nevertheless contain features that are generalizable and to some extent already generalized – after all, it speaks of 'time' and 'place', 'earlier' poems, 'genre', distinct 'predecessors' and their 'social' and 'cultural' roles, and so on. Such features point towards some formal 'model' of the internal connections between them, a model that may then be explicitly articulated while we are studying the *Aeneid*. The point here is that contextualizing knowledge is not just haphazard. It is already tending towards some kind of a 'model' that may turn the use of such knowledge into a proper comparison. We will take up this feature of historical criticism later when we turn to the purposes of comparison.

In addition to the two features that we have noted of historical comparison as a contextualizing practice, we also need to add a further insight from twentieth-century hermeneutics: that when we open the Greek New Testament for the first time, we come to that study with an enormous amount of '*later*' knowledge of that textual corpus itself. This 'pre-knowledge' (so eloquently developed in Gadamer's hermeneutics) is due to the texts' *Wirkungsgeschichte* in the later tradition, which constitutes a hugely important fact that we cannot just circumvent. Thus before we open the Greek New Testament, we not only know the texts themselves in translation: our intuitive understanding of them is also strongly influenced by the whole tradition of reading these texts for almost two thousand years.

---

[4] I am indebted here to Abraham Malherbe's insistence that we should speak of the 'context' instead of the 'background' of the New Testament writings. In June 1991, I organized a conference in Copenhagen on the topic of 'Paul and his Hellenistic background' with a number of scholars participating from the USA (including Malherbe), the UK and the Nordic countries. The resulting volume had a different title: *Paul in His Hellenistic Context* (ed. Troels Engberg-Pedersen; Edinburgh: T&T Clark, 1994).

We may summarize the situation so far by saying that empirically we come to the study of the New Testament with a huge amount of 'pre-knowledge' of two kinds: contextual and traditional. How, then, should we handle this knowledge in a rationally responsible way?

The result: historical criticism

The by now established answer is this: it is in the clash between reading the New Testament texts from the two very different directions we have noted – from the historical, contextual and comparative direction (our knowledge of the full historical context of the New Testament writings) and from our own intuitive understanding based on the post-original readings of almost two thousand years (the *Wirkungsgeschichte*) – that New Testament scholarship has its place and raison d'être. Wettstein himself made the point very clear when he stated that 'you can make no progress by means of any modern system, whether of theology or logic, or by means of opinions current today'. Instead, we have to go back *via* the imagination to the ancient world itself. But we must also remember our twentieth-century caveats: that we can never leave our modern conceptual schemes completely behind and that the same goes for the texts' own *Wirkungsgeschichte*, which will inevitably have an influence on our questions to those texts.

Let me give two examples of this understanding of New Testament scholarship. When – 150 years after Wettstein – scholars from the *Religionsgeschichtliche Schule*, such as William Wrede, found the very meaning of the New Testament texts in their ancient historical situation, they took the task of articulating the historical meaning of those texts to be in direct opposition to the meanings claimed for them by systematic theologians, whose work precisely reflected and drew on the tradition and reception of those texts during the almost two thousand years after they were written. This, of course, is the precise point of the 'historical' and 'critical' method of the investigation of the New Testament texts: 'critical' of contemporary uses of the texts by insisting on their 'historical' meaning. The second example is the development of the 'new perspective' on Paul in relation to Judaism inaugurated by E. P. Sanders in 1977.[5] This was done both by rejecting the picture of Paul that came out of the long, later tradition of reading him and also by a renewed comparison of Paul himself with a newly understood Judaism, in short, by freeing oneself from the tradition and going directly back to the ancient sources. In both cases, however, we must never forget the two insights we have noted from twentieth-century hermeneutics: that we can never leave our own conceptual schemes completely behind nor forget the impact of the texts' own *Wirkungsgeschichte*.

This whole approach – the 'historical-critical method,' but understood in the light of twentieth-century hermeneutics – has come to stay. It is a constituent part of the kind of self-reflectivity that has come to characterize the human sciences since the Enlightenment and that cannot be given up.[6] It is certainly not the only thing one may

---

[5] *Paul and Palestinian Judaism* (London: SCM Press).
[6] In *Ethics and the Limits of Philosophy* (London: Fontana Press/Collins, 1985), Bernard Williams speaks (163) of a 'growth of reflective consciousness' that 'goes deeper and is more widely spread in modern society than it has ever been before', and he adds the memorable phrase: 'There is no route back from reflectiveness', meaning that there is no intellectually sound *route* back, 'no way in which we can consciously take ourselves back from it' (163–4). (Personally and socially, by contrast, things are quite different.) He was right.

responsibly do with the New Testament writings, but it does articulate a necessary condition for any assertion about those writings to be scientifically worthwhile.

In all of this, I have presupposed (as did Wettstein) that by using our imagination and without actually *living* then we may in fact reach an adequate understanding of both the contextual material we will be studying and the New Testament writings themselves as ancient texts that differ in their overall profile from anything we ourselves would immediately say. I now turn to a set of queries that have been raised concerning the very possibility of reaching such an understanding and to some answers that have been given to defend that possibility. Here we will find a line of reasoning that makes it more and more doubtful whether understanding a 'worldview' that differs quite radically from one's own in either time or place is at all possible. The issue was raised implicitly in Gadamer's hermeneutics and brought more directly up front in discussions of rationality and relativism in Anglophone philosophy of the 1970s and 1980s – and has recently become acute in relation to New Testament scholarship itself.[7] I will be concerned to sort out the character and roles of 'rationality', 'tradition', 'social context' and 'way of life' in connection with 'understanding', 'believing' and 'living'. This will all be a way of spelling out what goes into the human capacity for 'imagination'. The basic argument will be that while a number of points made in different ways (by Gadamer and Alastair MacIntyre) concerning the role of 'tradition', 'social context' and 'way of life' for 'understanding' are both valid and important, they do not have the consequence (nor were they necessarily taken that way by their proponents) that 'cross-cultural understanding' through the use of the 'imagination' is impossible. Against this stands the character and role of human 'rationality' to be understood in the ways to be developed. By contrast, as I shall try to show, the position recently adopted in New Testament scholarship, which does query the very possibility of cross-cultural understanding and hence of comparison proper, cannot be sustained.

Justification

Kavin Rowe on the possibility of understanding

Before we turn to the earlier explorations of the conditions of understanding, it will be useful to have before us the basic features of Kavin Rowe's position on the same issue. One basic claim is that different worldviews – at least those that differ as much, according to Rowe, as a 'Christian' worldview and a 'Stoic' one – are *'incommensurable'* in the sense that they cannot both be lived by the same person at the same time. One might well query this claim by asking whether any human being *just* 'lives' in accordance with a single worldview. I personally doubt this very much. I also feel sure that the claim would not hold true, for instance, of the apostle Paul (who was famously criticized for being inconsistent) nor for his various types of addressees. So perhaps neither of them was after all 'fully' 'Christian'? However, let us accept for the sake of the argument

---

[7] See C. Kavin Rowe, *One True Life: The Stoics and Early Christians as Rival Traditions* (New Haven: Yale University Press, 2016), on which much more later.

that living as a 'Christian' and living as a 'Stoic' are in fact incommensurable: one cannot live in both ways at the same time.

Rowe's next basic claim is that this (supposed) fact is implied by the need to engage in a certain 'way of life'. Here the notion of a way of life is presumably to be understood as consisting of a set of practices, but the idea also seems to be that such a set will be impregnated with the set of *ideas* that go into the given 'worldview'. So, not only will a person *just* live either a 'Christian' or 'Stoic' life: it will also be the case that each of their lives will be a wholly monolithic one, a block or pillar that stretches from the earth (practices) to heaven (ideas) and in this form is 'incommensurable' with any other pillar.

Another way of articulating this conception is by claiming that *understanding* the ideas that go into any given worldview requires *believing* them in the way one does when one *lives* the relevant form of life. After all, did not Wittgenstein claim that the very meaning (of ideas) lies in the (practical) use? Thus Rowe draws his intended radical conclusion from 'incommensurability' to 'unintelligibility': that since living as a 'Christian' and as a 'Stoic' are mutually incommensurable, either form of life (including the basic ideas of its worldview) is *unintelligible* to the other. It is this conclusion that we must query.[8]

Gadamer and Habermas on understanding and believing

The challenge consists in the claim that in order to understand, say, Paul's whole 'theology', considered as a set of ideas that inform a set of social practices, the investigator must herself believe it and so assert and subscribe to that whole worldview and its corresponding practices. Such a claim might be said to form part, for instance, of Gadamer's overall hermeneutical understanding, which holds that we can only understand some comprehensive phenomenon back in history because we already 'stand in' that history (it is our *own* history) as also partly defined by the '*Wirkungsgeschichte*' of the given phenomenon within our tradition. Does this not mean that we can only understand, say, Paul's theology if we already *believe* in that theology as the best overall worldview among those that might in principle be available to us?[9]

In its general shape Gadamer's quite stark hermeneutical position immediately raises the question of how we may come to understand comprehensive phenomena *outside* 'our own' tradition. But then, should we not rather say that Gadamer has raised the bar for

---

[8] In an earlier review of Rowe's book (*JECS* 25, 2 [2017], 326-8), I could only present it and criticize three points in its interpretation of Stoicism. The present essay attempts to get to the root of the fundamental, philosophical issues. Rowe himself does not explicitly articulate the step from incommensurability to unintelligibility. But precisely that step must lie behind the whole of his 'Part III' (pp. 175-258). Here he enlists (Chapter 7: 'Can We Compare?') Alasdair MacIntyre in an attack on a belief in 'the translucifying [!] power of scholarly reason' (p. 175), but finally, as we shall see in some detail, has to leave even MacIntyre behind (Chapter 9: 'The Argument of Rival Traditions'). In between (Chapter 8: 'Traditions in Juxtaposition'), he develops an idea of 'narrative juxtaposition', which is the best one can do when one cannot 'live' both 'traditions'. In this way, he constructs a position based on the notion of incommensurability that *in fact* leads into mutual unintelligibility.

[9] This cannot in fact be Gadamer's idea. After all, he had a clear sense of the *multiformity* of 'our tradition'. But the temptation to understand him like that is great.

understanding too high, even if he did not outright stipulate the need for *believing*? Instead we might say this: while it is certainly true (as we know from the 'critical theory' of the Frankfurt School) that all human beings come with some (socially informed and normative) conceptual scheme that is local and leaves us with a number of blind spots to prevent us from seeing and understanding the viewpoints of others; nevertheless, we do have a set of faculties that allows us to overcome this limitation, namely, the faculty (or faculties) of the imagination and of rationality as a capacity for self-reflection. For that is precisely what defines rationality and goes into the imagination: that it allows us to hold our own conceptual scheme out in front of ourselves and to look at it as a sheer view of the world consisting of a number of 'propositions', but with the belief element (in the form of 'assertions' of those propositions) detached from it. When we activate that capacity in relation to times and places that differ from our own, we are reasoning imaginatively.[10]

That we do have this capacity was Habermas' claim against Gadamer in the extensive German debate that followed the publication in 1960 of Gadamer's *Truth and Method*.[11] Speaking of 'the transcending power of reflection',[12] Habermas noted that it shows itself in the fact that it 'can also reject the claims of tradition',[13] 'inasmuch as it [that is, reflection] not only affirms but also breaks dogmatic powers'.[14] 'This understanding [which is determined by prejudices (in Gadamer's sense)] rises to [the level of genuine] reflection when it makes the normative framework transparent, as it moves around within it.'[15] 'When the structure of prejudices has been made transparent, it can no longer function in the manner of a prejudice.'[16] What Habermas articulates here is the second-order character of rationality that allows its possessor to rise above the immediate (and normative) perception of the situation in which the person finds herself (call it 'the intuitive perception') – and hence also to move imaginatively into other times and places so as to understand them without necessarily believing what is understood.

MacIntyre on understanding and believing

The same issue was intensively discussed in Anglophone philosophy of the 1970s in a sharpened form that focused on the preconditions within anthropology for understanding 'indigenous people' who belong completely outside our own cultural conceptual schemes.[17] Here the earlier idea that we can never leave those schemes completely behind

---

[10] I leave aside here a closer consideration of the relationship between the 'two faculties' of rationality and the imagination: whether and if so how they differ.
[11] See *Hermeneutik und Ideologiekritik: Mit Beiträgen von Karl-Otto Apel, Claus v. Bormann, Rüdiger Bubner, Hans-Georg Gadamer, Hans Joachim Giegel, Jürgen Habermas* (Frankfurt am Main: Suhrkamp, 1971). (Habermas: 'Zu Gadamers "Wahrheit und Methode"', 45–56.)
[12] 'die transzendierende Kraft der Reflexion' (Habermas, 'Zu Gadamers', 52).
[13] 'den Anspruch von Traditionen auch abweisen kann' (Habermas, 'Zu Gadamers', 49).
[14] 'weil diese [die Reflexion] nicht nur bestätigt, sondern dogmatische Gewalten auch bricht' (Habermas, 'Zu Gadamers', 49–50).
[15] 'Zur Reflexion erhebt sich diese [von Vorurteilen bestimmte] Erkenntnis, wenn sie den normativen Rahmen, indem sie sich darin bewegt, selber transparent macht' (Habermas, 'Zu Gadamers', 49).
[16] 'Die transparent gemachte Vorurteilsstruktur kann nicht mehr in der Art des Vorurteils fungieren' (Habermas, 'Zu Gadamers', 49).
[17] See not least *Rationality* (ed. Bryan R. Wilson; Oxford: Blackwell, 1970) and *Rationality and Relativism* (eds Martin Hollis and Steven Lukes; Cambridge, MA: MIT Press 1972).

(but according to Habermas, we at least can bring them clearly into consciousness) was sharpened by the claim that such schemes are invariably tied to a specific 'social context' and a whole 'way of life'. The question now became raised head-on whether we are at all able to understand people living (whether in other times or places) with wholly different conceptual schemes.

As an example of this discussion I will consider an article by Alaisdair MacIntyre, not least because MacIntyre plays an important role as a kind of 'authority' in Kavin Rowe's argument. The article dates from 1964 and thus predates MacIntyre's sharpened position in books like *Whose Justice? Which Rationality?* (1988) and *Three Rival Versions of Moral Enquiry* (1990).[18] However, MacIntyre retained his claim from the earlier article that cross-cultural and cross-temporal understanding is in fact possible. It is worth seeing, therefore, how MacIntyre himself describes the overall issue in a manner that does *not* lead to a claim about unintelligibility.

In the article, which was reprinted in *Rationality*[19] with the title 'Is Understanding Religion Compatible with Believing?', MacIntyre addresses the role of believing in relation to understanding a religious worldview both back in history and also of a contemporary alien tribe (like Malinowski's Trobrianders and Evans-Pritchard's Nuer and Azande).

MacIntyre's question, which we need not consider directly, is this: 'in what sense, if any, can [a religious] sceptic and [a religious] believer be said to share the same concepts, and so to understand one another?'[20] In relation to what he takes to be Peter Winch's ('Wittgensteinian') view that 'you can only understand it [some form of religious activity] from the inside',[21] MacIntyre wishes to insist that 'sometimes to understand a concept involves *not* sharing it'[22] and so, while it may be true that some features of a worldview can only be understood from the inside, this does not imply that one must also *share* the worldview in order to understand it. To show MacIntyre's overall position I provide a long quotation:

> I have argued that to make a belief and the concepts which it embodies intelligible I cannot avoid invoking my own criteria, or rather the established criteria of my own society.... I have [also] argued that I cannot do this [that is, make a belief and the concepts which it embodies intelligible] until I have already grasped the criteria governing belief and behaviour in the society which is the object of enquiry. And I only complete my task when I have filled in the social context so as to make the transition from one set of criteria to the other intelligible.
>
> (1) All interpretation has to begin with detecting the standards of intelligibility established in a society. As a matter of fact no one can avoid using clues drawn from

---

[18] London: Duckworth, 1988 and 1990, respectively. MacIntyre himself saw the following article as marking a turning-point in his thought: 'Epistemological Crises, Dramatic Narrative, and the Philosophy of Science', *The Monist* 60, 4 (1977), 453–72. Compare the full discussion of MacIntyre's development by Christopher Stephen Lutz in the article on MacIntyre in the *Internet Encyclopedia of Philosophy*.
[19] See n. 17.
[20] p. 72. All page references are to the 1970 reprint.
[21] Ibid., 66.
[22] Ibid., 69 (emphasis mine).

their own society; and as a matter of exposition analogies from the anthropologist's society will often be helpful. But we have to begin with the [alien] society's implicit forms of self-description. It does not follow from this ... that the descriptions used or the standards of intelligibility detected will always be internally coherent. And, if they are not, a key task will be to show how this incoherence does not appear as such to the members of the society or else does appear and is somehow made tolerable.

(2) But in detecting incoherence of this kind we have already invoked *our* standards. Since we cannot avoid doing this it is better to do it self-consciously. Otherwise we shall project on to our studies ... an image of our own social life. Moreover, *if we are sufficiently sensitive we make it possible for us to partially escape from our own cultural limitations.* For we shall have to ask not just how we see the Trobrianders or the Nuer, but how they do or would see us. And perhaps what hitherto looked intelligible and obviously so will then appear opaque and question-begging.[23]

Note here that in the italicized sentence MacIntyre does recognize the possibility of reaching an understanding (even if only a partial one) of an alien culture.

Next, he transfers this picture of anthropological epistemology to the case of the modern understanding of a religious world view back in history. His aim is to identify the role played by the 'social context' for any given type of belief:

To take an obvious example, Christianity does not and never has depended upon the truth of an Aristotelian physics in which the physical system requires a Prime Mover, and consequently many sceptics as well as many believers have treated the destruction of the Aristotelian argument in its Thomist form as something very little germane to the question of whether or not Christianity is true. *But in fact the replacement of a physics which requires a Prime Mover by a physics which does not secularizes a whole area of enquiry. It weakens the hold of the concept of God on our intellectual life by showing that in this area we can dispense with descriptions which have any connection with the concept.*[24]

Armed with this notion of a 'social context' that is required to make medieval Christianity intelligible, MacIntyre proceeds to draw his quite radical conclusion:

For a sceptic to grasp the point of religious belief, therefore, he has to supply a social context [the medieval one] which is now lacking and abstract a social context which is now present [e.g. that of modern physics which does not operate with a 'Prime Mover'], and he has to do this for the mediaeval Christian, just as the anthropologist has to do it for the Azande or the aborigines. ... If I am right, understanding Christianity [on our modern premises] is incompatible with believing in it, not because Christianity is vulnerable to sceptical objections, but

---

[23] Ibid., 71–2 (emphasis mine).
[24] Ibid., 74 (emphasis mine).

because its peculiar invulnerability belongs to it as a form of belief which has lost the social context which once made it comprehensible. It is now too late to be mediaeval and it is too empty and too easy to be Kierkegaardian. Thus sceptic and believer do not share a common grasp of the relevant concepts any more than anthropologist and Azande do. And if the believer wishes to he can always claim that we can only disagree with him because we do not understand him. But the implications of this defence of belief are more fatal to it than any attack could be.[25]

Thus ends the article. MacIntyre makes four points in it, the combination of which is immensely relevant to our concerns. First, he insisted on the importance of 'social context' for the content of any given 'conceptual scheme'. It is not entirely clear whether 'social context' implies actual 'living' or merely 'sharing a comprehensive set of beliefs'. But the concept is at least strong enough to tie a given conceptual scheme to a specific social context. Second, MacIntyre recognized a basic similarity with respect to 'otherness' of cultures that differ from our own whether in time (the Middle Ages) or in place (the Trobrianders, etc.). On this point MacIntyre basically accepted the point about 'historical difference' that we saw to go back to Wettstein. Third, MacIntyre *accepted* the possibility of *understanding* across the gap between different cultural and temporal social contexts. It *is* possible for a person living within the present social context to *understand* a person who was living with a medieval, 'Aristotelian' cosmology. By contrast, and fourthly, it is impossible for the former person to *live now* with such a cosmology, that is, to believe in and have such a conceptual scheme, which was tied to an altogether different social context.

All of this makes excellent sense. What it shows is that MacIntyre was operating with two different forms of rationality itself: a substantive and a formal one. The substantive form is implied when he insists on the intimate connection between a conceptual scheme and a specific social context. Here something 'makes sense' *within* a certain social context. But there is also a formal form of rationality, which is what enables understanding *across* a temporal or cultural gap. This is the form of rationality that is a constituent part of the imagination, and MacIntyre does recognize that. In short, while we cannot live and believe in the way people did in the Middle Ages, we can in fact understand how they lived. Thus, incommensurability does *not* imply unintelligibility.

We noted earlier that MacIntyre retained this view in his later work. This is made clear by Kavin Rowe himself when – on the last three pages of his book – he articulates his own non-intelligibility point by explicitly departing from MacIntyre. Rowe gives a series of quotations from the later MacIntyre showing (in Rowe's correct summary) that 'it is . . . possible "through the exercise of philosophical and moral imagination" to acquire the "conceptual resource" needed to "transcend" the limits of a tradition'.[26] This is then rejected by Rowe himself:

---

[25] Ibid., 76–7.
[26] Rowe, *One True Life*, 256.

Doubtless we need imagination to engage another tradition. The trouble is that imagination is not a faculty or ability that exists independent of the way we reason – which is to say, ... the lives we live. MacIntyre speaks of imagination as if it were a special capacity that would allow us to overcome the difficulties that would otherwise stick with us. But there is no magical quality to imagination that somehow enables it to leap over the existential barrier erected by traditions that claim they must be lived to be learned.[27]

Instead, so we must conclude, we are each stuck within our own 'tradition' and way of life. I see this as a clear case of what one might call 'group solipsism'. Note also that Rowe's departure from MacIntyre on those last three pages[28] is only supported by two endnotes[29] that finally reveal his neo-orthodox, Christian position: 'If MacIntyre would discard the division between nature/grace and philosophy/theology, he could finally learn from Pascal and Kierkegaard that the way he describes traditions requires a robust theological account of conversion/reason.'

So, at the very end of a long argument in which Rowe invokes MacIntyre as an authority for a full-scale attack on positions that allow for the full intelligibility of 'rival' worldviews and ways of life, he is forced to acknowledge that MacIntyre himself makes the same allowance. Undismayed by this, however, Rowe takes a strangely supported step into his own position of unintelligibility, which is also (as he would himself probably recognize) a quite extreme position. I believe there is a pattern here. Rowe also from time to time invokes another (brilliant) philosopher, Bernard Williams, for the idea of the incommensurability of ways of life (historical or anthropological).[30] But Williams never took the additional step from incommensurability to unintelligibility.[31] Taking that step is Rowe's own move.

Rationality and beliefs

One conclusion to be drawn from this discussion in both its German and English forms is that rationality – as a constituent part of the imagination and a faculty that enables an understanding of historical or alien cultures – should not just be understood as standing for what makes coherent ('rational') sense *to us*, based on our own conceptual schemes, worldview(s) and indeed on our social context (what I called a 'substantive' form of rationality), but also much more broadly, as a formal faculty that is (i) wedded to a notion of (logical) coherence of beliefs and also (ii) enables the rational person precisely to *detach* the element of belief (or 'assertion') from any set of beliefs and to consider the coherence of the 'propositional content' of those beliefs on its own.

---

[27] Ibid.
[28] Ibid., 256–8.
[29] Notes 50 and 52 on p. 314.
[30] Williams is listed in Rowe's bibliography, but not in his index. He played an important role in the discussions at the Durham conference.
[31] Certainly not in *Ethics and the Limits of Philosophy*, in which he does develop the idea of incommensurability.

I have articulated the second feature of this understanding of rationality in terms of the modern philosophical concepts of assertion and propositional content of beliefs. It is noteworthy that a similar distinction was articulated in ancient philosophy, especially in Stoicism in the distinction between a *phantasia* (an 'appearance') and *synkatathesis* ('assent') to a *phantasia* that might turn it into a 'cataleptic' or 'cognitive' *phantasia* (a *phantasia kataléptikê*): one that expressed truth. Here the concept of *synkatathesis* presupposes the ability to 'consider' some proposition for its coherence with other appearances and beliefs *without* (yet) assenting to it. Similarly, when the ancient philosophical sceptics argued for the need for *epochê* or 'withholding assent', they, too, drew on the distinction between a kind of 'provisional' assent (in immediate appearances) and the full kind of assent that would give one truth (which the sceptics denied to be possible). In this debate the Stoics were insisting on precisely the human faculty of reason that allows us to hold out any immediate beliefs for more comprehensive and reflective investigation, which may then *end up* in a proper, rational assent. There will no doubt be some element of belief in the initial appearance, but reason is able to entertain the propositional content of the appearance on its own and to consider whether it should in fact be assented to. Here we are not so far from the understanding of rationality that we found in Habermas. These philosophers all appear to be on target.

Understanding and belief in relation to the New Testament

It seems likely that there has been for a very long time an unarticulated idea within New Testament scholarship to the effect that one cannot ('fully') understand the New Testament texts unless one subscribes to the worldview that they are expressing. This idea has now been articulated head-on by Kavin Rowe and turned into a cornerstone of his view on how comparison should be understood within New Testament scholarship. We have seen that such a claim constitutes a huge challenge to the way New Testament scholarship has been proceeding since Wettstein. But we have also seen that it neglects a number of apparent facts about the way human beings go about comparing and thinking. In particular, it neglects the formal shape of rationality: that as a capacity for reflection (including self-reflection) it is an ability to grasp the elements of an alien worldview by looking at the propositional content alone of the beliefs that express it and to consider the logical coherence of those elements.

But might not Rowe argue that if you leave out the element of assertion, you are also likely to leave out at least *some* propositional content – and so full belief is a necessary condition for *full* understanding? Whether there is this risk is a question that would require some discussion. Leaving that question aside, I will present a much broader argument that trades on the idea of an incontestable difference between then and now that we have seen to form a nucleus in New Testament scholarship since the eighteenth century. The argument draws on a number of lines of thought that we found in the early article by MacIntyre.

Here is the argument. Suppose somebody (call her 'the believer') claims A: in order fully to understand, say, Paul's 'theology', one must oneself believe it. Now (the first horn): if the notion of 'believing' in A is understood to imply 'living' with the whole social context that goes with it (cf. MacIntyre), then the believer is making a claim that is absurd. The believer is living in a wholly different social context from that of Paul. What she believes is something that a person living at present *can* believe. This excludes a large number of other worldviews, including sizeable parts of what everybody agrees went into Paul's own worldview. For instance, it *must* exclude Paul's belief that Christ was about to return to set in motion the apocalyptic events of the immediate future (cf. 1 Thess. 4.13–18; 1 Cor. 15.51; Rom. 13.11–14). Nobody living at present *can* believe that for the simple reason that it has not in fact come about. The believer cannot therefore believe 'just what Paul did'. The 'living' with its whole social context is just different. To claim otherwise would be absurd.

The second horn: if the notion of 'believing' in A is understood to be detached from living in the original social context, then the believer is *already* engaged in some form of 'interpreting' or reformulating the original set of beliefs in the light of the modern social context in which she lives. This operation may well include *rejecting* some of the original beliefs, e.g. those just mentioned. This presupposes, however, that the believer has in fact *understood* the original beliefs *without* sharing the original social context and without *believing* the original, full set of beliefs. It follows that 'believing' is not a necessary condition for understanding. The believer's claim, therefore, is self-refuting.

It also follows that there is no reason why the believer should not also be able to understand *other* worldviews (e.g. ancient ones like contemporary non-Christ-believing Judaism or Stoicism) that may be initially 'comparable' with Paul's theology. For while she may be *even more* distant from them than from the historical Paul, she has *already* taken the step towards understanding *without* (fully) believing, namely, in the case of Paul himself.

The only way to escape from this conclusion and uphold A would be for the believer to claim that she fully believes *everything* in Paul's theology (and that this is the reason why *she* alone understands it *fully*). But in view of the historical distance between then and now, such a claim would mean that she lives in the ancient world or is even identical with Paul (on the supposition that *he* – and *only* he – fully understood his own worldview). And then we are back with the first point: such a claim is absurd.[32]

In short, (the second horn): one either understands and accepts the quite real difference between then and now. In that case, the believer's claim A is self-refuting, and understanding is possible without believing. Or else (the first horn): one denies it. In that case, the believer's claim is absurd.

I have constructed this argument – drawing on the insight in MacIntyre, Williams and others that *we* cannot *live*, say, the life of an early Christian apostle – in order to demonstrate that underlying Kavin Rowe's emphasis on the necessity of living for understanding I detect the fundamentalist belief that we can in fact have the very same set of beliefs and live the very same way of life as the apostle Paul. If Rowe is not to be understood in this way, then he would be forced by the second horn of the argument to accept that understanding is possible without believing.

---

[32] Compare again Bernard Williams (*Ethics and the Limits*, 161): 'Many outlooks that human beings have had are not real options for us now. The life of a Bronze Age chief or a medieval samurai are not real options for us: there is no way of living them.'

So much for the justification of the historical, contextual practice of comparison. I now turn to consider its purposes.

Purposes

The basic paradigm (J. Z. Smith)

If both the possibility of and the need for contextualizing comparison for the purpose of understanding have been justified, we may still ask about different types of comparison as reflecting different purposes with it. Here we shall come across a number of concepts that are often connected with comparison: 'analogical' versus 'genealogical' and 'analogical' and/or 'genealogical' versus 'heuristic'. We shall also address the notion of a 'model' that plays an important role in reflection on comparison. Underlying these reflections will be one fundamental idea in J. Z. Smith's famous discussion of comparison: that comparison is a scholarly exercise that is fundamentally tied to the scholar herself; and consequently that for it to be intellectually responsible it must reflect the utmost clarity on what is being compared with what, in what precise respects, and for what scholarly purposes.[33] Here are a few quotations to remind us of Smith's points:

> there is nothing 'natural' about the enterprise of comparison. Similarity and difference are not 'given'. They are the result of mental operations.... comparison, in its strongest form, brings differences together within the space of the scholar's mind for the scholar's own intellectual reasons. It is the scholar who makes their cohabitation – their 'sameness' – possible, not 'natural' affinities or processes of history.... the statement of comparison is never dyadic, but always triadic; there is always an implicit 'more than', and there is always a 'with respect to'... 'x resembles y more than z with respect to ...' In the case of an academic comparison, the 'with respect to' is most frequently the scholar's interest, be this expressed in a question, a theory, or a model – recalling, in the case of the latter, that a model is useful precisely when it is different from that to which it is being applied.[34]

> A comparison is a disciplined exaggeration in the service of knowledge. It lifts out and strongly marks certain features within difference as being of possible intellectual significance, expressed in the rhetoric of their being 'like' in some stipulated fashion. Comparison provides the means by which *we* 're-vision' phenomena as *our* data in order to solve *our* theoretical problems.[35]

---

[33] J. Z. Smith, *Drudgery Divine: On the Comparison of Early Christianities and the Religions of Late Antiquity* (Chicago: University of Chicago Press, 1990), in particular chapter II, 'On Comparison'.
[34] Smith, *Drudgery Divine*, 51.
[35] Ibid., 52 (Smith's italics).

Smith then quotes with approval from F. J. P. Poole:

> Comparison does not deal with phenomena *in toto* or in the round, but only with an aspectual characteristic of them. Analytical control over the framework of comparison involves theoretically focused selection of significant aspects of the phenomena and a bracketing of the endeavor by strategic *ceteris paribus* assumptions ... The comparability of phenomena always depends both on the purpose of comparison and on a theoretically informed analysis. Neither phenomenologically whole entities nor their local meanings are preserved in comparison.[36]

Smith himself continues:

> It is the scholar's intellectual purpose – whether explanatory or interpretative, whether generic or specific – which highlights that principled postulation of similarity which is the ground of the methodical comparison of difference being interesting. Lacking a clear articulation of purpose, one may derive arresting anecdotal juxtapositions or self-serving differentiations, but the disciplined constructive work of the academy will not have been advanced, nor will the study of religion have come of age.[37]

In the light of this overall understanding, I will now distinguish three different purposes with the exercise of comparison. They all serve the aim of understanding, but they differ with respect to what is understood and to the logical form (historical and/or contemporary, descriptive and/or normative) of the comparison that is involved.

Parallel comparison: historical, descriptive stock-taking leading to deep parallelism

There is first a sheer historical, descriptive stock-taking of different worldviews seen in parallel. Here the investigator attempts to understand two or more worldviews (with the corresponding practices) from within and each on its own. The worldviews are selected because they initially appear to the investigator to be 'comparable'. This implies that they are taken to have certain similarities, which are initially posited by the investigator. In trying to understand each worldview from within, the investigator will next focus on certain features of each that make them different, but the focus will not so much be on the difference itself as on the role played by any differences *within* the two or more overall worldviews under investigation. If successful, this whole exercise may result in what we may call a '*deep parallelism*' of two or more worldviews, and the purpose lies in such initial stock-taking. Apparently, in that time and place there were two (or several) such worldviews with some similarities and some differences. This initial type of contextualizing comparison and stock-taking – call it 'parallel comparison' – should live up to what I have called the *lex Malherbe*: each worldview must be investigated on its own premises, without any bias of interest in one or the other of the comparanda.

---

[36] Ibid., 53. See 'Metaphors and Maps: Towards Comparison in the Anthropology of Religion', *JAAR* 54 (1986), 411–57, esp. 414–15.
[37] Smith, *Drudgery Divine*, 56.

A comparison that ends by setting out two or more worldviews in deep parallelism may proceed analogically without postulating any genealogical relationship between the investigated worldviews. Or else it may work with such a relationship. Whether it does one thing or the other is immaterial to the result since the purpose is fundamentally analogical: to see the two or more worldviews as deeply parallel to one another with all their similarities and differences, no matter how each worldview has come into being.

Heuristic comparison: sheer stock-taking that is heuristic and focuses on only one of the comparanda

Second, under sheer stock-taking there is also a *heuristic* use of comparison in order to make the investigator understand better a given historical phenomenon (A). This approach presupposes an understanding of two or more comparanda that yields a deep parallelism in accordance with the *lex Malherbe*. But now the comparison with other worldviews (B, C . . .) is skewed in the sense that its purpose is to throw further light on the one worldview (A) that is in primary focus. Here too a general similarity is postulated to begin with and the focus again is on the differences. But here the aim is to highlight the special shape (in terms of the differences) of the one worldview that is under investigation. The *lex Malherbe* still applies, but now as supplemented by a *lex Meeks*: the aim of the comparison lies in elucidating the one worldview that is being investigated (A).

Where 'parallel comparison' has a balanced aim, 'heuristic comparison' has a one-sided aim. That also explains a difference in type among the comparanda that may be brought in. Where parallel comparison usually finds its comparanda in what is broadly the same historical time and place, heuristic comparison may in principle find them in all times and places. The criterion for the success of the comparison lies exclusively in its result: whether it sharpens the investigator's understanding of the special shape of the worldview (A) that is in focus. The comparanda are brought in order to elucidate *that*.

By connecting the two preceding types of comparison with two names of well-known scholars, I may have suggested that these two scholars belong in an exclusive sense under either type of comparison. That is not actually the case. In fact, Malherbe regularly presented the paraenetic practice of the Graeco-Roman philosophers in deep parallelism with that of Paul – but for the purpose of throwing light on the latter. Still, the approach of parallel comparison is part of Malherbe's notion of a '*context*' that was shared by the philosophers and Paul taken together. Conversely, in his actual practice, Meeks did not stick exclusively to the heuristic approach. Instead, he remained wedded (in spite of his sociologically informed approach) to comparison among worldviews and social practices that were historically close to one another. A good example is one of the subtitles in his Chapter 4 ('The Formation of the *Ekklēsia*') of *The First Urban Christians*: 'Models from the Environment'.[38] Not only does Meeks here speak of the 'environment', thus matching Malherbe's focus on the (historical) 'context': he also uses the term 'models' not so much in a distinctly social scientific sense but rather as types of community in the historical context of the Pauline communities on which they might have been *literally* (even genealogically) 'modeled'. However, Meeks' actual

---

[38] *The First Urban Christians: The Social World of the Apostle Paul* (New Haven/London, 1983), 75.

practice in the whole of the chapter is rather more refined, as we shall see in a moment. Also, his heuristic approach did allow him to employ in addition some fully social scientific, *modern* 'models' for the comparative elucidation of Paul's social world. Here one in fact finds a practice that fits J. Z. Smith's fully theorized understanding of comparison even before the publication of the latter.

A fully heuristic understanding of comparison

Since in this essay I am arguing for the virtues of a *fully* heuristic understanding of comparison as practised by Meeks and articulated by Smith, I will look at an analysis by Edward Adams of the scholarship that followed on from Chapter 4 of Meeks' *First Urban Christians*. The aim is to show how difficult it is to arrive at a fully heuristic practice of comparison in its sharpest form: Meeks in fact did it, but his followers did not. I will end this section with a footnote on my own writings on Paul and John.

In his essay 'First-Century Models for Paul's Churches: Selected Scholarly Developments since Meeks',[39] Adams first rehearses Meeks' own understanding of what he is doing in his chapter. 'By "models" Meeks means *comparative* models or "analogies"'.[40] Having noted what Meeks says of his four comparanda (the household, the voluntary association, the synagogue and the philosophical or rhetorical school), Adams concludes as follows:[41] 'Meeks thus comes to the conclusion that "none of the four models ... captures the whole of the Pauline *ekklēsia*, although all offer significant analogies" (p. 84). ... However, in his view, the structures that characterized Paul's churches were "worked out by the Pauline movement itself" and may have been "unique" (p. 84).'[42]

As Adams further shows, Meeks' comparative work inspired his followers to investigate whether one or the other of the four 'models' (and a few more) might not, after all, be the model that 'fit best'. However, what Meeks had himself done was something rather different. His comparative work in this chapter only served as an introduction to a lengthy study, informed by sociological concepts, of the 'primary sources' that the Pauline movement 'has [itself] left us': the Pauline letters themselves.[43] Thus in Meeks' own case the comparison took the form of an initial exercise, whose purpose was to make the investigator look more carefully at the Pauline community formation itself as reflected in its own language.[44] This is where Meeks actually did

---

[39] In *After the First Urban Christians. The Sociel-Scientific Study of Pauline Christianity Twenty-Five Years Later* (eds. T. D. Still and D. G. Horrell; London/New York: T&T Clark International, 2009), 60-78.
[40] Adams, 'First-Century Models', 60 (on Meeks, *First Urban Christians*, 84).
[41] Adams, 'First-Century Models', 63.
[42] See n. 44 below on Meeks' use of 'unique' here.
[43] Meeks, *First Urban Christians*, 84.
[44] For the same reason Meeks' use of the term 'unique' on p. 84 does not fall foul of the (just) criticism of that term advanced by J. Z. Smith (*Drudgery Divine*, 36): 'The "unique" is an attribute that must be disposed of, especially when linked to some notion of incomparable value, if progress in thinking through the enterprise of comparison is to be made.' Compare also Dale B. Martin in *Biblical Truths: The Meaning of Scripture in the Twenty-First Century* (New Haven, 2017), 26: 'It is common knowledge among real historians that either (1) nothing in history ... is truly "unique," or (2) everything is.'

make a fully heuristic use of his 'models from the environment', even though he did not perhaps present his approach in quite that way.

In Adams' presentation of Meeks' followers, by contrast, where the comparison itself is more in focus, a certain problem arises regarding the proper understanding of the term 'model'. It seems that the term is employed in two different ways, either in a Weberian sense as equalling an 'ideal type' (*the* household, *the* voluntary association, etc.) or else as an entity on which the Pauline type of community had *literally* been 'modelled'. Where the former meaning lends itself to an exclusively 'analogical' comparison (and from there to a fully heuristic type of comparison), the latter also brings in a genealogical perspective. But these two senses and approaches must be kept apart. And they are not always so in the scholars mentioned by Adams.

Adams' own conclusion is more promising even though he does not quite take the final step. He first notes the 'lack of agreement' among scholars 'on what is the "best" first-century model for the Pauline churches' but also claims that this lack 'does not invalidate the comparative exercise, *though it may raise questions about fixating on any one, particular model*'.[45] This is exactly right, but it also reveals the error underlying the scholarship described by Adams: that the comparison is intended to ascertain that the Pauline community *was* (if only 'primarily') one among the four (or more) comparanda – primarily 'a' household or *primarily* 'a' voluntary association, and so on. That way of understanding the comparison, which will invariably contain genealogical features, will not do justice to the level of reflection reached in Smith's theoretical account and in Meeks' practice.

Adams also speaks of 'scholars' increasing recognition of the overlapping nature of households, associations, synagogues, and schools and thus suggests that 'more attention should be given in the comparative enquiry to the "generic" features of first-century groups':

> e.g., each involves the coming together of people on a regular basis; each is a distinct unit with a sense of social identity; in each members have or develop relatively close ties with each other; each has its own norms and ethos; in each meeting takes place in a regular physical setting, relevant to the group's activities; each imitates to some extent patterns in the wider civic arena.[46]

And he concludes: 'If the most telling similarities between the Pauline churches and the different comparative models are at the generic level, the quest for the single, most appropriate first-century analogy may be somewhat misguided.'[47]

One can understand what Adams is aiming to say and his scepticism concerning 'the quest for the single, most appropriate first-century analogy' is exactly right. But the route towards it (*starting* from that quest) is, I believe, conceptually wrong.[48] Instead, what he should have said is this: the so-called 'generic' features of first-century groups are those

---

[45] Adams, 'First-Century Models', 76 (my italics).
[46] Adams, 'First-Century Models', 77 and 77–8.
[47] Adams, 'First-Century Models', 78.
[48] Adams might of course defend himself by pointing out that the scholars he is analysing did engage in that quest. But he might have left them behind more directly by theoretical considerations.

that make the investigator engage in the comparison to begin with by making her hold those groups to be similar. Against that background, the investigator will look for differences either within those similarities (when the similarities are 'filled in' in each individual type of group as in 'parallel comparison') or outside of them. She will conclude that in *this* particular respect A differs from B, whereas in another particular respect A differs from C, and so on. Thus the comparison does not proceed by way of a distinction between certain features that are 'generic' and others that are 'specific'. Instead, the investigator *holds* certain features to be similar and uses the comparanda to bring out any differences. It is all a matter of the *heuristic* purpose of the whole comparison, as anticipated by Meeks – to bring out the specific shape of the group under investigation. Correspondingly, there is absolutely no reason to look for 'the *single, most* appropriate first-century analogy' (my italics).[49] It is all a question of how much is gained *for the understanding of A* in bringing in one, two or several other groups for comparison.

This, I think, is the proper understanding of 'heuristic comparison' to which Meeks' own approach in his Chapter 4 points, as do Adams' concluding remarks. It employs the notion of a 'model' in its Weberian sense of an ideal type and it may bring in as many models from as many times and places as one likes – as long as they will genuinely illuminate the specific shape of the group under investigation. In our example, one should not seek to discover what the Pauline congregation *was* (among other similar groups), but how best to *understand* it (and hence of course also what it in fact was) in its *own* shape.[50]

As a footnote to this discussion, let me mention two comprehensive types of 'comparison' from my own writings on Paul and John. In *Paul and the Stoics*,[51] I developed a 'model' for the relationship between the individual (called I), logos or Christ (called X), and the social (called S), which I then employed to elucidate Paul. Seen in hindsight, what I did was to focus on certain 'generic' features (à la Adams) of Stoic and Pauline thought, respectively, but precisely to be used as a 'model' – in the sense of my own scholarly model, as articulated by Smith – for describing *differences within* the posited similarity. In principle, it should certainly be possible to fill in this model by looking at Stoicism and Paul, respectively and independently, in a manner that would place the two patterns of thought in 'deep parallelism'. But my aim was rather to achieve the heuristic type of comparison in its fully Smithian form, using the model as my *own* model for *elucidating Paul* and seeing the model in that guise as *in principle* equal to a modern social scientific model.[52]

---

[49] Ibid., 78.

[50] The last parenthesis in this sentence is intended to indicate that a Smithian approach to comparison does not at all go against making genuinely historical claims about the material under investigation: what it *was* (as one now sees).

[51] Edinburgh: T&T Clark (2000).

[52] For a less extensive, but just as pointed, use of comparison (using a Stoic idea as a reading lens, trying to *find* something of importance in a Pauline text that can then be seen to be actually there), see my essay in conversation with Samuel Vollenweider: Troels Engberg-Pedersen, 'On Comparison: The Stoic Theory of Value in Paul's Theology and Ethics in Philippians', in *Der Philipperbrief des Paulus in der hellenistisch-römischen Welt* (eds J. Frey and B. Schliesser; WUNT 353; Tübingen: Mohr Siebeck, 2015), 289–308. For Vollenweider's own reflections on comparison, see his 'Lebenskunst als Gottesdienst: Epiktets Theologie und ihr Verhältnis zum Neuen Testament' in *Epiktet, Was ist wahre Freiheit? Diatribe IV 1* (ed. Vollenweider; SAPERE 22; Tübingen: Mohr Siebeck, 2013), 119–62.

Similarly, in my latest book, *John and Philosophy: A New Reading of the Fourth Gospel*,[53] I employ two basic ideas in Stoicism – a comprehensive epistemological and ontological theory of the interconnectedness of *logos* and *pneuma* and an understanding of what goes into a way of thinking that is genuinely philosophical – in order to see whether these ideas might help us to achieve maximal coherence in the Johannine text. Again, the approach is quite far from being 'genealogical.' Nor is it merely 'analogical' since I have little interest in placing the two sets of ideas (John and Stoicism) in any form of deep parallelism that might satisfy one's historical (or perhaps later, existential) curiosity. Instead, I have employed some important, Stoic ideas as a reading lens, trying to see in a fully heuristic comparison whether they throw new and convincing comprehensive light on John.

Existential comparison: from descriptive to normative

I have distinguished between two different purposes with comparison (of Malherbe and Meeks, respectively) and attempted to bring out the special profile of the latter in a sharpened form. There is a third purpose of comparison which leaves behind the level of mere understanding in the sense of a non-committed, historical stock-taking. Instead, *once* the investigator has set up two or more worldviews in deep parallelism, the question may arise which of them, if any, may have a stronger persuasiveness to be *believed* (when duly reformulated) as part of one's *own* worldview. This type of comparison is only rarely performed by New Testament scholars. Or if it is, it is done in a manner that precisely does not go *via* the two other types of comparison, but instead relies on a pre-existing (and wholly un-historical) bias in favour of some New Testament position or other. This is where J. Z. Smith's critique of 'arresting anecdotal juxtapositions or self-serving differentiations' becomes relevant.[54]

But here there are two things to be said. First, it is certainly entirely legitimate for scholars of antiquity to have a more than scientific, even existential interest in the material that they are studying. And the attempt to find intellectual stimulus in the ancient material is highly laudable – as long as the differences between then and now are not forgotten. But second, precisely because those differences must always be kept in mind, the attempt to find existential answers by looking at the ancient material must always go *via* one or the other of the two stock-taking types of comparison we have distinguished. Only then will the investigator be able to make those *reformulations* of the ancient material that are inescapably required by the differences between then and now.

Here too we may articulate a 'law', in this case a *lex Räisänen*: when in an existential quest one is addressing worldviews that differ from one's own, one must always proceed in a spirit of 'fair play,' giving each of them its due. The *lex Räisänen* is closely similar to the *lex Malherbe*, only the principle of fairness is applied to a search that is not just historical, but also existential.

Here, then, at the end of a long, critical road, one may end up with a 'belief' that is truly enlightened.

---

[53] Oxford: Oxford University Press (2017).
[54] Smith, *Drudgery Divine*, 53.

5

The Possibility of Comparison, the Necessity of Anachronism and the Dangers of Purity

Dale B. Martin

Human beings compare things. We compare ourselves to other people. We compare different people to one another. We compare living spaces. We compare groups of people, nations, countries, ethnic groups. We compare ideologies, languages, plants, animals, ways of being in the world. Comparison is just one of the fundamental ways we human beings think. We cannot *not* compare. Comparing similarities and differences is simply one of the fundamental ways that we organize our world. My mother has a saying we always took to be humorous. Whenever one of us would compare one person to another in any kind of disparaging way, she would raise her nose, as if smelling something unpleasant, and proclaim, 'Comparisons are odious.' But whether fortunately or unfortunately, we human beings cannot avoid comparing.

This is not to say that all ways we compare are good ways, especially when it comes to the comparison of what we call 'religions', as has been demonstrated in several books by Jonathan Z. Smith, among others. In his classic essays published as the volume *Drudgery Divine*, Smith concentrates on the twentieth-century academic discipline then called the 'history of religions'.[1] Reviewing some of the points he makes in that book can help us think of our own practices of comparing ancient Christianity to other social and religious systems or movements in antiquity and modernity.

Jonathan Z. Smith and *Drudgery Divine*

According to Smith and other scholars he quotes, comparison must first be recognized as the construction of the scholar, a product created in the study. Sameness and difference are not properties that simply exist 'in the things themselves' to be passively 'seen' or 'discovered' by the scholar. In Smith's words, 'It is the scholar who makes their cohabitation – their "sameness" – possible, not "natural" affinities or processes of history.'[2] Though Smith does not make the point in this context, the point should be made here: since

---

[1] Jonathan Z. Smith, *Drudgery Divine: On the Comparison of Early Christianities and the Religions of Late Antiquity* (Chicago: University of Chicago Press, 1990).
[2] Ibid., 51.

'sameness' or 'difference' are not properties of the phenomena themselves, the truth of a statement of comparison cannot be confirmed or denied by just pointing to the phenomena themselves. In other words, a comparison will be good or bad as judged by whether the comparison 'plays by the rules' of scholarly comparison or not, or whether the comparison 'does the work' the scholar wants it to do. This means that a 'correspondence theory' of language, in which a linguistic description can be judged by whether it 'corresponds' to reality or 'the thing itself', is inadequate. By showing that comparisons are products of scholars made to further their own purposes or goals, Smith is at the same time rejecting a 'correspondence theory' of language or truth.

Here, because I am about to discuss Smith's 'second observation', I should note that I am presenting his main points in a different order from the way he presented them in his book. I think my ordering of these several suggestions better helps us see how they fit together to form something of a 'method' of comparison.

My second reminder from Smith is that comparison, if it is to succeed, does not compare phenomena *in toto*, but by taking apart their parts and then 'redescribing' them for a different context. Proper comparisons resist the attempt to compare different things or systems in their entirety. Rather, good comparatists recognize that we, as scholars, break up complex systems (of course, they are 'systems' in the first place because we have construed them and constructed them as such) into many different component parts, and then we 'redescribe' them in a different context. Citing the use of the word 'redescribe' by Max Black, Smith explains,

> A comparison is a disciplined exaggeration in the service of knowledge. It lifts out and strongly marks certain features within difference as being of possible intellectual significance, expressed in the rhetoric of their being 'like' in some stipulated fashion. Comparison provides the means by which *we* 're-vision' phenomena as *our* data in order to solve *our* theoretical problems.[3]

Comparison selects certain parts of what we may think of as 'systems', lifts them out of their 'home' context and 'redescribes' them in another discourse *for the purposes of the scholar doing the comparing*.

To reiterate the point, Smith provides a long quotation from anthropologist F. J. P. Poole:

> Comparison does not deal with phenomena *in toto* or in the round, but only with an aspectual characteristic of them.... Neither phenomenologically whole entities nor their local meanings are preserved in comparison. What matters in comparison are certain variables that are posited by and cohere in theories and that are aligned with aspects of the phenomena to be compared through some set of correspondence rules.[4]

---

[3] Ibid., 52. Max Black, *Models and Metaphors: Studies in Language and Philosophy* (Ithaca: Cornell University Press, 1962), 230–8.

[4] J. P. Poole, 'Metaphors and Maps: Towards Comparison in the Anthropology of Religion', *JAAR* 54 (1986): 414–15; quoted in Smith, *Drudgery Divine*, 53.

Because no two complex phenomena or systems will be completely like one another, it makes no sense to insist that those systems must be compared only in terms of their entireties.

I have already mentioned what I will call Smith's 'third point', but it will be useful to emphasize it here: comparison is done to serve the interests of the scholar and what the scholar wants to 'do' with the comparison. Again, another long quotation, but this from Smith himself:

> It is the scholar's intellectual purpose ... which highlights that principled postulation of similarity which is the ground of the methodical comparison of difference being interesting. Lacking a clear articulation of purpose, one may derive arresting anecdotal juxtapositions or self-serving differentiation, but the disciplined constructive work of the academy will not have been advanced, nor will the study of religion have come of age.[5]

Comparison is created in the study to serve some end of interest to the scholar, but in order to be defensible from a disciplinary perspective both the purpose and the method must be clear.

Finally, or at least 'finally' for my initial treatment of Smith, for I shall return to him later, we note what I will call Smith's fourth observation. When attempting to compare two things or systems, it is never sufficient to refer only to two things. One must introduce a 'third thing', a *tertium quid*, to which both the other entities may be compared with regard to some particular characteristic. In Smith's words, 'The statement of comparison is never dyadic, but always triadic; there is always an implicit "more than," and there is always a "with respect to".'[6] The model of comparison should be, '*x* resembles *y* more than *z* with respect to ...' or '*x* resembles *y* more than *w* resembles *z* with respect to ...'.

The sensibility of this rule is easily demonstrated. Everyone in a debate usually will agree that there is *some* resemblance between things and that there is *some* difference. Several years ago scholars argued whether 'homosexuality' as we know it today in our culture existed in the ancient Mediterranean world. Some argued that what we know as 'homosexuality' was a modern invention, in the precise way we talk of it, especially the pervasive notion of 'sexual orientation' and the often assumed binary of 'homo' or 'hetero' sexuality.[7] Others argued that of course 'homosexuality' existed in the ancient world: we know that men were having sex with men, and though we encounter it much less in our sources, women were sometimes having sex with other women.[8] One side of

---

[5] Smith, *Drudgery Divine*, 53.
[6] Ibid., 51.
[7] Perhaps the best example is David M. Halperin, *One Hundred Years of Homosexuality: and Other Essays on Greek Love* (New York: Routledge, 1990).
[8] A 'classic' treatment that most scholars have believed emphasized the 'continuity' of homosexuality from ancient to modern times is John Boswell, *Christianity, Social Tolerance, and Homosexuality: Gay People in Western Europe from the Beginning of the Christian Era to the Fourteenth Century* (Chicago: University of Chicago Press, 1980); but see also Amy Richlin, 'Not Before Homosexuality: The Materiality of the *Cinaedus* and the Roman Law Against Love Between Men', *Journal of the*

the debate simply stressed the similarities, while the other side stressed the differences. That debate was never really resolved because each side could simply stress sameness or difference without some 'third thing'. One such comparison that introduces a 'third thing' may go like this: 'Sexuality in the ancient world was construed more like the way we moderns construe preferences for ice cream flavours than the way we construe sexual orientation.' The third thing – here modern 'tastes' – at least clarifies what exactly we are arguing about.

So to sum up for the moment, the four points I derive from Smith: (1) comparisons are the products of the scholar's own construction; (2) comparison does not attempt to compare entities *in toto* but in parts that are then 'redescribed' for another context by the scholar; (3) comparisons are done for the purposes or goals of the scholar, and those purposes and methods of taking apart and putting back together parts of the phenomena should be clear; and (4) comparisons should introduce a 'third thing' to which both the original entities may be also compared so that the degree of similarity or difference can be better gauged.

C. Kavin Rowe compared to Jonathan Z. Smith

Kavin Rowe's account of ancient Stoicism when considered with early Christianity could have benefitted by following Smith's methodological suggestions. In the first place, Rowe seems to be working with what I have called a 'correspondence theory' of language and truth. Rowe says, 'Learning that we cannot adequately conceive the Stoic/Christian relation from some vantage point outside of the shapes of life that they *are* may indeed complicate comparative work on the ancients to a rather startling degree. But it will also be *closer to the truth*.'[9] This is one place where Rowe's rhetoric allows his theory of language and truth to come to the surface in a more notable way, but I would argue that those assumptions pervade the entire book. The truth of an account of Stoicism or Christianity will be the extent of correspondence between the description and the thing itself. And his metaphor, at least if we give him some credit by reading it as a metaphor, that 'truth' is something we can get 'closer to', gives his assumptions away. If 'truth' were a place, we could judge whether we were getting 'closer' to it or not. But, of course, 'truth' is not a place. It is a construction that may be satisfactory or may not. And its satisfactoriness can be judged only, for historiography, by whether the scholar has 'played by the rules' of academic scholarship in 'doing history' or not, not by whether or not the scholar's account 'corresponds' to the ancient 'thing' or the 'past'. The ancient 'thing' is not accessible to us when we are discussing ideas or intellectual systems themselves. And the 'past' is radically inaccessible to us as modern human beings.

History of Sexuality 3 (1993): 523–73 (among others of her publications); and Bernadette J. Brooten, *Love Between Women: Early Christian Responses to Female Homoeroticism* (Chicago: University of Chicago Press, 1996).

[9] C. Kavin Rowe, *One True Life: The Stoics and Early Christians as Rival Traditions* (New Haven: Yale University Press, 2016), 205, emphasis added.

Second, it is a fundamental insistence throughout his book that comparisons of Stoicism and Christianity must compare each of those belief structures in their entirety, not in their parts. It is the 'Encyclopedists', in Rowe's jargon, who take parts or aspects of complex phenomena rather than their entireties in comparison. Stoics and Christians were offering 'readings of the world and styles of existence that were to be taken whole or not at all. This sort of claim is not the type that can be examined bit by bit, statement by statement, but the type that is either taken or left.'[10] Of course, if one must compare ancient Stoicism in its entirety with early Christianity in its entirety, they cannot be seen to be 'the same thing'. But then again, if one were to take Paul's thinking and assumptions *in its entirety* and compare it with Luke's or Justin Martyr's thinking and assumptions *in the entirety of each of them*, they would be, according to Rowe's method, incomparable and different from one another.

Next, Rowe seeks to compare Stoicism with early Christianity side by side. He never introduces a 'third thing' that can serve as a measure for similarity and difference. We can all agree, for instance, that πνεῦμα does not mean exactly the same for Stoics as it does, say, for Paul or the author of the Fourth Gospel. But we can make some progress in comparison and illustration by introducing a 'third thing'. I have done precisely this sort of comparison in some of my publications on the meaning of πνεῦμα in Paul and ancient thinkers, such as the Stoics, and Galen in particular. The πνεῦμα in Paul's thinking resembles πνεῦμα in Stoic or Galenic systems more than πνεῦμα resembles later Christian understanding of 'spirit' with regard to 'materiality'. Both Paul and the Stoics assume (more than explicitly agree, for Paul) that πνεῦμα is 'matter' or 'stuff', even though usually invisible and extremely rarified 'stuff'. Later Christian doctrine and theology would consider spirit (πνεῦμα), rather, to be non-matter, or 'immaterial substance'.

This kind of three-way comparison proves useful also in pointing out *differences* as well as similarities. Stoicism resembles Paul *less* than it does American ideology with regard to the assumed value of αὐτάρχης (as the Stoics put it) and the 'rugged individual' (as American ideology puts it). The Stoics taught that the virtuous wise man would be αὐτάρχης, ultimately self-reliant and truly dependent for his virtue on nothing else and no other person. Paul knew about αὐτάρχεια (see Phil. 4.11), but Paul seems to assume that all human beings are utterly dependent on one another and are their true persons only in community. For Paul, κοινωνία is much more important than αὐτάρχεια.[11] So when compared with Paul's theology, Stoic philosophy has much more in common with Ayn Rand than it does with Paul. But we might not see that as clearly if we were looking only at Stoics and Paul.

To take another example from Rowe's book: he points out, rightly I think, that the Stoics and at least many early Christians understood 'death' in very different ways.[12] For the Stoics, death is a natural part of the cycle of life and the world. It is not an 'evil' nor should it be feared. For apocalyptic early Christianity, death is usually taken to be an

---

[10] Rowe, *One True Life*, 244; but the claim recurs in some form or other throughout the book.
[11] See fuller treatment of this point in Dale B. Martin, *Sex and the Single Savior: Gender and Sexuality in Biblical Interpretation* (Louisville: Westminster John Knox, 2006), 73–6; Dale B. Martin, *Biblical Truths: The Meaning of Scripture in the Twenty-First Century* (New Haven: Yale University Press, 2017), 271–4.
[12] Rowe, *One True Life*, 231–2.

evil or at least something the Christian would hope to avoid, from which to be delivered, or something to be defeated. But if we introduce a 'third thing', the comparison becomes more complex and rich. I would say the meaning of 'death' in Stoicism resembles more the meaning of 'death' in the Wisdom literature of the Hebrew Bible than it resembles the meaning of 'death' in most of Paul's letters. Even here, we should not emphasize the 'difference' so much that we cannot see Paul and the Stoics as comparable. Even the Jewish apocalypticist Paul could speak of his own death as something he could reasonably choose, and not as something in itself 'evil': 'I am torn between the two possibilities. I have a desire to depart and be with Christ, which is surely the better for me, or to remain in the flesh for your sake' (Phil. 1.23-24). In summary, comparing only two things is methodologically hazardous and may even be simplistic.

Other problems with *One True Life*

Besides comparing Rowe with Smith, I would point to other aspects of Rowe's statements about comparison that I believe are not true, or at least exaggerated and misleading from a methodological and historiographical perspective. First, Rowe repeatedly insists that one can live only one life at a time.[13] This claim can of course be accepted if taken in a certain kind of literalist way, but Rowe is not using 'life' in a completely literalist way. He is speaking of a way of being in the world, a *way* of life. But simply as a statement, it is not true that we cannot or do not live different 'lives' even at the same time. I am a Christian, but I am also a historian. When acting as a historian, I do not stop being a Christian, though it is true that modern historiography cannot be used to verify many of the truths taught by Christianity. But then again, Christianity cannot be used to verify the truth claims about history or science. Christians, as Christians, do not need to affirm the truth of the big bang theory. But even while we are Christians, we can accept it or believe it or, if one is a better scientist than I am, explain it.

My point here is related to my dissatisfaction with Rowe's use of 'language' for the systems of sensibilities of complex phenomena such as Christianity or Stoicism. I would prefer the use of the term 'discourse' as used by discourse theorists such as Mikhail Bakhtin.[14] And though I would agree that one cannot express all Christian truths in ways commensurable with historical or scientific truths, I can indeed use them all and go back and forth among them *as discourses of truths* without being false or schizophrenic. So yes, I can talk like a Stoic sometimes and like a Christian at other times without claiming to say the same thing or without claiming that the two ways of talking are commensurable. I can live more than one life at the same time, as I do all the time. I am a Christian, a gay man, a rather amateur modern philosopher, a historian and a very amateur follower of modern science. I am a musician, but that does not mean I cannot at the same time be a theologian. And I do not have to be a 'theological musician'. I can and do operate in both discourses. Rowe's steady insistence that one

---

[13] Ibid., 1, *et passim*.
[14] I am thinking especially of M. M. Bakhtin, *Speech Genres and Other Late Essays* (Austin: University of Texas Press, 1986).

cannot live more than one 'life' at a time, unless he means the word 'life' in its most literal sense, is not true.

I just brought up the notion, which Rowe also uses repeatedly, of incommensurability. But it seems that Rowe actually equates his favoured 'incommensurability' with 'untranslatable'. He may be partially excused for this collapse of two notions because he is heavily dependent on Alasdair MacIntyre, who sometimes collapsed the two words into one another. But I have spent a 30-year teaching career trying to show my graduate students why these two words must not be confused. Indeed, we can get better use of each of them if we define them to have distinct meanings.

I take 'incommensurable' to mean that two different phenomena cannot be completely equated in all ways. To invoke the etymology, the two phenomena cannot be 'measured by the same standard' or 'co-measured'. The image is that one measure of something cannot be simply emptied into another container without any lack or spillover. Those of us who have become, at least at some time in our lives, fluent in more than one language often know the experience that something said in one language cannot be translated into another language perfectly without producing the feeling that the translation 'does not exactly capture the original'. We say, 'Well, I do not think an English translation completely captures the meaning or nuance of that phrase in Spanish.' The two languages are not completely 'commensurable'. That is, any translation will not be perfect. But note well: that does not deny the possibility of 'translation'. The fact that any statement from one language can actually be 'translated' into other languages is clear from simple empiricism: we do it all the time. 'Translation' is the shift of the meaning of language from one language to another. But it does not claim commensurability between the two languages. Concepts as well as words or phrases, properly understood, may 'mean' in somewhat different ways in two different languages. But there may still be a translation of more or less accuracy.

This confusion causes Rowe to make other mistakes about language. He implies that for a 'translation' to be sufficient, it must render things 'transparent' in meaning.[15] This is related to a common mistake made by scholars: that for a word to be useful or 'correct' from a scholarly point of view, it must be 'pure' of any 'taint' or incorrectness. Again related to a 'correspondence theory of language or truth', the term or description must be entirely 'right' or 'pure' to be true in any way. But language is never 'pure' or 'transparent'. There are no 'pure' words. All words are tainted. So of course, the Greek οἶκος does not completely 'reproduce' any of the 'houses' we see around our own neighbourhoods. Which is why we should sometimes translate the Greek as 'household', 'family', 'home' or 'house' – or in some cases, especially Roman, even a person's 'clients' and 'slaves'. That shows that translation is often complicated and variable; indeed, there is no perfect translation. But it also shows that translation is always possible.

In answer to similar arguments Rowe quotes Jeffrey Stout, and takes refuge in a truly strange idea: *since* Stoics and ancient Christians themselves may have insisted that one could not understand the truths of their own doctrines unless one took their teachings 'whole or not at all', *therefore* scholars cannot understand either system unless

---

[15] See, among other references, Rowe, *One True Life*, 203, 258.

they take them 'whole or not at all'.[16] Moreover, we cannot understand either Stoicism or Christianity unless we take on that 'life' as our own.[17] In other words, we must be 'convinced and converted' before we can 'understand' at all, just because that's what ancient Stoics and Christians may have claimed. But since when do scholars allow the object of their study to 'set the rules' for analysis of the object? If I am a biologist, I do not allow the life-forms I study to tell me how to study them. If I am a sociologist, I do not first ask my subjects what questions I will be allowed to pose to them. To insist that a system we want to analyse must be allowed to 'set the rules' for our analysis is ridiculous. It is not critical scholarship at all.

Another problematic assumption throughout Rowe's book is that 'comparison' seems to mean only 'resemblances' or 'sameness', and never 'difference'. Indeed, if I must analyse only phenomena in their 'entirety', and if I find any 'differences' even in details, and even if I must 'agree' with the system in order to 'understand' it or 'translate' it into some other discourse, then the only thing I can accept as demonstrating 'translatability' or 'understanding' is if the two different phenomena are 'the same'. I can discover 'difference' not at all.

Indeed, Rowe seems to be insisting on a radical re-definition of the very word 'understand'. Rowe argues that 'understanding' must be about 'acceptance'. I do not really 'understand' Stoicism or Christianity unless I accept their own truth claims as my own beliefs,[18] and in fact 'live' the life they advocate. This may indeed be the kind of argument made by a true believer or proselytizer. But critical scholars will buy that argument to their peril – and thereby give up any claim to *being* 'critical' scholars. Rowe seems to believe he can simply 'redefine' the meaning of the word 'understand'. But that is just not what most people mean when they say they 'understand'. I demonstrate that I understand what you mean when you say 'pass me the hammer, please' when I either pass you the hammer or decline to do so. I have no need to 'agree' with what you want to 'do' with the hammer to 'understand' the language.

In fact, for an author who cites Wittgenstein a lot, I was surprised to note the *absence* of two Wittgensteinian notions that I think are central for comparison. The first is what people call an 'ordinary language' notion of the function of language and use of words. Unless we have real methodological reasons for doing so, we should not be inventing a lot of new meanings for terms we use. We should at least start off with meanings of words as they would be used in 'ordinary', daily use of the language. By completely changing the meaning of 'understand', Rowe departs significantly from Wittgensteinian 'ordinary language' philosophy.

The second notion is Wittgenstein's famous introduction of 'family resemblance'. When I am deciding whether two men before me are members of the same family, there is no one particular item of their appearance I use to the exclusion of all others. I do not decide they are brothers just because of the colour of their hair, or because both are bald. Nor do I look only at height, skin tone, noses, mouths, eyes or any other body part. I also do not insist that they must look exactly alike *in their entirety*. I look

---

[16] Ibid., 244.
[17] Ibid., see, e.g., 193, 235, though the argument is repeated elsewhere.
[18] Ibid., 195, 198, 257, et passim.

at several of their features. And no one can say exactly *how many* traits I need to list before I can confidently say the two men are members of the same family. Three? Four? Eight? There is no 'line' I can draw that moves me over to being convinced they are from the same family. I just at some point come to a conclusion – yes or no.

Why is 'family resemblance' not the method used by Rowe in comparing Stoicism and Christianity? It is about as classic a Wittgensteinian methodological notion that one can cite. I believe Paul's notion of πνεῦμα is similar to, though not exactly the same as, the Stoic notion of πνεῦμα. I also have argued that Paul resembles the Stoics in their goal of the complete extirpation of 'desire' (in Paul's case, perhaps limited to erotic desire) and for some of them the belief that such extirpation was possible, at least for a very few. But I would still not put Paul and the Stoics in the same 'family'. Their views on death, as I have admitted, are different. Paul, unlike any Stoic I can think of – or mostly any ancient philosopher at all – assumes it is perfectly rational to depict a wrathful god who may indeed destroy human beings prompted by the passion of jealousy. I know of no ancient philosopher who would agree.[19] There are many other dissimilarities. But in doing such comparison, I admit both similarities and differences, and I work with Wittgenstein's notion of 'family resemblance' rather than 'purity' or 'perfection'.

I wish to bring up only one more observation about Rowe's method or claims, precisely because it will allow a transition to the final section of this chapter, where I wish to speak of my own methodological assumptions. Like most people who deal with historical movements or systems, Rowe is concerned with 'anachronism'. He criticizes Troels Engberg-Pedersen's intention to analyse ancient 'ideas as ideas' and says that that method commits 'gross anachronism'. Moreover, Rowe faults Engberg-Pedersen's method of interpreting ancient texts because it operates 'quite contrary to their authors' intentions' (195). This is wrong-headed for at least two reasons. First, it assumes that any interpretation of someone else's language that does not correspond to the 'author's intentions' is by definition wrong. But the ability of 'authorial intention' to control interpretation by another human being is empirically falsifiable: authorial intention factually has no ability to control interpretation, as I have demonstrated in many publications.[20] Moreover, we as interpreters have no moral compunction to interpret the language of others restricted by what we can surmise of their 'intentions', and we cannot discern with certainty their 'intentions' anyway.

And then there is the irony that although Rowe accuses others of 'gross anachronism', he uses a glaring anachronism throughout his book. He speaks repeatedly of 'pagans' as those in even Paul's and Luke's days who are not Christians. I will soon speak of why I believe we should make historical use of 'useful' anachronism at times. But this is a harmful and misleading anachronism rather than a helpful anachronism. To call *everyone* in the first century who is not a Jew or a Christian a 'pagan' gives the mistaken impression that there are only three classes of persons in the Mediterranean world of the first and second centuries: Jews, Christians and 'pagans'. It also exaggerates the presence, visibility and historical importance of Christians and Jews of that time. The

---

[19] This is a main theme of my book *Inventing Superstition: From the Hippocratics to the Christians* (Cambridge: Harvard University Press, 2004).
[20] See Martin, *Sex and the Single Savior*, 5–7; Dale B. Martin, *Pedagogy of the Bible: An Analysis and Proposal* (Louisville: Westminster John Knox, 2008), 29–45; Martin, *Biblical Truths*, 96–9.

ancient Mediterranean world did not 'divide up' into three 'demographics' (or 'religions' to use that other 'anachronism') of comparable size or importance. The word 'pagan' may be historically defensible when speaking of the late ancient Mediterranean of the fifth century or later. But to retroject it to the first century is unhistorical and misleading.

Anachronism

I want to move on, however, to one of my own concerns with comparison, one not addressed in the way I do so by Kavin Rowe or, to my knowledge, Jonathan Z. Smith: a defence of anachronism. If we want to construct 'histories' of cultures or social groups and movements from 2,000 years ago – and we are talking about several 'cultures' and 'social' entities, Greeks, Romans, Jews and Christians, to mention only the most obvious – and we are translating from Greek, Latin, Hebrew and Aramaic, we will almost never find the 'perfect' fit of language, concept or social form. All historical writing by modern English speakers of the ancient world will be anachronistic to some extent. The very use of modern English introduces anachronisms. It is unavoidable.

So I prefer to speak of good and bad anachronism. 'Good' anachronisms are those that do a better job of 'translating' language or phenomena in ways that do good work for the purposes of modern historiography. 'Bad' anachronisms are those that mislead our readers about the ancient world, usually by making that world look too much like our own. Good anachronism takes a modern term or concept and uses it to illustrate how we imagine a corresponding word or concept functioning in that culture in a way similar to the way the modern word or concept functions in ours, though the fit, of course, will almost never be perfect, especially when dealing with complex systems or phenomena.

To illustrate a good anachronism: I have often tried to explain what I take to be a common understanding of πνεῦμα in the ancient world, especially in Paul's writings, but also in much scientific writing and the Stoics, though I think the notion was assumed even in the 'common sense' of ancient persons in general. I have already noted that for Paul, the Stoics and Galen, πνεῦμα was not 'immaterial' but was matter indeed. It referred to very rare, fine and perhaps 'refined' 'stuff' (for Galen, the brain was basically a 'refinery' that turned air into πνεῦμα of various levels of refinement). It was nonetheless 'stuff'. In fact, to avoid 'misleading' anachronism, I often decline to translate πνεῦμα as 'spirit', preferring to import into English the Greek term πνεῦμα as something of a technical term or 'loanword'. If modern people think of 'spirit' as 'not material or physical', then 'spirit' would be a misleading anachronistic translation.

In order to help people grasp my point, though, I compare these ancient notions of material πνεῦμα with how we usually think of oxygen or electricity.[21] Oxygen and electricity are to us invisible, but we still assume that they are material or physical. Moreover, both oxygen and electricity are supremely significant for the functioning of our material world and our bodies. We could not live without our bodies constantly depending on and using oxygen for life and thinking. Electricity causes our brains to function and shoots throughout our bodies at unimaginable speed. Oxygen and electricity make our

---

[21] My most recent treatment of this topic is in *Biblical Truths*; see esp. 201–3, 225–6, 305

world work and our bodies live. It just so happens that those activities in the ancient world, especially in several of the sciences, were attributed to πνεῦμα. Though it is obviously anachronistic to think that any ancient person understood our modern notions of oxygen or electricity, those are perfectly useful terms for explaining the ancient notions of πνεῦμα. It is a good, useful, creative anachronism.

Of course, there are anachronisms I see as a bit more problematic. As Brent Nongbri demonstrated, at least to my satisfaction, in his book *Before Religion*, even the word 'religion' may commit some harmful anachronisms when used for ancient Graeco-Roman societies.[22] There are no social institutions in the Graeco-Roman world that correspond in truly satisfactory ways to what we moderns call 'religion' in general or 'religions' in particular. This is one anachronism that doesn't bother me too much. I still use the term 'religion' or 'religious' for the ancient world, but I make clear that I am not thinking of the twentieth-century definition of a social entity that has all of three components: doctrine, ethics and ritual. I explain that by 'religion' when used of the ancient world, I mean merely 'technologies for dealing with gods or other "superhuman" beings'. Thus, I take 'religion' to be an anachronism, but one that does not do *too much* harm for modern historiography.

In fact, I think it is useful, especially when teaching students, and graduate students in particular, for scholars to address the issue of anachronism. And one helpful way to do so is to group different words into different classes. I have done this by listing (1) 'terms I have problems with and won't use' for the ancient world; (2) terms about which I resist calls for getting rid of them; we could call them 'useful' or even 'unavoidable' anachronisms; (3) terms I do not like but sometimes still use; and (4) things or concepts I am perfectly willing to 'read into' the ancient world.

(1) First, those I have done my best to give up or argue against. For example, I resist speaking of Paul's 'conversion'. That completely and wrongly implies that Paul left one 'religion' to 'join' another. Paul never saw himself as founding a 'new religion'. He never stopped being a Jew. If Paul knew the terms 'Christianity' or 'Christian', I think he would have rejected the former and been at least wary of the latter. Paul did not 'convert'. Paul describes whatever happened to him as a prophetic call, not a conversion. Similarly, I also resist using the title 'Christ' when talking about the historical Jesus.

In spite of some respectable scholarship to the contrary, I do not use the word 'race' for any group or taxonomy of people in the ancient world. I think the English word 'ethnicity' is much better. No one in the ancient world thought to take all the different peoples or ethnic groups in the world and put them into three or five or eight 'races' that are fewer than however many 'ethnicities' there were. They simply did not group demographics into anything approaching the few 'races' we think of: white, Asian, black, Latino or Hispanic, Native American, or whatever. To use the word 'race' for the ancient world is an anachronism that distorts what good scholars recognize about ancient taxonomies of human beings.

I also insist that retrojecting 'middle class' into ancient society is misleading anachronism. I say this even though I am perfectly willing to use the category of 'class'

---

[22] Brent Nongbri, *Before Religion: A History of a Modern Concept* (New Haven: Yale University Press, 2013).

and even 'class conflict' or 'class oppression' for the ancient world. Yes, there were 'the poor' as well as what I think are fairly called 'the destitute poor'. There were obviously 'the rich' of different levels. And there were no doubt some people in between. But those people 'in between' were, I think, few, and they never constituted a 'class' in the modern economic sense of the term – that is, as a social formation that played a role in a special and significant way in the ancient modes of production. The bourgeoisie became an important and distinct class in Europe in the early modern era. The 'middle class' is a later term, much preferred in English language and especially American economic discourse. It is inaccurate and misleading to think of anyone in the ancient Graeco-Roman society as occupying a 'middle class'.

Likewise, I do not believe 'capitalism' existed in ancient societies. Capitalism is an invention of modernity. Of course, there were people who invested money and made money with money. But as Karl Marx's extensive analyses should have proven to everyone, the specific economic modes of production that make up capitalism did not exist in the ancient world, and 'making money by investing in industry that made profit that was then reinvested in the mode of industrial production' is a misleading way to think of the ancient economy.

I have already given some indication why I believe the word 'pagan' is a harmful anachronism for the first few centuries of the Roman Empire and all its subcultures. For other reasons, I refuse to use the word 'supernatural' for any reference to ancient beliefs or phenomena. As I have explained elsewhere, ancient people assumed that if there were gods at all – and I have never come across a real 'atheist' in the modern sense in any premodern society – those gods, or beings like gods because they are superior to human beings, existed not 'outside' nature, but 'in' nature. The gods and similar beings were part of nature, not above nature. In the place of 'supernatural', I will sometimes use the term 'superhuman', though I admit that has its own problems.

Note that it is not enough to say that I do not want to use these words because they do not accurately correspond to the ancient reality. Nothing will. Nor is it enough to say that they do not 'sufficiently' capture the ancient meaning, without saying what *would* count as 'sufficient', for what purposes, and why. Rather, one must make a case for why these words mislead in significant ways that other terms would avoid. So 'superhuman' may be better than 'supernatural'. 'Polytheistic' may be preferable to 'pagan'. Or what would be even better, just replace 'pagan' with more specific options, such as 'Roman', 'Greek' or 'Graeco-Roman'. My main point is that alternatives must be offered and defended as *less* misleading than the words we are rejecting.

(2) Then there are terms or concepts some would call misleading anachronisms, but which for various reasons I continue to use. Some have argued that 'Jews' should be replaced by 'Judeans' or something similar. While I agree that the full 'religion' or identity we think of as 'Jews' today is a complex product of a long history, not least after the 'watershed' of the rise of 'rabbinic Judaism', I think it is too difficult to avoid calling people of Israel 'Jews' also for times before the Rabbis. 'Judean' seems too geographically limited. Likewise, I have no problem referring to 'Judaism' for social movements, ethnicity and religious identity and practices even in the Second Temple Period and the first few centuries of the Roman imperial period. Similarly, when I am speaking of a Jewish or Christian context, I have no problem using the term 'gentiles' for those who

are not Jewish, even though of course 'gentiles' themselves would not refer to themselves like that, unless they were also embedded in a Jewish context by their own choice.

Though I noted earlier that Paul either did not recognize or perhaps would have rejected the terms 'Christianity' and 'Christians', I am willing to use those terms for those people *we today* would identify as Christ-believers, though I do that less when speaking of Paul's churches and writings.

There has been much debate in the past several years about the term 'Gnosticism' or 'Gnostics' (in either lower-case or capitalized forms). Though I would not want to talk about a 'Gnostic' church or coherent 'movement', I do find it useful to continue using the term Gnostic for what we scholars may recognize as a cluster (think, again, 'family resemblance') of myths, themes, motifs or literary forms from the third and fourth centuries we discern in certain texts. 'Gnostic' when I use it refers neither to a church nor a person, but to a scholarly created cluster of similar ideas and texts.

Though I hesitate to use 'orthodoxy' and 'heresy' for forms of Christianity in the first or second centuries (though I will sometimes refer to something or someone as 'proto-orthodox' for that period), I am willing to commit what I see as a 'useful anachronism' in using those terms for the third and fourth centuries, even though I recognize that as still something of an anachronism before the fifth or sixth centuries and later.

I have already explained why I am willing to use categories of 'ethnicity' and 'religion'. Similarly, I actually enjoy speaking of ancient 'science' even though there would be many people, not least of them modern practising scientists, who believe that is anachronistic. The reason I do so is because I do not believe that there is for all of modern science an actual 'scientific method'. There are only many such kinds of practices for many different kinds of disciplines that we would take today to be 'science'. I use 'science' for many ancient technologies and systems of knowledge in order to demonstrate that the ancients themselves self-consciously attempted to differentiate certain professionally formed technological systems (τέχναι) from popular ideas or beliefs or amateur practices or bricolage. I use this 'helpful anachronism' because I want to point out the 'constructedness' of the modern category of 'science' itself. I intentionally use a problematic term *because it is problematic*.

(3) There are perhaps several terms I do not particularly like when used of the ancient world, but which I nonetheless sometimes am willing to use. The most important of these, I think, would be my use of 'homosexual' as an adjective for the premodern world. I am uncomfortable speaking of 'homosexuals' or 'homosexual persons' in classical antiquity because I do not think that could serve as an 'identity' for them in anything like it is an available identity for us today in the West. And I still believe that 'homosexuality' carries too many complex systems of meaning related to politics, 'heterosexuality', psychology and even sometimes medical discourses to be anything but a misleading anachronism for the ancient world. Yet I do not think it is too misleading to speak of 'homosexual acts' or 'deeds' or the like. So one may see that this is very much a 'borderline' case for me.

(4) Lastly, there are those terms or concepts that I am perfectly willing to 'read into' the ancient world. I have already mentioned that I talk about 'classes' when speaking about ancient society, persons and even economics, and that in what I consider a (classical or perhaps 'neo') Marxist sense. In my book *The Corinthian Body*, I explained

that whereas I realize that classes in antiquity did not function in the same way classes function in capitalist systems, I use the term in a rather simplified way. Put in its simplest formulation, as I had it, 'those who live off the surplus labor value of others ... are members of the propertied, or upper, class, whereas those whose labor provides the surplus value that supports the livelihood of others are members of the exploited class or classes'.[23]

I am also willing to speak of 'colonialism' for the Greek, Roman and Graeco-Roman contexts. I recognize that some scholars have believed this to be an inaccurate anachronism since the shape and function of 'colonies' in ancient societies, economic exploitation and political domination was significantly different from such issues and dynamics in modern colonialism, say in the fifteenth to twentieth centuries. Yet Athens and other Greek city-states did self-consciously found 'colonies' of their own people or other peoples in different places, and to a great extent Athens controlled and even dominated them. Moreover, Rome did economically exploit its 'colonies' even if not in precisely the same ways modern colonizing empires did. For me, and here my case just sometimes has to be made on an individual basis, we get more out of talking about ancient 'colonialism' than we hazard with the term.

Of course, as historians – and 'comparers' – we must remain aware that 'anachronism' and specific 'anachronisms' must be recognized and treated carefully. My point is that all historiography that has the historian separated much at all by time, language, and culture from the subject or object of study is going to use anachronism. Which is why it behooves us as scholars to think theoretically and pragmatically about how we will *use* anachronism – and how to differentiate the 'good' from the 'bad'. And as teachers, we should take it upon ourselves to work with our students to help them learn to think about these issues for their own work and their future productions of 'anachronistic' description. Since there is no 'purity' of language, speech, or translation, we must be pragmatists, not purists.

A return to Jonathan Z. Smith and C. Kavin Rowe

I would like to close this essay with a question rather than a claim, and return to Smith and Rowe to do so. In speaking of different methods in comparison, contrasting scholarship that insists on comparing complex phenomena *in toto* with scholarship that insists on taking apart complex systems, analysing their constituent parts and then reorganizing the result as a 'redescription', Smith quotes Karl Mannheim, a sociologist of the early twentieth century and a founder of the sociology of knowledge:

> Early nineteenth century German conservatism ... and contemporary conservatism, too, for that matter, tend to use morphological categories which do not break up the concrete totality of the data of experience, but seek rather to preserve it in all its uniqueness. As opposed to the morphological approach, the analytical approach characteristic of the parties of the left broke down every

---

[23] Dale B. Martin, *The Corinthian Body* (New Haven, Yale University Press, 1995), xvi.

concrete totality in order to arrive at smaller, more general, units which might then be recombined.[24]

Smith concludes, 'Religious studies, with its bias towards the "unique" and the "total", expressed methodologically through its deep involvement in morphology, phenomenology and, more recently, in a morality of regard for local interpretations, has been a discipline profoundly and not unsurprisingly of the "right".'[25] Mannheim and Smith locate the insistence on comparing complex systems *in toto* with conservative scholarly tendencies, and they identify what they characterize as a more 'analytic' approach with 'the left'.

I do not know Kavin Rowe well enough to know whether the methodological approach he outlines in *One True Life* springs from a conservative attempt to portray early Christianity as historically 'unique' – or 'true' – in contrast to Stoicism or any other 'way of life'. I do not feel confident about Rowe's personal beliefs to decide on any possible theological or ideological motives of his method. But I do think the issue should be raised. Does one have to be a conservative, as opposed to a liberal or progressive or leftist scholar or even Christian, to end up portraying Christianity as somehow unique? Methods and ideologies, or theologies, sometimes link up.

---

[24] Karl Mannheim, *Ideology and Utopia* (New York, n.d.; reprint), 274; quoted in Smith, *Drudgery Divine*, 52.
[25] Smith, *Drudgery Divine*, 52.

6

Beyond Compare

or: Some Recent Strategies for Not Comparing Early Christianity with Other Things

Matthew V. Novenson

Introduction

Comparison is, notionally, a rational or even *wissenschaftlich* undertaking: we take two or more things, observe them side by side (whether in a laboratory or in our minds) and enquire in what relevant respects they are alike or different, in the hope that we will understand one or more of them better as a result.[1] In vernacular usage, however, claims to compare, or not to compare, often function rhetorically as valuations, as expressions of praise or blame for the thing in question. According to this rhetorical commonplace, to say that x is comparable to y is to denigrate x, to put it in low company, while to say that x cannot be compared to y, that x is *beyond compare*, is to praise x. In regard to the former, consider the internet-era axiom known as Godwin's law, which states that 'as an online discussion grows longer, the probability of a comparison involving Hitler approaches 1'. To say that x is in any way comparable to Hitler is to heap scorn on x. In regard to the latter, consider Shakespeare's immortal Sonnet 18: 'Shall I compare thee to a summer's day? Thou art more lovely and more temperate', and so on. The denial of comparability is the poet's way of extolling the beloved.

This rhetorical use of claims to compare, or not to compare, is a feature not only of popular discourse but of academic discussions, which brings us to the theme of the present essay. My purpose here is to examine the ways that some recent, important books in our field have coped with the comparability of early Christianity with its counterparts. (By 'its counterparts', here I mean other Graeco-Roman philosophies and

---

[1] This essay emerged from my conversations with the other contributors to this volume at the Durham colloquium in June 2017. I have also presented parts of it in draft form at the SBL Annual Meeting, the Nottingham Theology and Religious Studies Seminar, and a meeting of my Edinburgh graduate students. It is much better than it would have been without the incisive feedback of Larry Hurtado, Kavin Rowe, Margaret Mitchell, Francis Watson, Dale Martin, Troels Engberg-Pedersen, Philippa Townsend, David Frankfurter, Kyle Harper, Tom O'Loughlin, Simeon Zahl, Jon Hoover, Sara Parks, Matt Sharp, Ryan Collman, Brian Bunnell, Patrick McMurray, Benj Petroelje, Daniel Jackson, Sofanit Abebe, Sydney Tooth, and most of all John Barclay. Any remaining deficiencies are my own fault.

religions, in particular Stoicism, although, as I will argue later, the notion of a counterpart for comparison is in fact entirely artificial, stipulated by the scholar for her own heuristic purposes.) As I mean to suggest by my subtitle, 'Some Recent Strategies for *Not* Comparing Early Christianity with Other Things', these recent, important books perpetuate – although admittedly in new and sophisticated ways – a longstanding scholarly anxiety at the prospect of comparing early Christianity with other Graeco-Roman philosophies and religions. The two books to be discussed here – Larry Hurtado's *Destroyer of the Gods* and Kavin Rowe's *One True Life*[2] – take very different approaches to the issue; their authors would, I expect, disagree sharply with one another at many points. But both, in their respective ways, illustrate the phenomenon with which I am concerned here, namely, strategies for not comparing.

On Larry Hurtado, *Destroyer of the Gods*

The title of Hurtado's 2016 book *Destroyer of the Gods* is actually a line lifted from the second- or third-century *Martyrdom of Polycarp*. The narrator places these words in the mouths of the angry Smyrnean crowd who call for the aged bishop to be thrown to the lions:

> The proconsul ... sent his herald into the center of the stadium to proclaim three times, 'Polycarp has confessed himself to be a Christian'. ... [And] the entire multitude of both Gentiles and Jews who lived in Smyrna cried out with uncontrollable rage and a great voice, 'This is the teacher of impiety, the father of the Christians, *the destroyer of our own gods* [ὁ τῶν ἡμετέρων θεῶν καθαιρέτης], the one who teaches many not to sacrifice or to worship the gods.'
>
> Mart. Poly. 12.1–2[3]

By this epithet, θεῶν καθαιρέτης, the crowd means that Polycarp teaches against traditional cult and sacrifices. In that sense he destroys – or, alternatively for καθαιρέω, deposes or undermines – the old gods. Hurtado cleverly picks up this *ad hominem* complaint against Polycarp (as imagined by the hagiographer) and repurposes it as an image of the decline of paganism and the rise of Christianity. The dust jacket of the book reads: 'How Christianity destroyed one world, and created another'; although, of course, neither Polycarp nor any of Hurtado's protagonists could have imagined that Christianity would displace traditional religion as thoroughly as it eventually did.

As it happens, I can remember quite clearly the first time that I read the work of Larry Hurtado. It was the mid-2000s, and I was a student in a graduate seminar on early Christian Christology, and our assigned text for the week was Hurtado's opus

---

[2] Larry W. Hurtado, *Destroyer of the Gods: Early Christian Distinctiveness in the Roman World* (Waco: Baylor University Press, 2016); C. Kavin Rowe, *One True Life: The Stoics and Early Christians as Rival Traditions* (New Haven: Yale University Press, 2016).
[3] Text and trans. Bart D. Ehrman (ed.), *The Apostolic Fathers* (LCL 24; Cambridge, MA: Harvard University Press, 2003).

Lord Jesus Christ: Devotion to Jesus in Earliest Christianity, which had recently been published.[4] I recall being strongly impressed by the erudition on display in that book and aspiring to know all the myriad ancient texts that Hurtado knew. I also recall a vague sense of dissatisfaction with Hurtado's habit of characterizing the Christ cult with terms like astonishing, incomparable, unprecedented, unparalleled, and without analogy. Now, by sheer accident of intellectual biography, it was around the same time that I first read Jonathan Z. Smith's *Drudgery Divine: On the Comparison of Early Christianities and the Religions of Late Antiquity*,[5] which provided me with categories for making sense of my misgivings about Hurtado's emphasis on incomparability. As is well known, Smith argues in *Drudgery Divine* that scholarship on early Christianity has not yet really reckoned with the problem of comparison, encumbered as it is with received notions of Christian uniqueness. Smith does not appear in the notes of *Destroyer of the Gods*, but I suspect that Hurtado may have had him in mind at some points. *Lord Jesus Christ* had specifically to do with the Christ cult, while *Destroyer of the Gods* takes a wide view of early Christianity as a social phenomenon, but the red thread, it seems to me, is Hurtado's intellectual fascination with anomaly. If Hurtado were a naturalist, then his special expertise would surely be the duck-billed platypus or ambulatory fish or some such.

In *Destroyer of the Gods*, Hurtado presents early Christianity as the ambulatory fish of ancient Mediterranean religions (thus the subtitle: 'early Christian *distinctiveness* in the Roman world'). His thesis, in brief, is that 'Early Christianity of the first three centuries was a different, even distinctive kind of religious movement in the cafeteria of religious options of the time.'[6] On his way to this conclusion, Hurtado makes five key moves, corresponding to the five chapters of the book. In Chapter 1, he examines characterizations of early Christians by hostile outsiders – the early Paul, Tacitus, Suetonius, Pliny the Younger, Galen of Pergamon, Marcus Aurelius, Lucian of Samosata and the philosopher Celsus – concluding that Christianity was widely perceived as 'objectionably different'. In Chapter 2, Hurtado argues that early Christianity was effectively 'a new kind of faith', aberrant enough to have been denied the title 'religion' by ancient and modern observers, but deserving the title nonetheless – albeit a new, hitherto unseen kind of religion. In Chapter 3, he addresses the category of identity, arguing that early Christianity bestowed a novel *religious* identity on its adherents, leaving their respective *ethnic* identities unchanged, partly analogously to what an exotic foreign cult (e.g. of the Magna Mater) might do, except that Christianity also forbade the offering of cult to one's own ancestral gods. In Chapter 4, Hurtado explicates what he calls the bookishness of early Christianity; that is, the prominence accorded by Christians to their holy books and accompanying paraphernalia: scribes, lectors, homilies, codex technology, and so on. In Chapter 5, finally, Hurtado argues that certain early Christian ethical scruples – in particular, the condemnation of infant exposure, of

---

[4] Larry W. Hurtado, *Lord Jesus Christ: Devotion to Jesus in Earliest Christianity* (Grand Rapids: Eerdmans, 2003).
[5] Jonathan Z. Smith, *Drudgery Divine: On the Comparison of Early Christianities and the Religions of Late Antiquity* (Chicago: University of Chicago Press, 1990).
[6] Hurtado, *Destroyer of the Gods*, 183.

gladiatorial games, of the sexual use of children, and of extramarital sex generally – put them conspicuously out of step with their contemporaries and constituted 'a new way to live'.

At the risk of belabouring the zoological metaphors, I am sure that I am not the only reader of *Destroyer of the Gods* who will have found him or herself thinking of William James's indignant crab. James famously wrote in *The Varieties of Religious Experience*, his Edinburgh Gifford Lectures for 1901–2, 'Probably a crab would be filled with a sense of personal outrage if it could hear us class it without ado or apology as a crustacean, and thus dispose of it. "I am no such thing", it would say; "I am *myself, myself alone*."'[7] Early Christianity, Hurtado urges, cannot be classed without ado or apology as an ancient Mediterranean religion. It is *itself, itself alone*. To be fair, that is a slight overstatement on my part. Hurtado carefully avoids speaking in absolute terms of Christian uniqueness, opting instead for the language of difference, oddity, strangeness, newness, and especially distinctiveness. But even in this more cautious register, the persistent rejection of all putative analogies and insistence on distinctiveness amounts to a protest against taxonomy.

And this inevitably raises ideological questions. As James comments in his explanatory gloss on the crab's protest:

> It is true that we instinctively recoil from seeing an object to which our emotions and affections are committed handled by the intellect as any other object is handled. The first thing the intellect does with an object is to class it along with something else. But any object that is infinitely important to us and awakens our devotion feels to us also as if it must be *sui generis* and unique.[8]

James's concern is that the human sciences struggle to give an account of religious experience because human beings – including, of course, scholars of religion – subconsciously perceive religion as something 'infinitely important to us', something that 'awakens our devotion', something to which 'our emotions and affections are committed', rendering it unclassifiable and, therefore, strictly speaking, unintelligible. Hurtado, for his part, is pleading for the distinctiveness not of religious experience but of early Christianity. But readers might be forgiven for wondering, in a Jamesian manner, whether his plea is for something infinitely important to the author, something that awakens his devotion, something to which his emotions and affections are committed. And in fact, Hurtado writes in his opening chapter, 'One should not and cannot pretend to have a superhuman objectivity or even a lofty disinterest in the subject [of early Christianity] ... I would be inclined to distrust any claim to such disinterested objectivity.'[9] This postmodern caveat aside, however, Hurtado insists that what he is doing is not religious advocacy but historical description: 'I ... wish to approach the question of how early Christianity was distinctive, doing so neither in the

---

[7] William James, *The Varieties of Religious Experience: A Study in Human Nature* (New York: Mentor, 1958), 26.
[8] Ibid., 26.
[9] Hurtado, *Destroyer of the Gods*, 6–7.

service of Christian apologetics nor from an aggressive and skeptical stance toward Christian faith.'[10]

I take Hurtado at his word here, but I also think that the claim that early Christianity was different from everything else – because of the particular differences such a claim chooses to highlight and the particular samenesses it chooses to pass over – has a quite particular rhetorical (not to say apologetic) effect, regardless of the author's intentions. (There is another postmodern caveat for you.) The principal objection invited by Hurtado's argument – namely, that he ignores aspects of Christian sameness that would be inconvenient for his thesis – lies in plain sight almost from the first page. This is not Hurtado's first rodeo, so he anticipates this objection and bats it away repeatedly throughout the book. For instance: 'Of course, I note again that early Christian exclusivism in matters of worship was not totally unique. It echoed the stance of the Jewish religious matrix... But, nevertheless, I think that we can distinguish [the former from the latter].'[11] And again: 'In ascribing a distinctiveness to early Christianity in certain social and behavioral practices, I intend no stereotype of the Roman era – for example, as one of simple decadence and a moral wasteland ... But, all the same, it was... a time when people legally and without qualms ... engaged in some practices that... we would regard as abhorrent.'[12] And again: 'Early Christianity was distinctive, but not absolutely so or in every respect. At a certain level of generalization, we could note [some similarities].'[13] And again: 'Certainly, Christianity did not fall from the sky like some foreign object. It was a historical phenomenon and can be studied as such. But it would be facile, and poor historical analysis, to ignore the very real ways in which early Christianity was a novel and distinctive development.'[14] Taken together, however, these numerous concessions add up to a quite different thesis than the one Hurtado argues: Christianity is very much *like* other ancient Mediterranean religions in being a historical phenomenon, in not having fallen from the sky, and so on.

And what about the many other, more specific samenesses? Again to his credit, all along the way, Hurtado dutifully records numerous examples of what a critic might take to be defeaters for his hypothesis, that is, points at which ancient Jews, Greeks, Romans, and others actually share what are ostensibly Christian distinctives. The Christians refuse to offer cult to the pantheon of gods, but so do the Jews. The Christians orient their ritual lives around sacred books, but so do the rabbis. The Christians look after the material needs of their comrades, but so do the trade guilds and burial associations. The Christians urge voluntarist devotion to a god other than one's ancestral god, but so do the mysteries of Isis or Mithras. The Christians believe in a transcendent high god, but so do the Platonists. The Christians condemn the exposure of infants, but so do the Stoics. The Christians condemn the gladiatorial games, but so, again, do the Stoics. The Christians condemn sex acts with children, but so, yet again, do the Stoics. (What is it about these Stoics? We shall return to them later.) Hurtado concedes each of these cases, and others besides, but he nevertheless persists in

[10] Ibid., 7.
[11] Ibid., 89.
[12] Ibid., 144.
[13] Ibid., 186.
[14] Ibid., 187.

characterizing such features as Christian distinctives. He reasons that the rabbis, or the trade guilds, or the Stoics do not hold belief x or undertake practice y in just the way that the Christians do. And that is of course true. But the converse is also true: The Christians do not condemn pederasty in just the way or for just the reasons that the Stoics do; hence, by the same logic, we could speak of condemnation of pederasty as a Stoic distinctive.[15]

Or we could, as I found myself doing while reading *Destroyer of the Gods*, think of religious distinctiveness, of the kind Hurtado is trying to get at, as a property inhering not in particular features but in clusters of features, or, we might say, cocktails of features. Consider the cocktail metaphor. The Manhattan, an enthusiast might say, is utterly distinctive among all its cocktail brethren. It is a sublime combination of rye whiskey, sweet vermouth, and aromatic bitters. Yes, but, a killjoy comparativist might interject, an Old Fashioned also has rye. And a Negroni also has vermouth. And an Amaretto Sour also has bitters. So the Manhattan is not really so distinctive, after all, is it? But perhaps the distinctiveness that the Manhattan enthusiast wants to praise lies not in the rye, nor in the vermouth, nor in the bitters, but in their being mixed in just those amounts, at just that temperature, and so on. That is what makes the Manhattan so very Manhattan-y. And I can imagine an analogous explanation of what makes early Christianity so very Christian, or Stoicism so very Stoic, or the Mithras cult so very Mithraic. But it would be a rather different explanation than the one Hurtado offers.[16]

As for the explanation that Hurtado offers, two questions, in particular, merit further reflection. First, was early Christianity, *viewed as a social whole*, really so conspicuously different as Hurtado suggests? He says that early Christianity *as such* forbade offering cult to the old gods, taking multiple sexual partners, and so on. But of course we have ample anecdotal evidence from antiquity of lay Christians doing and approving just these (ostensibly forbidden) things. For Hurtado, however, 'early Christianity' is represented by the epistles, homilies, and treatises of orthodox, orthoprax spokesmen: by the apostle Paul, not his Corinthian gentiles-in-Christ who celebrated temple meals to the old gods; by the Bithynian Christians who refused Pliny's instruction to burn incense to the emperor, not those who consented to do so; and so on. This decision about what one allows to count as 'early Christianity' is – to indulge in understatement – not the only one that a historian of early Christianity might make.[17] To paraphrase and repurpose Paula Fredriksen's *bon mot* about Judaism and Jews: early Christianity did not teach anything; early Christians did.

---

[15] Cf. the apt example cited by Smith, *Drudgery Divine*, 40: 'Such formulations are necessarily relative *and* reciprocal. If the Gospel of Mark is different from Iamblichus's *Life of Pythagoras*, so is Iamblichus different than Mark, so are both different from the Gospel of Matthew, and from Porphyry's *Life of Pythagoras*. Difference abounds.'

[16] Consistently with this metaphor, I think it best, as a rule of thumb, not to speak of 'Christian distinctiveness' at all, because doing so masks (either naively or deceptively) the artificiality and reciprocity of the comparison.

[17] For a hint of the other possibilities, see Elizabeth A. Clark, 'From Patristics to Early Christian Studies', in Susan Ashbrook Harvey and David G. Hunter (eds), *The Oxford Handbook of Early Christian Studies* (New York: Oxford University Press, 2008), 7–41; Karen L. King, 'Which Early Christianity?' in ibid., 66–84.

Second, even if we agree, for the sake of argument, to let 'early Christianity' mean the austere religion of a Paul, a Polycarp, or a Justin, do the standard pagan criticisms thereof actually treat it as something *sui generis*? To be sure, it is, in Hurtado's nice turn of phrase, 'objectionably different', but in fact, objectionably different religions are themselves a genus, indeed, a genus with old, conventional names in both Greek and Latin: δεισιδαιμονία and *superstitio*.[18] When Tacitus, Suetonius, and Pliny call Christianity a *superstitio*, so far from declaring it unlike anything else on offer, they are expressly classing it within a well-populated subset of Graeco-Roman religions. From their perspective, the Christians are emphatically not unprecedented or unparalleled; they are like Chaldean astrologers, or Thessalian witches, or, indeed, Jews (a barbarian *superstitio*, according to Cicero, of course [*Flacc*. 67]). To be sure, the Christians fall afoul of traditional εὐσέβεια or *pietas*, but there have always been groups that do that. That is why we have the words δεισιδαιμονία and *superstitio*. Viewed from this angle, Christianity is not a new kind of faith, but an old kind of deviance.

A few years ago, there was a brief but fascinating exchange of letters in the *New York Review of Books* between two titans of late antique scholarship, Ramsay MacMullen and Peter Brown. In response to a glowing review by Brown of Alan Cameron's *The Last Pagans of Rome*,[19] MacMullen wrote a letter to the editors entitled 'The Tenacity of Paganism', urging that paganism was not eclipsed by Christianity but persisted for centuries in myriad forms of popular Christian piety.[20] In reply to MacMullen's letter, Brown wrote:

> Whether everything that average Christians did was automatically 'pagan' and a 'survival' of pagan practice is less certain for me than it is for Professor MacMullen. His work seems to take too seriously the denunciations of the clergy – for whom any practice other than their own austere version of Christianity seemed suspect and vaguely 'pagan'. I would call it, simply, human.[21]

Hurtado's *Destroyer of the Gods* excels at describing historical particularity, but by driving a wedge between Christianity and everything else, it allows for precious little of the human in early Christianity.

On Kavin Rowe, *One True Life*

Kavin Rowe's 2016 book *One True Life: The Stoics and Early Christians as Rival Traditions* likewise has problems with the category of the human, but they are a quite different set of problems. This is what I mean:[22] humanistic scholarship, in all its varied fields of study, proceeds on the assumption that we can, with hard work, achieve a degree of

---

[18] See Dale B. Martin, *Inventing Superstition: From the Hippocratics to the Christians* (Cambridge, MA: Harvard University Press, 2004).
[19] Peter Brown, 'Paganism: What We Owe the Christians', *New York Review of Books* (7 April 2011).
[20] Ramsay MacMullen, 'The Tenacity of Paganism', *New York Review of Books* (9 June 2011).
[21] Peter Brown, reply to Ramsay MacMullen, *New York Review of Books* (9 June 2011).
[22] Bits and pieces of the following are excerpted and revised from my review of *One True Life* in *ExpTim* 129 (2018): 238.

understanding of people who are separated from us by oceans, centuries, beliefs, and otherwise. *Humani nihil a me alienum puto*, as Terence put it. Or, closer to home, τοῦ γὰρ καὶ γένος εἰμέν, as Aratus put it, and Paul (according to Luke) agreed.[23] We are not ourselves Vestal virgins or stylite monks, but by careful study and sympathetic imagination we can begin to understand the lives they lived and the choices they made. Or can we? Rowe thinks that we cannot, at least not in regard to traditions of life (Rowe's term, repurposed from Alasdair MacIntyre)[24] such as Stoicism and Christianity. A tradition, Rowe claims, is the kind of thing that cannot be understood except by living it exclusively and in full.[25] When it comes to Stoics and Christians, on Rowe's account, it takes one to know one.[26]

But if this is the case, then no one person could be both Stoic and Christian, nor could a Stoic and his Christian neighbour experience an actual meeting of minds about their respective traditions. They could relate to one another only as rivals, or not at all. Historically, Stoics and Christians did in fact relate to one another; hence Rowe concludes that they were (and are) rivals. In one corner, Rowe gives us a chapter each on Seneca, Epictetus, and Marcus Aurelius representing the Stoics, and in the other corner, a chapter each on Paul, Luke, and Justin Martyr representing the Christians. These chapters are meticulously researched and artfully written. But Rowe's ambitious claim that the relation among these thinkers can only be conceived as a two-sided, zero-sum contest would have come as news to Tertullian, Origen, and Jerome, among other ancient Christians, who famously regarded Stoic teachers (e.g. Seneca) and Stoic

---

[23] The latter reference here is a bit mischievous, since Rowe has argued eloquently elsewhere (C. Kavin Rowe, 'The Grammar of Life: The Areopagus Speech and Pagan Tradition', *NTS* 57 [2011]: 31–50) that, at least in Luke's appropriation of it (Acts 17.28), Aratus's maxim does not mean what I am suggesting it means. Rowe's argument is eloquent, but not convincing.

[24] See Alasdair MacIntyre, *Three Rival Traditions of Moral Enquiry: Encyclopaedia, Genealogy, and Tradition* (Sound Bend, IN: University of Notre Dame Press, 1990), e.g. at 59–61: 'A third possibility [is] ... that reason can only move toward being genuinely universal and impersonal insofar as it is neither neutral nor disinterested, that membership in a particular type of moral community, one from which fundamental dissent has to be excluded, is a condition for genuinely rational enquiry and more especially for moral and theological enquiry.... For part of what put the philosophical tradition which runs from Socrates to Aquinas at odds with the philosophical thought of modernity, whether encyclopaedic or genealogical, was both its way of conceiving philosophy as a craft, a *techne*, and its conception of what such a craft in good order is.'

[25] Rowe, *One True Life*, 184: 'A tradition of inquiry, for MacIntyre, is thus a morally grained, historically situated rationality, a way of asking and answering questions that is inescapably tied to the inculcation of habits in the life of the knower and to the community that originates and stewards the craft of inquiry through time. *Tradition* in this sense is the word that best describes the forms of life that were ancient Christianity and Stoicism.' And ibid., 204: '[The] inability to live more than one tradition at a time means that in a crucial and, truth be told, rather sobering sense, even the central patterns of reasoning in one tradition—as that tradition understands them—will not be understood in another.'

[26] On this notion, see Jeffrey Stout, 'Commitments and Traditions in the Study of Religious Ethics', *JRE* 25 (1997): 23–56 at 34–5: 'The epistemology behind the ecumenical model of religious scholarship tends to be, as Henry Levinson once put it, that it takes one to know one. . . . [But] all serious work in the humanities is predicated on the maxim—call it Levinson's law—that it *does not* take one to know one. Religious ethicists would do well to nail this aphorism to the lintels of their office doors, that every student might see it there. Understanding ancient texts, distant cultures, or strange mores is intrinsically valuable, potentially useful, and likely to be difficult. The faith that such understanding is, in principle, possible is a normative assumption as well as a hopeful one, but it is implicit in the work of all scholars in the humanities.'

ideas (e.g. *autarkeia*) not with enmity but with profound sympathy.[27] Now, we might reasonably wonder whether these ancient Christians were over-sanguine in their presumption of Stoic-Christian *homonoia*, and we can agree with Rowe that, for the most part, even they still envisioned an optimal state of affairs where Seneca or Musonius Rufus converted fully and finally to Christianity. But Tertullian, Origen, and Jerome knew their Stoics, they knew that they knew them, and they did not remotely think it an epistemic impossibility to do so.

This is an important point, because one of Rowe's key claims in *One True Life* is that the ancients would have agreed with his existentialist, sectarian account of epistemology, and that only naïve modern encyclopaedists (Rowe's preferred term, on which see later) would disagree with it. He writes, 'The ancients put it to us moderns in a way that makes us uneasy or even squirm. They would give us a pill that neither Stout nor MacIntyre, Malherbe nor Engberg-Pedersen, Levering nor Cochran, can swallow. It is, frankly, just that difficult for us to believe that if we will not enter a way of life, the door to understanding is shut upon us.'[28] Let us leave aside for the moment Rowe's remarkable claim to stand outside modernity, on the side of the ancients, from whence he would diagnose the rest of us as moderns.[29] In fact it is Rowe himself, not the ancients, who would have us swallow this pill. To be sure, Seneca, Epictetus, Marcus Aurelius, Paul, Luke, and Justin make strong truth claims, and, at least in a significant number of cases, they think that believing these truth claims entails existential kinds of commitment. But contrary to Rowe's too-easy generalization, they do not insist that a person cannot understand them except by living their lives. This lattermost claim is not Luke's or Seneca's or even MacIntyre's, but Rowe's and Rowe's alone.

On Rowe's idiosyncratic premises, not only can a Stoic not understand a Christian, nor a Christian a Stoic. Neither, for that matter, can any human being (Stoic, Christian, Platonist, Hegelian, Muslim, Buddhist, agnostic, or otherwise) stand outside Stoicism and Christianity and compare the two. Stoicism and Christianity are, as far as human minds are concerned, *incomparable*. Of course, it is an empirical fact that scholars of

---

[27] Rowe denies that they did so. See Rowe, *One True Life*, 260-1: '[I] redescribe what the Christians have been doing.... The Christians have been treasure hunting. The treasures they find are the words in the Stoic texts, not the Stoic 'thoughts' that are somehow independent from the Stoic grammar in which thoughts have their shape and meaning.' Against this, however, ancient Christians did not need Stoic texts to find the words *pneuma, autarkeia, philanthropia*, and so on. Those words were available before and apart from the Stoics. It was the way the Stoics used these widely current words that ancient Christians appreciated and with which they sympathized.

[28] Rowe, *One True Life*, 257.

[29] In regard to this claim, Jeffrey Stout's comment about Alasdair MacIntyre and John Millbank applies equally well to Rowe: 'I applaud such openness [viz. that of MacIntyre and Millbank about their normative commitments], but I wonder whether we in religious ethics have been as suspicious of their rhetorical stratagems as we ought to have been. These writers announce themselves as debunkers of *modern* ethical discourse, as champions of a *traditional* alternative to it. Evidently, a large distinction is at work—on behalf of normatively charged business. We participate in modern ethical discourse, do we not? It behooves us to be on our guard' (Stout, 'Commitments and Traditions', 38). And again, '[MacIntyre] belongs to a prominent strand of romantic ethical discourse that has never been far to find in the modern period and has always relied, in just the way MacIntyre does, on the rhetoric of ruin and fragmentation. It is a very modern form of ethical discourse, but also a form that has a stake in not being able to recognize itself as belonging to the setting against which its criticism is directed' (ibid., 45).

ancient philosophy and religion compare Stoicism and Christianity all the time. But Rowe argues that all such research is in vain, that to undertake it is a fool's errand. Modern comparativists – Rowe rightly identifies Troels Engberg-Pedersen and the late Abraham Malherbe as exemplars – are tried and found guilty of the epistemic sin of encyclopaedism, which Rowe borrows from MacIntyre's *Three Rival Versions of Moral Enquiry* (MacIntyre's Edinburgh Gifford Lectures for 1988), inflating it for his own polemical purposes.

Encyclopaedism, according to MacIntyre, was the dominant theory of knowledge among late-nineteenth-century intellectuals in Britain, a faith in

> the assent of all educated persons to a single substantive conception of rationality, ... the elaboration of a comprehensive, rationally incontestable scientific understanding of the whole, ... [and a vision of] their whole mode of life, including their conceptions of rationality and of science, as part of a history of inevitable progress, judged by a standard of progress which had itself emerged from that history.[30]

For MacIntyre, quite plausibly, the exemplars of encyclopaedism were the Victorian editors of the ninth edition of the *Encyclopaedia Britannica* (1875–89), while for Rowe, less plausibly, its exemplars are more or less all contemporary New Testament scholars. Rowe writes, 'My basic critical contention is that we cannot hope to understand the Stoic/Christian relation if we continue to read them in the way we usually have. Encyclopedic inquiry – the name for the epistemic assumptions of the vast majority of modern scholarly work on the Stoics and the New Testament – is dead and gone. We should take notice.'[31]

MacIntyre's threefold rubric of modes of enquiry is not immune to criticism.[32] But let us grant, for the sake of argument, that it is. Even so, Rowe's application of it to contemporary scholarship on Stoicism and Christianity does not follow and is in fact mistaken. Consequently, a colossal straw man looms. To demonstrate: Here is Thomas Spencer Baynes, chief editor of the ninth edition of the *Encyclopaedia Britannica*, in his 1875 prefatory note to volume 1, the fullest statement of the epistemology presupposed by the makers of the Encyclopaedia:

---

[30] MacIntyre, *Three Rival Versions*, 23–4.
[31] Rowe, *One True Life*, 2.
[32] See especially the author's postscript in Jeffrey Stout, *Ethics after Babel: The Languages of Morals and Their Discontents* (2d edn; Princeton: Princeton University Press, 2001), here 350: '[MacIntyre's *Three Rival Versions* examines] the styles of moral inquiry associated with the *Encyclopaedia Britannica*, with Nietzsche, and with modern Thomism. The point of the exercise is to vindicate Thomism's superiority to its rivals. But suppose we grant that Thomism wins this three-sided contest. The exercise reinforces MacIntyre's account of modernity only if the encyclopedists and the Nietzscheans are the best modern competitors one could find to test the strength and weaknesses of Thomism.... We do well to remind ourselves that those years [1875–1900] also include [historic contributions from Walt Whitman, Frederick Douglas, William Morris, William James, Frances Willard, John Ruskin, John Dewey and John Muir]. MacIntyre's three rivals are important ones, but they do not adequately represent the ethical vitalities of the age.'

The work, while surveying in outline the existing field of knowledge, was able at the same time to enlarge its boundaries by embodying, in special articles, the fruits of original observation and research. The Encyclopaedia Britannica thus became, to some extent at least, an instrument as well as a register of scientific progress.... [The Encyclopaedia] has to do with knowledge rather than opinion, and to deal with all subjects from a critical and historical, rather than a dogmatic, point of view. It cannot be the organ of any sect or party in Science, Religion, or Philosophy. Its main duty is to give an accurate account of the facts and an impartial summary of results in every department of inquiry and research.[33]

And here is MacIntyre, in 1988, giving his account of Baynes's theory of knowledge: 'The encyclopaedist's conception is of a single framework within which knowledge is discriminated from mere belief, progress toward knowledge is mapped, and truth is understood as the relationship of *our* knowledge to *the* world, through the application of those methods whose rules are the rules of rationality as such.'[34] A bit overwrought, perhaps, but not grossly unfair to Baynes and his collaborators, in any case.

Now, here is Troels Engberg-Pedersen, in the introductory 'Essay in Interpretation' of his 2000 *Paul and the Stoics*, a landmark in the study of ancient Stoicism and Christianity:

The approach adopted here has three logical parts: (i) In its existentially neutral, historical-critical aspect it is dedicated to making as much historical sense as possible of Paul's thought-world taken in its entirety.... (ii) By almost exclusively focusing on ideas, it differs from an approach like Meeks' [on social history]. But otherwise it should be understood as being informed by an underlying concern just like Meeks' to provide a methodologically-based, comprehensive picture of the intrinsic connections between the various levels of Paul's thought world and between those taken together and his social world. (iii) In its existentially interested aspect it cuts out a sizeable portion of Paul's thought world – the 'anthropological' and 'ethical' one – and attempts to elucidate that both as part of the more comprehensive perspective on the Christ-believing form of life that Paul aims to present to his addressees – but also as constituting a real option for us.[35]

And here, finally, is Rowe, marking Engberg-Pedersen's *Paul and the Stoics* as exhibit A of a putative twenty-first-century encyclopaedism:

[According to Engberg-Pedersen,] modern scholars can focus on ideas as ideas; these ideas are expressed in a universally intelligible 'natural' language; this natural language corresponds intellectually to the etic discourse of modern scholarship; modern scholarship is itself, therefore, the universal language, the most conceptually

---

[33] T. S. Baynes, 'Prefatory Notice', *Encyclopaedia Britannica*, 9th edn, vol. 1 (New York: Scribners, 1878), v, viii.
[34] MacIntyre, *Three Rival Versions*, 42, emphasis original.
[35] Troels Engberg-Pedersen, *Paul and the Stoics* (Edinburgh: T&T Clark, 2000), 28.

comprehensive discourse, that which can restate, or translate, all emic expressions/claims in its own terms.... [Engberg-Pedersen illustrates] the more fundamental assumptions and intellectual parameters of an entire modern scholarly project – that of mistaking traditions for entries in an encyclopedia.[36]

Not to put too fine a point on it, if Engberg-Pedersen's introduction to *Paul and the Stoics* is encyclopaedism, then I will eat my hat. Engberg-Pedersen robustly affirms the unity of intellection and life, the recognition of ancient Stoicism and Christianity as forms of life, and the legitimate existential interest of modern interpreters in those same forms of life, all of which Rowe accuses him of denying. Rowe is accurate, to be sure, in noting Engberg-Pedersen's willingness to hazard a historical-critical, existentially disinterested reading of a Paul or a Seneca. But that is not encyclopaedism, just sympathetic historical imagination, which does exist, Rowe's protestations notwithstanding.[37] Rowe speaks repeatedly and contemptuously of how 'encyclopedic enquiry is dead and gone'. The epistemology of MacIntyre's Victorians is indeed dead and gone, as are the Victorians themselves. But Engberg-Pedersen's position (and, *mutatis mutandis*, the position of other present-day comparativists) is not that epistemology.[38]

One True Life is an exciting book, bracing to read and useful to think with. It crackles with the same earnest moral energy that one feels when reading Rowe's heroes, MacIntyre and Blaise Pascal. This is the kind of passage I mean: 'Pascal was finally right. We cannot know ahead of the lives we live that the truth to which we devote ourselves is the truth worth devoting ourselves to. So we wager our lives, one way or the other. The tradition of life that is Stoicism is a certain kind of historically dense and elongated wager; so is Christianity. If our being is in becoming, then the wagers we make are on the patterns of life that make who we are. Our being is caught up in them, and we are what we become.'[39] As this passage suggests, the burden of Rowe's book really is to exhort his readers to be, or to become, Christians. Or, theoretically, Stoics. (To his credit, Rowe does not claim that Christianity is unique and therefore incomparable. Rather, he claims that both Christianity and Stoicism – and presumably other traditions of life, too, although we do not hear about them – are equally incomparable.) But because Stoicism is not a live option in the way that Christianity is, it is not really a fair fight. A book that did the same thing with, say, Islam and Christianity would be more so. It had not occurred to me until I heard her say it, but Margaret Mitchell is exactly right in her judgement that Rowe's book is a *protreptikos* every bit as much as Clement's book by that name.[40] Not an apologetic, crypto- or otherwise, but a straight-up invitation to live a Christian life.[41] Rowe's invitation will no doubt strike some readers

---

[36] Rowe, *One True Life*, 191.
[37] See ibid., 256: 'There is no magical quality to imagination that somehow enables it to leap over the existential barrier erected by traditions that claim they must be lived to be learned.'
[38] See Engberg-Pedersen's Chapter 4 in this volume.
[39] Rowe, *One True Life*, 258.
[40] See Mitchell's Chapter 7 in this volume.
[41] Rowe, *One True Life*, 261: 'The grammars of traditions that claim truth in the way the Stoics and Christians do are inherently invitational or kerygmatic. The invitation to enter is simultaneously the condition of true understanding; invitation, that is, names the fact that conversion is the inevitable goal of all traditional speech toward outsiders.'

as old-fashioned. It is certainly unusual for a twenty-first-century biblical studies monograph, though not at all unusual for a sermon. For my part, I have no principled objection to this kind of religious advocacy, and I find Rowe's way of doing it genuinely moving. But I do object strongly to his claim that it is the only possible way of talking about ancient Stoicism and ancient Christianity. If *One True Life* is exciting, it is also wrong in this crucial respect.

A sympathetic reader might think that what Rowe really *means* is just that an inhabitant of one tradition is incapable of understanding another tradition *fully*. And indeed, in his essay in the present volume, Rowe comes out somewhere close to this claim.[42] I consider this a welcome development, because it is closer to the truth. But – in the interest of dealing with Rowe as he wants to deal with the Stoics, taking seriously the difference of another's view and not assimilating it to one's own – that is not the position he takes in *One True Life*. His admirably consistent thesis in the book is that an inhabitant of one tradition is incapable of understanding another tradition, full stop.[43] Rowe even out-MacIntyres MacIntyre himself by denying the capacity of imagination to surmount this difficulty.[44] What Rowe says is that comparison of traditions cannot be done. What he ought to have said is that it can be done but that he, Rowe, finds it not worth doing; that it is too pedantic, superficial, or existentially unimportant to be worth his intellectual energy. He might also think that comparing traditions is not worth anyone's intellectual energy, that converting to and practising a tradition of life is more than enough to occupy any human being.[45] But that would amount to a renunciation of all the arts and sciences, which is further than I, at least, am willing to go. We can agree with Rowe's affirmation that the study of philosophy and religion is, or can be, a matter of existential concern, and yet reject Rowe's denial (which

---

[42] Rowe, Chapter 3: 'Making Friends and Comparing Lives' (p. 23). 'I do not deny and do not think we should deny that human beings who live in roughly the same time and place share all sorts of things in common... [and thus] can understand each other in a regular and important way at the bank or supermarket or pagan festival, and so on'; ibid., [p. 27]: 'We might speak here of a kind of understanding: we understand one another as friends do, even if the grammars of our traditions remain grammars of conflict and summons.'

[43] Rowe, *One True Life*, 204: 'Short of conversion, we are literally shut out of one [tradition] by the life we live in another. Rival rationalities are not surmountable by learning'; ibid., 262: 'The argument of this book rejects the conception of both the human being and traditions of life that would allow us to picture ourselves as able to move noetically between traditions without living different lives. In this significant sense we are stuck in the traditions in which we live.' As far as I can tell, the closest the book gets to the concession made in the essay is at Rowe, *One True Life*, 260: '[Ancient Stoics and Christians] lived in roughly the same time and place, after all, and could not help but share some assumptions about this or that; it would be nothing short of stunning if they did not. Such shared assumptions are not, however, as significant as they have been said to be. The most significant assumptions and convictions of each tradition—tradition comprising assumptions and convictions—are precisely those that keep them apart.'

[44] Ibid., 256.

[45] Ibid., 1: 'At its heart, this book is about the fact that we can only live one life. The track from birth to death can be run—or walked, or crawled, or held in the arms of others—only once. However much we speak metaphorically of aging as an eventual return to the dependence of childhood, no human being has ever grown from an adult to an infant. We all go only one way, toward death. How we should travel this one-way road—if in fact there is a *should*—is a question as old as human reflection on the journey itself. Is there a best or right or true way to live? To what should we entrust ourselves? Can we find healing for what ails us? Can we make it up as we go? Can we waste our lives?'

is, anyway, a *non sequitur*) of the possibility of comparison. The human mind can *both* compare phenomena *and* make existential decisions. We see human minds do both all the time. Indeed, when we read *One True Life*, we see Kavin Rowe's mind do both. The only problem is his insistence to the contrary.

Stategies for not comparing

I single out *Destroyer of the Gods* and *One True Life* for comment not because they are easy targets but because they are not. Both books make their respective cases about as powerfully as I can imagine these cases being made. Hence, if there are problems, those problems are likely to be with the core claims themselves. And this is in fact the case. Both Hurtado and Rowe demonstrate a thorough command of the mass of ancient evidence, but they organize that evidence selectively and partisanly so as, finally, to recommend early Christianity and thereby (implicitly for Hurtado, explicitly for Rowe) modern Christianity, too. There is a fascinating irony here. Hurtado wants to compare early Christianity with its counterparts but, insofar as he repeatedly vindicates it over against all of them, does not really do so. Rowe, by contrast, wants *not* to compare early Christianity with its counterparts (indeed, he declares such comparison an impossibility), but in fact he executes a number of fruitful comparisons. (He just calls them 'juxtapositions,' a distinction without a difference.)[46] In short, Hurtado tries to compare but fails; Rowe tries not to compare but succeeds at comparing in spite of himself. The two agree, however, in judging early Christianity to be beyond compare. For Hurtado, it is beyond compare in a poetic sense: when we compare early Christianity to its counterparts, again and again it stands apart from them all. For Rowe, it is beyond compare in a literal sense: it cannot be compared; it can only be converted to and lived.

Why this hang-up? Why should it be such a problem simply to compare early Christianity with other things? The answer includes at least a conceptual and an ideological aspect. First, the conceptual. When comparison goes awry, it usually does so in one of two directions. This is not a novel observation, and it has recently been spelled out with particular clarity by Aaron Hughes, the American scholar of medieval Judaism and Islam.[47] Because comparison always involves making judgements about relative similarity and difference, failures of comparison usually involve a preoccupation with and privileging of *either* similarity *or* difference. In the academic study of religion, the former kind of failure (privileging of similarity) is typical especially of phenomenologists (e.g. Rudolf Otto, Joseph Campbell, Mircea Eliade), who, when they compare bits and pieces of religion, discover the same, universal Numinous or Sacred. The latter kind of

---

[46] About comparison, Rowe writes, 'The modern comparative project depends upon a philosophical mistake in which a profound abstraction is taken for a real thing and believed to provide the categorical sense in which the work of comparison can be done' (ibid., 192). And about juxtaposition: 'If Stoicism and Christianity are seen as traditions of inquiry, the most constructive way to conceive their relation is to think them in direct narrative juxtaposition, face to face. Traditions are of course considerably complex things, but such complexity will always be related to the narrative that makes the tradition what it is' (ibid., 199). But Rowe's 'modern comparative project' is a straw man (see my comments earlier), and what he here calls 'juxtaposition' is just comparison by another, more sectarian name.

[47] See Aaron W. Hughes, *Comparison: A Critical Primer* (Sheffield: Equinox, 2017), especially 51–76.

failure (privileging of difference) is much more common in the history of research on early Christianity and is the besetting problem with both Hurtado's and Rowe's work. As Smith showed to devastating effect in *Drudgery Divine*, scholars of early Christianity have a congenital habit of thought, an instinct, for claiming Christian uniqueness.[48] Within the logic of this habit of thought, to study early Christianity is nothing other than to explain how it is different from everything else. The scholar of early Christianity knows that her job (in a lecture, an article, a monograph) is done when she has reached and underlined the point of difference. But this is simply the mirror-image of the phenomenologist's error, the non-rational choice to fixate on one part of the comparative task – either identifying similarity or identifying difference – and to ignore the other.

Which part of the comparative task the scholar chooses to fixate on, and which to ignore, most often comes down to ideology. By ideology, I mean the whole range of religious, theological, ethical, political, and other kinds of commitments that bear on the scholar's subjectivity. When one or more of the things being compared is, or is perceived to be, closely related somehow to an aspect of the scholar's subjectivity (as in the case of James's crab: 'any object that is infinitely important *to us* and awakens *our devotion*'), then it becomes proportionately more difficult for the scholar to think comparison. This phenomenon is more common in the humanities and social sciences than in the laboratory sciences (though it is not absent from the latter), which is why, as Marcel Detienne comments, 'When researchers choose to study comparative anatomy, they do not begin by passing a value judgment on the various organs that they plan to consider.'[49] A classic example in our subfield is the conspicuous apologetic strand documented by Smith in modern research on the New Testament and the mystery religions. That research, undertaken overwhelmingly by Protestant scholars, laboured under a need to demonstrate the ancient Christian sources' freedom from any stain of *pagan* (used as a cipher for *Catholic*) influence. When these scholars compared baptism in the Pauline Christ groups with Mithraic initiation rites, they were really comparing their own piety with that of their Catholic contemporaries. The outcome of this *sogenannte* comparison was decided before the work was even begun.[50]

---

[48] Smith, *Drudgery Divine*, 38: '[As used in religious studies,] the "unique" is more phoenix-like, it expresses that which is *sui generis, singularis*, and, therefore, *incomparably* valuable. "Unique" becomes an ontological rather than a taxonomic category; an assertion of a radical difference so absolute that it becomes "Wholly Other," and the act of comparison is perceived as both an impossibility and an impiety.... The most frequent use of the terminology of the "unique" in religious studies is in relation to Christianity; the most frequent use of this term within Christianity is in relation to the so-called "Christ-event."'

[49] Marcel Detienne, *Comparing the Incomparable*, trans. Janet Lloyd (Stanford: Stanford University Press, 2008 [French original 2000]), ix.

[50] Smith, *Drudgery Divine*, 34: 'The pursuit of the origins of the question of Christian origins takes us back, persistently, to the same point: *Protestant anti-Catholic apologetics*. It will be my contention, in the subsequent chapters, that this is by no means a merely antiquarian concern. The same presuppositions, the same rhetorical tactics, indeed, in the main, the very same data exhibited in these early efforts underlie much of our present-day research, with one important alteration, that the characteristics attributed to "Popery," by the Reformation and post-Reformation controversialists, have been transferred, wholesale, to the religions of Late Antiquity. How else can one explain, for example, the fact that the most frequent distinction drawn in modern scholarship between the early Christian "sacraments" (especially the Pauline) and those of the "mystery cults" is that the latter exhibit a notion of ritual as *ex opere operato*?'

Religious commitments like these are one powerful kind of comparison-skewing ideology, the most common kind in our field, perhaps, but they are not the only kind. The classicist Detienne, writing about comparative methodology in his field, expresses analogous worries about nationalism among twentieth-century historians: 'Societies that lacked civilization and writing were brushed aside. If comparison was to be done, it would be of the "we have .../they have" variety, provided that the "they" designated some opposing nation, and it was understood that "we" had received the lion's share.'[51] And just as many modern Christian scholars see themselves as heirs of and coreligionists with the ancient Christians and reason that the latter must have been finally different from other ancients, many modern, Western humanists have done likewise with the ancient Greeks: *we* are the cultural heirs of *them*; hence *they* must have been finally different from their own contemporaries. Detienne writes, 'The experimental comparativism of the earliest anthropologists was not able to resist the pressure of western values that insisted on a direct transmission from Greek universality characterized exclusively by Reason, Science, and the incomparable Greek Miracle.'[52]

Larry Hurtado tries, far more subtly than his twentieth-century forebears but in continuity with them nonetheless, to trace the lines of the incomparable Christian Miracle. Kavin Rowe, more subtly still, demurs from calling Christianity unique, or even distinctive, but then outstrips Hurtado by claiming that Christianity is literally incomparable, that it does not admit of comparison by human minds. Both Hurtado and Rowe trade in that rhetorical use of the language of comparison that I noted at the beginning of this essay. Like the psalmist to God ('Who is like unto thee?'), or the poet to the beloved ('Shall I compare thee to a summer's day?'), they praise early Christianity by avoiding comparing it with other things, by putting it out of reach, beyond compare. Some forty years ago, Smith wrote that 'the possibility of the study of religion depends on [the] answer' to Wittgenstein's question, 'How am I to apply what the one thing shows me to the case of two things?';[53] that is, on a theory of comparison.[54] It did, and it does.[55] We could, of course, opt out of the study of religion entirely, as Rowe effectively suggests we do, but short of that self-segregating option, there is nothing for it but to wade in and compare early Christianity with other things: Stoicism, Judaism, platypuses, fish, crabs, cocktails, and anything else that helps us to understand.[56]

---

[51] Detienne, *Comparing the Incomparable*, x.
[52] Detienne, *Comparing the Incomparable*, 7.
[53] Ludwig Wittgenstein, *Philosophical Investigations* (trans. G. E. M. Anscombe et al.; 4th rev. ed.; Oxford: Wiley Blackwell, 2010) §215.
[54] Jonathan Z. Smith, 'In Comparison a Magic Dwells,' in idem, *Imagining Religion: From Babylon to Jonestown* (Chicago: University of Chicago Press, 1982), 35.
[55] My own purpose in this essay is not to give a new, theoretical answer to Wittgenstein's question, but to argue, with Smith and against Hurtado and Rowe, that Wittgenstein's question pertains to early Christianity every bit as much as it does to anything else. For an artful theoretical answer to Wittgenstein's question, see, in addition to Smith, John Barclay's essay in the present volume.
[56] Once more, Smith, *Drudgery Divine*, 51: 'There is nothing "natural" about the enterprise of comparison. Similarity and difference are not "given." They are the result of mental operations.... Comparison, in its strongest form, brings differences together within the space of the scholar's mind for the scholar's own intellectual reasons. It is the scholar who makes their cohabitation—their "sameness"—possible, not "natural" affinities or processes of history.'

7

On Comparing, and Calling the Question[1]

Margaret M. Mitchell

Ancient Christianity is unthinkable without comparison. It is unthinkable either for them or for us. From the earliest extant sources – the letters of Paul – forward, Christ-believing missionaries expressed its distinctive teaching in relation to 'Jews' and 'Greeks'. 'Jews ask for signs (σημεῖα) and Greeks seek wisdom (σοφία), but we proclaim Christ crucified, a stumbling block to Jews and foolishness to Greeks. But to us, the very ones who are called – both Jews and Greeks – Christ is the power of God and the wisdom of God' (1 Cor. 1.22–24).[2] The author of this text, Παῦλος κλητὸς ἀπόστολος Χριστοῦ Ἰησοῦ (1.1), deftly articulates in a crisp formulation that reflects his bi-cultural position as a Hellenistic Jew the characteristic cultural-religious quests of Jews as σημεῖα and Greeks as σοφία, and he makes the audacious claim that a crucified messiah (Χριστὸς ἐσταυρωμένος) constitutes the fulfilment of both those quests. This Christ is, correspondingly, θεοῦ δύναμις and θεοῦ σοφία – that is, in the eyes of those who, like himself, whether Jews or Greeks, are κλητοί. Paul's role as ἀπόστολος is to ensure the 'invited' know that they are 'invited' (cf. Rom. 10.14–15), and, if we may peek at 1 Thess. 1.9 for a moment, heed the summons and 'convert' (ἐπιστρέφειν) to the one true god (πρὸς τὸν θεὸν ἀπὸ τῶν εἰδώλων δουλεύειν θεῷ ζῶντι καὶ ἀληθινῷ) and place their πίστις in the story of the son whom he raised from the dead, Jesus, that Paul calls his εὐαγγέλιον.

The Christian κλητοί, as described on the socio-religious map of a Jew who sees the world according to Jew/Gentile distinctions in 1 Cor. 1.22–24 (though he can readily adopt the majority culture map of 'Greek and barbarian' in Rom 1.14, as well), have found their truth in the crucified Christ, Paul proclaims. Although Paul does not yet quite have the *tertium genus* of Tertullian,[3] he had laid out in these two carefully crafted

---

[1] This chapter is based on the paper prepared for the conference on comparison organized by Professor John M. G. Barclay, University of Durham, UK, June 22–23, 2017. I thank all the participants for good feedback, and especially wish to express appreciation to Kavin Rowe for excellent conversations on that occasion and in the years since then about the important issues involved, and a friendship forged amid honest, respectful dialogue on real disagreements.

[2] Greek text from Nestle-Aland²⁸; translation mine, as throughout.

[3] *Ad nationes* 1.8.1 (*Plane, tertium genus dicimur* [text CCSL, various editors, 1954]), etc. But see 1 Cor. 10.32, which is heading in that direction: ἀπρόσκοποι καὶ Ἰουδαίοις γίνεσθε καὶ Ἕλλησιν καὶ τῇ ἐκκλησίᾳ τοῦ θεοῦ.

Greek sentences that have a very long life ahead[4] its intellectual logic and sociological self-positioning: 'Christianity' is to be both embedded within yet separate from the categories 'Jew' and 'Greek', and their respective methods and criteria for discerning what is true.

To prove that Christ accomplishes the σημεῖα Jews expect (i.e., the fulfilment κατὰ τὰς γραφάς mentioned in 1 Cor. 15.3–4) requires comparison and comparative exegesis to establish this as more than a 'stumbling block' assertion. To demonstrate that Christ is the answer to the σοφία Greeks expect requires comparison and comparative exegesis to establish the claim as more than mere 'foolishness'. As Paul allows within this classic formulation, both sets of comparisons must emphasize continuity *and* discontinuity; the crucified Christ is both an obvious fit and a thoroughly unexpected and incongruous one. Paul, the Hellenistic Jewish self-styled μιμητὴς Χριστοῦ (1 Cor. 4.16; 11.1), began this work by choosing two terms that are themselves bi-culturally understood, and hence already inaugurate not just two separate or separable proof structures and persuadable communities, but a bold bid for cross-cultural confirmation: σημεῖα is biblical (LXX Exod. 7.3; Deut. 34.11) *and* part of the vocabulary of ancient Greek religion and philosophy;[5] σοφία is both readily understood as the Greek φιλοσοφία of Peripatetics, Stoics and others,[6] *and* as the personified biblical figure of divine wisdom active in creation (of Prov. 8 and Ps. 1.7, etc.). As so often, the wordsmith Paul's lexicon derives its power from its flexibility and multi-valence, and from the way he sets up homologies between the everyday *koinē* diction of non-Jews (and Jews) and his biblical vocabulary for a double-down effect. In this way, 1 Cor 1.22–24 is not meant to imply two separate or separable forms of proof, but rather proofs on both sides that, properly understood, should aggregate the plausibility of the crucified Christ as God's power and wisdom. At the same time, within this formulation is powerful vituperation against those Jews and Greeks *not* among the κλητοί as being fundamentally and absolutely wrong, even dead wrong,[7] in that they see the exact opposite from what they should: a stumbling block rather than an avenue to truth; foolishness rather than wisdom. Sprinkled throughout Paul's letters and in those written in his name we find explanations for such error and a set of invective *topoi* applied to the errant (as foolish,[8] ignorant,[9] blind,[10] sick,[11] dead or on a path to destruction,[12] demon-possessed,[13] etc.), but, strikingly, not at this

---

[4] This argument is consistent with the larger emphasis of my book *Paul, the Corinthians, and the Birth of Christian Hermeneutics* (Cambridge: Cambridge University Press, 2010) on the importance of the reception of the Corinthian correspondence in early Christian thought in regard to biblical interpretation, in particular.

[5] See LSJ I.A.2, 'sign from the gods, omen' (where they also list some LXX references) and II.3.b, 'in Stoic and Epicurean philos., sign as observable basis of inference to the unobserved or unobservable' (with references from Epicurus, Philodemus, and Zeno).

[6] Again here LSJ A.3 points to uses of σοφία as 'learning, wisdom' or 'speculative wisdom' (e.g. Arist. *NE* 1141a19; *Metaph.* 282a2, etc., and *Stoicorum Veterum Fragmenta* [ed. von Arnim 1903] 2.15).

[7] As in the earlier part of this argument, upon which 1.22–24 builds, in 1 Cor. 1.18: οἱ ἀπολλύμενοι.

[8] 2 Cor. 11.19, etc.

[9] E.g. Rom. 10.2–3; Gal. 3.1; 1 Tim. 6.2; 2 Tim. 3.6.

[10] 2 Cor. 4.4.

[11] 1 Tim 4.2; 6.2, and throughout the PE for those who resist the ὑγιαινοῦσα διδασκαλία.

[12] 1 Cor. 1.18; 2 Cor. 2.14; 4.3, etc.

[13] 2 Cor. 4.4; 11.13–15; 2 Tim. 2.26, etc.

moment. Paul instead goes on to make the case by a grand theological comparison, as he expresses it in the following verse, using genitives of comparison: 'God's foolishness is wiser than people, and God's weakness is stronger than people' (1 Cor. 1.25). Christ meets, and exceeds, all expectations, because God is greater than mortals and surpasses their standards even when one pits his lowest against their highest. The hyperbole shows there is 'no comparison', even when God fights with both hands behind his back.

Just as the early Christ-believing Gentile movement that develops from the historical person Paul through the historical-epistolary Paul and into authors such as the pseudepigraphers of Ephesians, 2 Thessalonians and the Pastorals, the author of Acts, Ignatius of Antioch and others, is unthinkable without Paul,[14] it is also unthinkable without comparison, because its truth claims are comparatively formed. While Paul did not advance his comparative argument in his extant letters as much with Greek philosophical evidence as with the Greek scriptures of Israel, in which he finds both σημεῖα and σοφία, later authors with a higher level of philosophical training and social stature will seek to carry forward and fulfil Paul's comparative religious claims by supplying even more proofs. One such text is the Προτρεπτικὸς πρὸς Ἕλληνας written by Clement of Alexandria, who was born about one hundred years after Paul wrote and sent 1 Corinthians.

Clement of Alexandria, Προτρεπτικὸς πρὸς Ἕλληνας

Cast not in a letter, but in a προτρεπτικὸς λόγος[15] used by philosophers to invite adherents to their school or system,[16] Clement seeks to carry out in longhand and with full documentation the terse claim to comparative superiority as Paul had laid it down in 1 Cor. 1.22–24. The text as we have it is, to say the least, substantial, more than three times the length of 1 Corinthians. The argument, true to form, is both of προτροπή (persuasion to) and ἀποτροπή (dissuasion from). As is well known, Clement's *Protreptikos* is a work of inestimable importance for the study of ancient religion and philosophy, because Clement brings into his argument a trove of quotations of comparative materials (some of which are no longer extant in any other source or manuscript tradition). Clement's facility in and knowledge of Greek philosophy,

---

[14] For a fuller argument (and explanation of the distinction between Paul and the 'historical-epistolary Paul'), see Margaret M. Mitchell, *Paul and the Emergence of Christian Textuality: Early Christian Literary Culture in Context* (Collected Essays, volume 1) (WUNT 393, Tübingen: Mohr Siebeck, 2017), xiii–xvi.

[15] The term refers to a type of deliberative argument chiefly found among philosophers that seeks to persuade its hearer to (προτροπή, προτρέπειν) a way of life, and away from (ἀποτροπή, ἀποτρέπειν) another. There is considerable literature on protreptic; a convenient entrée may be found in Herwig Görgemanns, 'Protreptics', in *Brill's New Pauly*, Antiquity volumes ed. Hubert Cancik and Helmuth Schneider, first published online, 2006; http://dx.doi.org/10.1163/1574-9347_bnp_e1011490, consulted online on 14 June 2017; Diana M. Swancutt, 'Paraenesis in Light of Protrepsis: Troubling the Typical Dichotomy', *Early Christian Paraenesis in Context*, ed. James Starr and Troels Engberg-Pedersen (BZNW 125; Berlin/New York: de Gruyter, 2004), 113–53, along with discussion of key issues in the history of scholarship.

[16] In some, but not all cases, the language of 'conversion' (ἐπιστρέφειν) is used.

religion and culture are evident on every page, and are a key part of his ἦθος as a persuasive speaker. His goal via comparison, he says in the long and lyrical *prooimion*, is to show that Christ is the true 'troubadour' (ᾠδός), who far exceeds such legendary bards as Amphion of Thebes, Arion of Methymna, Orpheus or Eunomos of Locris, whose songs supposedly brought about such wonders in the animal kingdom as summoning a dolphin as a water-taxi, a wild animal to domesticity, or a cicada to replace a broken lyre-string with its natural, cadenced chirping.[17] Such stories (μῦθοι) are believed by 'the Greeks' (οἱ Ἕλληνες). Clement then turns to his readers and fires:

> How then is it that you have believed (πεπιστεύκατε) in empty myths (μύθοις κενοῖς[18]), supposing that animals can be charmed by music? And yet it is only the bright shining face of truth (ἀληθείας ... τὸ πρόσωπον τὸ φαιδρὸν μόνον) that apparently seems to you to be false (ἐπίπλαστον)[19] and you subject it to unbelieving eyes (τοῖς ἀπιστίας ... ὀφθαλμοῖς)?![20]

Via this σύγκρισις, 'rhetorical comparison',[21] as Clement has constructed it, 'the Greeks' have it exactly backwards: they regard truth as falsehood and falsehood as truth. The contrast is absolute, the binary set up to be mutually reinforcing (perfectly aligned with belief and non-belief). In line with this opening diagnosis, the goal of Clement's προτρεπτικὸς λόγος is to demonstrate through a superabundance of proofs where proper πίστις/πιστεύειν should be placed (προτροπή), and should not (ἀποτροπή), to put the stark choice before their eyes (and ears) and call on them to make it. There is a paradox to the comparability,[22] of course, since from the outset Clement has indicated that there is 'no comparison' between truth and falsehood. Still, he will dare to compare, and will prove the superiority of Christianity. In the conclusion (some 80 pages later in the GCS edition), Clement will, as expected in the genre of προτρεπτικὸς λόγος, call the question:

---

[17] *Protr.* 1.1.1–3 [Stählin 3, 1–22] (cited first by chapter, section and subsection, and then, inside brackets, by page and line numbers in Otto Stählin's 1905 GCS edition); all translations are mine.

[18] A significant concern in the Paulinist tradition, which tries to dichotomize truth and myth, as in the 'de-conversion' depicted in 2 Tim. 4.4; καὶ ἀπὸ μὲν τῆς ἀληθείας τὴν ἀκοὴν ἀποστρέψουσιν, ἐπὶ δὲ τοὺς μύθους ἐκτραπήσονται.

[19] Literally, a 'fabrication'.

[20] *Protr.* 2.1.1 [Stählin 3, 23–6].

[21] Clement clearly knows the rhetorical form, as taught via the προγυμνάσματα in school, and found ubiquitously in ancient literature, oratory and philosophy, and he uses it throughout this treatise. Theon of Alexandria (perhaps ca. 125, though there is debate) defines σύγκρισις as follows: 'Comparison is an argument that places the better or the worse side by side' (Σύγκρισίς ἐστι λόγος τὸ βέλτιον ἢ τὸ χεῖρον παριστάς [*Prog.* 9; text ed. L. Spengel, Teubner, 1854, 2.112, 20–1 (cited by volume, page and lines)]; translation mine, as throughout).

[22] According to Theon, σύγκρισις requires that there be similarity between the two *comparanda*, and genuine doubt about which is best. 'First, let it be stipulated that comparisons are not made of things that have a huge difference with one another ... but should be made of things that are similar, and about which we are in doubt as to which should be preferred, because one cannot see any superiority that one has when set alongside the other' (πρῶτον δὲ διωρίσθω, αἱ συγκρίσεις γίνονται οὐ τῶν μεγάλην πρὸς ἄλληλα διαφορὰν ἐχόντων ... ἀλλ' ὑπὲρ τῶν ὁμοίων, καὶ περὶ ὧν ἀμφισβητοῦμεν, πότερον δεῖ προθέσθαι, διὰ τὸ μηδεμίαν ὁρᾶν τοῦ ἑτέρου πρὸς τὸ ἕτερον ὑπεροχήν [Spengel 2.112, 27–113.2]).

I suppose that's a long enough set of verbal arguments (λόγοι), even if the reason I've gone on so long spewing them out is the deep love for humanity (φιλανθρωπία) that I received from God, given that I am issuing an invitation (παρακαλῶν) to the greatest of all goods (τὸ μέγιστον τῶν ἀγαθῶν) – salvation (ἡ σωτηρία). . . . But the final decision (πέρας) still is left to you (ὑμῖν δὲ ἔτι τοῦτο περιλείπεται), to choose (ἑλέσθαι) what is to your advantage (τὸ λυσιτελοῦν), either judgment or grace (ἢ κρίσιν ἢ χάριν). But in my view (ὡς ἔγωγε), I think there's no doubt at all (οὐδ' ἀμφιβάλλειν ἀξιῶ) about which of the two is superior (πότερον ἄμεινον αὐτοῖν).[23]

In protreptic fashion, Clement turns to his readers, those he has invited to embrace the truth, and says the choice now is theirs, to opt either for divine judgement and condemnation, or grace and gift. There is no middle option, no third alternative. As is customary to the genre (as a part of deliberative rhetoric), Clement appeals to them to choose what will be most to their advantage (τὸ λυσιτελοῦν).[24] He adds a final testimony of his own to weight their choice: really there is no doubt at all[25] about which of the 'two things' (as we shall see in a moment, he has bundled all of 'paganism' or 'traditional culture' into a single whole against which Christianity wins – in each set and match) is the superior. Exactly what it means for them to choose (ἑλέσθαι) grace (χάρις) is not spelled out here, which is one among several elements of the work that may indicate that its main addressees are less 'outsiders' who will convert and be baptized and change their lives, than 'insiders'[26] who have enjoyed seeing their Christian truth so ably defended by an erudite champion against all contenders. Whatever its actual addressee and purpose in Clement's own context,[27] the work has surely been received and enjoyed in the latter fashion. After issuing his summons to choose, Clement closes the long work with a final sentence that is itself a *topos*, and perhaps for him a deliberately ironic one. After pages and pages of comparative proofs through λόγοι (including arguments, testimonials and rhetorical appeals), Clement closes by saying, 'indeed, it's not fitting for life (ζωή) to be compared (συγκρίνεσθαι) with everlasting doom (ἀπώλεια)'.[28] Thus this monumental, carefully wrought work of early Christian comparative religious rhetoric ends – with the incomparability *topos*.

But Clement has throughout the work deliberately set up a host of comparisons between the power and truth of 'his troubadour', Christ, and avatars and sages of Greek religion and philosophy, organized in various groups for consideration. Clement chose each of them because they are, apparently, *in some way* comparable, or at least regarded

---

[23] *Protr.* 12.123.2 [Stählin 86, 24–30].
[24] Compare Theon, *Prog.* 9: 'next we should speak of the advantages [ὠφέλειαι] that result from each of the things we are comparing' [Spengel 2.114, 1–2].
[25] Note that Clement uses similar language about 'doubt' as in Theon, *Prog.* 9 (cited above, n. 22).
[26] As argued by Swancutt, 'Paraenesis in Light of Protrepsis', 149–51, among others (citing Wayne A. Meeks in n. 74 on p. 149). But it is not completely certain. An authority like Eric Osborn, *Clement of Alexandria* (Cambridge: Cambridge University Press, 2008), 18, 32, 34, etc., still presumes an intended broader Greek readership.
[27] It is also the first part of a trilogy with the *Paedagogos* and *Stromateis*, which raises other sets of interpretive issues (that we cannot take up here).
[28] *Protr.* 12.123.2 [Stählin 86, 30].

by him (and presumably by the audience, at least in principle) as a source of competition for the singular plea he is making for Christian truth claims. But at the same time he wants to employ them as witnesses – often unwitting – to the truth of his own position. Hence Clement's stance towards his *comparanda* is not exclusively negative, but complexly variegated. In what follows I give an all-too-brief analysis of the flow of the argument according to its main headings,[29] with a particular focus on the crucial role of comparison in the *Protreptikos*.

Prooimion: invitation to the 'true troubadour' (1.1.1–1.10.3)

In his elaborate opening, Clement compares the songsters of 'the Greeks' with Christ, the one true troubadour, whom Clement will present as μοῦ τὸ ᾆσμα τὸ σωτήριον, 'my song that saves', a song that is both new and old at the same time. Then comes a transition in which he issues the protreptic invitation, 'if you desire to see God as he truly is' (σὺ δὲ εἰ ποθεῖς ἰδεῖν ὡς ἀληθῶς τὸν θεόν), followed by a summons to come find this access through Clement's speech: the gates to Christ, the λόγος, are reason (λογικαί), and 'belief' (πίστις) rightly placed (1.10.3). Clement employs the metaphor of initiation as a call to the right truth, in Christ, 'through whom alone God is beheld by initiates' (δι' οὗ μόνου θεὸς ἐποπτεύεται, 1.10.3). This forms a neat bridge to the first set of *comparanda*.

Proofs via *Synkrisis* (2.11.1–12.117.5)

Mystery cults (2.11.1–2.25.3)

Clement treats these first, since, as he later says, they are 'the height of ignorance' (ἀμαθία) and demonic deceit. He demonstrates his broad knowledge of a range of mystery sanctuaries and rites, including those to the gods Dionysus, Demeter, Persephone, Aphrodite, Attis and Cybele, and the Cabeiri, before concluding that these are actually godless cults frequented by the god-bereft (ἄθεοι), who are guilty of a two-fold crime of folly: ignorance of the one true god, and believing things that don't even exist to be gods (2.23.1–2). Clement's argument is a mix of description and detail, analysis and invective. He never admits that there is any real challenge here to the Christian claims. He offers as witnesses to this argument of dissuasion by appeal to the absurdity of the mysteries a sage from the Greeks, Heracleitus of Ephesus (2.22.2), and one from the Jews, Moses (2.25.1–2), the first of many places in the work where we can see that the comparison, though set up as a binary, can be tri-fold (as with Paul's 1 Cor. 1.22–24) and that Clement uses that triangulation to best advantage, sometimes summoning witnesses even from potentially rival camps when they can be useful. Hence, in rhetorical σύγκρισις the line between competitors and allies is flexibly and strategically constructed, and by no means absolute.[30]

---

[29] I give an overview of the full argument so the parts can be seen in relation to the whole, but will provide a more detailed analysis of the section on the philosophers, given the focus of this essay and the engagement with the Rowe book that will follow in the last part of the chapter.

[30] For instance, sometimes he can use the Egyptians' worship of animals as an extreme example of idolatry, and in other cases say the Egyptians don't go as far as the Greeks (even within the same sub-argument; see *Protr.* 2.39.4–6).

Apparent gods, which are actually idols (2.25.4–4.63.5)

Because the race of human beings from its origin had 'an ancient fellowship with heaven implanted into it' (ἦν δέ τις ἔμφυτος ἀρχαία πρὸς οὐρανὸν ἀνθρώποις κοινωνία),[31] how did such ignorance (ἀμαθία, ἄγνοια) and atheism arise, which have reached grotesque expression in the mystery cults with their strange and vacuous customs and assumptions (2.2.3), and even in the cults involving all the Greek gods, their temples, rites and statues? Clement's answer here is not just custom (νόμος), as earlier with the mysteries, but cognition (ἔννοια): 'thoughts that are errant and lead away from what is correct, thoughts that are truly deadly' (ἔννοιαι δὲ ἡμαρτημέναι καὶ παρηγμέναι τῆς εὐθείας, ὀλέθριαι ὡς ἀληθῶς).[32] This is key to his argument, of course, since he writes in order to fix their misguided thoughts about the gods and their statues. Clement tackles an array of questions in this long section of proof spanning three books of the twelve, again showing his cultural virtuosity by the breadth of his knowledge of traditional cult, lore and myth, as well as philosophical speculation about where the gods came from, why they are called as they are, and whether they are hypostatized emotions like love or joy or fear, or are explained by Euhemerism or hero cult. He gives no less than seven different explanations in 2.25.4–26.8, which is also meant to show the confusion and hopeless lack of unity in the Greeks' accounts of their own gods. Clement explains that his purpose in telling all this is to demonstrate the 'slippery and ruinous routes that lead away from the truth' (αἱ ὀλισθηραί τε καὶ ἐπιβλαβεῖς παρεκβάσεις τῆς ἀληθείας).[33] The binary of the λόγος προτρεπτικός is well in view here, as there is a path that leads to truth (that the speaker is beckoning people to, via προτροπή) and one that leads away (from which they must be dissuaded, via ἀποτροπή). Clement has mapped this onto a cosmological geography, such that the human being by nature was originally oriented properly to heaven (where God is) but idolaters have been trapped in error and deceit (πλάνη), and need to be reoriented. Here Clement offers a kerygmatic antidote that casts the Christians as having once been part of that Greek story, but now restored in Christ (quoting Eph. 2.3–5). So the Christians are no longer a part of the story of error, but have 'pulled ourselves away from error, and darted back to the truth' (οἱ τῆς πλάνης ἀπεσπασμένοι, ᾄσσοντες δὲ ἐπὶ τὴν ἀλήθειαν).[34] In contrast, the Greek gods are immoral, shameful, servile, swayed by their passions, cruel, age badly (poor Zeus, look at him now![35]), and have some embarrassing bodily defects. And the worship of their images is wrong, on religious, philosophical, aesthetic and practical grounds. In contrast, 'our God' is not a statue made of sense-perceptible materials, but a νοητὸν ἄγαλμα (4.51.6). Once again, Heraclitus makes a cameo to serve as a supporting witness for Clement (2.34.5; 4.50.4), as does 'the prophet' Moses (4.62.2), and 'the prophet' David (4.62.4–63.5). Within the tumble of arguments the direct protreptic appeal to make a choice shows up occasionally to remind the audience of what is at stake in the sea of *comparanda*: 'Even now, forget

---

[31] *Protr.* 2.25.4 [Stählin 18, 29–19,1].
[32] *Protr.* 2.25.4 [Stählin 19, 9–10].
[33] *Protr.* 2.27.1 [Stählin 20, 3].
[34] *Protr.* 2.27.2 [Stählin 20, 12–13].
[35] *Protr.* 2.37.1–4 [Stählin 27, 23–8, 12].

this superstitious worship of demons!' (ὑμεῖς δὲ ἀλλὰ κἂν νῦν δεισιδαιμονίας ἐκλάθεσθε).[36] Given that the temples 'the Greeks' worship these gods in are really tombs, if they don't turn away from them in shame, 'then you are going around completely dead, since you believe in things that are truly dead' (νεκροὶ ἄρα τέλεον ὄντες νεκροῖς [ὄντως] πεπιστευκότες περιέρχεσθε).[37] Having demolished pagan cult (in his view), Clement ends book four in an exhortation that provides an elegant transition to the next heading: 'it seems that there is only one refuge left for the person who is going to reach the gates of salvation: divine wisdom (σοφία θεϊκή).'[38]

The philosophers (φιλόσοφοι) on the gods (5.64.1–6.72.5)

'Now, if it seems right to you, let's run through the opinions that the philosophers (οἱ φιλόσοφοι) declare with confidence about the gods,'[39] Clement announces at the outset of book five. On the one hand, he is moving to higher-level *comparanda* in doing so, but he is also a bit scathing about ways in which self-styled 'philosophers', in their teachings that identify τὰ στοιχεῖα with gods, wind up less the metaphysicians they imagine themselves and more actually 'worshipers of matter' (τὴν ὕλην προσκυνήσαντες); as a result they are as ἄθεοι ('god-bereft') as the crude devotées of the mystery cults.[40] Clement (the Platonist) mentions with more implied approval those who are less rooted in physical matter and seek τι ὑψηλότερον καὶ περιττότερον ('something higher and more extraordinary') that is, abstractions like 'the infinite' (ἄπειρον), 'mind' (νοῦς) or 'images' (εἴδωλα); but these, too, are guilty of shamelessness (ἀναισχυντία), he concludes.[41] Missing, conspicuously, from Clement's list here is 'the Good' (τὸ καλόν) for he is (mostly) moving from the lower grades (in his estimation) to the higher. (Hang on, dear reader, Plato will appear later!) It is in this context (comparing the sensible with the insensible) that he dispenses quickly with the Stoics: 'Nor shall I pass by the Stoics who, in saying that the divine pervades through all matter (ὕλη), even the most dishonorable, simply heap shame on philosophy.'[42] The Peripatetics deserve a bit longer treatment, since their πατήρ (Aristotle) did not mentally perceive (νοεῖν) the Father god, creator of all (τῶν ὅλων πατήρ), and thus regarded the 'highest' (ὕπατος) as the 'world soul' (ψυχὴ τοῦ παντός). While he is at least raised above the crass materialism of the others, Aristotle nonetheless fails for not understanding the cosmic extent of God's providence (πρόνοια). This leads (predictably) to the Epicureans, whom Clement dismisses with even more invective than the Stoics for their denial of providence and lack of piety (ἀσέβεια). In all these arguments, Clement is drawing upon debates among and between the philosophical schools and their critiques and invective tags, using the internal συγκρίσεις against each in turn to bury the whole lot (i.e. the category of 'philosophers').

---

[36] *Protr.* 3.44.3 [Stählin 34, 7–8].
[37] *Protr.* 3.45.5 [Stählin 35, 7–8].
[38] *Protr.* 4.63.5 [Stählin 48, 25–7].
[39] *Protr.* 5.64.1 [Stählin 48, 30–1].
[40] *Protr.* 5.64.3 [Stählin 49, 7]. Of course, these were not actually distinct groups (philosophers did sometimes become initiates), but Clement is fashioning an internal comparison to suit his purposes.
[41] *Protr.* 5.66.1–2 [Stählin 50, 13–22].
[42] *Protr.* 5.66.3 [Stählin 50, 24–7].

But there is an exception. Expressing his concern about how even philosophers, as though they were children, attend to myths, Clement fashions a dialogue with φιλοσοφία herself. He tells her, 'I am searching (ἐπιζητεῖν) for God. Who among those who are devoted to you should I take as my co-worker (συνεργός) in this search (ζήτησις)? For we haven't given up on you completely, philosophy!' She replies, on cue, 'If you wish, Plato.'[43] Clement now turns his gaze to philosophy's chosen avatar: 'Well, then, Plato, in what way should we trace the path to God?'[44] The Plato of *Timaeus* 28C provides both the answer and a co-lament from Clement's συνεργός: 'it is work (ἔργον) to find the Father and Maker of this entire universe (πατὴρ καὶ ποιητὴς τοῦδε τοῦ παντός), and, once he is found, it is impossible to declare him to everyone.' 'But, in God's name, why?' Clement asks. Plato replies (this time from *Ep.* 7.341c): 'Because it is incapable of being put into speech' (ῥητὸν γὰρ οὐδαμῶς ἐστιν). 'Bravo, Plato, you have touched on the truth (εὖ . . . ἐπαφᾶσαι τῆς ἀληθείας)! But don't lose heart. Take up the search for the Good with me!'[45] Clement then again proffers a theory of knowledge, to the effect that 'an outpouring of the divine (τις ἀπόρροια θεϊκή) has been placed in all people, and especially those who devote their time to careful arguments (λόγοι)'.[46] This means that everyone, but especially the philosophers (despite their deficits as just recounted at some length), confesses – even if involuntarily (ἄκοντες δὲ ὁμολογοῦσιν) – certain things about God: he is one, indestructible, unbegotten, dwells above the heavenly skies and is eternally existing.[47] A bit later in the dialogue Plato will admit that he had received the truth in a second way (alongside its being instilled in all humanity), from 'the races of the barbarians'.[48] Clement goes further and insists that Plato received his teaching about God and about the laws from 'the Hebrews' (cf. Moses in Deut. 25.13-15 quoted earlier, and *Sib. Or.* 3.586-8, 590-4). This is a bid to ensure that the strong blood lines of the Christian patrimony, as both Jewish and Greek, were unified from the start (the Paul of 1 Cor. 1.22-24 would say, *Touché!*).

Now that the pivot has been made, and the protrepticist has turned from *condemning* the philosophers to *offering them as witnesses for his own case*, Clement calls on φιλοσοφία once again and asks her to aid his effort by bringing forward other Greek philosophers who, inspired by the right conception of God (κατ' ἐπίνοιαν αὐτοῦ), have 'laid hold of the truth' (εἴ που τῆς ἀληθείας ἐπιδράξαιντο) and 'announced that the one true God alone is God' (τὸν ἕνα ὄντως μόνον θεὸν ἀναφθεγγόμενοι θεόν).[49] And here they come: Democritus, Antisthenes, Xenophon, Cleanthes and the Pythagoreans. It is Cleanthes the Stoic who plays a key role to anchor this argument. He receives unmitigated praise for having set out, not a 'poetic theogony' (θεογονία ποιητική) but a 'true theology' (θεολογία ἀληθινή).[50] Replicating the dialogical feeling in Clement's own text, the fragment from Cleanthes answers the question 'you ask me what the

---

[43] *Protr.* 6.67.2-68.1 [Stählin 51, 25-7].
[44] *Protr.* 6.68.1 [Stählin 51, 27-9].
[45] *Protr.* 6.68.1 [Stählin 51, 30-52, 2].
[46] *Protr.* 6.68.2 [Stählin 52, 2-4]. As always with Clement, λόγος here can mean words, arguments, reasons, etc.
[47] *Protr.* 6.68.3 [Stählin 52, 4-7].
[48] *Protr.* 6.70.1 [Stählin 53, 11-12].
[49] *Protr.* 6.71.1 [Stählin 53, 27-9].
[50] *Protr.* 6.72.1 [Stählin 54, 15-16].

good is like?' (τἀγαθὸν ἐρωτᾷς μ' οἷον ἐστ';) with a list of some 29 characteristics, among which are εὐσεβές, καλόν, δέον, λυσιτελές, ὠφέλιμον, εὐάρεστον, φίλον, ὁμολογούμενον, and ending with ἀεὶ διαμένον.[51] Where others may 'hint' (αἰνίττεσθαι)[52] at the truth, Clement argues, it is the Stoic master who declares with utter clarity (σαφῶς) the nature of God.[53] Cleanthes serves at last (surprisingly, over Plato!) as proof of the consummate wisdom with which God has inspired human beings, providing a guide for all people who wish to examine the truth (διαθρεῖν ἀλήθειαν).

In this key section of comparison with the Greek philosophers, Clement deftly plays with part and whole, variously configured, such that the same thinker or school can at times stand for the whole of philosophy, and at others serve as a foil for or corrective of the others. Unlike with mystery cults or idolatry, the proof by appeal to philosophy ends on a note of commonality, both among the philosophers and between them and the Christians, about the unity and nature of God.

The poets (7.73.1–7.76.6)

Clement begins on a Platonic note by saying the poets normally traffic in falsehood (τὸ ψεῦδος). He then calls ποιητική forward to testify to her prior lies, on the one hand, and to show, on the other hand, that the poets (e.g. Aratus, Hesiod, Sophocles, Orpheus) often spoke with some truth, if not clearly, but figuratively (αἰνίττεσθαι). They did not reach the fullness of understanding (οὐ ἐφικόμενοι τοῦ τέλους),[54] Clement insists, but their glimpses of the truth prove that the power of the truth has not been hidden (ἀποκεκρυμμένη). And, in turn (using an internal comparison), Clement argues that it is the comic poets in particular (such as Menander) who have given especially forceful expression to the truth[55], as they offered deliciously scathing send-ups of the traditional gods and other cults like that of Attis and Cybele. Maybe, he urges, the comic poets can shame you into rejecting them and turn to the way of salvation!

Prophets and scripture (8.77.1–9.88.3)

Moving from the poets of the Greeks to the prophets of the ancient Hebrews (as read in Greek), Clement argues that they were the foundation of the truth (θεμελιοῦσι τὴν ἀλήθειαν), and the divine scriptures are what 'gives a clear *protreptikos* to the salvation that is before your eyes' (προτρέπουσαι δὲ ἐμφανῶς εἰς προῦπτον σωτηρίαν). The Sibyl, for instance, teaches by the method of σύγκρισις, setting error and truth, light and darkness side by side, and declaring the choice one must make (ἄμφω δὲ παραθεμένη τῇ συγκρίσει, τὴν ἐκλογὴν διδάσκει).[56] A colloquy of voices, from Jeremiah, Hosea, Isaiah, Wisdom (in Prov. 8.22), and Moses shows again and again the falsehood of the idols. Moses in the Shema (Deut. 6.4) and elsewhere is ἀποτρέπων εἰδωλολατρείας

---

[51] *Protr.* 6.72.2 [Stählin 54, 18–55, 4].
[52] *Protr.* 6.68.5; 6.70.1; 6.71.3 [Stählin 52, 21; 53, 10; 54, 5], of Plato and Xenophon.
[53] *Protr.* 6.72.3 [Stählin 55, 5].
[54] *Protr.* 7.74.7 [Stählin 57, 8–11].
[55] *Protr.* 7.75.2 [Stählin 57, 15].
[56] *Protr.* 8.77.3 [Stählin 59, 27–8].

ἁπάσης,⁵⁷ dissuading from all idolatry. In this way, the Christian orator's words are meant to join, in both form and content, the protreptic work of scripture herself. All of book nine continues, offering a cascade of biblical protreptic passages (αἱ προτροπαί), with a strong presence of 'the blessed apostle' (Eph. 4.17-19; 1 Tim. 4.8; 2 Tim. 3.15), urging their hearers to seek truth rather than falsehood, freedom rather than slavery, salvation instead of death, eternal life instead of punishment. The voice calls out ἥκετε ἥκετε ὦ νεολαία ἡ ἐμή ('come, come, my young people!').⁵⁸ But the most astonishing προτροπαί, and the greatest 'calling of the question', comes from the Lord himself, in Matt. 4.17 ('the kingdom of the heavens has drawn near'), by which he 'converts people when they approach out of fear' (ἐπιστρέφει τοὺς ἀνθρώπους πλησιάζοντας τῷ φόβῳ).⁵⁹ Christ is joined first by the apostle Paul (Phil. 4.5) and the Psalmist (34.8, 11-12) and then a hymn to the cosmic harmonic unity of all humanity 'following the Word as its choral-leader and teacher, coming to rest in the truth itself (αὐτὴ ἀλήθεια), saying, "Abba, Father"'.⁶⁰

Serving God in truth, rather than in custom (i.e. idolatry) (10.89.1-10.110.3)

In this long section of proof, Clement returns, in chiastic order, after the philosophers, to the problem of idolatry. As a part of his call to conversion, he takes up the anticipated objection from his auditors that he is calling for them to abandon their ancestral customs. Clement says, indeed, that is exactly what he is calling for: 'leave behind the custom that is wicked, lustful and godless' (τὸ ἔθος καταλιπόντες τὸ πονηρὸν καὶ ἐμπαθὲς καὶ ἄθεον).⁶¹ This means, in turn, its exact opposite, towards which he calls them: 'shall we not turn toward the truth' (ἐπὶ τὴν ἀλήθειαν ἐκκινοῦμεν)?⁶² Casting his would-be converts who rejected his λόγοι as wild horses refusing a bridle, Clement adopts the mantle of the 'charioteers of life' (οἱ ἡνίοχοι τοῦ βίου) who will steer one aright: away from custom and towards truth; from madness to sanity; from evil to goodness; from punishment to life; from destruction to salvation; from ignorance to knowledge; from drunkenness to sobriety. As with the proofs that preceded, he can mix supporting evidence from Elijah and Democritus⁶³ (i.e. Jew and Greek) one after another, who alike critique the ignorant who dwell in darkness (10.92.3-4). Clement sounds the exhortation directly at 10.93.1: μετανοήσωμεν οὖν καὶ μεταστῶμεν ἐξ ἀμαθίας εἰς ἐπιστήμην ('So, then, let's repent, and let's change from ignorance to knowledge!').⁶⁴ And Moses in the life and death covenantal formula in Deut. 30.15 joins the array of voices. Then Clement again singles himself out and calls for his readers to take him as their advisor (σύμβουλος), as he will lay before them an abundance of persuasive arguments for the true Word, and, switching the metaphor, call them to strip down and ready themselves for the ἀγών against 'the godless devotées

---

⁵⁷ *Protr.* 8.80.4 [Stählin 61, 19-20].
⁵⁸ *Protr.* 8.82.4 [Stählin 62, 18].
⁵⁹ *Protr.* 8.87.3 [Stählin 65, 14-15].
⁶⁰ *Protr.* 9.88.3 [Stählin 65, 29-66, 1].
⁶¹ *Protr.* 10.89.2 [Stählin 66, 13-14].
⁶² *Protr.* 10.89.2 [Stählin 66, 15].
⁶³ And, later, Theocritus of Chios (*Protr.* 10.97.1 [Stählin 70, 29-71, 2]).
⁶⁴ *Protr.* 10.93.1 [Stählin 68, 15-16].

of demonic idol worship' (δεισιδαιμονίας ἄθεοι χορευταί),[65] where the Logos is the umpire (βραβεύς), and God is the master of the games (ἀγωνοθέτης).

The implied dialogue with the possible convert is raised to the surface at 10.100.1, where she or he asks (via Clement's *prosopopoiia*) how she can find the way (ὁδός) to heaven. Predictably, Clement offers Jn. 14.6 (ἐγώ εἰμι ἡ ὁδὸς καὶ ἡ ἀλήθεια καὶ ἡ ζωή) and Matt. 7:13–14 to answer the question: the narrow (στενή) way that leads to heaven is Christ. The tension between a wisdom from outside and that within the human person re-emerges, as Clement returns to the earlier ideas that the human being is by birth and nature akin to God (πέφυκε γὰρ ὡς ἄνθρωπος οἰκείως ἔχειν πρὸς θεόν),[66] and to Plato's right conception of God as Creator and Father of the Universe (ὁ τῶν πάντων δημιουργὸς καὶ πατήρ) who should be known by all his children – that is, unless they are mired in ignorance, darkness and disability.[67] The true hymn promised in the opening of the *Protrepticus* is now offered, if his hearers 'have their beastly brutality removed by its beguiling charms' (ἀλλ' ὑμεῖς γε κατεπᾴσθητε τὴν ἀγριότητα), and receive 'the gentleness that is found in our Word/word' (παραδέξασθε τὸν ἥμερον καὶ ἡμέτερον λόγον).[68] The book soars to a crescendo of the hymn to the Word as the sweetest medicine, the way to salvation, peace and 'an ocean of good things' (πέλαγος ἀγαθῶν).[69]

The Christian story saves (11.111.1–11.117.5)

'Now please look closely, at least in brief, at the story of God's beneficence from the very beginning.'[70] Thus begins book eleven, in which, nearing his final call to decision, Clement largely eschews comparison, providing instead a dramatic telling of the kerygmatic narrative (τὰ διηγήματα)[71] of salvation from Adam and Eve, through the fall, the incarnation, the death of Christ and his vanquishing of death. 'Oh marvelous mystery!' (ὦ θαύματος μυστικοῦ), he exclaims. Having moved again in chiastic order back to the first comparandum,[72] Clement proclaims the Christian tale and song as the replacement for, and sum total of, all mystery cults. Now comes some strong rhetoric of displacement directed at the philosophers, not due to their complete error, but on a developmental, partial to whole, schema: 'Now that the Word has come to us from heaven, there is no longer any need for us to go to a human teacher, meddling about in Athens, or other parts of Greece or Ionia.' Indeed, 'the whole world has become Athens and Greece due to the Word.'[73] Clement calls on the hearers as proof against themselves in the same terms as at the opening of the *Protreptikos*: if they believed (ἐπιστεύετε) in legends about Minos of Crete, surely they will not disbelieve (οὐ ... ἀπιστήσετε) that the

---

[65] *Protr.* 10.96.3 [Stählin 70, 25].
[66] *Protr.* 10.100.2 [Stählin 72, 24–5].
[67] *Protr.* 10.105.1 [Stählin 75, 14].
[68] *Protr.* 10.106.1 [Stählin 75, 28–9].
[69] *Protr.* 10.109.1–110.3 [Stählin 77, 23–78, 24].
[70] *Protr.* 11.111.1 [Stählin 78, 25]: Μικρὸν δέ, εἰ βούλει, ἄνωθεν ἄθρει τὴν θείαν εὐεργεσίαν.
[71] Clement uses this term in 11.113.4: Σώσει σου τὰ διηγήματα, παιδεύσει με ἡ ᾠδή [Stählin 80, 9].
[72] As also with a return to the new song, which harks back to the opening, in *Protr.* 1.1–7.1 [Stählin 3, 1–7, 20].
[73] *Protr.* 11.112.1 [Stählin 79, 7–12].

disciples of Christ have now received 'the wisdom that is really true' (ἡ ὄντως ἀληθὴς σοφία), which the best of the philosophers only hinted at' (ἣν φιλοσοφίας ἄκροι μόνον ᾐνίξαντο).[74] Those disciples received that true wisdom and proclaimed it in the world. Paul's sentiment in 1 Cor. 1.22-24 is certainly in view here, but then Clement turns especially to the Paul of Gal. 3.28[75] to cement his claim the 'Christ is not divided' (ὁ Χριστὸς οὐ μερίζεται; cf. 1 Cor. 1.13), but 'there is neither barbarian nor Jew nor Greek, nor male and female; but there is a new human being refashioned by the spirit of God'.[76] Here Clement's σύγκρισις is dissolved in a claim for a unitary community of truth, made up of all races of peoples. Furthermore, he maintains, Christian teaching issued a single and universal προτροπή to all humanity that the chief end of human life is θεοσέβεια, 'godly piety'.[77] The Christian protrepticist calls his audience to embrace the light, reject ignorance and darkness, and, taking up πίστις, ensure for themselves the greatest reward, true salvation, eternal life (11.115.2-11.1174.1). Summing up his entire argument Clement asks, 'Toward what am I persuading you by my protreptic (τί δὴ σε προτρέπω)? I am urging you to be saved! (σωθῆναί σε ἐπείγομαι).'[78]

Epilogos: flee Bacchic revelry and come to the true mysteries (12.118.1-123.2)

The poetic-infused conclusion to Clement's *Protreptikos* begins with the often-invoked image of Odysseus avoiding the Sirens in book twelve of the Odyssey, to forge his *apotrope* from the 'custom' (συνήθεια) of idol worship (cf. book 10). 'Custom', he argues, offers her own corresponding *apotrope* – leading people away from the truth (τῆς ἀληθείας ἀποτρέπει).[79] By that binary logic, one must be like Odysseus, Clement urges, and 'Sail right by that song, for it produces death,'[80] once again alluding to the opening image of the work, which set forth the stark comparison between two songs – those of 'the Greeks' and of Christ. Clement cannot resist developing the nautical image for his hearer: lash yourself not to the mast (like Odysseus), but to the cross of Christ (cf. *Od.* 12.184-5). The Word of God will serve as your pilot; the Holy Spirit will bring you into the harbours of heaven (12.118.4). And then Clement shifts gear back into the theme of the true mysteries. While Paul is his visionary muse (1 Cor. 2.9), he fashions a σύγκρισις with the Dionysiac mysteries to urge his Christian hearers to avoid the mad, drunken and violent fate of Pentheus (Euripides, *Bacc.* 918-919). First comes the *protrope* to Christianity as possessing the true mysteries to which Clement beckons his hearer, and then the *apotrope*: 'Flee Thebes!' He promises, 'I shall show you the Word and the Mysteries of the Word, giving an account that fits your own cult image' (δείξω

---

[74] *Protr.* 11.112.3 [Stählin 79, 12-16].
[75] Cf. also Rom 1.14; 1 Cor. 12.13; Eph. 4.24; Col. 3.9-11.
[76] *Protr.* 11.112.3 [Stählin 79, 18-19]: οὔτε βάρβαρός ἐστιν οὔτε Ἰουδαῖος οὔτε Ἕλλην, οὐκ ἄρρεν, οὐ θῆλυ· καινὸς δὲ ἄνθρωπος θεοῦ πνεύματι ἁγίῳ μεταπεπλασμένος.
[77] *Protr.* 11.113.1 [Stählin 79, 22-4].
[78] *Protr.* 11.117.3 [Stählin 82, 31-2].
[79] *Protr.* 12.118.1 [Stählin 83, 10].
[80] *Protr.* 12.118.4 [Stählin 83, 24]: παράπλει τὴν ᾠδήν, θάνατον ἐργάζεται.

σοι τὸν λόγον καὶ τοῦ λόγου τὰ μυστήρια, κατὰ τὴν σὴν διηγούμενος εἰκόνα).[81] Before calling his hearer to make the choice in the final lines ('But the final decision [πέρας] is left to you [ὑμῖν δὲ ἔτι τοῦτο περιλείπεται], to choose (ἑλέσθαι) what is to your advantage [τὸ λυσιτελοῦν], either judgment or grace [ἢ κρίσιν ἢ χάριν]'),[82] Clement recasts the Christian mysteries ('Oh, truly holy mysteries!'),[83] marked by a pure light, a torch-lit path to a heavenly vision of God. Clement says of himself, 'I become holy by becoming initiated' (ἅγιος γίνομαι μυούμενος), and beckons each hearer individually, 'if you wish, become initiated, too!' (εἰ βούλει, καὶ σὺ μυοῦ).[84] Joining his own voice with that of Homer (Il. 17.220) and Christ himself (Matt. 11.28-30), Clement calls upon 'the whole human race' (τὸ πᾶν ἀνθρώπων γένος καλῶ)[85] to answer his urgent summons to conversion to the true mysteries.

Yet Clement ends his *Protreptikos*, not in the guise of the μύστης, but the φιλόσοφος, not with revealed truth, but reason. He does this because the *Protreptikos* is grounded in an appeal to the human capacity to choose what is better over what is worse – unless, that is, one is drunk or mad or corrupted or dead. As such, it is crucial to emphasize, Clement insists, that φιλοσόφων παῖδες,[86] 'the sons of the philosophers' recognize that the foolish cannot come to wisdom, but only the wise. With this image of the Stoic wise man comes the promise of the *topos*: κοινὰ τὰ φίλων ('friends have all things in common'). Ultimately, he argues, the purpose of the protreptic is to get people to be wise, and to choose what is to their advantage – choose the Christian God and the Logos, and all good things will be yours.

Clement's *Protreptikos* is a complex, learned and carefully crafted text that ingeniously employs σύγκρισις, 'rhetorical comparison', throughout, in whole and in part, in a way that recognizes fully the competitors to Christ and his church at Clement's time (in order of ascending importance: the mysteries, image-worship of the gods and the philosophers) but does not by any means reject them wholesale. He splits the possible adversaries by accenting their differences, thereby using them as witnesses against one another; but he also has a grand conception that all of humanity has the capacity to know the divine truth, because the human is created by the divine. Hence the philosophers and even the poets have offered glimpses of the truth, but not its complete form. Their testimony is a key part of Clement's comparative rhetoric of persuasion to his hearers that the Christian truth claims are the highest and best, and hence should be chosen. These cultural forms are so powerful and evocative that Clement has enmeshed his understanding of Christianity thoroughly in all three of them, as a mystery cult of the very highest order, a competitive image-cult (cf. Gen. 1.26-7; 2 Cor. 4.4), and the true philosophy of the Greeks seeking wisdom (that had had Hebrew signs in the past) brought now to its fulfilment.

---

[81] *Protr.* 12.123.2 [Stählin 84, 6–7].
[82] *Protr.* 12.123.2 [Stählin 86, 28–9].
[83] *Protr.* 12.120.1 [Stählin 84, 23]: Ὢ τῶν ἁγίων ὡς ἀληθῶς μυστηρίων.
[84] *Protr.* 12.120.1–2 [Stählin 84, 24–8].
[85] *Protr.* 12.120.2 [Stählin 84, 33].
[86] *Protr.* 12.122.1 [Stählin 86, 1].

Propositions on comparison in the study of the New Testament and ancient Christianity

Out of this (lengthy but still far too brief!) discussion of how Clement employs σύγκρισις throughout his *Protreptikos*, I would like next to offer a dozen propositions about academic comparison in the study of ancient Christianity[87] as I understand it. They do not, of course, result solely from this analysis, but reflect the assumptions of my broader scholarly work and my own understanding of the field.[88] However, I think one can see how most of these principles have been illustrated in or follow from my foregoing analysis of Clement's προτρεπτικός:

1. Comparison is ubiquitous within early Christian sources because of the projects of self-definition and self-understanding of this multiply hybrid movement (or set of movements) and the nature of its claims, from Paul (the first extant Christian author and inaugurator of its literary culture) forward.
2. Early Christian use of σύγκρισις (one of the *progymnasmata* taught in school among the tools of literacy) involves constructing interested claims of *both* similarity and difference, continuity and discontinuity, often complexly intertwined (and played off of one another).
3. The role of scholarship is not to accept these comparisons at face value, but to analyse them as efforts that are theological, rhetorical, political, philosophical, literary, sociological, cultural, linguistic, etc.
4. In the study of ancient Christianity the terms or elements of many comparisons are given already in our sources (because of points 1 and 2), others are not (because of new sources, new questions, new methods); both should be pursued.
5. Comparisons within our sources often demonstrate that our authors themselves were aware of ways in which early Christian thought, rituals, ethics, community forms were not unique; sometimes in comparing it was to their advantage to emphasize the commonality, sometimes the opposite.
6. Comparison is both a rhetorical form and an analytical one (i.e. a place for thinking), both for the ancients and for us; it does not have to be exact or absolute for us to learn from it.

---

[87] In this I am following the lead of my Chicago colleague Bruce Lincoln in his 'Theses on Comparison', in *Gods and Demons, Priests and Scholars: Critical Explorations in the History of Religions* (Chicago: University of Chicago Press, 2012), 121–30, 121–3, but making statements of particular relevance to the study of ancient Christianity. There is much (though not absolute) agreement in my theses with Lincoln's call for disciplining comparison in what he regards as the '(un)discipline of religious studies', such as the following four points: 'it is time we entertained comparatism [sic] of weaker and more modest sorts that (a) focus on a relatively small number of comparanda that the researcher can study closely; (b) are equally attentive to relations of similarity and those of difference; (c) grant equal dignity and intelligence to all parties considered; and (d) are attentive to the social, historical, and political contexts and subtexts of religious and literary texts.'

[88] I understand the field to be New Testament and Early Christian Literature, with no separation out of 'New Testament' as an area distinct from the study of early Christian literature, history, culture, religion and theology more broadly.

7. Every act of comparison is selective, both in whole (τὸ ὅλον) and in part (τὸ μέρος)[89] and in the decisions about how to navigate between them; in scholarly analysis it is crucial to attend to what is brought in and what is not, what highlighted and what diminished – and the cogency of the reasons given for doing so.
8. It is up to the modern researcher to justify a comparison s/he wishes to make, explain the terms of that comparison (this includes the third term,[90] but also the body of questions being asked and the assumptions on which the comparison proceeds) and argue for why his/her interpretation of either *comparandum* is compelling or is of analytical benefit.
9. Every act of comparison we construct as scholars, as with the ancients, which involves both similarity and difference (so especially Jonathan Z. Smith[91]), is for a particular purpose (σκοπός), and often with counter-comparisons actively in view[92] (or, at other times, they need to be reconstructed out of the silence). These ancient arguments need to be read in context, with attention to the logical and rhetorical ἀκολουθία,[93] not sampled piecemeal.
10. Since, as Theon insisted, we compare 'like things' (τὰ ὅμοια), we need categories[94] in order to compare (e.g. Clement's προτρεπτικός includes holy places, rituals, cult objects, ideas about the gods, moral codes, poems, stories, promises, benefits, etc.); these categories are always provisional (though necessary) and open to contestation and/or refinement (or rejection) in ongoing debate.
11. The denial of comparability (as in Clement's ἐπίλογος) is a rhetorical *topos* (that in fact depends upon its contrary to be true). Saying something is incomparable does not make it so.
12. Whether or not a magic still dwells[95] in comparison, it is certainly not dead.

---

[89] As Menander Rhetor para. 376 shows, synecdoche (reasoning from part to whole) is a key part of the logic of σύγκρισις.

[90] As insisted by Jonathan Z. Smith, 'In Comparison a Magic Dwells', in *Imagining Religion: From Babylon to Jonestown* (Chicago Studies in the History of Religions; Chicago: University of Chicago Press, 1982), 19–35.

[91] Ibid., and throughout his oeuvre, especially (for the present study) *Drudgery Divine: On the Comparison of Early Christianities and the Religions of Late Antiquity* (Chicago: University of Chicago Press, 1990). See also Lincoln, *Gods and Demons*, 123 (quoted in n. 87).

[92] Within what I call 'the agonistic paradigm of interpretation' (*Paul, the Corinthians, and the Birth of Christian Hermeneutics*, 25–7.)

[93] This refers to the structure and progression of a rhetorical argument, which are essential to meaning. That is why I provided such an analysis of Clement's *Protreptikos* earlier in this chapter.

[94] 'All generalization depends on comparison, although the latter is usually pursued in ways inadequate to the task. Still, the only alternatives are (a) a discourse whose generalizations remain intuitive, unreflective, and commonsensical, that is without basis, rigor, or merit; and (b) a parochialism that dares speak nothing beyond the petty and the particular' (Lincoln, 'Theses on Comparison', 121 [Thesis #3]).

[95] So the volume ed. Kimberley C. Patton and Benjamin C. Ray, *A Magic Still Dwells: Comparative Religion in the Postmodern Age* (Berkeley: University of California Press, 2000), playing on the title of Jonathan Z. Smith's famous essay, 'In Comparison a Magic Dwells'.

C. Kavin Rowe's *One True Life*

Professor C. Kavin Rowe's book *One True Life: The Stoics and Early Christians as Rival Traditions* (2016) is presented at first glance as a scholarly argument about forms of comparison of ancient religion, in interaction with select modern philosophical voices (prominently Alasdair MacIntyre, Charles Taylor and Jeffrey Stout, occasionally Martha Nussbaum[96] and A. A. Long). In fact, the work is a λόγος προτρεπτικὸς[97] εἰς ἀλήθειαν Χριστιανικήν,[98] in which Rowe calls on his readers to embrace the one true path of life; delivers denunciations of the opposing view as errant,[99] blind,[100] self-deceived,[101] proffering damaging distortions,[102] obscurantist,[103] dead[104] and fossilized;[105] and, on both exegetical and testimonial bases, seeks to show the superiority of the Christian life because it is incomparable, unique, isolated in its truth claims, still alive,[106] and a rival – as it always has been, from antiquity forward – to any other regime of truth. Rowe ends the book by calling the question on his reader, with a modern version of the 'two ways' tradition, an appeal to Kierkegaard's leap of faith or Pascal's wager, a summons to choose (phrased at one point, embedded within an argument about the basis of truth, as 'Come join!'[107]), while offering a final caricature of his opponents as arrogant

---

[96] Nussbaum's *The Therapy of Desire: Therapy and Practice in Hellenistic Ethics* (Princeton: Princeton University Press, 1994), is invoked at various points in the exegesis of ancient Stoics. That Professor Nussbaum is a champion of the liberal arts and humanistic engagement (as well as global efforts for religious equality and tolerance) – of very much the kind Rowe seeks to repudiate in the book – is not acknowledged.

[97] Despite its fit in purpose and genre, the words protreptic or *protrope* do not appear in *One True Life*. The words 'change' and 'convert' (and associated nouns) and 'reject' (e.g. 'the need to reject encyclopedic reasoning as an illuminating way of knowing the ancient texts and construing their relation' [p. 191]) do, frequently. The form of protreptic was used by ancient Stoics, such as Persaeus of Citium, Ariston of Chios, Cleanthes, and Posidonius (all lost; mentioned by Diogenes Laertius, *Vit.* 7.36, 163, 175, 91, respectively) and Christians, such as Clement of Alexandria, examined above.

[98] 'A protreptic argument for Christian truth' (the Greek phrasing and translation are mine). We shall turn at the end of this essay to the question of πρὸς τίνας ('directed towards whom?').

[99] Page 194.

[100] 'The second error concerns the way in which the claim to be able to render particular traditions via modern scholarly languages produces a very specific kind of blindness' (p. 194).

[101] 'Modern projects of [encyclopedic] absorption are, in brief, self-deceived' (p. 195).

[102] 'This will allow us to specify the more fundamental distortions that arise from the strangeness of studying traditions as if they were something else' (p. 185). See also the section 'Encyclopedic Distortions' (pp. 191–8), that begins, 'it nevertheless remains for us to specify and elaborate the most damaging distortions of this type of mistake'.

[103] Pages 185, 193, 198.

[104] As announced on p. 2: 'Encyclopedic inquiry – the name for the epistemic assumptions of the vast majority of modern scholarly work on the Stoics and the New Testament – is dead and gone. We should take notice.' See also p. 179: 'The encyclopedia lives on and continues to form structurally the way we learn and think – even though it is quite dead.' Rowe characterizes his own approach as follows: 'This is what comparative scholarship is that refuses to live among the dead' (p. 204). The dead here presumably refers both to scholarly peers who lack his insight and to the ancients (whom those scholarly peers, on this account, treat as though they were dead).

[105] Page 243 ('the fossil-like thinking of today's encyclopedists').

[106] Despite the emphasis on living tradition, Rowe does not attempt to show how one might 'convert' and live as a Stoic in twenty-first-century America.

[107] Page 257; this echoes back to p. 221: '"Come join us, for we know the truth" is inherent to the political vision of the Christian story and produces the tension that indelibly marks Christian existence.' See also p. 245 for another formulation: 'seizing on a way of life believingly, lovingly, through thick and thin'.

positivists (thinking 'humanistic scholarship[108] can render all forms of life transparent'), blind to difference in their misguided quest for human universals, not 'more scholarly or philosophically rigorous', but (especially in comparison with selective modern philosophers like MacIntyre and Stout) 'hopelessly out of date' and 'voguishly cosmopolitan' (p. 258). The final sentence[109] ("Talk really is, after all, as deep as life' [p. 258]) suggests that they are sophists when compared with a real philosopher like himself: they mistake words for playthings, since such scholars are superficial and lacking in 'depth' about what life is really about. Clearly, they are not good guides and should be rejected. Follow my path to one true life!

Rowe's *protreptikos* proceeds on two levels, what I shall term *Protrope* A and B. *Protrope* A is an urgent call to a different kind of scholarship in New Testament studies that rejects the current, 'encyclopedia-based' attempts to document and analyse similarities between Christian thinking and that of its imperial period philosophical contemporaries, most conspicuously, Stoics. This is crystalized in the protreptic call on p. 204: 'There is no other choice … It is time to change the way we think' (= *Apotrope* A). The position to which *Protrope* A urges readers is to 'reject' the comparative project entirely in its present form,[110] because it is impossible to understand any tradition unless one is 'inside' it, and because traditions are, in fact, 'mutually incompatible' (p. 250) and 'mutually exclusive' (p. 259). They are also largely 'untranslatable', because (Rowe categorically states) one simply cannot live inside[111] more than one tradition at a

---

[108] For Rowe, the humanistic disciplines are the opposition, as he acknowledges in his response to Objection 1 (in the 'Appendix: Objections and Replies'), which states, 'Your argument flies in the face of the crucial epistemological assumption that funds the vast majority of religious studies programs and humanistic scholarship more generally', i.e. by dismantling the idea that human beings can understand one another across belief systems, linguistic systems, cultural difference, etc. Rowe replies: 'Yes, the argument of this book does entail the rejection of the dominant way of thinking about our knowledge of lived difference of traditions of life' (p. 259).

[109] That is, before the 'Appendix: Objections and Replies', which documents Rowe's unyielding to the criticisms, either brought against the manuscript by the editorial reviewers at Yale University Press, or as anticipated by the author (or both). The rhetorical form of the Objections suggests a kind of testimonial *confessio* for the 'extreme' formulations (p. 261) of his 'academically surprising' arguments (p. 259) that 'fly in the face' of what most scholars think (five of the eight Objections use this same phrase). In n. 2 (on p. 315) Rowe points to precedents for this form (including in one of his earlier books), and puts these in the line of 'dialectical reasoning' back to Plato. And yet it is quite jarring to see dialectic brought in at the end, when the logic of the larger argument of the book is based in antithetical reasoning, in line with its protreptic purpose. This is less dialectic or dialogue (something eschewed in the book – see, e.g., p. 224: 'Conversation on the basis of shared substantive commitments [among Stoics and Christians], is, quite frankly, impossible') than a restatement of Rowe's positions. The final objection (#8, on violence), however, introduces something new, to which I wish I could devote attention in this essay (but cannot, for space purposes), for it raises the crucial issue of what Rowe is willing to risk for his proposal, especially in terms of historic and present enactments of Christian exclusivist truth claims in political, military and other forms. Rowe argues that 'the early church knew … well' that there is clear normative guidance in the New Testament against violence, but 'we cannot claim to have remembered it faithfully through our history' (p. 262). While one appreciates the acknowledgement, this is not a satisfactory answer, on historical, theological, ethical, or practical grounds.

[110] Or mostly; there is some wavering here, given that Rowe (like Clement) wishes to employ comparison in order to demonstrate incomparability.

[111] Rowe exhibits a kind of 'hardened-Hadotism' (my formulation), turning the latter's keen insight that ancient philosophy was 'a way of life' into a rigid epistemological prescription that the condition for all knowing, and any knowing worth achieving, must come from 'living its way of life'. The other difficulty in Rowe's application of this, as far as I can see, is that it is an 'all or nothing at all' (you are in or out/converted or not) whereas much of ancient philosophy (certainly with the Stoics on

time.¹¹² Comparative arguments in contemporary scholarship that get caught up in small details ('minutiae') overly emphasize surface-level similarities and do not recognize that traditions are 'rivals' among which one *has* to choose; they thereby distort the evidence, and mislead their audiences. This leads to the second goal of Rowe's λόγος προτρεπτικός.

Protrope B is a purportedly gentler summons to any who read the book to recognize that 'The human condition is such that you have to choose¹¹³ how to live from among options that rule one another out' (p. 1), and hence one must convert, take the leap of faith (pp. 257–8¹¹⁴) to find the life that is true (the 'One True Life' of the book's title). Not only can one ultimately not compare (or only in a limited way that may not work), but one cannot be 'cosmopolitan', embracing a range of 'traditions'. One simply has to choose, and scholarship needs to put that choice emphatically before its readers' faces; scholarship that 'avoids' this conviction (or, this fact) wilfully misrepresents ancient Christian and Stoic voices that insist one has to choose (p. 257).

Although there is not a direct sentence to this effect, Rowe's *Protrope* B (you must choose!) must entail a summons *to embrace Christianity*, not an evenhanded one to find one's truth by leaping into Stoicism (or Platonism, or Judaism,¹¹⁵ or Buddhism, Islam, existentialism, or atheism) because Rowe has gone to considerable pains in this book to deny his ability to comprehend fully or translate any tradition that is not his. He has not 'converted' to Stoicism.¹¹⁶ So, both logically and methodologically, as well as in terms of the genre he has adopted, Rowe could not issue a προτροπή towards the school of the Stoa, the school of Zeno, Cleanthes and Chrysippus (and Seneca, Epictetus and Marcus Aurelius), because he is not one of them. Even though Rowe presents himself as making an honest effort 'to reason Christianly about Roman Stoicism as my second first language while acknowledging that because I can do this only as an outsider, the way

---

προκοπή, 'moral progress', as well as Christian spiritual traditions), emphasized that life is a *progression* towards wisdom, God and truth. In other words, when, exactly, one is 'living' the Stoic or Christian life is in reality far less clear than Rowe's argument allows.

¹¹² I would posit that if one cannot, then Paul is impossible, as is Clement, the focus of the earlier part of this chapter. Biculturalism and bilingualism are major contestations of this point, one that also presumes its own categories of what constitutes a 'tradition' (for instance, is 'Roman Stoicism' one tradition, or two? Is 'Hellenistic Judaism'?). With Alasdair MacIntyre, Rowe allows for learning 'a second first language', but he goes even further beyond him to say that, 'Short of conversion, we are literally shut out of one by the life we live in another' (p. 204).

¹¹³ This is of course a classic statement of a λόγος προτρεπτικός, insisting that one must choose, and must choose now. Given that, the semi-disclaimer in n. 1 (p. 263) is a part of the rhetorical cast of the argument: 'Of course, *choose* might be too strong a word: we can slip or slide or fall into a certain type of life, or just drift along.' Rowe isn't denying the urgency of the choice by this statement, but, on the contrary, is insisting that one cannot, by *not* choosing, avoid it.

¹¹⁴ The *prooimion* and *epilogos* of the book, and hence crucially important statements (as argued above with Clement's *Protreptikos*).

¹¹⁵ The special case of 'Judaism' in Rowe's hands will be treated below.

¹¹⁶ Or, in the terms of *Protrope* A, to humanistic scholarship. It is not clear whether Rowe has 'converted' from humanism. He mentions in the Introduction that 'by training ... I am a scholar of the New Testament and its environs' (p. 1). Given the pervasiveness of the 'encyclopedic' form of knowing in New Testament studies that he critiques in this book, it is not quite clear whether he was once, by his training, one of the deceived, or, despite the persuasive force of that training he was always among the unconverted.

may in fact be closed'[117] (p. 204), he writes throughout as a self-declared Christian[118] living a Christian life within the Christian tradition in America today, and, consequently – for undefended reasons – a 'native speaker',[119] able to understand both ancient and modern[120] Christian lives.[121] Although he decries the 'encyclopedists'' naïve conception of 'a single, unitary rationality',[122] Rowe seems to operate with a single, unitary conception of 'Christianity', past and present. Unlike *Apotrope* A, however, the form of *Apotrope* B is not 'reject Stoicism!' (which is, for Rowe, no longer really a live modern option as it was in antiquity[123]) but, 'don't avoid your choice, but make the leap now to join the Christian tradition[124] so as to know and appreciate its unique truth (as only one can, as I have) from the inside once you get there.'[125]

The binary required by προτροπή/ἀποτροπή explains why Rowe is so ungenerous towards Abraham J. Malherbe and Troels Engberg-Pedersen in *Apotrope* A. One of the two 'rival' scholarly approaches must be true, and the other is false, 'distorted', obsolete and

---

[117] This statement comes after the reader has been given an account of Seneca, Epictetus and Marcus Aurelius (one that is in many ways indistinguishable from other 'encyclopedic' accounts) by him some hundred and fifty pages earlier.

[118] '[The narrative accounts of Stoicism and Christianity that follow in Chapter 8] are, rather, an account by a Christian who reads as a Christian' (p. 204). This statement (which I do not doubt is true), presumes a unified identity and reading practice of 'Christians' that belies the complexity and diversity of the tradition, both in antiquity and today.

[119] By this logic, Rowe presents himself as a native speaker for all its dialects across time. Rowe critiques Troels Engberg-Pedersen for positioning himself as an 'etic' rather than 'emic' thinker of Stoicism and ancient Christianity (pp. 190–1), but Rowe's own position as 'emic' to Christianity (whether modern or ancient) is merely presumed as true.

[120] Given the jabs at 'liberal Protestantism' sprinkled throughout the book (e.g. pp. 27 ['yet such confidence does not result from a kind of naïve liberalism that believes in the inherent resilience of humanity in the face of all that assails us'], 125 ['nor does the Father-language (of Luke-Acts) arise from a Harnack-like conception of the universal 'Fatherhood of God' – 'Our Father who art in heaven' refracted amorphously off the lens of liberal Protestantism'], 162 ['Not for Justin is today's liberal Protestant discomfort with fates unpleasant to contemplate']), one wonders if Rowe would grant that liberal Protestants, too, are living the 'one true life' of 'Christianity.' In our conference the term 'strong traditions' was used often in discussion by Rowe. The phrase is found at the beginning and end of the book (p. ix, 262), and seems to be identical with a tradition that admits of no compromise with another tradition (hence a kind of tautology). Beyond that, I wondered if there was not a conscious appeal to 'strong' traditions as a part of the self-identification of some Christians in the American context, as 'strong Christians', a formulation that sets itself over and against presumably 'weaker' ones (such as 'liberal Protestants'). Of course, this rhetorical language goes back to Paul, and 1 Cor. 8 and 10! In conversation Rowe said he was not making such an allusion, which I accept fully, but one wonders if readers of the book might not make such an association.

[121] Still nebulous is the formulation, 'one human life – its pattern or style of existence' (p. 245). What are the criteria of a 'Christian life'? How do we know one when we see one? Like truth, is it 'criterionless' (p. 257)?

[122] With MacIntyre, p. 176.

[123] But neither is the account given here particularly compelling or complete as a way of life. For example, the cosmological differences between Stoicism and a modern scientific worldview, that are of course striking, are pointed out by Rowe on p. 208; however, the pre-Enlightenment world views of Paul, Luke and Justin are not rendered as nakedly or problematically. Nor can Stoicism today meet the criterion of appropriating a tradition that Rowe adopts from MacIntyre, of having living communities and teachers, since these largely no longer exist. Hence, the double σύγκρισις is uneven, since the 'live option' that either 'Stoicism' or 'Christianity' represented in the first and second centuries (as studied in Part One) is not similarly 'alive' in the twenty-first century.

[124] The final pages of the book contain an account of 'Christian conversion' but not Stoic (p. 254).

[125] This is my own *prosopopoiia* of the viewpoint of the book as it reaches its close.

dead[126] (things Rowe does not say overtly about either Stoicism, or Judaism). This is characteristic invective fare, but it also requires that Rowe overlook the significant contributions those scholars have made, and denigrate their form of scholarship by classifying it as 'encyclopedism' à la MacIntyre in the most disparaging terms, as epistemically and methodologically invalid, bankrupt and embarrassingly out of fashion.

And yet, when we turn to Rowe's three chapters in Part One of the book on Seneca, Epictetus and Marcus Aurelius we find that his approach to the Stoic thinkers, presenting their thought on various topics,[127] in some sense mimics that of the *Stanford Encyclopedia of Philosophy* (*SEP*), a valuable tool upon which Rowe likely drew (or, if not, he should have!).[128] Rowe tells the reader that he has chosen his five themes for Seneca because they 'are recurrent emphases'[129] (what I shall call rationale #1) *and* because 'some of [them] provide illuminating points of continuity and/or juxtaposition with our other two Stoics and our chosen Christians' (p. 14) (rationale #2). There is no attempt to explain which category is which, or to integrate these two, quite different reasons for the choices, and the different modes of analytical comparison each implies. Hence, the possible circularity in method, and the potential for rationale #2 to distort the evidence's own emphases (rationale #1), are left unaddressed.

The five topics that Rowe treats by culling from throughout Seneca's *epistulae morales* and select other works are, in his order: 'death, Fortuna, God,[130] the passions, and philosophy'. The corresponding five sections of his chapter on Seneca are every bit as 'encyclopedic' or digestive of bits out of the letters (and a few other writings) as what Rowe critiques in others (Malherbe, Engberg-Pedersen). Rowe's list of five topics for understanding Seneca is by no means self-evident or uncontroversial, either in what he has included and left out, or in its order of treatment. For instance, Rowe announces that he will deal first with death, on the assumption that 'for Seneca it is

---

[126] See further adjectives of denigration (and documentation) on pages 20–1 of this essay.

[127] This has apparently necessitated the order of the book. For instance, in Part III he critiques Engberg-Pedersen for seeking to compare 'God' among Stoics and Paul, as follows: 'Scholarly analysis of "God", for example, in both Stoicism and Christianity presupposes the ability to know something that is logically distinct from the specific ways in which *God* receives its meaning in particular religious/philosophical traditions. Engberg-Pedersen speaks of a "God" that is identical neither with the Christian use of the word nor the Stoic. What then is it? It is the scholar's idea of God, or – to put it only slightly differently – the God of modern scholarly grammar, a way of speaking that implicitly claims to be more conceptually capacious, or determinative, than the specific ways of knowing endemic to the two traditions under analysis' (p. 190). Had he *followed* this with his treatment of Seneca, with its confident section 'God and Nature', the contradiction would have been more glaring. But what concept of 'God' did Rowe use to organize the material he pulled together in Part I, chapter one, on pages 27–30?

[128] Those who have written encyclopedia entries (given the explosion of reference works in academic publishing these days it seems hard to judge the genre dead!) know that in some ways these are the hardest to write, because they require many choices and an economy of expression. In saying this I realize that what Rowe means by 'encyclopedic' is not just the form (though the exemplum of the *Encyclopedia Britannica* is key for MacIntyre) but also the conceptualization of the intellectual enterprise it enshrines. But the two go together, and hence comparing with *SEP* is fully justified.

[129] On p. 224 when he revisits the point he refers more loosely to 'the drift of the individual texts'. But in all the cases there weren't individual texts, but text corpora, and 'drift' is hardly an argument for analytical choices and prioritizations.

[130] The heading within the book, however, calls this 'God and Nature' (p. 27).

death above all else that requires philosophical response'[131] (p. 14, rationale #1). But is that true? Or must it be true for Rowe, in order to compare Seneca and Paul//Stoics and Christians on their view of one true life (rationale #2)? And, in turn, is treating death before either 'the passions' or 'philosophy' the best way to understand Seneca's thought? The *SEP* entry 'Seneca' by Katja Vogt[132] provides an illuminating contrast to Rowe's own 'encyclopedic' approach:

1. Life and Works (same as with Rowe, 'Letters', pp. 13–14[133])
2. Seneca's Stoicism
   2.1 Philosophy as Practice (Rowe treats last, #5)
   2.2 The World of Philosophy: Seneca's Cosmopolitanism (Rowe does not mention this, for obvious reasons![134])
3. Philosophical Psychology
   3.1 The Stoic Account of the Soul
   3.2 The Will and the Self
   3.3 The Therapy of the Emotions (Rowe #4)[135]
4. Virtue[136]

---

[131] Rowe's treatment of his source materials does not establish this claim, on the one hand, and makes it harder on the reader to test it, on the other. He sprinkles passages from various letters into his own retelling, but never, for instance, tells the reader how many of the 124 letters preserved from Seneca to Lucilius are principally concerned with death, and how many others contain either major or incidental references to it. He provides no analysis of a single letter from Seneca's corpus, so how and where and why death is treated in these letters (e.g. how often in consolations, in other epistolary types or among what topics, like aging) is not addressed.

[132] https://plato.stanford.edu/entries/seneca/ Published online 17 October 2007, revised 24 December 2015 (accessed 12 June 2017). Vogt is Professor of Philosophy at Columbia University (in the City of New York).

[133] In the 'Life and Works' part of her *SEP* entry, unlike Rowe, Vogt notes at the outset that the treatment of death seems to vary from Seneca's tragedies to his other writings (letters and treatises). Rowe says he focuses on the letters, but in a footnote on his treatment of Seneca Rowe tells his readers that lots of work has gone on 'behind the scenes' (p. 267), such as looking at Seneca's other works (tragedies, satires), but that is not included in the book.

[134] Rowe expresses disdain for 'cosmopolitanism' throughout the book (pp. 175, 178, 179, 193, 194, 203, 258), and seeks to locate it strictly in modernism: 'The judgment behind this chapter is that it would be largely useless to begin yet another discussion of the Christians/Stoics under the same set of assumptions that have determined the majority of modern scholarship. Re-evaluating the same evidence on the same terms may lead to something that looks like more knowledge, but in fact it would be only one more small shift of the pieces in a predetermined shape of inquiry. That shape is "cosmopolitan modernity": the complex cluster of co-commitments that makes it possible to believe in the translucifying power of scholarly reason vis-à-vis any text from any tradition' (p. 175; cf. p. 262: 'the current canons of cosmopolitan liberal theory'). The Stoic concept of cosmopolitan understanding is deeply rooted in cosmology and anthropology, as Vogt writes in her entry on Seneca in *SEP*: 'In Stoic philosophy, cosmopolitanism includes a view of the nature of human beings: human beings are, by virtue of the kind of beings they are, connected.' This is precisely what Rowe is at pains to deny and reject in his book, in favour of a segmented set of human communities in 'lives' that are only (or virtually only) intelligible to themselves and like-minded others. How can such a contradiction simply be avoided tout court?

[135] It is under this heading that Vogt treats death [Rowe's #1], but not as the foremost concern of Seneca: 'Next to anger, Seneca pays most attention to fear and grief, emotions that tend to dominate human life due to human mortality.'

[136] Interestingly, the index to Rowe's book under 'virtue' puts its longest treatment at pp. 31–7, where Rowe's topic is 'Passions'.

4.1 Appropriate and Correct Action
4.2 Benefitting Others
4.3 The Good
5. Physics and Theology
5.1 The Practical Side of Natural Theology
5.2 The Natural Law (here is where Vogt treats death once again)
5.3 God (Rowe #3)[137]

In comparison with Vogt's presentation of Stoicism, Rowe moves in the opposite direction, i.e. from some topics towards 'philosophy', whereas hers moves from 'philosophy as practice' into that practice. One could argue, on Rowe's own criterion of seeking to render a tradition in some sense as a whole, that Vogt has done so better, both on the level of ideas and life, and their necessary integration.[138] Most striking is that Rowe's account of Seneca's Stoicism is oddly tilted against ethics (neither 'virtue' nor 'ethics' is among his five key elements[139]). This is, of course, in deliberate contrast to the group of scholars he targets in *Apotrope* A (Malherbe, Engberg-Pedersen). More can be said about the particulars of interpretation at each point,[140] but this comparison should serve to show what a selective and somewhat odd account Rowe has given of Seneca,[141] both in terms of method (applying some of the same encyclopedic approach he decries in others) and substance (not differentiating the two rationales, which shows the merging of *Protrope* A and B). Hence one must reckon with the possibility that his decision about non-comparability between Roman Stoicism and 'Christianity' reflects his own encyclopedic choices in analysing his chosen authors, and not necessarily the sources themselves.

This extends to the most conspicuous case where the two accounts (Rowe and *SEP*) do not overlap at all. Vogt in her account does not make an attempt to identify an underlying 'narrative' to Seneca's Stoic philosophy. Rowe provides a rationale for doing so on pp. 199–201 (mostly from MacIntyre), and then fashions his own comparative narratives on pp. 207–15 ('A Tradition of Life: The Stoic Story') and pp. 215–24 ('A Tradition of Life: The Christian Story'). One can offer significant critiques of the

---

[137] Rowe has separated fortune/fate from God (#2 and #3).
[138] It is helpful to test Vogt's organization of knowledge vis-à-vis Rowe's five 'issues' or 'areas' against his criterion as articulated on p. 193: 'To the degree that we compare parts without the density of the whole, we continue to project modern abstractions onto the ancient sources and obscure the fact that what is really juxtaposed in the question of "comparison" is a full way to live.'
[139] 'Ethics' or 'morality' is an abstraction that Rowe regards as an illegitimate modern imposition (see, e.g., p. 192: 'The fact that there is no word for morality as such in any ancient or medieval language should already caution us against the assumption that we know what ancient morality in general could be ... The reason is strikingly simple: it did not exist'). That ethics (τὰ ἠθικά) was a standard part of the philosophical curriculum (as even Rowe notes on p. 54!) does not seem to have mitigated this problematic claim.
[140] E.g. one might also contest Rowe's emphasis on 'Fortuna', which is not mentioned in the *SEP* entry on Seneca. Interestingly, Rowe has largely neglected natural law (the term is not found in the book, though a less precise use of the adjective 'natural' often is). This may render a peculiar account of what the Stoic means by *fortuna*.
[141] One might go on to analyse similarly the entries on Epictetus and Marcus Aurelius, but I shall not have the space to do that here.

particulars of Rowe's renderings of each narrative. A rather easy one is that what Rowe calls '*the* Christian story' (p. 218, etc., italics added) is one such telling, that has sanded away the kinds of 'paradoxes' or 'tensions' (the 'indicative' and 'imperative' of salvation, for instance, or the problem of evil and free will) that *are* accented in his telling of the Stoic narrative (such as the wise man paradox, on p. 213). But the even larger problem is that several different senses of 'narrative' are in view, in particular the relationship between a story *of* the tradition (like, say, Diogenes Laertius' *Vitae et sententiae philosophorum*) and a cosmic story (i.e. myth and its explications) that is promulgated *within* a tradition.[142] I would argue that one of the most striking features of early Christian literary culture is that it combines these two features (the sacred story and the story about the success of the sacred story as εὐαγγέλιον), as already is done by Paul in 1 Thess. 1.9–10; 1 Cor. 3.10–16, etc., and in Acts. In expecting Stoicism to have a narrative and, at that, one that combines what Paul somewhat surprisingly does, Rowe has skewed the comparison. And, in turn, the role of the myths for Stoics (and their famous allegorization of them) does not get much attention in Rowe's account (because that is not what he means by 'Stoic narrative' here).

By telling the Christian story Rowe is adopting its very own missionary strategy[143] (as with Clement in book 11 of his *Protreptikos*). In fashioning the 'Stoic narrative' Rowe has provided an ill-fitting, Christian-designer garment for Stoics (on the assumption that it must have some correlate to what 'ancient Christianity' had). Perhaps if Rowe had exegeted a text like Cleanthes' *Hymn to Zeus*[144] and tried to derive from it a narrative sub-structure one might have a comparative exercise worth considering alongside the Pauline εὐαγγέλιον (or at least this particular rendering of it).[145] But it is faulty to assume that the Stoic story is trying to answer the same problem as Paul, or Luke (or Augustine, or others), even as to cast Stoicism in terms of a soteriological narrative is, at the least, a disputable rendering of the tradition. Clearly all this comes under Rowe's rationale #2 and not rationale #1, which has disappeared as a meaningful criterion. The substantive point needs to be addressed: does narrative really function the same in these Roman Stoics as it does in the Paulinist tradition? And, related to this, is it the case that Stoicism presented itself as the one true life in the same way that Christianity did?[146] If not, has this approach not been every bit as much an imposition on the materials of some categorical universal as Rowe claims the encyclopedists do?

---

[142] See the fuller argument in Mitchell, *Paul and the Emergence of Christian Textuality*. It is not clear that this can or should be generalized onto all 'traditions'.

[143] On p. 201 Rowe states, 'not one of the six figures treated in this book tells us directly what the Stoic and/or Christian narrative is', but, of course, Paul (1 Cor. 15.3f., etc.) and Luke sure do it a lot! This is also why he refers to it as 'kerygmatic' on pp. 257 and 261.

[144] On which see Johan Carl Thom, *Cleanthes* Hymn to Zeus: *Text, Translation and Commentary* (STAC 33; Tübingen: Mohr Siebeck, 2006).

[145] It is surprising that Rowe's account of Stoicism does not give attention to Stoic allegorizing and etymologizing of the Greek myths.

[146] In our conference I asked Rowe if he could point to any Stoic texts that say anything like John 14.6 ('I am the way, the truth and the life; no one comes to the father except through me') to insist that their 'way' is the only way to truth, incompatible and incommensurable with any others. In asking this I made reference, for instance, to the obvious problem of Seneca's continual citation of tags from Epicurus in his letters to Lucilius, that seem to call into question whether Seneca claimed Stoicism

Within the argument about non-comparability that Rowe sets up are also sprinkled some overtly protreptic arguments for the historical superiority of Christianity, such as:

> As influential as the Stoics treated in this book have been, even their cumulative weight is virtually insignificant compared with St. Paul's ... Down through the centuries from his time to ours no less than theology, philosophy, politics, law, literature, architecture, and visual and material art – in short, the whole field of human life we call culture – experienced the gravitas of Paul (p. 85).

Surely readers are meant to infer (for *Protrope B*) that when one makes the single choice that one must, one should choose a prominent rather than an insignificant, a living rather than a dead, tradition for one's one true life. As in some arguments in

---

was exclusive, or exclusive in the same way as Rowe's rendering of the early Christian sources. Rowe pointed instead (as he does in the book) to the authority of A. A. Long, in reference to a quotation from Long's 'Stoicism in the Philosophical Tradition: Spinoza, Lipsius, Butler', in Brad Inwood (ed.), *The Cambridge Companion to the Stoics* (Cambridge: Cambridge University Press, 2006), 365–92, to the effect that 'in the eyes of its greatest exegete Chrysippus, it was an all-or-nothing system' (p. 367), and 'the idea, as stated by Cicero on the school's behalf, that Stoic philosophy is coherent through and through – a system such that to remove one letter would be to destroy the whole account ... No modern philosopher, as far as I know, has ever taken this Stoic claim to complete coherence seriously, but I believe it is the key to the original system and to much of its appeal' (p. 368) (as cited in Rowe p. 310, n. 16). In addition to the problem of not being able to ground his point in the primary sources, this key quotation from Long (an expert modern interpreter of Stoicism) is in some ways taken out of context to support Rowe's own insistence upon incompatibility, incommensurability and untranslatability that is in fundamental ways at variance with Long's own approach. First, Long makes clear that the 'all or nothing' is a reference to the 'original' Stoic system as expounded by Chrysippus (3rd century BCE), not to Roman Stoicism of the first and second centuries CE (the object of Rowe's own enquiry because contemporary with early 'Christianity'). Furthermore, Long's own point in this essay, which focuses on the reception of ancient Stoic thought in the early modern period, is about why Stoic reception was hindered in modernity. The third of three reasons Long gives for this, is that, because at least in some forms, it claimed to be 'coherent through and through', 'no fully fledged representative of the ancient Stoa has emerged in Neo-Stoicism' (p. 367). One would not know from its rendering for Rowe's project that the second of the reasons Long gives for why 'Stoicism as systematic philosophy has hardly been refashioned at any time' (p. 366) is that 'Stoicism was easily conflated or assimilated, on casual acquaintance, to ideas associated with the much more familiar names of Platonism and Aristotelianism. The conflation is not, of course, wholly mistaken. Outside metaphysics and technical logic, the three philosophies do have much in common' (p. 367). Long goes on to name figures such as Antiochus (the Academic), Philo, Plotinus and Clement as examples of how Stoicism was conflated with other philosophical schools and systems. And even more detrimental to Rowe's point is that Long does not take the claim for systematization of the 'original' Stoic thought as a methodological restriction for his own research; indeed, he goes on to provide precisely what Rowe's book denies one can: subtle and thoughtful analyses of Spinoza, Lipsius and Butler that exemplify comparativism at its best, sensitive to similarity and to difference, and to part and not just whole (hence, Spinoza and the Stoics share 'a broadly similar conception of reality' [p. 374], but also they are 'poles apart' in regard to 'teleology and divine providence' [p. 377]). Therefore, rather than substantiating a principle of incommensurability, Long's essay exemplifies both its possibility and fruitfulness. On Stoicism and Christianity in particular, Long is fully attentive to the complexities of their confluence: 'First, much that had been distinctively Stoic in origin was absorbed into the complex amalgam of Judaic and Greek teaching that became Christian theology and ethics. So Stoicism is a part, but a largely unacknowledged part, of the Christian tradition. Second, the assimilation of Christian and Stoic ethics tended to blur the profound differences that really exist between the two belief systems, to the detriment of the Stoics' originality' (p. 367). Long simply does not support Rowe's more extreme position of incomparability and incompatibility.

Clement's *Protreptikos*, here the Stoics stand in (*pars pro toto*) for all of ancient philosophy. And 'Christianity' is clearly the superior choice for 'the one true life'.

Rowe is a bit more ambiguous when it comes to the other competitor, 'Judaism'. In a footnote to the chapter on Justin, we find a paean to Daniel Boyarin (and his famous claim that Justin Martyr 'invented Judaism'). Here Rowe says, 'Boyarin – probably better than any other current scholar – helps us to remember that the forms of life we describe as "Christianity" and "Judaism" were in antiquity far more intertwined and inseparable than we (scholars) are accustomed to thinking and than they later became' (p. 293 n. 51). The point is far too important to be hidden in a note, and its impact on the argument of the present book potentially enormous, even devastating, since it undermines – rightly, in my view – the presupposition of fixed, separable, mutually exclusive and mutually unintelligible traditions that is the basis for the comparison between 'Stoicism' and 'Christianity'. If, on the same logic, Justin's 'Christian philosophy' were allowed also to blur the lines between 'Christianity' and 'Stoicism' (or 'Platonism'), the entire binary argument, together with its claims about being only able to inhabit one tradition at a time, collapses (as, I think, it should). Within his analysis of Justin's *Dialogue with Trypho*, Rowe allows a form of comparison between 'Judaism' and 'Christianity'[147] that includes both agreement and disagreement, which he terms and spells in the hyphenated fashion 'dis-agreement'.[148] But why could one not understand Justin's *Apologies* (as well as significant parts of the *Dialogue* itself) as also exemplifying 'dis-agreement' between Hellenistic philosophy and 'Christianity'?[149] Indeed, doesn't all comparison (in religion, in other matters as well) involve such 'dis-agreement'[150] (hence this is hardly a special case)? It is only in Rowe's conception of them,[151] and this powerful protreptic altar call, that these 'traditions' were complete and utter 'rivals', completely unintelligible to one another; but it was not universally so in antiquity, in

---

[147] On which see, most recently, Matthijs den Dulk, *Between Jews and Heretics: Refiguring Justin Martyr's* Dialogue with Trypho (Routledge Studies in the Early Christian World; London: Routledge, 2018).

[148] On the neologism 'dis-agreement', applied in the case of 'Judaism' and 'Christianity' in the book (but only to 'Stoicism' and 'Christianity' in a heading title on p. 235, which allows of a single point of 'dis-agreement' – the claim to alone represent the true life) see p. 166: 'Still, it is hard to miss what is the most distinctive feature of Justin's relation to Judaism, that of a complexly interwoven and profound dis-agreement. Characterizing Justin's relationship to Judaism as dis-agreement may well be orthographically awkward, but it is conceptually necessary for the simple reason that the hyphen gets to the truth of the matter: the simultaneity of agreement and disagreement occurs at the deeper level of things and cannot be dissolved (or, for that matter, resolved in ordinary time).' Twice later Rowe will use '(dis)agreement' (pp. 192, 260, perhaps to indicate the same, or the ambiguity). Quite frequently in the book Rowe appeals to what is 'deeper' or 'more complex' to handle exceptions or problems in his argument.

[149] That is not to presume that comparison between 'Judaism(s)' and forms of Christ-believing thought, ritual, community form, expression would or must be essentially the same when it comes to Stoic or other Hellenistic philosophy. Comparison reveals both similarity and difference, and may be carried out with different categories (as emphasized in my twelve propositions earlier).

[150] As I have stipulated as proposition #9 on comparison.

[151] To frame an analogy, for Rowe the pool (whether the ancient Mediterranean world, New Testament scholarship, or 'life') has clearly demarcated lanes within which swimmers move; one may perhaps (though how is unclear) move from lane three to lane six (i.e. 'convert'), but one must be in a lane. The chief point is that it is all swim meet all the time, rivals racing each other to the finish; there is no such thing as 'open swim' (or even competitive water polo!).

actual persons, as we see so well with Clement,[152] the Christian philosopher. And yet, even still, it is significant that the rhetoric of rivalry has a limit, for Rowe, when it comes to 'Judaism'.

Later in the book Rowe refers to 'Judaism' (now without quotation marks) in contradistinction to Stoicism, not – at least overtly – as a 'rival tradition', but a tradition whose contestation with Christianity 'makes sense' in a way the Stoic one does not. But he hedges the point by an appeal to eschatology: 'Whether Christianity is in fact the correct extension or completion of the Jewish tradition is obviously an argument that will not be settled until the end of human life' (p. 255[153]). Rowe does not apply here the binary logic of the λόγος προτρεπτικός and complete the argument in the expected mode of his adopted genre (and tenor of the book and its conclusion): while alive, you need to 'wager' and 'make a choice' as to whether the 'Jewish' or 'Christian' tradition is the one true life.[154] This would be especially true on Rowe's own terms (as well as on Pauline ones), emphasizing lived commitments and praxis, that one must choose whether ἐθνικῶς or Ἰουδαϊκῶς ζῆν (Gal. 2.14).[155] This inconsistency in application of the (otherwise intractable) binary between rival versions of a true life in a book wanting to 'fly in the face' of most received wisdom is striking (and in my view better than the alternative, surely!). It echoes also with his reading of the end of Justin's *Dialogue* with Trypho, as not a rivalry but a positive dialogue: 'the parting at the conclusion of the Dialogue could hardly be friendlier' (p. 169). Rowe recognizes that in the *Dialogue* is some 'strong language' against Jews (he lists, but does not quote, 38.1;[156] 48.2;[157] 93.4[158]) and then suddenly, and tellingly, he leaps into the present: 'Modern readers, for reasons

---

[152] See how Clement, though he can treat all philosophers as similar in some respects, can also parlay differences among philosophers in regard to the status of matter, for instance in *Protr.* 5.66.3 [Stählin 50, 24–7], quoted p. 102.

[153] Cf. earlier in the Justin chapter: 'Truth claims of this sort are just more complex, Justin might have said to his modern readers. They cannot be resolved by swinging an ideological bully stick or, in fact, by any criteria external to the traditions between which the truth about God is contested. Unless one converts to the other's way of life, dis-agreement between Justin and Trypho will continue until the coming/return of the Messiah' (p. 170). If these are discrete traditions, and only one of them can be true, and one can only live inside one of them, or convert to the other, why (on the logic of Rowe's argument) is this too, not a 'rivalry of traditions'?

[154] My purpose in raising this issue is emphatically not to force Rowe to apply his binary logic further, but instead to rethink it. But I focus on it here to ask whether he can allow for an exception to the inescapable ultimatum the book sets forth.

[155] Of course, what exactly that means and where the differentiation markers are (dietary halachah, Shabbat observance, circumcision, etc.) was up for much contestation from the 50s (when Paul wrote Galatians) forward.

[156] I think this should be 38.2.

[157] [οἱ ἀπὸ τοῦ γένους ὑμῶν], οἵτινες τὰ τοῦ θεοῦ οὔτε νοῆσαι οὔτε ποιῆσαί ποτε βεβούλησθε, 'those from your race who have never wanted either to understand or to act upon God's teachings' (text Edgar Johnson Goodspeed, *Die ältesten Apologeten* [Göttingen: Vandenhoeck & Ruprecht, 1914]; my trans.).

[158] ὑμεῖς δὲ οὔτε πρὸς θεὸν οὔτε πρὸς τοὺς προφήτας οὔτε πρὸς ἑαυτοὺς φιλίαν ἢ ἀγάπην ἔχοντες οὐδέποτε ἐδείχθητε, ἀλλ', ὡς δείκνυται, καὶ εἰδωλολάτραι πάντοτε καὶ φονεῖς τῶν δικαίων εὑρίσκεσθε, ὡς καὶ μέχρις αὐτοῦ τοῦ Χριστοῦ τὰς χεῖρας ἐπιβαλεῖν ὑμᾶς καὶ μέχρι νῦν ἐπιμένειν τῇ κακίᾳ ὑμῶν, 'But you have never been shown to have friendship or love, neither for God, nor for the prophets, nor for yourselves, but, as is clearly shown, you are found to have always been idolators and murderers of the just, even to the point of your laying hands on the Messiah, and even now remaining in your wickedness' (text Goodspeed; my trans.).

both sound and sentimental, bristle at the strong language such difference evokes ... But in the ancient world vigorous, even harsh, polemic was the norm' (p. 169). At that point Rowe has added a footnote with a telling then-and-now comparison:

> In our time, it is difficult to be polemical about others' beliefs. We can be horrid in political races, attack a person's character, family, personal appearance, decisions made as an adolescent and everything else. But we can't say 'your religious beliefs are wrong'[159] without incurring the wrath of the 'offended'. But the ancient world was nothing like this, and vigorous polemic was the norm. It was given, and it was taken – and it was expected (p. 293, n. 55).

Here in this nostalgic note[160] there seems to be the explanation for the intertwining of *Protrope* A and B in *One True Life*, and how the polemic and invective against Abraham J. Malherbe and Troels Engberg-Pedersen (and all humanists, presumably) in *Protrope* A is meant to serve the goals of *Protrope* B (Christianity alone against all its rivals). Since in the modern world religious polemic[161] is less tolerated, it must be carried out by indirection, even as one is still called to proclaim the singular truth of 'Christianity' against its rivals, wherever they are to be found.

One True Life should not be taken as a contribution to method in comparison in the study of New Testament and ancient Christianity, but as a rhetorical *tour de force* meant to bring the enterprise to a close with the sweeping and tautologically formulated claim that Christianity and Stoicism are simply incomparable and incommensurable. This raises a final point for consideration: to whom, then, is this λόγος προτρεπτικός addressed? Given the rhetorical cast of Rowe's argument, one can hardly imagine that he expects Malherbe, his students, Engberg-Pedersen, Betz,[162] or others, to be persuaded by this form of argument (*Protrope* A) to repent and change their ways and no longer engage in comparative study of religion or philosophy that doesn't insist on rivalry and incommensurability. This is because Rowe chose a rhetorical form that treats them as the foil in such dismissive terms (i.e. more like Clement treats the mysteries than he does Plato or Aristotle) that scholars who inhabit or even just respect this line of scholarship will be all the less likely to accept it at face value. It did not have to be so, of course. Rowe could have written a book that might have called for and instantiated a

---

[159] I wonder if Rowe would still hold to this statement in the current, Trump presidency in the United States (Rowe's book was published before the election in November 2016), with a marked and frightening increase in both popular and political anti-Islamic and anti-Semitic rhetoric and actions (as documented, e.g., by the Southern Poverty Law Center). From my conversations with him, I imagine he is as deeply troubled by this as am I. How would that affect the argument made here?

[160] In contrast to his nostalgia for religious 'polemic', Rowe is withering about inter-religious dialogue: 'Justin had not tasted the modern sap that frequently accompanies lowest-common-denominator attempts to deal with religious difference' (p. 170, a cast-away sentence for which no examples of 'sap' are given).

[161] One yearns for some acknowledgement here that 'polemic' is not the only way for different traditions to engage one another, but, on the terms of Rowe's argument, 'dialogue' is, in the end, impossible (see also previous note).

[162] Surprisingly, Hans Dieter Betz is never mentioned in the book, nor, unless I missed it, the Corpus Hellenisticum Novi Testamenti project (extending back to W. C. van Unnik).

treatment of ancient Stoicism and ancient Christianity along the lines of comparative philosophy of religions that takes seriously the truth claims of the arguments and sets them in conversation with select modern philosophical voices.[163] But those projects are deeply instantiated in the practices and values of humanistic enquiry, predicated on the assumption that human beings can – in some sense and with proper humility – understand one another. But Rowe's goal is *protrope* and *apotrope*; reproach, not rapprochement. And *Protrope/Apotrope* A will hardly lead to 'conversions' by the 'encyclopedists'.

It seems clear that Rowe's rhetoric (both *Protrope* A *and* B) will be most effective on those who are already inside (or at least presume that they are), who will feel that as committed Christians they have been intellectually, theologically and spiritually championed by an erudite, philosophically sophisticated contemporary who slays both the dragons of nitpicking philological obscurantism[164] and of syrupy multicultural dialogue painting over difference, and diluting or compromising Christian truth claims. Rowe wishes to call his readers to, or, rather more likely in many cases, reaffirm them in, a conversion to the one true life to be found in 'Christianity'. One of the logical problems of the book is whether or how 'conversion' is even possible,[165] given that one can only live one life (at a time) and that 'rivals' share almost nothing in regard to things

---

[163] As is done, for instance, in the comparative work by Daniel A. Arnold, *Buddhists, Brahmins, and Belief: Epistemology in South Asian Philosophy of Religion* (Columbia University Press, 2005) and *Brains, Buddhas, and Believing: The Problem of Intentionality in Classical Buddhist and Cognitive-Scientific Philosophy of Mind* (Columbia University Press, 2012).

[164] The conference version of this chapter documented Rowe's generally dismissive attitude towards philological precision and 'minutiae' (see, e.g., pp. 7–9), as strikingly accompanied by his own almost complete reliance on the text and the translations of the Stoic authors in the Loeb Classical Library volumes by Gummere on Seneca and Haines on Marcus Aurelius (both of which are over 100 years old, and for which texts newer critical editions of the Latin or Greek have appeared in the meantime). He justifies his method in footnotes at the back of the book, on the grounds that 'the Loeb editions are as close to the base as it gets' (p. 265), and, later, he stipulates: 'In all cases I adjust as I see fit based on both interpretive and philological considerations. Because it would be extraordinarily tedious and distracting, I do not always provide justification for my translations' (p. 266, but note that he has just allowed on the previous page that they are not in fact 'his translations'). This problem with Rowe's method and writing procedure needs to be pointed out here, not only because of the role of denigration of philology in his characterization of his scholarly opponents, but because the issue lies at the heart of the enterprise – comparison depends upon precision, including philological accuracy, and justification for choices made at every turn (this would be true of any study of ancient religion, but it all the more vital when a central claim of the book is that it is impossible to 'translate' from one tradition to another!). While I fully accept Rowe at his word that he has done further background work that is not shown here (though as far as I can tell the actual 'translations' are rarely much different from the LCL), the reader of the book is given a false and dangerous assurance that there is some easy distinction between philology and interpretation that can simply be leaped over. See the following: 'I am well aware, of course, of the bazillions of linguistic, textual, and critical problems for almost every passage of each text of our six authors. Still, for projects of *interpretation* at some point we have to get on with trying to say what they were trying to say' (pp. 7–8, italics original). But how do we know what they were trying to say without close philological analysis?

[165] Rowe stipulates that 'an inexpungible existential wager – and possibility of conversion – is at the heart of all rivalry between traditions' (p. 259). The statement seems to entail some self-contradiction, for if the wager is 'inexpungible' it cannot be changed (hence it is also, 'incontrovertible'). But this is part of the rhetoric of protreptic: to call the hearer to change to a new position (that will then be 'inexpungible', but, of course, if it could be changed once, why not again?). And is all conversion so effective that it wipes away the prior 'life' entirely?

that most matter. How could one construct an argument that might appeal to another when one has no common language, concepts, ideas, values or commitments? Rowe does not explain, except to say that it must be a 'leap of faith', a leap that cannot even be a 'reasoned conversion' (so MacIntyre, quoted and rejected on p. 257), but just a blind leap for which there is only 'retrospective reason' (p. 254) after the fact about how one's former life (Stoicism, Judaism) was either enslavement or incompleteness, respectively. What exactly entering a 'new way of life' must include in order to arrive 'inside' it and know it as true is not stated; the altar call remains very general, which leads one to assume that those to whom it is primarily addressed already know to what Rowe is referring. A λόγος προτρεπτικός calling the question on *Protrope* B as a rhetorical bid to insiders to hold fast and have confidence in their choice for Christian truth that both matches and utterly eclipses all rivals was, of course, what may have been the intention and effect of a work like Clement of Alexandria's προτρεπτικὸς πρὸς Ἕλληνας, as well, some 1800 years ago, even as both share the performative paradox of comparing what they will inevitably declare to be incomparable.

8

A Response to Friend-Critics

C. Kavin Rowe

Wittgenstein once remarked, 'An honest religious thinker is like a tightrope walker. He almost looks as though he were walking on nothing but air. His support is the slenderest imaginable. And yet it really is possible to walk on it.'[1] I wrote *One True Life* as an attempt to display what an honest religious thinker looks like. To some, it may look like I have walked on air. But it is not so. The support may be slender, indeed *almost* imperceptible, but it is nevertheless there, real, can be seen, touched, and even walked on.

I take 'honest religious thinker' to be a way of naming what scholarship is that works with the questions that question us. To encounter ancient Christianity and Stoic philosophy is, if nothing else, to encounter questions that question us. Read the old texts well, and we will find ourselves exposed. We may, of course, then choose to hide. Or we may not. *One True Life* argues by structure and discourse that intellectual and existential judgements are not two decisions, but one. It is an attempt not to hide, especially not behind the veil of learning.

Some direct replies

I am honoured by the attention given to *One True Life* both at the conference and in these essays.[2] Although I may have put some of the cookies a little high on the shelf, I did not write the book so that it would 'automatically separate those who understand it from those who do not'.[3] Nevertheless, apart from a passing reference in Jonathan Linebaugh's treatment of Hamann's hermeneutics, *One True Life* has been misunderstood and misrepresented in some materially significant ways.

Because I obviously cannot go point by point for each of the essays that engage *One True Life*, I will respond by focusing on six substantive issues and leave lesser matters

---

[1] Ludwig Wittgenstein, *Culture and Value* (London: Wiley-Blackwell, 1995), 7.
[2] It is important for readers of the essays to know that even though the arguments can be sharp (especially between Mitchell and me), there is plenty of room for conversation, discussion, and even genuine friendship and warmth. But the issues are complicated, serious, and evoke all kinds of reactions from all of us. That is, I think, to be expected.
[3] Wittgenstein, *Culture and Value*. Besides, as he says shortly thereafter, 'telling someone something he does not understand is pointless, even if you add that he will not be able to understand it' (ibid.).

for another occasion.[4] The following issues are indispensable for an intelligent reading of the book, whether one agrees with its central claims or not.

Do we compare things?

Several of the essayists insist that we humans really do compare things. And the essayists insist and/or imply further that this truth somehow runs against the argument of *One True Life*, in which I am alleged to have severely problematized or rejected comparison of all kinds. To be blunt: I find this reading of the book bizarre. Of course human beings compare things and cannot not compare/contrast. But *One True Life* is about lived religious/philosophical traditions. I do not think we have trouble comparing apples to apples, or even to oranges or mangoes, or fruit to vegetables or to trees or trains – and countless other things – but I do think traditions of life cannot be conceptualized in the way that modern comparative enquiry requires us to assume that they can be. Whether they can or not is the only issue worth talking about.

I would be foolish indeed if what I thought was 'we cannot compare' and then actually forgot that and wrote Parts I and II of the book, placed them next to each other on purpose, and went on to argue against myself in Part III. What I think is this: comparison is of course unavoidable, but comparison of traditions of life under the philosophical conditions I describe is best conceived as juxtaposition. Juxtaposition turns out to be the way difference/similarity is construed; language the way we think through the construal; narrative the way we know how language games work; existential truth the way narratives are lived and life made sense of; incommensurability the name for the lack of a common measurement that would allow rational evaluation of difference over life; and Kierkegaard the best thought I know of that corresponds to the condition we humans find ourselves in, in which we cannot rationally adjudicate between different lived claims to existential truth.

I argue further that there is no intellectually more fundamental place outside of the traditions that can hold them at bay, set them up side by side, and evaluate them in

---

[4] For example, in n. 166 Mitchell misreads my sentences about the Loeb series translations and confuses the question of philology with that of philosophical 'translation' that I discuss later in *One True Life* (224–6). What I say about the Loeb series was, I thought, rather clear: for the sake of the reader's convenience, I cite the Loeb whenever possible, adjusting as I see fit. The fact that many citations of Seneca et al. correspond to the Loeb is thus entirely unsurprising since that is (a) what I intended, and (b) what consistent practice in line with such an intention would reveal. That is, 'as close to the base' means 'as close to what you'll regularly find in this book' not 'the Loeb series is *the* critical edition; I know about no others, and no others were consulted'. I actually wrote not only with various texts open but also, when applicable, while reading multiple 'translations' in English, German and French. So I very much believe in the importance of philology, and the conference version of her essay 'demonstrated' no such thing as she claims ('dismissive attitude' – yet another attempt to divine my psychological/emotional posture, something about which I say more later in this response). In fact, one of the major points of my book is that language and thought are inseparable. But I also believe – correctly, as it turns out – that many readers of *One True Life* are not as interested in the 'minutiae' of extensive philological analysis as they are in being able to go read through some of the texts that I treat. Since not all readers of my book can do philological analysis or read Greek or Latin, I preferred to aid them in reading the editions that are widely available. I did not imagine it would be controversial to say that it is possible to get too far down in the weeds in a book that is aiming to do something else.

comparative enquiry. There is a position that says that this larger place of knowing exists, and this epistemic possibility inescapably entails philosophical positions on the human being (what sort of self we are/have that can know in this way, the significance of historical conditioning for what we know and what we take ourselves to be as knowing subjects, the importance of time and death for the limits of knowledge, and so on). In both its original Enlightenment and updated forms, it is the encyclopedia. I deny that this is a true account of the way we can know or compare traditions of life. I maintain instead that summons and conflict, or invitation and conversation, or display and critique, are the way incommensurable religious/philosophical traditions interface with each other. The 'come now, we really do compare things' objection is a serious distraction from the main issue involving traditions of life. One can argue for a reinstantiation of the encyclopedic mode of knowing – in more contemporary dress, of course – or one can go another direction. But insisting that we compare things is akin to insisting on the wetness of water. Who would deny it?

Incommensurability and invitation

There is, next, the question of incommensurability and how it relates to the book as a whole. Followed by Novenson, Mitchell maintains that *One True Life* is a *protreptikos*. Like Clement (an honour, really), I use learning not to compare things as I should but to preach to the already-converted about the superiority of Christianity. My argument is less an argument about how traditions of life relate to one another than it is an altar call.

There are many replies to such an astounding reading, but I focus here on two in particular. First, to say that traditions are incommensurable is automatically and necessarily to say that you cannot argue for the superiority of one over another. Why? Because there is no shared standard of measurement by which such superiority could be shown to exist. That is what incommensurable means. The conceptual arrangement and entire argument of Mitchell's essay presuppose that this most basic point has been missed.[5]

The structure of my book, the repeated affirmations throughout, and the Kierkegaardian conclusion make clear that the two traditions of life stand face to face, that they both exist inseparably with grammars of invitation and commitment, of claim and conflict, that they both insist on living the *philosophia* to know what true knowledge is, and so on – *and that there is no way rationally to resolve the rivalry*.

I suppose Mitchell's misreading may result partly from my straightforward admission that I am a Christian. But, of course, that I admit this and that I take it to be indispensably significant for how I reason is part of the overarching claim about traditioned rationality in the first place. Mitchell misunderstands what is a philosophical claim about the possibility and subsequent shape of human reason vis-à-vis traditions

---

[5] It is also interesting to note that none of the essayists actually give an account of incommensurability as a feature of traditions. Perhaps they think such a thing does not exist, that it is simply a figment of the imagination. But, if so, they would need to give the narrative that allows the traditions' narratives to be subsumed.

and confuses the matter by (unintentionally, I assume) relocating this question within guesswork about a sort of quasi-personal piety as that which underlies the book's purported exhortative genre.[6] I take it to be constitutive of rationality that we reason from within the traditions that turn out to make rationality what it is. It is thus rather basic to the understanding of *One True Life* that arguing rationally in the absence of a shared standard will not – because it cannot – produce a defeat of a tradition since rationality itself will be traditioned. There is no rationality to which we can appeal that exists above or lies beyond what rationality is in the traditions; if we could appeal to it (either as a formal capacity or as a set of principles/beliefs or whatever), we would of necessity invoke a shared standard.[7]

Informing readers that I am a Christian is thus nothing more, but also nothing less, than a naming of the shape of rationality that I take to be possible. This is so both historically: the language we have been given that is the antecedent condition of our thought – and anthropologically: the only thinking self that exists is the self that is embedded in the traditions that make the thinking self what it becomes through time. Incommensurability is a way of saying that there is no self and no history that can take you back behind the human condition of your knowing to something purer, more pristine, more thought as *thought*. Your knowing life is the only place from which you can know. All this – and much of what it might entail – has also been missed.

Second, the language of these religious/philosophical traditions is both proclaiming and invitational, which is to say that the Stoics and the early Christians took themselves seriously enough as possessors of the truth that they fashioned their speech accordingly. The grammar of their texts displays not the existential indifference of much current academic discourse but an intensity of purpose; they have something to offer the world. Indeed, it is virtually inconceivable that these traditions could ever have gotten off the ground without this sense about their claims. I say explicitly that I am trying to write in something akin to Ricoeur's second-naïveté, that I am attempting to think with the sources and reproduce this sense rather than simply reporting on them.

---

[6] A key example is her reading of Wittgenstein as me (n. 107, 'seizing on a way of life believingly, lovingly, through thick and thin.'); she also thinks I'm 'nostalgic'. This turn to see into my mind or my spiritual disposition ('fundamentalist'; Engberg-Pedersen) or political leanings (possible 'conservative'; Martin) or psychological state ('anxious'; Novenson) is characteristic of the essays that miss large parts of the philosophically constructive moves of *One True Life*. Since I am sceptical of the ability to know the things about other people through their writings that the essayists claim to know about me, I do not know exactly why they turn to things they cannot know about me (and, as it turns out in fact, are incorrect). But it is guesswork, a little run at mystical telepathy to go with some arguments. The conceptual lines to follow are those that could be traced primarily between MacIntyre, Wittgenstein, Kierkegaard, and Gadamer. Tracing some of these lines would not necessarily result in agreement, of course, but it could aid in a better reading.

[7] Mitchell seems to think that because Stoicism is no longer alive in the way that Christianity still is I *ipso facto* present Christianity as superior. But I nowhere say anything like this. Moreover, *One True Life* is focused on the Christianity of Paul, Luke, and Justin, which is quite different from ours today (*contra* Engberg-Pedersen's assertion that I see no difference). Stoicism is a permanent possibility of sorts, runs deep in the modern world, and always lies close at hand. Will it re-form with teachers, schools, etc.? Who's to say? There is no reason – metaphysical, logical, historical – that it cannot (as if there were something written into the structure of the universe that prevented Stoics from existing). There are of course dedicated Stoics today (see, e.g., modernstoicism.com), but they are not really a school or a scheme in the sense that the ancients were.

Contrary to Mitchell's assertion, this style does not entail a denigration of academic reporting.[8] If I have re-displayed the grammatical nature of these traditions of life – their claim and conflict, their proclamation and invitation – I count that as a success. It is what an interpretation looks like that allows the questions of the sources to mingle, linger, and reside within our own questions – which, I still maintain, is historically closer to the animating moves of the texts of both the Roman Stoics and the early Christians.[9] To miss this point about the grammar of traditions of life and replace it with psychological gestures about my intentions in writing is once again to confuse a philosophic claim about the working-end of a tradition's language with what might have been going on in my mind or heart or wherever it is we come up with intentions (which, of course, we do not know, cannot know, and therefore cannot assess in another person).

Non-compossibilty and one life to live

Several of the essayists question whether we actually live only one life. Dale Martin, for example, notes that he is an amateur musician, philosopher, and so forth, and believes this means that he lives more than one life. Frankly, this is baffling. It is Dale Martin who is/does these things, and exactly to the degree that he can name them as his activities, he presupposes the unity across, in, and between them that is he himself.[10] These are things that Professor Martin does/is. 'Dale Martin' picks out the one who is/does these various things through time.

If we change the example to sickness and death, say, the anthropological point emerges more sharply. Who is it that gets sick? Who dies? Imagine this brief exchange: 'John Doe is sick. *Is he at home?* 'No, he is in the hospital.' *Will he make it?* 'Alas, likely not...'[then later] 'John died this afternoon.' The unity presupposed in the exchange is Mr Doe's life and death. Whose life can you live but your own? Whose death can you die but your own? As it applies to the existence of individual human beings, I find the notion of living only one life so basic that I cannot fathom Prof. Martin's form of

---

[8] Mitchell also suggests I denigrate regular scholarship. But this is untrue. I have often written the 'regular' scholarly way. The hermeneutical point is something else entirely. To my mind, there are many other puzzling features in her essay. For example, she takes my remarks about Paul's influence on Western tradition to be an argument about spiritual/religious superiority. But I took them to be simply a matter of the historical record. The remarks are descriptive, not jubilant exaltation, and, as far as I can see, historically incontestable.

[9] I don't think the way the grammar works is the same for everything in the world – choreography, baseball, swimming, say – but I do think this would be the case for religious/philosophical traditions of the sort that are under discussion to begin with. Claiming truth is ingredient to their identity as particular traditions. My understanding of hermeneutics also owes much to what George Steiner has called 'answerable understanding' or 'answerability' or 'responding responsibility' wherein we become 'answerable' to the texts we read. Reading well means we become 'answerers in action'. Too often academic work avoids exactly this critical, more fully human dimension of hermeneutics. The ancient Stoics and Christians were interested precisely in 'answerers in action'. See George Steiner, *Real Presences* (Chicago: Univ. Chicago Press, 1989).

[10] Both the *idem* and the *ipse* in Ricoeur's language (see his *Oneself as Another* (Chicago: University of Chicago Press, 1995)).

denial.¹¹ Kavin Rowe lives the life that only – and precisely only – Kavin Rowe can live. And when Kavin Rowe dies, it is only – and precisely only – Kavin Rowe who dies. Kavin Rowe names in shorthand the life and death that I am through time in all the various things I have done/do/will do/permanently cease doing.¹² It is this sort of human life, the only one that we can live along the trajectory from birth to death, that rival traditions attempt to claim and for which they compete.

What I can better understand, I think, is the question about the unity of life as it pertains not to individual identity in a stricter sense but to the ability to live the pattern of more than one tradition of life at a time. Engberg-Pedersen, for example, 'personally doubts very much' whether 'any human being *just* "lives" in accordance with a single worldview'.¹³ And Mitchell speaks of Paul's 'bi-cultural'.¹⁴ But the point in *One True Life* was not to deny that we all inhabit complex cultures, that we draw from this piece here and that piece there in our daily activities, and so on. It was rather to insist on non-compossibility as an essential way these particular traditions of life exist and what they claim for those who would join them. Can one, for example, worship the God of Israel and not worship the God of Israel, or take Jesus of Nazareth to be God's Messiah and take him to be not the Messiah but a pretentious Galilean Jew, and cultivate love as the rightly ordered wellspring of virtue and endeavour to eliminate love in a self-risking way, and dozens of other things besides – all at the same time in the same pattern of one human life? I think not.¹⁵

One of the outstanding strengths of Martha Nussbaum's *Therapy of Desire* is her depiction of Nikidion's philosophical journey as change through existential formation and re-formation: Niki does not simply learn to think differently when she changes philosophical schools; her very self is actually constituted and reconstituted by the new life she learns she must begin to live as she moves from school to school.¹⁶ Her life-

---

¹¹ There is a sophisticated form of denial: genealogists who would deny inherent identity between the masks that we choose to wear for whatever reasons we choose to wear them. The mask is the thing itself, as it were, and there is nothing – no human, no continuous life – behind it. But, again, just to the extent that the genealogist employs language that requires a subject who *is* (not who *wears*) the mask, he presupposes a person that subsists through time, and he therefore undermines the attempt to get free of a unified life.

¹² The connection to narrative here is indissoluble. Even to begin to answer the question, 'who is [Kavin Rowe]?' one will necessarily begin to tell a story or, perhaps if the situation already provides some initial clarity, to point to pieces of a human identity (e.g. 'the first violinist') that derive their specific intelligibility from the narrative that is the background answer to the question 'who?'

¹³ P. 46, emphasis original.

¹⁴ P. 95.

¹⁵ Even successive stages display the existentially exclusive shifts that must take place, say, for example, from the lived affirmation that Jesus is the Lord, to the realization that Pliny's coercive pressure is too much, to a subsequent denial and sacrifice and return to pagan life (Jesus is not the Messiah after all).

¹⁶ Martha Nussbaum, *Therapy of Desire* (Princeton: Princeton University Press, 1996). Bernard Williams notices this in his review of Nussbaum, though Williams thinks it is a detriment to Nussbaum's style. By contrast, I think it is an advantage and that Williams missed a chance to see how the 'not much remains constant' with Nikidion relates to Nussbaum's depiction of the re-formation of the self. Mitchell also notes that I do not mention Nussbaum's work on toleration, etc. and – perhaps – suggests that I do not know of it or for some inexplicable reason choose not refer to it. I do know it, but the reason I do not mention it is simple: I do not find it particularly helpful. There are several reasons for this, but the principal one to name is that despite the elegance and passion of her work, Nussbaum appears to me to presuppose a philosophically liberal notion of the human person, and I take that anthropology to be self-defeating in attempts to argue for toleration/tolerance. Though I could write only several pages about toleration/tolerance, I worked extensively through this question in both the Graeco-Roman world and the modern period for my book *World Upside Down: Reading Acts in the Graeco-Roman Age* (New York: Oxford University Press, 2009).

shape is the way she acquires the knowledge she must gain. And Pierre Hadot, though often known only for his description of 'spiritual exercises', also compellingly depicted philosophical life as one of attraction and lived response.[17] Earliest Christianity is unintelligible apart from the sense that it, too, 'called' people of all stripes to be transformed in the patterns of their lives. Even to acknowledge these most basic matters is *already* to have granted the point that traditions of life were schemes into which adherents were inducted and taught to live. To argue that the Christian scheme and the Stoic scheme were compatible in one human life is then to erase the anthropological limitations of induction, transformation, and time, and, implicitly at least, to argue for a fantasy: an elastic view of the self undetermined by body, time, and death; indeed, one that finally abstracts the self from the life lived by the person whose self it is. These traditions involve the sort of existentially thick claims to truth that mean one has to choose a life that turns out to make truth what it comes to be for the self that also itself comes to be[18]; and this choice will, moreover, simultaneously involve choosing against – again, in an existentially thick sense – other forms of life that claim their own truth. One simply cannot live in the cluster of things that make for a Christianly patterned existence and the cluster of things that make for a Stoically patterned existence at one and the same time. Non-compossibility is thus finally less a theory about the exclusivity of traditions and human finitude than it is an acknowledgement of phenomenological fact.[19]

[17] Hadot's project can be seen most clearly in four books: a brief study of Plotinus called *Plotinus or The Simplicity of Vision* (Chicago: University of Chicago Press, 1994), a more detailed work on Marcus Aurelius named *The Inner Citadel* (Cambridge, MA: Harvard University Press, 1998), a collection of essays entitled *Philosophy as a Way of Life* (New York: Blackwell, 1995), and the programmatic history *What is Ancient Philosophy?* (Cambridge, MA: Harvard University Press, 2002). Taken together, these books display not only deep historical knowledge but also a systematic philosophical interpretation of ancient philosophy itself. This is not, of course, to say that Hadot treats every twist and turn of each ancient thinker or his school, but rather that Hadot's historical readings aim at something much more difficult and philosophically significant: he attempts to grasp the whole of what ancient philosophy actually was and, subsequently, to reintegrate ancient wisdom into modern intellectual life. (In *The Veil of Isis*, which is more about the history of the idea of 'nature' than about ancient philosophy, and in *The Present Alone*, which is a series of conversations and statements of his views, Hadot presents his own philosophy/ideas through the testimony of the ancients, but he does not offer the kind of interpretations present in the other books.) Mitchell suggests that I 'harden' Hadot and turn his insights about philosophy and life into a 'rigid epistemological prescription that the condition for all knowing, and any knowing worth achieving must come from 'living its way of life' (n. 113). Again, I say nothing of the kind. The book treats religious/philosophical traditions, not all kinds of knowing. I imagine that people from various traditions of life or who position themselves outside any tradition could agree on any number of things worth knowing (whether prednisone helps asthmatic flares, or when the French Revolution occurred given conventional dating schemes, or the significance of resilin in a flea's legs for its jumping ability, or when the Cubs last won the World Series ...) but would require a different, existentially engaged sort of posture vis-à-vis such questions as raised by the Christian and Stoic traditions: Was Jesus of Nazareth the Messiah of the Jews? Should one strive to extirpate passion? Is the cosmos eternal? Can death finally be overcome? and so on ... As Hadot himself put it, the problem that animates religious/philosophical traditions is 'not the problem of knowing this or that, but of *being* in this or that way' (*What is Ancient Philosophy?*, 29, emphasis original).
[18] See the discussion of understanding as 'a becoming' in my 'Making Friends' in this volume.
[19] I take it to be a phenomenological fact of both past and present that there are competing ways to live and that many of these ways force choices. There may well be no metaphysical necessity to this reality: it could, insofar as we know, have gone differently. One may have theories about why such a phenomenon is not *really* the way things *are*, that the choices amount to the absence of difference in God's eyes (e.g., John Hick's pluralism) or do not matter that much as long as we can get along in the public square. But who would deny that this is the way the world appears to us? In my view, the phenomenon is rooted in the finitude of the creature. We really do have to live just one life. The schemes are instances of the way this life is ordered towards its perceived end.

Words, stories, and more words

It is quite surprising that not one of the critics of *One True Life* really addresses the question of the interdependence of words, narrative, and translation in the philosophical sense in which I discuss it.[20] In fact, the essayists proceed almost as if this question does not exist or could be by-passed in the discussion of how we think comparatively.

But the truth is that we cannot think without words. The words that we think with are the thoughts we have.[21] Paying close attention to the way words work, therefore, is a *sine qua non* for thinking about what comparison entails. *One True Life* argues by way of repeated case-by-case demonstration that words work in particular ways in the language games in which they are played (i.e., the texts and narratives of the traditions in which they play their roles).[22] Let this point sink in: in order to counter these arguments, one would have to show that the words work differently from how I say they do, that in fact the same words (or those closely clustered with them) work the same way in different traditions, and that there is thus the same narrative that allows the words to work the same way. One cannot simply *assert* that incommensurability or untranslatability is not the way traditions relate to each other. One must show that the words work the same way for the instances – and eventually the totality – of the things one is trying to align. That is, one would have to display the complicated interconnection of words, lived traditions, and narrative, and all in a way that meant same-saying – and therefore the possibility of translation in the philosophical sense – was what had been discovered.

Once one understands the connection between words, language games/texts, narrative, and traditions, one will see that this 'word-study' section is the one place in *One True Life* where case-by-case counter-arguments would complicate or even

---

[20] On this point, see my essay 'Making Friends and Comparing Lives', Chapter 3 in this volume. Martin mentions *pneuma* but his discussion illustrates the *problem* I describe: they do not mean the same thing with the word. Martin also wonders why I do not employ Wittgenstein's notion of family resemblance. The reason is uncomplicated. Wittgenstein thought of family resemblance in relation to the meaning of words: he wondered why words that do not have the exact same meaning all the time – they do not have a core or an essence – can nevertheless be seen to have something like a similar meaning from context to context. They have a family resemblance. This is manifestly *not* the case with words such as *theos*, *cosmos*, etc. when looking at the Christian and Stoic use. Family resemblance works best within traditions (the theological grammar of the New Testament documents, e.g., has a family resemblance). Francis Watson's paper in this volume, e.g., may work with a notion of family resemblance inasmuch as Watson treats Christian texts that can be read profitably together. In short, family resemblance is an excellent way to think but it is precisely the sort of language that illustrates the real difference between the sort of comparison Watson engages in and what I am talking about with the language of rival traditions. The Gospel of Peter and the canonical Gospels may be part of the same family – at least it's debatable who belongs to this family, who's a brother or sister, who's an extended relative, or long lost cousin and so on – but Stoicism and Christianity are not part of the same family in any real sense. If we personalize the image a bit, Seneca and Paul are not brothers or first cousins or distant relatives from the same family; they are friends. Martin's discussion of *pneuma* is *not* family resemblance in Wittgenstein's sense.
[21] If you disagree with this, tell me the thoughts you have with the words you need to tell me the thoughts you have without words. You will be telling me your thoughts with words, i.e., the words that are your thoughts. Or: try telling me the thoughts you have without the words you need to tell me the thoughts you have without words. This, of course, you can't do. The words are your thoughts.
[22] See *One True Life*, 226–35, on *theos*, *cosmos*, *anthropos*, etc.

potentially defeat my sense of comparison. But no one took up the challenge. Not a single argument of this sort has been forthcoming. I can assume only that this is because the significance of the linguistic/narrative point was not grasped, or perhaps the language-game demonstration was completely persuasive (though if so, the significance of such persuasiveness was missed).[23] If I were to write against myself, I would start here.

A clarifying way to put the whole question of words/narrative and theological/philosophical knowledge is in relation to natural theology.[24] In the appendix to *One True Life*, I say that I reject natural theology. I would rather have said that I prefer to rename natural theology as 'the reader's knowledge of how the story really goes'. This way of putting it acknowledges the importance of narrative and plays on dramatic irony and the difference in knowledge between the characters in the story and the readers of the story. I do not, that is, deny that the words in pagan texts were and can be read to express Christian truth ('the father and maker of all'; 'we are his offspring'; 'God is near you'; and countless other phrases) – that is the reader hearing the words in light of how the larger story really runs. But I do deny that the authors of those pagan texts would have meant what Christians mean, and that they would agree with the Christian extraction and transformation of their lines (the meaning of the words in the context of the texts in which we originally find them is different from the meaning of the same words in the Christian texts). So arguments that run 'if they [authors/words] speak truly, they speak truly of the one God since there is no other of whom they could truly speak and be true' strike me as exactly correct; it is simply that the truth that the words speak is not according to character but according to reader. Casual understandings to the contrary, this is not the same thing as affirming 'insights' or granting the order of being/order of knowledge division as it has historically been used. 'Insights' are what the Christians read in the words. The order of being/knowledge distinction says that while the statements of a Seneca, e.g., are true according to being, Seneca himself does not know this. In my judgement, this distinction assumes something false, viz., that there is a univocal meaning of the words: i.e., that the words mean in Seneca's text what they mean to the order-of-being-reader. While I see that words can mean Christian things (used for true statements about the order of being in light of Christian theological knowledge), I think that there are two meanings of the words, and these meanings are not the same at all. There is the Stoic meaning and the

---

[23] Mitchell drastically misunderstands the final sentence of the book, and accuses me of arrogance, inexplicably suggesting that the Yale Press readers were ignored (they were not since they raised other matters than the ones that bother Mitchell). The point – once again, philosophical – is about the unity of words and life; it encapsulates, in fact, my criticism of MacIntyre in light of how I read Wittgenstein. One wishes that this type of philosophical scrutiny had been possible at several points. I did not expect all the right echoes to be heard, but somehow Mitchell seems to have heard many of the wrong ones. How exactly this happens is complicated: some of it may be my direct way of writing, some a lack of philosophical analysis, and some a genuinely perplexing misfire on both parts. We are working on it.

[24] I wince even as I write 'natural theology', for the term is itself equivocal, of course, as is its close cousin, natural law. Among others, see Russell Hittinger, *A Critique of the New Natural Law Theory* (Notre Dame: University of Notre Dame Press, 1987).

Christian meaning, and no amount of order of being/knowledge distinction can make the same words say the same thing.[25]

So, yes, of course there is extensive borrowing, use, quotation, and so forth.[26] There is a Philo, and a Clement, and dozens of others. But all the piling up of cross-references in the world will still show the same basic hermeneutical difference: the words mean different things in the different texts/traditions.[27] What makes the difference in meaning? The narrative that makes 'Christian' and 'Stoic' make sense as particular religious/philosophical traditions in the first place. Words, narratives, knowledges: these must be seriously tackled if there is to be advanced discussion on the question of rival traditions. But these matters, too, have, alas, been missed.

Traditions of life, rival traditions, and Judaism

Several of the essayists raise questions in one way or another about the interdependent matters of my understanding of tradition, my use of Alasdair MacIntyre, and my view

---

[25] There are or can be of course many more than 'two meanings'. I simply use two to make the difference apparent. Noticing this difference in word meaning problematizes the use of 'concepts' to describe what the Christian readers found in the pagan texts. What they found were words. When these words were resituated within Christian discourse, they expressed the concept needed for the discourse to work. That is, you can't know what the concepts are apart from the words that are used, and when you look at the words used in the pagan texts you see that they don't have the thought that you count as an insight since their words do not work the way the same words work in what you mean by 'insight'.

[26] Augustine's famous image is finding gold among the Egyptians (*De Doctrina Christiana*, 40ff.). The words are the gold.

[27] An example from the Stoic material is Seneca, who frequently recommends something from Epicurus for Lucilius to meditate on: Seneca clearly says, I think, that it is the comprehensiveness of the Stoic take on the world that allows him to borrow the maxims from others (e.g. Ep. 6; 8.7ff.; 9.19ff.; 33; 90; 95). The Stoic tradition assimilates to itself whatever it wants/needs/finds useful. It does not simply 'agree with' what it finds in other philosophical traditions. It 'makes use of' what it finds in ways that fit the purpose at hand. Mitchell notes the occurrence of other philosophical material in the Stoics but cannot get past a kind of 'citation-means-same-meaning-of-words-and-therefore-agreement' hermeneutic. It is as if merely finding the words of tradition A in a text from tradition B indicates conceptual overlap, agreement, and so on, when in fact it does no such thing at all. The accumulation of examples of cross-tradition citation is thus philosophically useless. It simply means that one has more of what one already knows exists. It is like getting more and more and more blood tests with the same reading. The question is what to make of them. And for this, one will have to make something of the interpretative register that makes the particular interpretation make the sense it makes. Here is, I suppose, as good a place as any to address briefly the questions raised in her comments on A. A. Long's essay (n. 146). First, I remember the question/answer at the time of the conference somewhat differently, and we did have a productive exchange about the texts and Long's essay afterward in which I attempted to say a good deal more than what is reported in her footnote. Second, what I say about Long is not that he is my source for what I think about all things Stoic – indeed, Pohlenz and Veyne and others have made similar points to the one I took Long to make – but that Long's comment about philosophical unity should apply to the Roman Stoics. I cannot read them as a dilution of Chrysippus, though there is a strain in the scholarly literature that sees them that way. I read Long's essay differently from Mitchell, but for the sake of the main point, let it be said: if Long thinks the Roman Stoics cannot be read as examples of the philosophical comprehensiveness of Stoicism, then I disagree with him. There are too many texts that speak against the dilution thesis on this point: to point only to Epictetus, see *Disc.*, 1:16.17; 2.12.3; 2.20; 4.1.131; 4.4.39, all of which speak of and/or presuppose Stoicism's philosophical comprehensiveness and its truth as the 'one way' to life (*mia hodos*). By attempting to recruit Long's essay to her side of the argument, Mitchell pays admirable attention to an important essay but misses the larger hermeneutical question altogether.

of early Christianity vis-à-vis Judaism. Four larger points are in order. First, my understanding of tradition is obviously and heavily MacIntyrean. But it is not MacIntyre *simpliciter* for reasons that are critical to understand. The 'of life' is my attempt both to extend and criticize MacIntyre's understanding of traditions specifically in light of the ancient insistence on the indispensability of living for what we make of how we think. Of course, MacIntyre is well known for his insistence on the inseparable connection between social practice and thought, but when it comes to his analysis of the epistemological conditions of incommensurable traditions and their rivalries, he retreats to his basic views about nature, the clear division between theology/philosophy, and so forth, and resorts to quasi-metaphorical descriptions of the resolution of rivalry by natural reasoning ('imagination' or 'sympathy'). The best reason he offers for this move is that the inability rationally to resolve conflict between traditions would require us to assume criterion-less choice as our only option in the face of rivalry.[28] Which is to say that MacIntyre realizes quite clearly that his explanation of rival traditions could lead to Kierkegaardian conclusions. But MacIntyre himself, at least on this matter, recoils from Kierkegaard. I do not.

I think, instead, that if you follow MacIntyre's basic account of traditions, and if you embed thought as fundamentally in the human being's finitude – its actual living and dying – as the ancients would have us to do, you must embrace Kierkegaard as the best articulation of the impossibility of a rational resolution between incommensurable traditions.[29] In short, the 'of life' is the Kierkegaardian side of my departure from and disagreement with MacIntyre about nature, theology/philosophy, the limits of traditioned rationality in the life of the knower, and so on.[30] It is this attempt to hold MacIntyre and Kierkegaard together in a dialectical move about traditions/living/rationality that generates the complexity of my position and its conclusions. I may be wrong that Kierkegaard and MacIntyre can be dialectically held together but if so it is certainly not because of simplistic reassertions of Stout's view of scholarship or yet another, though thoroughly thoughtful, insistence on 'propositions' as a way to get at

---

[28] This somewhat depends on what we mean by criterion. I can, for example, find something attractive in the life of another and simply desire to do it, too, or be like that, too, without being able to articulate rationally why his life is superior to mine and thus makes a better choice. After the change, reasons may be given. But that means that the rivalry has been resolved in the life of the 'convert' before rational resolution is possible; moreover, the 'ratio' with which the convert works post-conversion is the traditioned ratio of the new way of life. For the way our life experience conditions genuine ignorance/knowledge in relation to 'major' decisions of life, see also philosopher L. A. Paul, *Transformative Experience* (New York: Oxford University Press, 2014).

[29] This entails the judgement that MacIntyre himself is inconsistent. I think in order to avoid Kierkegaard he has to soften his account of rivalry, traditioned rationality, and translation. Novenson's claim that I out-MacIntyre MacIntyre is puzzling for these reasons among others and, at the least, suggests the need for a more thorough exposure to philosophical options.

[30] Engberg-Pedersen quotes MacIntyre's earlier work, pp 48-54. Though it is not its purpose in Engberg-Pedersen's essay, this citation foreshadows MacIntyre's problem, or at least the place where I think differently from him. Engberg-Pedersen thinks my departure from MacIntyre is strange and unsupported. Is what is meant that he does not like it? It has plenty of support, as MacIntyre himself recognizes (see his response essay in *Kierkegaard After MacIntyre*). I grant that if you think 'reason' (*histrionicus*) is what Engberg-Perdersen thinks it is, traditioned rationality may appear strange.

the essence of human reasoning.³¹ It would be instead because I am wrong about the inescapable weight of time and death upon human thought (I think it is heavier and more limiting than it is) and the Thomists more or less right in their claims about the natural potential and tendencies of human thought *qua* thought.³²

Second, Professors Barclay and Mitchell note that the ancients did talk about morality and query my rejection of 'morality' as an abstraction. The point, however, is not that the terms *mores* or *ethē* are absent in ancient literature, since of course they are not, but that the sense of *mores/ethē* is not what 'morality' has come to be in modern ethics. Morality in the modern sense is what MacIntyre and Bernard Williams both reject as a philosophical option and what Kantians and utilitarians believe in and try to argue about. It is a domain of action with its own discernible rules in which we all equally share and to which we contribute by our conduct and views about such conduct. Ethics is the directive logic of morality. One can see this conception at work clearly in current discussions in bioethics, for example, where we behave as if we can get content-full or content-rich agreements;³³ we behave this way because we assume that there is a realm of enquiry/behaviour that is detachable in some significant sense from religious convictions or knotty metaphysical puzzles or quantum physics or botany or emotional commitments to important people in our lives (or whatever). *Ethē*, whatever else it means in ancient traditions, does not mean morality in this modern sense. My point is simply, but importantly, that there is no larger arena than the traditions themselves, no isolatable sphere with behavioural norms in which all humans participate equally irrespective of the traditions in which they otherwise live.³⁴ The norms generated by the traditions are not instances of some larger universal human ethics. Scholars who make it look like there is such an arena in which all ancients work philosophically, pastorally, etc. reproduce a modern way of avoiding the depth of traditioned enquiry for what human action should entail. In this way, they create both historical and philosophical problems. Morality is tradition all the way down.

Third, Mitchell in particular asserts that I 'operate with a single, unitary conception of Christianity'.³⁵ But in the conceptual sense so does every person who thinks

---

[31] Engberg-Pedersen's slippage between 'a set of faculties', a 'capacity', a 'faculty', 'faculties' of 'rationality' and 'imagination' is typical, perhaps inevitable, when one ties rationality to propositions (see p. 48 and esp. n. 10). Engberg-Pedersen treats propositions (belief assertions, etc.) as if one can know what they mean without the narrative that tells one how the words work. One can, for example, 'entertain' and 'assent' to propositional content 'on its own'. But in fact propositions, no less than individual words, simply say *histrionicus histrionicus histrionicus* until you know the narrative that interprets the words. If one grants this, and one should, one grants, linguistically/hermeneutically speaking, the whole ball of wax.

[32] Perhaps I should say that there are plenty of days where I go back on myself and think the Thomists are essentially right about reason. Of course, to say Thomist is already to say traditioned reason, but it is traditioned in a way that gives an account of different possibilities.

[33] See H. Tristan Englehardt's work, for example, *The Foundations of Bioethics* (2nd edn; New York: Oxford University Press, 1996).

[34] When Malherbe, for example, writes about morality in the ancient world, he constructs a spectrum that makes it look like the various traditions/texts he discusses are participants in a larger arena called the moral. In case one wonders: neither for MacIntyre nor for Williams (nor for the pragmatist Stout) does negating the modern sense of morality rule out the pursuit of common goods. We can simply pursue common goods without the background notion that it is something called Morality that binds us together with specific obligations, norms, etc.

[35] P. 114.

Christianity is an identifiable tradition. Conceptually speaking, the plural *Christianities* is given its intelligibility by the narrative that allows one to see pluriform instances of some specific thing. In the very nature of the case, one cannot answer 'how specific?' because the pluriformity is ingredient to the tradition itself; following MacIntyre, I say explicitly that traditions are in part constituted by their different instantiations, arguments, contests, and so on, through time. But if one did not presuppose a Christian tradition, one would not be able to speak of its variations. The variations would, that is, simply be different traditions or different forms of life and one would need different words for them. If one calls variations of Christian life *Christian* variations, one has already invoked the narrative presupposition that tells one that these are *variations* rather than something else.[36] I have no quarrel with Mitchell in thinking that there are internal complications, contestations, and developments of almost unimaginable variety within Christianity. But, to put it simply now, if you do not have a singular conception of a religious/philosophical tradition, you would not know what you were looking at and would not have the word for it. This is not 'essentializing' but simply the way that concepts work.

Fourth, some of the essayists assert that *One True Life* problematizes Judaism as a possible conversation partner for the early (and contemporary?) Christians. This is very odd for two different but related reasons. First, *One True Life* is not about Judaism and Christianity but Roman Stoicism and early Christianity; and, second, I explicitly deny that the relation between the Stoics and the Christians is the same as that between

---

[36] This, of course, is the conceptual answer to Mitchell's pointed question about whether or not I would take Liberal/liberal Protestants to be Christians (!). By speaking of a part of the Christian tradition as L/liberal Protestants, I have *already* named them as Christians. Perhaps I am too hard on them, but I do not at all mean 'liberal' in today's American culture-war sense. I mean it in relation to philosophical commitments within certain forms of Protestantism that stem from notions of the self which go back at least to Locke and are underwritten by convictions about the existence and subsequent importance of autonomous individuals and their voluntary participation within certain democratic practices. That such commitments can lead to more fully developed 'liberal' positions that I reject as good options – not 'weak', something I nowhere say – should be no more surprising than the realization that there are conflicting options in any *inner*-tradition philosophical negotiations. (On the origins of the various conceptions of the self that are still with us, I am unaware of any better account than Charles Taylor's now classic work, *Sources of the Self: The Making of Modern Identity* (Cambridge, MA: Harvard University Press, 1989)). So, too, Mitchell seems to confuse questions of 'in and out' with that of being able to speak of a tradition at all and labels my willingness to speak of Christianity as a tradition as 'exclusivist' (n. 111). Mitchell may not mean it this way in the least, but I regard such contemporary jargon as part of a wider moralizing grammar that substitutes implicit accusations for a description of more serious positions. We could talk about 'in and out' in many different ways, but any discussion that would touch on what I think about this question would have to include, among other things, the central theological importance of the New Testament's claim about Jesus as the Second Adam – i.e., all humans are 'in' – Karl Barth's reconstruction of the doctrine of election, which I take as a dogmatic development consonant with an Adam/Christ typology; the implications of being 'in' for non-violence (and/or just war) vis-à-vis friends, strangers, and enemies; the work done by the distinction between the visible and invisible church; the importance of the virtues, and so forth. The question of how to locate a tradition so you can speak of it and the question of who is in and out of a tradition are of course linked, but they are not the *same* question. I am quite willing to speak of Christianity as a tradition since, conceptually speaking, one has to do so if one thinks there is such a thing as 'Christian' anything, but reasoning theologically about in and out must range much more widely.

Christians and Jews. Had I written a book about Christians and Jews, I would not have conceived the question in terms of rival traditions. Why? Because I do not take them to be rival traditions.

In contrast to Mitchell's attempt to force me to dissolve the differences I see and say that Jews and Stoics stand in the same relation to Christians, I maintain that the Christian/Jewish relation constitutes a very complex, complicated, and chronologically continuous argument about how to carry Israel's story forward from the advent of Jesus of Nazareth.[37] Not only Jesus but the earliest Christians were themselves Jews and claimed that they were continuing God's purpose in the election of Israel by following his Messiah. Whether they were right about this or not was initially an ongoing argument between Jews who thought not and Jews who thought so; in short, what was contested was where Israel's history was now to go. There was a shared history, texts, theological grammar, and so forth. A 'yes, Messiah' or 'no, not Messiah' judgement about the significance of Jesus for Israel's history obviously had and has massive consequences for hermeneutics, doctrine, practice and many other critical matters. But it is precisely in the tension of the yes and the no that the ongoing argument about the true trajectory of Israel's election subsists.[38]

To say it this way is, I think, both historically defensible and a specifically Christian way of framing the issue. A Christianity that does not see itself as a continuation of Israel – an ongoing, historically dense argument about that very history and its *telos* – is a Marcionite Christianity and one that I regard as both historically and theologically indefensible. It was hardly, therefore, an oversight or a mistake not to write about choosing between Judaism and Christianity but a particular theological commitment to seeing at the heart of the Jewish/Christian relation an argument about Israel's history rather than incommensurable difference.

I speak of *eschatological* resolution of this difference because I follow Paul's reasoning in Romans 9–11, because both Jewish and Christian traditions look towards eschatological disclosure of God's final truth about the world to come, and because it maintains indefinitely the *connection* – not the dissolution – of Christian and Jewish history.[39] Speaking of eschatology is a way of naming the specific character of the argument as a real argument: there are shared agreements about a great many things (especially over against any form of pagan life about which we know much of anything

---

[37] Mitchell's arguments here are puzzling for the chief reason that she acknowledges that I do not say what she thinks I should say but then goes on to argue that I really mean what she says I should have said.

[38] The question of non-compossibility is also different in the Christian/Jewish relation. Obviously you cannot eat pork and not eat pork at exactly the same time, but it is possible to be a Messianist Jew, as Messianist Jews themselves attest. The early church also had Torah observant 'Christians', whose pattern of life is reflected in one way or another in most of the New Testament texts. The arguments about whether Torah observance was/is necessary simply amplifies my point. For an excellent analysis of these matters in relation to John's Gospel, see Christopher Blumhofer, *The Gospel of John and the Future of Israel* (SNTSMS; Cambridge: Cambridge University Press (forthcoming, 2019)). Blumhofer's book should reopen the question of how best to interpret John vis-à-vis Judaism.

[39] On this point, see Bruce Marshall, 'Christ and Israel: An Unsolved Problem in Catholic Theology', in Gary A. Anderson and Joel S. Kaminsky (eds), *The Call of Abraham: Essays on the Election of Israel in Honor of Jon D. Levenson* (Notre Dame: University of Notre Dame Press, 2013), 330-50.

at all and over against many of the more powerful currents of modernity). But these agreements are exactly the sort that make the discussion incapable of resolution apart from the disclosure from God's side of things of the true identity of the Messiah.

Traditions of life, cosmopolitanism, conversation, and education

Because Mitchell thinks I 'wish' to 'dismantle' the humanities, because it was a topic much discussed at the conference, and because I was (and am) regularly asked about it thereafter, it is important to point out that certain critical features of the Kierkegaardian either/or are intrinsic to the humanities and cannot be dismissed simply as extreme or as if they have been overcome or as if they bring humanistic study to an end. They exist at the heart of serious humanistic education.[40] The either/ors are now hidden, however, by the sense that the real life-shape of the human being is not what is at stake in philosophical or religious (etc.) education. (What is at stake may be hard to specify but it is not cynical to say a good job.) The profound differences of religious/philosophical traditions that one learns about are subsumed by the structure in which the larger sense that thinking and study are all equally the same thing is generated and subsists.[41] Students are not educated to choose between a Nietzsche, an Augustine, a Kant, an Epictetus, or any of the others – which are existential as much as intellectual choices, not possibilities of combination. One can live either as Kant or as Nietzsche declare you should/can, but not both. This absorption of difference by combination is cosmopolitanism writ large – a universal, untraditioned rationality written into the institutional structure that delivers the sense of what education is or should be. Students can simply move from course to course mentally absorbing information as they go (hopefully on the way towards a successful career). Cosmopolitanism in this instance is the implicit understanding that makes intelligible the sense that all these differences can be taken in without having to make choices that would impinge on the trajectory of a life.[42]

---

[40] My point was not that the humanities should come to an end but that they should be conceived more closely in line with the human being itself and the choices we have to make based on the knowledges that expose us as choice-bound creatures. Mitchell cannot seem to take philosophical objections as objections about thinking/existence and continues to refer to what I 'wish' to do. Her quotation of me illustrates the problem, not what she claims I wish to do.

[41] Individual teachers may think differently, of course, and doubtless many do; the point is about the structure of departments, universities, etc. That is, insofar as teachers who think differently about what they are doing are themselves absorbed by the larger pattern of students-consuming-information-as-they-go, the teachers, too, are absorbed by the effect of the cosmopolitan.

[42] Cosmopolitan is not a cheap shot at the Enlightenment way of knowing (there are many obvious gains) but the best word I know that gestures towards the narrative that delivers a philosophical anthropology that says persons can overcome incommensurable but conflicting claims of religious traditions in their knowing and non-compossible claims in their being/becoming. Obviously I have in mind certain kinds of modern research universities and not, for example, specifically religious colleges that may well have a normative vision that transcends the departments. Of course, 'cosmopolitan' modernity hardly explains everything about current university educational structure. But I do think it is what renders the sense that it makes to take courses in everything and come out of all of them with information. Education is the acquisition of lots of information – important to be sure, but information all the same.

Traditioned reason, on the other hand, displays that there are massive, existentially determining choices that all humans have to make simply to get through life as a human being – whether they know it or not, like it or not, want it or not, and so on. One decides, implicitly or explicitly but always by practice, whether to keep Kosher or not. One cannot *not* go one way or the other. Traditioned reason thus allows for, indeed, insists on, the human in the humanities. The Kierkegaardian either/or cuts to the heart of the promise and risk of education: send your children to the university, and they might just choose to change their lives.

The question then often comes: if traditioned reason shapes our thinking, how do you justify conversation between different traditions of life or existential choices? Why talk to others? My view is that you do not need a theory for talking with other people. You simply talk with them. (Perhaps only academics would require a theory for conversation.) Why would you talk to people from other traditions if comparison works in the ways you have suggested? My view is: why wouldn't you? Again, human existence is simply denser and more complicated than any theoretical account that would purportedly grant permission for us to say why we would be interested in talking to people from other traditions of life. Perhaps you share an office, play tennis together, or like the same fried chicken, slaw, and hush puppies. Or maybe your kids play middle infield together on the same baseball team and you watch them turn double-plays. Or maybe you have always been interested in things foreign, like the way foreign-accents sound, or hope to learn about something new to eat. Or maybe for reasons you cannot articulate to yourself you simply like another person's company. Or maybe you really do *not* like his company and think to yourself that you need to grow out of your dislike and mature. Or maybe you are friends because you have joined a diverse group that works against poverty. Or maybe ... a thousand other things. ... What theory can account for conversation that comes from life?[43]

There is also the assumption, implicit perhaps, that the only way you can criticize your own tradition – or that anyone else can criticize your tradition – is if you ascribe to a certain modern strain of epistemic criteria and then in this vein study another tradition. Well, maybe that helps, maybe it does not. There's no necessary connection, no metaphysical or intellectual law that makes it help. What is a necessary and perceivable connection, however, is the 'fit' between claim and life, which is to say that hypocrisy is always a critique and self-critique. 'You say we are to have all things in common, but you yourself have a private bank account from which you buy all sorts of things when you think no one is looking.' 'You claim to get free of passion. We see your life is wildly otherwise.' This is both public and internal critique.

A final statement

By now it should be clear: I take comparative enquiry to be less of a question about specific method than it is about being human in a world with competing accounts of

---

[43] If the question is, 'Why *study* other traditions?', there are again many answers. Some of them would be as simple as: one enjoys reading Seneca. A more important one is given in my essay in this volume, Chapter 3: 'Making Friends and Comparing Lives'.

what that is.⁴⁴ Comparative enquiry is a way that we try to take seriously the seriousness of the competition between divergent accounts and to get at their significance for the lives that we have to live. Several of the essayists believe that the essence of comparative practice is best grasped by boiling it down into some laws (three), some operations (three), some theses (twelve). Perhaps. But I rather doubt it. Techniques of this and that sort are simply a part of thinking – about the ancient world and a great many other things besides. Moreover, the most important question – some might think the most obvious one – has been left out, that of truth.

In a brilliant book on being human, Robert Sokolowski wrote, 'We cannot help but take ourselves and one another as involved in truth, but what it means to be so implicated remains obscure to us.'⁴⁵ *One True Life* tries to make explicit what it means to be implicated in certain kinds of truth, viz., traditions which claim that our implication in truth requires our commitment – and, even more pointedly, that tie truth and commitment together in a way that necessitates either/or choices. Intellectual, existential, incommensurable, non-composible, truth. How do we compare *that*?

Drawing on Feuerbach's well-known critique of religion, Bernard Williams coined the term 'Feuerbach's axiom': if religion is not true, it cannot explain anything and is itself in need of explanation.⁴⁶ How right he was. What the traditions of life invite us to discover is whether fundamentally they explain or must themselves be explained, which is the same thing, they might have said, as discovering in our lives whether they are true or not. That we cannot discover the truth merely by reflection, or through a collection of like terms, or by the making of scholarly models, is endemic to the claim. To recognize this is already to engage in historically rich comparative enquiry *and* to make far-reaching decisions about the kind of thinking-thing the human being is. Come and live, they say, and you will know the truth. Or not.

---

[44] Mitchell's triumphal declaration that *One True Life* should 'not be taken as a contribution to method in comparison in the New Testament and ancient Christianity' is thus unproblematical for me: I am not trying to make a contribution to an established method but to reshape the question. Once again: the reaction to the book shows, I think, that at least some of its arguments struck home. Exactly to the degree that my arguments cannot simply be absorbed by Mitchell, Engberg-Pedersen et al. and turned into yet one more instance of contemporary methodological discussion do they illustrate the inability of encyclopedic reasoning to capture that which rejects it.

[45] *Phenomenology of the Human Person* (Cambridge: Cambridge University Press, 2008), 1. Some of Sokolowski's formulations run towards 'nature' in a more Thomistic sense than I would take them. But I take his phenomenology – that we appear in the world like this to ourselves and to others – to be fundamentally correct.

[46] By other things: psychological projections, social dynamics, etc. Williams often discussed religion/Feuerbach/etc., but he coined this phrase in his review of Charles Taylor's *Sources of the Self*, in *Essays and Reviews 1959–2002* (pp. 308, 310).

9

Relational Hermeneutics and Comparison as Conversation

Jonathan A. Linebaugh

'Where does the riddle of a book lie? In its language and content? In the plan of its author or in the mind of the interpreter?—' Johann Georg Hamann asked this question in a Christmas letter in 1784. It still haunts hermeneutics.[1]

Hamann's question identifies three possible locations for the 'riddle of a book': the text, the author, the interpreter. Does a text mean, in other words, as words on a page ('language and content'), as a mediation of the *mens auctoris* ('the plan of the author') or as a reader's interpretation ('the mind of the interpreter')? The form of Hamann's question, however, resists the alternatives. Instead of an answer, he offers an em dash: '—'. But consider the context of the question:

> God, nature, and reason have as intimate a relation to one another as light, the eye, and all that the former reveals to the latter, or like the center, radius, and periphery of any given circle, or like author, book and reader. Where does the riddle of a book lie? In its language and content? In the plan of its author or in the mind of the interpreter?—

The riddle of the book, for Hamann, is not located in author or text or interpreter; it is the 'relation' between author and text and interpreter.

There is a story here. Hamann's relational hermeneutic, while present from at least 1759, takes its most suggestive form in a 1762 essay entitled *Aesthetica in nuce*. Hamann was prompted to write, in large part, in response to Johann David Michaelis' pioneering research on philology and biblical interpretation following the Danish expedition to Arabia.[2] Hamann countered Michaelis' scholarly pilgrimage, which aimed at resurrecting scripture through understanding the 'extinct' Hebraic languages, with his

---

[1] J. G. Hamann, *Briefwechsel* (eds W. Ziesemer and A. Henkel; 8 vols; Wiesbaden/Frankfurt: Insel Verlag, 1955–75), 5, No. 784, 272: 14–18 (hereafter ZH). English translation from G. Griffith-Dickson, *Johann Georg Hamann's Relational Metacriticism* (Berlin: de Gruyter, 1995), 338.

[2] See Michaelis' *Beurtheilung der Mittel, welche man anwendet, die ausgestorbene Hebräische Spache zu verstehen* (Göttingen, 1757). The expedition was funded by the King of Denmark and led by Karsten Niehbur, but it was undertaken at the behest of Michaelis whose research was part of an emerging historical approach to interpretation associated with figures such as Siegmund Jakob Baumgarten, Johann August Ernesti and Johann Salomo Semler.

own 'philological crusade'. His quest was also a question: not so much about how scholarship can resurrect the language of scripture, but rather how can the language of the 'poet of heaven and earth' resurrect us?[3]

This debate is programmatic, positioned as it is at the dawn of modern biblical scholarship. For Michaelis, comparative research is indispensable: it deepens linguistic understanding, colours in historical contexts, and can disclose genealogical connections. But this study, as undertaken by Michaelis, is governed by what Hamann labels 'monastic rules', method as a medicine proscribed to protect against 'passion'.[4] For Hamann, by contrast, philology, interpretation and comparison are more dynamic – more self-involving and passionate, more relational.

With hindsight, Michaelis' approach looks like the forerunner of much comparative research, whether genealogical or analytic – that is, whether the aim is to determine derivation and influence or to arrange texts synoptically and explore their similarity and difference. But Hamann is a reminder that there might be another way. This essay does not pretend to offer a comprehensive history, theory, method or rationale for the practice of comparing texts. It will, rather, remember Hamann's relational riposte. Hamann's relational hermeneutic invites a form of comparison in which texts are not so much placed side by side and observed as they are brought by an engaged interpreter into relationship, face, to face – and because the interpreter is a relational participant we have to add to face. After considering the salient features of Hamann's relational account of interpretation (in occasional dialogue with Ricoeur, Gadamer and Bahktin), I will suggest a relational approach to comparative research in which comparison is understood as a conversation between the comparanda as well as with the comparator. Finally, a comparative sample drawn from my previous study of *Wisdom of Solomon* and *Romans* will attempt to put some flesh on the theoretical bones by hosting and participating in a conversation between and with the texts.

Relational hermeneutics with J. G. Hamann

Hamann's relational approach to reading and writing is on display from the opening dedication of his initial authorial experiment, the *Socratic Memorabilia* (1759). This 'flying leaf', as Hamann called his writings, has a 'double dedication': to 'nobody' and 'to Two'.[5] The two here are Hamann's 'friends', Christoph Berens and Immanuel Kant. Hamann hopes that their relationship will enrich their reading, whether that results in 'biased praise' or 'biased criticism'.[6]

This may seem like an incidental detail, but it gestures towards a fundamental aspect of Hamann's hermeneutic. The language of friendship recurs in the *Socratic Memorabilia*

---

[3] *Aesthetica in Nuce* was published as part of a collection entitled *Crusades of a Philologian*.
[4] J. G. Hamann, *Sämtliche Werken*, ed. J. Nadler, 6 vols (Vienna: Verlag Herder, 1949–57), 208: 20 (hereafter N).
[5] N II, 57. For English translations, in addition to Griffith-Dickson, *Relational Metacriticism* see J. G. Hamann, *Writings on Philosophy and Language*, ed. K. Haynes (Cambridge: Cambridge University Press, 2007), 3.
[6] N II, 61.32–3.

in relation to the interpretation of its titular subject: 'Socrates often visited the workshop of a tanner who was his friend' and who 'was the first to have the idea of writing down the conversations with Socrates'. Hamann's hope is to 'understand my hero as well as Simon the tanner', to understand Socrates as a friend.[7]

In the *Socratic Memorabilia*, this hermeneutic of friendship entails passionate commitment to the friend, what Hamann calls 'a thirsting ambition for truth', and also the capacity to feel with the friend: 'as one must oneself know the affliction [of hypochondria] to understand a hypochondriac ... perhaps one must have sympathy for ignorance in order to understand the Socratic variety'.[8] In addition to these relational postures, Hamann also suggests a relational procedure: an 'interpreter must' place 'texts' in 'connection with others', must 'couple' them because 'words' and so texts mean in 'relations'.[9] Texts are compared – or 'coupled' – because, as Griffith-Dickson writes, they 'achieve their meaning and power when viewed in their relations', and this 'relational fertility is such' that 'new light is shed on both by their new relation'.[10]

All of these themes reappear and are developed in *Aesthetica in nuce*. If Hamann's relationship with Kant and Berens occasioned the *Socratic Memorabilia*, this 1762 essay from his *Crusades of a Philologian* is part of an ongoing engagement with Michaelis. Hamann's earlier *Cloverleaf of Hellenistic Letters* had already interacted with Michaelis, whose scholarship he seems genuinely to have admired and whose philology he worried was too truncated. His appraisal of Michaelis in these 'letters' does at times, as Hamann admits, 'extend frankness into impertinence'.[11] But Michaelis also seems to have inspired Hamann. Between 1759 and 1763, Hamann did indeed undertake a philological crusade: in addition to studying a range of authors from Horace to Luther, this 'great study scheme' included Greek, Hebrew and Arabic.[12]

This intensive study is evidence that Hamann's relational hermeneutic is not a replacement for linguistic and contextual research. Rather a relational understanding of reality means that research has to be less about 'monastic rules' and more a 'rhapsody', less constrained and more 'kabbalistic'. These unexpected descriptions, taken from the subtitle of the essay ('a rhapsody is kabbalistic prose'), are not an exercise in obscurantism; they name the genre and genealogy of the hermeneut. Interpretation is kabbalistic because an interpreter is not a reader after the order of Melchizedek – 'without father or mother, without genealogy, without beginning of days or end of life' (Heb. 7.3). Kabbala gestures towards tradition and transmission, and for Hamann is a reminder that each

---

[7] N II, 65. 24–31.
[8] N II, 63.34; 70.28–32. See also Griffith-Dickson, *Relational Metacriticism*, 381, 388.
[9] N II, 71.25–34. The most significant 'comparison' in *Socratic Memorabilia* is Hamann's coupling of the inscription at Delphi ('know thyself') and the Socratic confession of ignorance.
[10] Griffith-Dickson, *Relational Metacriticism*, 65.
[11] *Writings on Philosophy and Language*, 59. Perhaps the most obvious example is Hamann's remark that a 'reader who hates the truth may find much in *Opinion on the Means Used to Understand the Defunct Hebrew Language* to comfort him' (*Writings on Philosophy and Language*, 53). These 'letters' also afforded Hamann the opportunity to express his original take on the then *en vogue* question about the quality of New Testament Greek: the Greek of the New Testament is humble because the '*stylus curiae*' of the self-giving God is 'the *genus humile dicendi*' (*Writings on Philosophy and Language*, 40).
[12] For fuller details, see Griffith-Dickson, *Relational Metacriticism*, 76.

interpreter has a location and a life, an inheritance and a history. As a rhapsody, Hamann's philological and comparative research is like the poems of the rhapsodists, both in the sense that they selected and 'stitched together' pieces of previous poetry and in that they were, as Hamann's reference to Plato's *Ion* indicates, 'interpreters of interpreters'.[13]

If the kinds of relationships that go under the name research involve selection, coupling and interpretation – if research is a kabbalistic rhapsody – then, for Hamann, the moments and movements of these relationships can also be specified. Francis Bacon, who is among the muses of *Aesthetica in nuce*, divided learning into three: history with memory, philosophy with reason and poetry with phantasy. Hamann followed suit, but added some job descriptions or jurisdictions: with regard to the data (Hamann would say *dicta*) of nature and history, which are forms of 'address' and yet heard as 'jumbled verse', it is 'for the scholar to gather these; for the philosopher to interpret them; to imitate them – or even bolder – to bring them into order is the poet's part'.[14] Within this division of labour, Michaelis' research has an essential role, but it also oversteps its limits when it imagines archaeological research and exegetical rules can resurrect the language of 'the poet at the beginning of days'.

For Hamann, research is reception, interpretation and response. These moments are not so much a method as modes of relating: of listening, of engaging and of speaking. This suggests a fundamental anthropological asymmetry: the human creature is addressed and only so able to answer, is receptive and only so responsive, is a reader and only then a writer. Hamann's relational hermeneutic, in other words, is part of a more comprehensive relational anthropology. In an age in which the unions between contingent and necessary truth, subject and object, and rationality and sensuousness were being dissolved by what Hamann criticized as 'the art of divorce' (*Scheidekunst*), he insisted on the 'art of marriage' (*Ehekunst*).[15] This is ultimately a Christological contention, rooted in the '*communicatio* of the divine and human *idiomata*' and reflected in the title of a 1784 essay that references both the self-emptying and exaltation of Jesus, *Golgatha und Scheblimini*.[16] But this is not a narrowly Christological confession. For Hamann, the Christological *communicatio* discloses a relational understanding of reality: it is a 'fundamental law and master-key of all our knowledge and of the whole visible economy'.[17]

---

[13] N II, 217. 20. See Griffith-Dickson, *Relational Metacriticism*, 82–3 for an excellent discussion of the significance of the subtitle.

[14] N II, 199.13. John Milton, in *Areopagitica*, writes of 'Truth' being 'hewed ... into a thousand pieces and scattered to the four winds' such that the 'sad friends of Truth,' like 'the careful search that Isis made for the mangled body of Osiris,' must go 'up and down gathering up limb by limb' the scattered 'members' of 'virgin Truth'.

[15] On this theme, see O. Bayer, *A Contemporary in Dissent: Johann Georg Hamann as a Radical Enlightener* (trans. R. A. Harrisville and M. C. Mattes; Grand Rapids: Eerdmans, 2012), xii–xiii and 14; Griffith-Dickson, *Relational Metacriticism*, 1–15.

[16] *Scheblimini* is taken from Psalm 110:1 and means 'sit at my right hand'. The quotation is from 'The Last Will and Testament of the Knight of the Rose-Cross' (1772), N III, 27.11–14.

[17] N III, 27.11–14 (see *Writings on Philosophy and Language*, 99). Goethe, for whom Hamann was 'the brightest mind of his time', was among the first to interpret Hamann along the lines of the necessity of unification and the problem of isolation. Goethe's estimation of Hamann was shared by many and surpassed, perhaps, only by Kierkegaard who named Hamann, along with Socrates, as the 'most brilliant minds of all time'. For these and other descriptions of Hamann, see J. R. Betz, *After Enlightenment: The Post-Secular Vision of J. G. Hamann* (Oxford: Wiley-Blackwell, 2012), 2–3.

In *Aesthetica in nuce* this 'whole visible economy' is interpreted as an 'address (*Rede*) to the creature through the creature'.[18] For Hamann, then, to be a creature is to be addressed, to be one 'whose existence is relative' or 'constituted by a relation' of reception and response.[19] The human person lives from an address and as an answer.[20] For this reason, as Oswald Bayer argues, 'hermeneutical' characterizes Hamann's understanding of human existence: it points to 'the linguistic character of ... communication', the way this communication requires 'time' and 'translation', and theologically the 'cascade from the speaking God to the receptive human being'. Here Hamann anticipates Gadamer. Hermeneutic describes life as interpretative existence – the relational reality Hamann would call 'being created'.[21] Furthermore, Hamann's relational hermeneutic resonates with Gadamer's insistence that reading is a relationship: a text, for Gadamer, is *'ein echter Kommunikationspartner'* and thus to describe reading he speaks *'vom einem hermeneutischen Gespräch'*.[22]

Hamann makes the same point: while author and reader are among the communication partners who participate in the hermeneutical conversation, interpretation is also and always a relationship with 'the given letters' – with the text.[23] This attention to the given resists what Bayer calls 'a twofold impatience', the interpretative urge to get behind or away from the text to either 'the self-understanding of the author' or 'the self-understanding of the reader'.[24] As Ricoeur puts it, interpretation occurs 'before the text' – along the 'detour' of attention to 'signs' and 'symbols'.[25] In this sense, it is possible, indeed necessary, to talk about the 'relative autonomy of the text over against the author as well as over against the reader'.[26] To quote Milton's *Areopagitica*, 'books are not absolutely dead things, but do contain a potency of life ... they are as lively, and as vigorously productive, as those fabulous dragon's teeth.' This does not mean, as Griffith-Dickson points out, that the text is a 'self-sufficient' subject: a text derives from an author and depends on a reader. But it is not dominated by either.[27] Precisely as a text – as signs, symbols and detour – it detains; it resists and relates. Relative autonomy, in other words, is 'relational autonomy'.[28] Hamann

---

[18] N II, 198.29.
[19] O. Bayer, 'God as Author: On the Theological Foundations of Hamann's Authorial Poetics', in L. M. Anderson (ed.), *Hamann and the Tradition* (Evanston, IL: Northwestern University Press, 2012), 165.
[20] Hamann would call the address the human lives from the Word or grace and the answer life is lived as either unbelief or faith and love: faith and love are engendered by the antecedent address and are modes of relating to another, whether that other is God (related to in faith) or the neighbour (related to in love). Here, as Hamann said he was always doing, he 'Lutherizes' (ZH 307, quoted in Betz, *After Enlightenment*, 33).
[21] Griffith-Dickson, *Relational Metacriticism*, 354.
[22] Hans-Georg Gadamer, *Wahrheit und Methode: Grundüzge einer philosophischen Hermeneutik, Gesammelte Werke* 1 (Tübingen: J. C. B. Mohr [Paul Siebeck], 1990), 364, 391.
[23] From a letter to Jacobi, cited in Griffith-Dickson, *Relational Metacriticism*, 129.
[24] O. Bayer, 'Hermeneutical Theology', *SJT* 56.2 (2003): 131–47 (144).
[25] P. Ricouer, 'Erzählung, Metapher und Interpretationstheorie', *ZThK* 84 (1987): 232–53, quoted in Bayer, 'Hermeneutical Theology', 143.
[26] Bayer, 'Hermeneutical Theology', 143. Related to this is Gadamer's contention that 'understanding is never a subjective relationship towards a given "object", but belongs rather to the effective history' of the text or artefact (*Wahrheit und Methode*; ET *Truth and Method* (New York: Continuum, 1997), xix).
[27] See Griffith-Dickson, *Relational Metacriticism*, 129–30. As Hamann reads Socrates, he imagines him talking back to his interpreter: 'What does this young fellow', Plato in this case, 'mean to make of me?' (N II, 65: 29–30).
[28] Bayer, 'God as Author', 173.

is just as opposed to an 'exegetical materialism' that forgets the author as an 'other' as he is to an 'exegetical idealism' that leaps over the 'given letters'.[29] Author, text and reader – these are the communication partners who engage in a hermeneutical conversation.

As in the *Socratic Memorabilia*, the relational hermeneutic of *Aesthetica in nuce* entails passion, but also participation. 'Do not', Hamann warns, 'venture into the metaphysics of the fine arts without being initiated into the orgies and Eleusinian mysteries.'[30] Passion, in other words, is not a problem but a prerequisite: Michaelis 'sets monastic rules – Passion alone gives abstractions as well as hypotheses hands, feet, wings'.[31] The contrast with Michaelis is telling. According to Hamann's diagnosis, strict exegetical methods – 'monastic rules' – are motivated by 'fear': fear of subjectivity and of misinterpretation, but also 'fear of the spirit and life of the prophets'.[32] While Hamann's relational hermeneutic calls for rather than prohibits passion, he is resolutely opposed to a one-sided subjectivity, to those who 'flood' the text by 'dreaming up their own inspiration and interpretation'.[33] His solution, however, is not rules; it is the relationship. Hamann talks about an interpreter being 'true' to their communication partners, of sympathy and of reading as a form of relating as a 'friend'. What this amounts to, as Griffith-Dickson puts it, is that the 'safeguards' against exegetical 'abuse . . . arise from the respectful relationship with the author and the text'. And she adds, 'There are no further safeguards for this than there are against misunderstanding in any other relationship.'[34]

The flipside of this is that the possibilities of understanding are the same as in other relationships. Hamann's hermeneutic emphasizes certain capacities and practices that enable us to come to know another. Perhaps the most essential, for Hamann, is being addressed or, more simply, listening – the patient mode of receiving the other as they give themselves to us. But coming to know another also requires empathy and engagement. Hamann talks about 'sympathy' and 'initiation', forms of relating that require imagination and experience. George Eliot's explanation of the role of realism in literature resonates with Hamann: 'We want to be taught to feel . . . for the peasant in all his coarse apathy and the artisan in all his suspicious selfishness.' Art, according to Eliot, can engender this 'feeling for' because 'it is a mode of amplifying experience and extending our contact with our fellowmen beyond the bounds of our personal lot.'[35] At the limits of the imagination, Hamann also invites initiation 'into the orgies and Eleusinian mysteries' – into relationships and experiences. As Melville puts it in *Moby-Dick*, if you want to understand 'the experience of whaling', then 'go a-whaling'.[36] There are, to use a term employed by many religious and philosophic traditions, 'ways' of life

---

[29] The terms are Griffith-Dickson, *Relational Metacriticism*, 129, 337.
[30] N II, 201.12–14.
[31] N II, 208.20–1.
[32] N II, 204.26–7.
[33] N II 207.22 and 208.6.
[34] Griffith-Dickson, *Relational Metacriticism*, 128.
[35] *Essays of George Eliot*, ed. T. Pinney (Routledge & Kegan Paul, 1968), 170–1.
[36] Consider also the note found next to Martin Luther's deathbed: 'No one can understand Virgil in his Bucolics and Georgics unless he has spent five years as a shepherd or farmer. No one understands Cicero in his letters unless he has served under an outstanding government for twenty years. No one should believe that he has tasted the Holy Scriptures sufficiently unless he has spent one hundred years leading churches with the prophets', *D. Martin Luthers Werke: Kritische Gesamtausgabe, Tischreden* (Weimar, 1912–21), no. 5677; 317.

that to know are to live. That this is so, and that a person only lives one life, is the central insight of Kavin Rowe's *One True Life*. This does not mean, as Rowe is sometimes misread as suggesting, that 'rival traditions of life' cannot converse. Rather it specifies, in such cases, the relationship that comparison is: a relation between rivals who can nevertheless be friends in sympathetic but still honest conversation.[37]

This kind of conversation brings us back to comparison. Mikhail Bahktin says, 'The text lives only by coming into contact with another text.'[38] Hamann could almost have written that. He would agree that a text only lives by coming into contact with another, though that other could be a reader rather than another text. Drop the 'only', however, and you have Hamann: the text lives by coming into contact with another text. Stitching together or 'coupling' texts and traditions is a hermeneutical act that is both rhapsodic and relational. 'By creating new relationships', writes Griffith-Dickson, the interpreter 'creates a new world of possible meanings and insights', a world in which 'new light is shed on both [texts or traditions] by their new relation'.[39] This relational and rhapsodic approach resists forms of comparison in which material is simply juxtaposed and analysed by a personally uninvolved interpreter. For Hamann, texts and traditions should not, in this side-by-side sense, just be compared; they should be coupled: brought into relationship, face to face.

But again, because the interpreter is also engaged in the relationship, this comparative relation is best described as face-to-face-to-face. And this suggests that the illumination that occurs in the comparative relationship does not apply only to the texts. The interpreter also 'lives by coming into contact with another'. Hamann explores this theme under the question of self-knowledge. Through reading and comparative research – that is, by relating to others – we come to know not just the other but also ourselves. 'Self-knowledge begins with the neighbor, the mirror.'[40] As Hamann's stitching together of Socratic and Pauline ignorance suggests, however, this knowledge is less about 'knowing something' than it is about 'being known' by someone (1 Cor. 8.2–3). 'Self knowledge comes from being known.'[41] To read and compare and relate to others is, in T. S. Eliot's words, to 'explore' the 'unknown', the 'unremembered' and the 'half-heard'. But the 'end of all our exploring' is not only a better understanding of others. The 'end' is the self-knowledge that comes from being known – the end 'will be to arrive where we started, and know the place for the first time'.[42]

---

[37] It is essential to stress that strong traditions that invite living as the deepest mode of understanding can nevertheless converse and relate, can share experiences and empathize. It is precisely a lack of the kind of empathy suggested by Eliot, an 'incapacity to think ... from another person's point of view', that Hannah Arendt diagnoses as the 'banality of evil' in *Eichmann in Jerusalem: A Report on the Banality of Evil* (London: Penguin Books, 2006 [1963]), 252 and xiii.

[38] M. Bakhtin, 'Toward a Methodology for the Human Sciences', in C. Emerson and M. Holquist (eds), *Speech Genres and Other Late Essays*, trans. V. W. McGee (Austin: University of Texas Press, 1986), 159–72, (162).

[39] Griffith-Dickson, *Relational Metacriticism*, 65, 133. Within the larger theological horizon of *Aesthetica in nuce*, this coupling is underwritten by and ultimately hears 'the testimony of Christ', the 'divine word' that both interprets scripture and is the 'master-key' that unlocks the books of nature and history. Hamann's hermeneutic is thus characterized by the relationship between the one and the any: the one word of Christ makes legible and can be read in any book, whether it be the book of scripture, nature, or history.

[40] ZH 6: 281.

[41] G. Griffith-Dickson, 'God, I, and Thou: Hamann and the Personalist Tradition', in L. M. Anderson (ed.), *Hamann and the Tradition* (Evanston, IL: Northwestern University Press, 2012), 56.

[42] From 'Little Gidding', which is the last of Eliot's *Four Quartets*.

Engaged exegetical eavesdropping: comparison as conversation

After suggesting that 'the text lives... by coming into contact with another text', Bahktin adds a significant gloss: 'joining a given text to a dialogue' creates 'the point of ... contact between texts' at which 'a light flashes'.[43] This description of comparative research resonates with Hamann's relational hermeneutic. For Bahktin, texts are not just studied in juxtaposition; they are joined. And this joining or, in Hamann's word, this coupling creates a point of contact, a conversation.

The aim of this section is to suggest that this understanding of comparison as conversation provides a way to conceive and conduct comparative research that is informed by Hamann's relational hermeneutic. Comparison is a dynamic relationship between the comparanda and with the comparator. This relational dynamism, however, resists the attempt to translate Hamann's hermeneutic into a fixed comparative method. Living relationships cannot be controlled by 'monastic rules'. What Hamann invites, rather, is a consideration of the relationship that comparison is and the conditions by which an interpreter might facilitate and participate in that relationship. One way to capture this relationship is to call it engaged exegetical eavesdropping.

First, exegetical eavesdropping: texts sound different when they talk, not just to a reader, but to another text. This is the insight behind Bahktin's insistence that 'joining a given text to a dialogue' creates 'the point of... contact between texts' at which 'a light flashes'. Texts come alive when they connect, when they converse about what they share and where and why they differ. Hamann's description of the act of interpretation as a rhapsody points in the same direction: stitching texts and traditions together introduces a 'couple' that engages in a conversation and 'creates a new world of possible meanings and insights'. The relational results of this flash of light or new world of possible meanings cannot be controlled or predicated: familiar sentences may become strange, once insignificant passages may speak with surprise and urgency, apparently novel ideas may prove commonplace, and claims that seem routine may emerge as radical. But whatever the results, the relationship between the texts can impact the relationship the reader has with the texts. As the texts talk to each other, their otherness – their demand of a detour and their difference as given letters – resist and relate to the reader by requiring an act of reception, of listening. Exegetical eavesdropping describes this movement of comparative interpretation: comparison involves listening in on a conversation between the comparanda.

But texts do not just talk to each other. As Jonathan Z. Smith puts it, 'It is the scholar who makes their cohabitation... possible.'[44] The interpreter, in other words, creates the conversation through the 'postulation of similarity which is the ground of methodological comparison' and by 'bringing differences together'.[45] Comparison is a relationship not just between texts but also with the interpreter. Exegetical eavesdropping is thus

---

[43] 'Toward a Methodology for the Human Sciences', 162.
[44] J. Z. Smith, *Drudgery Divine: On Comparison of Early Christianities and the Religions of Late Antiquity* (Chicago: University of Chicago Press, 1990), 51.
[45] Smith, *Drudgery Divine*, 51.

necessarily engaged: the comparator listens to but also facilitates and participates in the conversation. Hosting the conversation entails 'bringing together' the comparanda and 'the focused selection of significant aspects of the phenomena' being compared; participating in the conversation includes, in Hamann's terms, the kind of interpretation and response that involves friendship, passion, empathy and experience.[46]

Both of these relational roles raise possible problems. E. P. Sanders argues in his comparison of Paul and Palestinian Judaism that 'the two principal difficulties' of placing texts in conversation can be 'summarized by the words imbalance and imposition'.[47] The former, 'imbalance', refers to the problems associated with comparing a single text or author with a more expansive tradition and the tendency such disproportion has towards over generalization. Reducing a diverse tradition to a common denominator that is useful for comparison may conceal rather than capture the tradition or texts in question. The second difficultly, 'imposition', identifies a temptation in comparative research to allow one participant in the relationship, whether one of the comparanda or the comparator, to function as the control or canon – the standard according to which the other communication partners are measured.[48] There are some procedural strategies that can alleviate these problems: limiting the comparanda to two or three texts that can converse reduces the risks of imbalance and reading the texts that bear less family resemblance to the reader first and without initial reference to the other text(s) mitigates against imposition. But methodological rules, for Hamann, are 'a negative quality' that can reduce risk but can 'never replace' the relationship.[49] As Volker Hoffman describes Hamann's hermeneutic, 'an element comes into interpretation that cannot be reduced to a rational method; indeed only through this it seems can the aliveness of interpretation be guaranteed'.[50] Any attempt to gain 'analytic control over the framework of comparison' amounts, in Hamann's view, to a return to Michaelis' 'monastic rules'.[51] Both the risks and the possibility of reducing them stem from what reading is: a relationship.

---

[46] Smith, *Drudgery Divine*, 51, 53; cf. his endorsement of F. J. P. Poole's remark that 'comparisons do not deal with phenomena *in toto* or in the round, but only with the aspectual characteristic of them'.

[47] E. P. Sanders, *Paul and Palestinian Judaism: A Comparison of Patterns of Religion* (Minneapolis: Fortress Press, 1977), 19.

[48] Sanders' own study is a telling example of this error: the normative status of Pauline patterns of soteriology result in the conclusion that, to quote Westerholm's summary, 'Jews are said, in effect, to have been good Protestants after all' (*Perspectives Old and New: The 'Lutheran' Paul and His Critics* (Grand Rapids: Eerdmans, 2004), 341).

[49] Griffith-Dickson, *Relational Metacriticism*, 128. Thus, while I agree with Engberg-Pedersen that comparative work requires deep familiarity with 'each figure to be compared', I am reluctant to call this requirement a rule or, as he does, a *lex* ('Self-Sufficiency and Power: Divine and Human Agency in Epictetus and Paul', in J. M. G. Barclay and S. J. Gathercole (eds), *Divine and Human Agency in Paul and His Cultural Environment* (London: T&T Clark, 2008), 118).

[50] V. Hoffman, *Johann Georg Hamanns Philologie: Hamanns Philologie zwischen enzyklopädischer Mikrologie und Hermeneutik* (Stuttgart: Verlag W. Kohlhammer, 1972), 190 (quoted in Griffith-Dickson, *Relational Metacriticism*, 128).

[51] See Smith, *Drudgery Divine*, 53. For Hamann, it is 'fear' that motivates method, and Smith does at least seem to have a concern: if comparison lacks 'analytic control' and 'a clear articulation of purpose', one may derive arresting anecdotal juxtapositions... but the disciplined constructive work of the academy will not have been advanced, nor will the study of religion have come of age' (53). I suspect Hamann would respond to this academic eschatology with an ageless aesthetic: 'Let us now hear the conclusion of this newest aesthetic, which is the oldest: Fear God and give Him glory...' (N II, 217.15–17).

One way to express the freedom and constraints that shape the hermeneutical relationship is to say that the reader is responsible, or better: response-able. That a reader is *able* to respond indicates a critical and creative freedom; that this freedom is a *response* indicates that it depends on and is constrained by an antecedent word.[52] This dialectic of 'freedom in response' can be seen in the way similarity and difference play out in comparative research.[53] Smith insists, 'there is nothing "natural" about the enterprise of comparison. Similarity and difference' are not properties of a single text; they exist in the act of comparison that creates the 'cohabitation' of texts that makes 'sameness' and 'difference' possible. But even Smith concedes the 'postulation of similarity' involves 'the selection of significant aspects of the phenomena'.[54] Therefore, as Hamann says of knowledge, similarity is 'neither mere invention nor mere recollection'.[55] Similarity is specified and named as such by an interpreter, but what is selected as similar is supplied by the texts or traditions. This 'sameness', in other words, is at once activated by the interpreter and anchored in the texts. And as Smith suggests, 'similarity ... is the ground of methodological comparison', it makes it possible.[56] In relational terms, similarity enables dialogue by providing the points of continuity between texts that serve as conversational commonplaces – topics for the texts to talk about. But as Poole puts it, if 'similarity makes [comparison] possible', then 'difference makes [it] interesting'.[57] Difference, however, like similarity, is neither simply created nor uncovered, 'neither mere invention nor mere recollection'. Rather, the interpreter invites texts into a dialogue so difference can be discovered. This difference is found by the interpreter, but it is found in the 'given letters' as they detain and address, resist and relate. To adapt Poole, similarity makes dialogue possible; difference invites an interesting form of dialogue: debate.

It is these relational dynamics that I am attempting to capture with the phrase engaged exegetical eavesdropping. Comparison, in this relational frame, involves the interpreter facilitating a conversation between texts but also participating in a conversation with texts. The comparative form is thus face to face – as the texts talk to each other – and to face – as the interpreter brings together, listens to, and talks with the texts.

---

[52] This notion of responsibility within an interpretative relationship bears some resemblance to Habermas' concept of 'Mündigkeit' as the criterion of truth within an 'unconstrained dialogic relation'. For Habermas, however, all communication is both ordered to and, because 'reason can become transparent to itself', capable of understanding (see both *Knowledge and Human Interests* (Cambridge: Polity Press, 1987), 287 and the introduction to the fourth edition of *Theory and Practice* (London: Heinemann, 1974), 17). But reason, as Hamann pointed out in his *Metakritik* of Kant, is not a hypostatic something that can vaccinate us against our histories and traditions. Rather, reasoning is a human activity that is preformed by persons who think and converse in language and as those who have a life and location.

[53] The phrase is the title of a collection essays by Oswald Bayer, *Freedom in Response* (Oxford: Oxford University Press, 2007).

[54] Smith, *Drudgery Divine*, 51, 53.

[55] N III, 41.11–12.

[56] Smith, *Drudgery Divine*, 53

[57] F. J. P. Poole, 'Metaphor and Maps: Towards Comparison in the Anthropology of Religion', *JAAR* 54 (1986): 411–57 (417). One thinks of Mr Darcy, in Jane Austen's *Pride and Prejudice*, whose love for Elizabeth Bennet is less interested in the ways she is like other woman than it is in the ways she is different and so distinctively her.

Wisdom and Romans (and me) in conversation

A comparison of *Wisdom of Solomon* and Paul's letter to the church in Rome is a particular relationship. These are texts that share a language, social and religious locations, a scriptural inheritance, and a set of theological concepts and concerns. The particularities of this relationship are also affected, in this instance, by the fact that I am conducting this comparison between *Wisdom* and Romans. I have a long and studied relationship with *Wisdom* and, in Hamann's words, feel like a 'friend' to this text and its tradition. But I am a Christian. I read Paul within a confession that is both shared with and shaped by Paul's letters. Specifying all of this neither rules out comparison nor means that 'monastic rules' are necessary to control the conversation. What this naming does, to quote Luther, is to 'call a thing what it is'. This comparison is a real relationship – between *Wisdom* and Romans and with me.

Wisdom and Romans have a lot to talk about. Both texts consider the relationship between Jew and non-Jew, both explore the meaning and operations of God's righteousness and grace, and both think theologically in conversation with Israel's scriptures. But as an icebreaker, consider Jacob. For *Wisdom*, Jacob is 'righteous' (δίκαιος) and so when Sophia 'guides' and 'gives to' him (*Wis.* 10.10) this beneficence exemplifies a theological maxim: 'Wisdom rescues from trouble those who serve her' (10.9) and 'she seeks those who are worthy (ἄξιος) of her' (6.16). In Romans, Jacob is again a recipient of divine blessing, but here the rationale is not his righteousness. Rather, as Paul's exploitation of the prenatal promise emphasizes, Jacob's election is 'not based on works' but only on 'the one who calls' (Rom. 9.9–13). This continuity together with contrast invites a conversation.[58]

Wisdom is a sermon addressed to sufferers. It is difficult to reconstruct the socio-historical details alluded to by *Wisdom*, but the tone and content of the pastoral address indicate that the situation was serious enough to generate a series of questions about the moral order of the world, the patterns of history, and the past, present and future justice of God. Into this crisis – a crisis that appears to be characterized by the present flourishing of the ungodly and the suffering of the righteous (*Wis.* 2–5) – the author of *Wisdom* announces a word of hope: the God of illimitable love is ineluctably just.[59]

This is bedrock: 'You are just and you rule all things justly' (12.15). It is this God who 'arranged all things by measure and number and weight' (11.20). Within this precisely calibrated cosmos, justice has a reliable shape: the non-condemnation of the righteous (12.15) and 'God's fitting judgement' (ἀξίαν θεοῦ κρίσιν) of the unrighteous (12.26). The

---

[58] For my attempt to facilitate this conversation between *Wisdom* and Romans, see *God, Grace, and Righteousness in Wisdom of Solomon and Paul's Letter to the Romans: Texts in Conversation* (Leiden: Brill, 2013).

[59] The consensus, which is probable though not definite, places *Wisdom* in Alexandria between 220 BCE and 20 CE; see C. Larcher, *Le Livre de la Sagesse, ou La Sagesse de Salomon* (Paris : Gabalda, 1983) 1.141-61; D. Winston, *The Wisdom of Solomon* (AB, 43; Garden City, NY : Doubleday, 1979), 20-25; H. Hübner, *Die Weisheit Salomons* (ATD Apokryphen 4; Göttingen: Vandenhoeck and Ruprecht, 1999), 15-19. While it is difficult to have an explicit relationship with anonymous or unknown authors, sensitivity to social setting and occasion helps to avoid treating the text in what Griffith-Dickson calls an 'anti-human fashion' and remembers that language and its truth is not just correspondence and representation, but communication and relationship.

paradigmatic instantiation of this pattern is the Exodus. At the Red Sea, the 'righteous' and the 'ungodly' (10.20) encounter, respectively, deliverance and destruction: 'Sophia led the righteous through deep waters, but she drowned their enemies' (10.18–19). In *Wisdom*, this correspondence is a criterion. Whether *Wisdom* is diagnosing the present, remembering the past, or promising a future, the shape is the same: as in the Exodus, God's justice is evident in the congruence between the form (judgement or mercy) and object (ungodly or righteous) of God's action. Adam, Noah and the patriarchs are rescued and rewarded by Sophia because they are, in some sense, 'worthy of her' (10.1–14; cf. 6.16).[60] Solomon receives Sophia as a 'gift' (χάρις, 8.21), but this giving is conditioned by correspondence: Solomon was 'good' (ἀγαθός, 8.20). In *Wisdom's* telling of the events of the Exodus, there is symmetry between the judgement experienced by the 'ungodly' Egyptians and the mercy shown to Israel, a 'holy people and blameless race' (*Wis.* 10.15–19.22). And the final hope is anchored in a promise that the eschaton will be like the Exodus: the present chaos will be overcome by correspondence as the God of justice acts to judge the unrighteous oppressors and vindicate the righteous sufferers (*Wis.* 2–5).

As the Exodus shapes *Wisdom's* theology and hermeneutic, it also necessarily shapes its anthropology. The symmetry of divine justice requires both the righteous and the unrighteousness. This is assumed throughout *Wisdom*, but it is argued in Chapters 13–15. The extended polemic against Gentile idolatry and immorality serves to pick out Israel as the innocent and so reinforce the irreducible difference between Israel *qua* the righteous and non-Israel *qua* the ungodly. 'All people' might be 'ignorant of God' (13.1), idolatrous (13.10–14.11, 15–21; 15.7–13) and so immoral (14.12–14, 22–9), but not Israel: 'We will not sin, knowing that we are counted as yours ... For the evil intent of human art has not deceived us' (15.1–4). The Exodus enacts justice because it is judgement for the ungodly and 'deliverance' for Israel *qua* a 'holy people and blameless race' (*Wis.* 10.15). Again, the Red Sea crossing gives the criterion. The Egyptians are named the 'enemy' (ἐχθρός, 10.19) and the 'ungodly' (ἀσεβής, 10.20) and so they suffer 'God's fitting judgement' (ἀξίαν θεοῦ κρίσιν). Israel is 'holy' (ὅσιος, 10.17) and 'righteous' (δίκαιος, 10.20) and her rescue is thus, precisely as grace, 'a reward (μισθός) for her labours' (10.17). The Exodus embodies justice: judgement for the unrighteous and mercy for the righteous. For *Wisdom*, this is the protological order, the canonical past and the promise: as it was in the beginning, even if it is not now, it ever will be. This is hope – for the righteous.

But here Romans interjects: 'all, both Jew and Gentile, are under sin' (Rom. 3.9). *Wisdom* 13–15 and Romans 1.18–32 are connected by vocabulary and an argumentative sequence. Both texts argue from a squandered creation-related knowledge of God (*Wis.* 13.1–9; Rom. 1.19–20) to a corresponding turn to idolatry (*Wis.* 13.10–14: 11, 15–21 and 15.7-13; Rom. 1.21––3), which in turn occasions a litany of immorality (*Wis.* 14.12–14, 22–9; Rom. 1.24–31) and invites a fitting exercise of divine judgement (*Wis.* 14.30-31; Rom. 1.32). At the end of this argument, however, *Wisdom* insists on Israel's innocence; Paul announces Israel's inclusion. 'We will not sin' and 'human art has not misled us', writes *Wisdom*. At this very moment in the argument, in what Richard Hays

---

[60] In most cases, this worthiness is identified as being 'righteous', though in the case of Adam it is his status as the 'first formed father of the world' (10.1).

has called a 'rhetorical sting operation', Romans asks, 'Do you think, you human being, when you judge others who do such things and yet do the same things yourself, that you will escape the judgement of God?' (Rom. 2.3).⁶¹ For *Wisdom*, the polemic against Gentile idolatry and immorality serves to reinforce a distinction: the non-Jewish world is ungodly, Israel is righteous. According to Romans, however, 'there is no distinction' (Rom. 3.22). The story of sin that Paul proclaims in Romans 1.18–32 is *human* history. God's wrath is revealed against the unrighteousness and ungodliness of human beings (ἄνθρωπος, 1.18), and the creational context (1.19–21) and echoes of both Eden and Israel (1.23) universalize Paul's diagnosis: 'none are righteous' (3.9) and 'all sinned' (3.23).⁶² Thus, in contrast to *Wisdom*'s polemical insistence on the irreducible difference between righteous Israel and the ungodly Gentiles, Paul's proclamation reduces that anthropological fraction to a single denominator: he announces the human and names a common condition – *homo peccator*.

For *Wisdom*, this can only have one conclusion. Because God's justice meets ungodliness with judgement, universal unrighteousness can only end in universal condemnation. And at Romans 3.20 Paul appears to agree: 'No human being will be justified before God by works of the law'. But, Paul declares, 'the righteousness of God is made manifest', with the result that those who 'sinned and lack the glory of God' are 'justified as a gift by God's grace' (Rom. 3.21–4). This announcement is uttered in language *Wisdom* also speaks: θεός, δικαιοσύνη and χάρις. But the configuration and usage of the words are off. The enactment of God's righteousness, in *Wisdom*, entails judgement for the sinner and grace for the righteous. But Paul's 'good news' proclaims a revelation of divine righteousness that is grace for the sinner. In Romans, then, grace is not, as it is in *Wisdom* (and most of Graeco-Roman society and Jewish theology), an unearned yet fitting gift given to a worthy recipient. Grace, in Romans, is the incongruous gift God gives at the site of sin and death that creates out of the opposite: righteousness and life (cf. Rom. 4.4–5, 17).

For Paul, however, this definition of grace is not a given; it is, rather, deduced from a specific gift God gave. As Romans 3.24 puts it, sinners are re-created as righteous by receiving the incongruous gift that is 'the redemption that is in Christ Jesus'. This, for Paul, is the event that enacts and establishes the righteousness of God (Rom. 3.21–2, 25–6) and the event that is the grace of God (see, e.g., Rom. 8.32; Gal. 2.21). This suggests that while the language Paul uses is contextual and canonical, his lexicon is

---

⁶¹ R.B. Hays, *The Moral Vision of the New Testament* (San Francisco: Harper, 1996), 389.
⁶² A telling contrast is that whereas *Wisdom* avoids the golden calf episode, Romans 1:23 alludes to it:

> And they exchanged the glory (καὶ ἠλλάξαντο τὴν δόξαν) that was theirs for the likeness (ὁμοίωμα) of a grass-eating ox (Ps. 105:2 LXX)
> And they exchanged the glory (καὶ ἤλλαξαν τὴν δόξαν) of the immortal God for the likeness (ὁμοίωμα) of the image of a mortal man and of birds and four-footed animals and creeping creatures (Rom. 1:23)

> This echo includes Israel in the history of Adamic sin, a link which is further developed in Romans 5:12-14 (and arguably Romans 7). Furthermore, as Simon Gathercole notes, Romans 2:21-24 and 3:9-18 provide what he calls 'phenomenological evidence' and 'scriptural evidence' for Israel's inclusion in the story of sin (*Where is Boasting? Early Jewish Soteriology and Paul's Response in Romans 1-5* [Grand Rapids: Eerdmans, 2002], 2011).

Christological. In Karl Barth's words, 'The Christian message ... recounts a history ... in such a way that it declares a name.' And 'this means that all the concepts and ideas used in this report can derive their significance only from the bearer of this name and from his history ... They can serve only to describe this name – the name of Jesus Christ.'[63] Righteousness and grace, as descriptions of the history of Jesus Christ, announce the event in which God both judges ungodliness and thereby justifies the ungodly in Christ – the 'one who loved me and gave himself for me' (Gal. 2.20), the one who 'died for us while we were sinners' (Rom. 5.8), the one who is 'our righteousness' (1 Cor. 1.30). Paul's Christological definitions of divine righteousness and grace would no doubt cause *Wisdom* to say, as Victor Hugo does in *Les Misérables*, 'he had his own strange way of judging things'. But Paul could respond just as well with Hugo's next words: 'I ... acquired them from the Gospel.'

This suggests that, from the perspective of Paul, the divide between *Wisdom* and Romans runs along a Christological fault-line. But if their points of contrast are Christological, the source of their common ground is, in large part, canonical. As Francis Watson writes, 'Paul and his fellow-Jews read the same texts, yet they read them differently.'[64] The shared language and *loci communes* that characterize the conversation between *Wisdom* and Romans are not coincidences but are the family grammar given by a shared scriptural tradition. But if this similarity makes the conversation possible, it is the different readings that make the conversation interesting. To use Watson's words, what connects *Wisdom* and Romans is a canon – they read the same texts – what differentiates them is a hermeneutic – they read these texts differently.

Wisdom reads the Red Sea crossing as the paradigm of divine justice and rewrites the rest of pentateuchal history according to this criterion: as the righteous were delivered and the ungodly were destroyed, so Adam, Noah and the patriarchs were the worthy whom *Wisdom* rescued, and so righteous Israel was only tested but finally blessed in the wilderness while the ungodly Egyptians where judged by the plagues that fittingly befell them (*Wis.* 10–19). In Romans 4 and 9–11, by contrast, the hermeneutical criterion does not seem to be correspondence but rather incongruous and creative grace. God's gift to Abraham is not a reward but a re-creation of him as righteous (Rom. 4.4-5, 17), nor is the birth of Isaac a rewarding of the righteous but rather a resurrection from the dead (4.19-25). Whereas *Wisdom* identifies the worthiness of Jacob that ensures that his blessing is just (*Wis.* 10.10), Paul insists that in the cases of Isaac and Jacob no genealogical, social or moral worth can account for their calling, which is anchored only in the God who promises and calls without condition: 'not the children of the flesh, but the children of the promise'; 'not by works, but by the one who calls' (Rom. 9.7-13). *Wisdom*, at this point, would want to ask Paul's own question: 'Is there injustice with God?' (Rom. 9.14). Paul, as *Wisdom* would hope, says 'by no means', but he does so on the basis of God's words to Moses in the aftermath of the golden calf: 'I will have mercy on whom I have mercy and compassion on whom I have compassion' (Rom. 9.14-15). This is unexpected mercy at the site of sin, not the

---

[63] Karl Barth *CD* IV/1, 16–17.
[64] F. Watson, *Paul and the Hermeneutics of Faith* (London: T&T Clark, 2004), ix.

predictable pattern of fitting judgement and grace that *Wisdom* calls justice. Paul, I suspect, would grant that this is unpredictable, but precisely so full of promise.

It is the unlooked for and incongruous mercy of God that 'calls those who are not my people my people' and 'her who was not loved, loved' (Rom. 9.25). And it is this unconditioned and creative grace – this pattern of promise that shapes the Christological present and the canonical past – that funds Paul's hope for the future: 'all Israel will be saved' (11.26), not because Israel is righteous and will be rewarded, but because Israel, though stumbling and trespassing (11.11–12), is at the site of God's salvation: though disobedient and dead, God has mercy and makes alive (11.15, 32). In Romans, then, as in *Wisdom*, there is a rhyme scheme and a righteousness that shapes history. For *Wisdom* the pattern is the predictable and just correspondence that orders the cosmos, is exemplified in the Exodus, and so will shape the eschaton. For Paul, the history of Jesus Christ that embodies God's righteousness and is God's gift that justifies the ungodly unveils a calculus of incongruity that means the grace of God is never predictable, but is always a promise: 'He shut up all in disobedience, so that he can have mercy on all' (Rom. 11.32).[65]

The comparison might end here, but not, as Hamann reminds us, the relationship. In his terms, by gathering and interpreting I have done the work of the 'scholar' and the 'philosopher', but the work of the 'poet' – that is, the work of the person – remains. I have played an active role in the dialogue between *Wisdom* and Romans, curating the conversation through selection and interpretation, but Hamann insists that the relationship that research is includes reception, reflection *and response*.[66]

To use Hamann's language, I can 'sympathize' with *Wisdom*. In a context of social oppression and suffering, the memory and promise of God's judgement against the enemy and mercy for the marginalized is hope. The Pauline gospel of God's justification of the ungodly through the incongruous gift of Christ, in this space, sounds 'scandalous and foolish' – it sounds like less good news than today's horrifying headline. And yet, for me, a sermon to righteous sufferers does not quite get to the bone. When I read *Wisdom* and Romans together, Paul's diagnosis reveals too much and resonates too deeply for me to hope that mercy for the righteous means mercy for me. Listening to Romans, I feel more like *Wisdom*'s Egyptians than its Israelites, more like the Pauline ἄνθρωπος, more like Janet in George Eliot's *Janet's Repentance* who knew how 'weak and how wicked' she was and who was left with only one question – my question: 'Is there any comfort – any hope?' Paul's 'word of the cross', though 'scandalous and foolish',

---

[65] For more on these readings of Romans 3.21–26 and Romans 9–11, see my 'Righteousness Revealed: The Death of Christ as the Definition of the Righteousness of God in Romans 3: 21–6', in B. C. Blackwell, J. K. Goodrich and J. Maston (eds), *Paul and the Apocalyptic Imagination* (Minneapolis: Fortress Press, 2016), 219–37 and 'Not the End: The History and Hope of the Unfailing Word in Romans 9–11', in T. D. Still (ed.), *God and Israel: Providence and Purpose in Romans 9–11* (Waco: Baylor University Press, 2017), 141–63.

[66] If such engagement seems out of place as part of what Kierkegaard calls 'a scientific aloofness from life', I would quote some further words from this most famous fan and follower of Hamann: 'the sort of learning that is "indifferent"' is 'an inhuman sort of curiosity' and can be contrasted with 'concern' which implies a 'relationship to life' (*Sickness unto Death* (New York: Doubleday, 1954), 142). For Kierkegaard's admiration of and (imperfect) attempt to follow Hamann, see J. R. Betz, 'Hamann before Kierkegaard: A Systematic Theological Oversight', *Pro Ecclesia* 16.3 (2007): 299–333.

is a sermon not just for sufferers, but a sermon for sufferers and sinners – for Israelites and Egyptians, for me. And so, while I can sympathize with *Wisdom*'s likely conclusion that the Pauline gospel 'turned the world upside down' (Acts 17.6), I can also confess with Paul that the 'good news' of God's incongruous and creative grace in Christ is 'the power of God unto salvation' (Rom. 1.17).

10

Comparing Like with Like?

The New Testament within Its Christian Literary Environment

Francis Watson

As he opens his demonstration that the Son is greater than angels, the author to the Hebrews cites two scriptural texts to make the same point. God never said to any angel, 'You are my son, today I have begotten you', or 'I will be to him a father and he will be to me a son' (Ps. 2.7, 2 Sam. 7.14, cited in Heb. 1.5). Readers are invited to *compare* the two texts and to conclude that these divine utterances refer to the same unique individual. If, however, we are to be convinced that God would never say anything of the sort to angels, we need to overhear the kind of thing God does say to angels: for example, 'Let all the angels of God worship him' (Deut. 32.43, cited in Heb. 1.6). Comparing this citation with the previous two suggests a contrast: God speaks of (or to) a Son quite differently from the way he speaks of angels. The Son is acknowledged as such by the Father, and the role of the angels is to worship him. Through the juxtaposition of similar and contrasting texts, a heavenly hierarchy is constructed.

In both cases, readers are required to compare texts extracted from quite different scriptural locations. Where the emphasis lies on *similarity*, differences will also come to light. One of the two sonship texts takes the form of second person address and announces an act of divine begetting; the other is couched in third-person language and stresses the mutuality of the father/son relationship. The two texts are employed to make a single point, but the second does more than merely repeat the first. Where the emphasis lies on *contrast*, there will also be a common basis for that contrast. Both the Son and the angels are the objects of a divine speech which assigns them their respective places within the heavenly hierarchy. Similarity always also entails difference, just as difference always also entails similarity, and every act of comparison must take both into account. Comparison itself originates simply and naturally out of the juxtaposition of any two texts.

Hebrews' readers and interpreters may extend the comparisons far beyond those the text itself requires of them. Many such comparisons will be intra-canonical. In expounding the Christology of the opening verses, commentators may refer their readers to the Johannine prologue (Jn. 1.1–18), or to the Colossians 'hymn' (Col. 1.15–20), which seem to establish a 'New Testament context' for the Hebrews passage.[1] If the comparisons are pursued, the same dialectic of similarity and difference will come to light in each case. Comparisons with extra-canonical material may also be ventured. Commentators rightly refer to the Wisdom of Solomon, a text excluded from the standard protestant scriptural canon, or to passages in the voluminous works of Philo of Alexandria or from the Qumran literature. The intention of such comparative work is to identify the sources or antecedents of the Christology of Hebrews 1, a primarily historical operation in contrast to the more theologically oriented focus on a so-called 'high Christology'. In practice these intra- and extra-canonical comparisons complement one another, and a single footnote may give succinct expression to both.

Intra-canonical comparison is already practised within the Epistle to the Hebrews, and it remains an indispensable and taken-for-granted interpretative tool. Extra-canonical comparison is more characteristic of the modern scholarly tradition, which rightly argues that texts that became canonical remain profoundly embedded in the general and specific historical contexts that gave rise to them. A canonical text may have far closer links to a non-canonical text from a similar time and place than to most of its canonical counterparts. Nevertheless, extra-canonical comparisons as conventionally practised are limited by a boundary almost as sharply defined as the canonical boundary itself. The early Christian movement created a great mass of gospels, epistles, apostolic acts and apocalypses, and many of these texts survive in whole or in part. Attributions to apostles or other revered figures represent a claim to participate in 'canonical space', and the fact that some texts established their claim whereas others did not has more to do with decisions taken over several centuries of use than with qualities inherent to the texts themselves. Yet the discipline of 'New Testament scholarship' acts as though the texts themselves determined their own 'canonical' or 'apocryphal' status.[2] 'Apocryphal' texts are said to be later than and dependent on their canonical counterparts.[3] Thus most of the canonical texts are typically dated no later than 100 CE, while an origin in the second century or later becomes a defining characteristic of the apocryphal.[4] The assumption of a qualitative difference between the first and second centuries is itself the

---

[1] Cf. F. F. Bruce, *The Epistle to the Hebrews* (NICNT, Grand Rapids: Eerdmans, 1964), 4; Paul Ellingworth, *The Epistle to the Hebrews* (NIGTC, Grand Rapids: Eerdmans, 1993), 98.

[2] So Markus Bockmuehl, *Ancient Apocryphal Gospels* (Louisville: WJK, 2017), *passim*. For Bockmuehl, canonical gospels are 'unique and distinctive' (226) whereas non-canonical ones are 'epiphenomenal and supplementary' (29, italics removed). There is no recognition here of the role of readers or reader-communities in determining how (and whether) texts are used.

[3] Thus John P. Meier views the Gospel of Peter as 'a 2d-century pastiche of traditions from the canonical gospels' (*A Marginal Jew: Rethinking the Historical Jesus*, volume 1, ABRL (New York: Doubleday, 1991), 117). The Gospel of Thomas 'took shape as one expression of 2d-century gnostic Christianity' (127), but at the same time it 'fits perfectly into the larger picture of 2d-century Christianity' (131) in its dependence on the canonical gospels. Such texts were 'produced by the pious or wild imaginations of certain 2d-century Christians' (115).

[4] In Bockmuehl's chronology of gospel origins, the synoptic gospels were composed in the years 60–90 CE (*Ancient Apocryphal Gospels*, 7) and were being cited as authoritative 'before *any* of the extant non-canonical gospels were composed' (6, italics original). The idea of a fourfold gospel emerged in the first half of the second century (9) while non-canonical gospels only began to proliferate 'in the later second and third centuries' (25). Little evidence is offered to support this apologetically oriented chronological schema, which serves to establish the absolute distinction between the canonical four and their 'epiphenomenal' (i.e. superfluous or redundant) non-canonical neighbours.

product of the canonical/apocryphal distinction, and most early Christian texts are in any case impossible to date with precision.[5] If dependence on canonical texts were an objective criterion of apocryphal status, Matthew and Luke would be apocryphal in view of their dependence on Mark. Yet New Testament scholarship appears to assume that the twenty-seven books that form its primary object of study somehow selected themselves for inclusion from the very moment of their origin. The New Testament is falsely seen as a first-century collection rather than what it truly is: a selection of relatively early texts that remained under dispute throughout the fourth century and beyond. The practical outcome is that the ties that bind New Testament texts and other early Christian literature are severed, and comparative work that crosses the canonical boundary is marginalized. Extra-canonical comparisons are sought in Jewish or Graeco-Roman texts prior to or contemporary with New Testament texts, but only rarely with the Christian texts that are actually their closest literary neighbours: non-canonical gospels, epistles, apostolic acts and apocalypses.

For a preliminary illustration of this point, we may return to the Epistle to the Hebrews. Any significant commentary on this text is likely to relate the hymn-like Christological statements at its opening to the personified Wisdom of the Wisdom of Solomon, depicted as 'a pure emanation of the glory of the Almighty [τῆς τοῦ παντοκράτορος δόξης] ..., a reflection [ἀπαύγασμα] of eternal light' (Wis. 7.25–6). Similarly in Hebrews Christ is 'a reflection of [God's] glory [ἀπαύγασμα τῆς δόξης ... αὐτοῦ]' (Heb. 1.3).[6] Clearly there is a link between the two passages, and a comparison might seek to show how significant it is. Is this a case of a 'Wisdom Christology', or just a borrowing of terminology?[7] How far does the presentation of Wisdom as a second alongside God provide a fruitful analogy to the pre-existent Christ of Hebrews and other early Christian texts?

This is all well and good, but the commentator's almost obligatory reference to Wisdom 7 is not normally accompanied by comparative material from non-canonical Christian sources. In 1 Clement 36, we read that Christ is

> the reflection [ἀπαύγασμα] of [God's] greatness, being as much greater than the angels as the name he has inherited is superior. For thus it is written: 'The one who makes his angels winds and his servants flames of fire.' About the Son the Lord speaks thus: 'You are my Son, today I have begotten you, ask of me and I will give

---

[5] Thus Richard I. Pervo argues that 'one can better understand Acts as a product of the decade 110–120 than of the decade 80–90' (*Dating Acts: Between the Evangelists and the Apologists*, Santa Rosa, CA: Polebridge Press, 2006, 346). That Luke-Acts may belong to the early 2nd century is also suggested by Steve Mason's convincing demonstration that Luke knew Josephus's *Antiquities* 18–20, completed in 93 CE (*Josephus and the New Testament*, Peabody, MA: Hendrickson, 20032, 251–93).

[6] Cf. Herbert Braun, *An die Hebräer* (HNT, Tübingen: J. C. B. Mohr (Paul Siebeck), 1984), 24; Harold W. Attridge, *Hebrews* (Hermeneia, Philadelphia: Fortress Press, 1989), 42–3; Erich Grässer, *An die Hebräer (Hebr 1–6)* (EKKNT XVII/1, Zurich/Neukirchen-Vluyn: Benziger/Neukirchener, 1990), 60; William L. Lane, *Hebrews 1–8* (WBC 47a, Dallas, TX: Word, 1991), 12–13; Craig R. Koester, *Hebrews* (AB 36, New York, NY: Doubleday, 2001), 179–80; Gareth Lee Cockerill, *The Epistle to the Hebrews* (NICNT, Grand Rapids: Eerdmans, 2012), 94.

[7] According to Lane, 'the functions of Wisdom are in Hebrews assigned to the Son...[The author] simply clothes the Son in the garb of Wisdom' (*Hebrews 1–8*, cxxxix). In contrast, Bruce writes: '[W]hile our author's language is that of Philo and the Book of Wisdom, his meaning goes beyond theirs' (*Hebrews*, 5).

you Gentiles as your inheritance and the ends of the earth as your possession.' And again he says to him, 'Sit at my right hand until I make your enemies a stool for your feet.' Who then are these enemies? Those who are evil and oppose his will.

1 Clem 36.2–4

In this passage the reworking of material drawn from Hebrews 1 is unmistakable.[8] Precisely because the relationship is so close, however, the differences are all the more interesting. Hebrews 1 includes two texts relating to angels, one of which 1 Clement omits, the other of which it highlights. The citation from Psalm 2 is more extensive than in Hebrews, linking Christ's sonship with his universal rule and thus providing a thematic connection with Psalm 110.1, with its reference to the exalted Christ's future triumph over his enemies – here tacitly identified with the rebel faction in the Corinthian church. This sharp focus on Christ's authority over the human sphere is facilitated by the absence of more diverse Christological themes from the Hebrews 1 catena, and by the reduction of references to angels from six to just two. Comparison of the two passages serves to highlight the broad scope of Hebrews 1 and the distinctiveness of its contrast between Christ and angels.

1 Clement is a text that has much in common with Hebrews, and it may stem from a similar milieu.[9] The point of citing it here is that, while the link between Hebrews and this extra-canonical Christian text is much closer and at least as interesting as its link with Wisdom 7, it is rare to find it taken seriously in the exegesis of Hebrews 1.[10] In conventional New Testament scholarship the canonical boundary opens up to the reception of prior comparative material from non-Christian sources, but it remains a significant barrier to free interchange with non-canonical Christian literature.[11]

If the resources of early Christian literature are to be effectively exploited, reading practices are required that focus not just on the individual extra-canonical text but also and above all on its interconnectedness with its literary neighbours. In what follows, the purpose is to introduce three important but relatively unfamiliar early Christian texts, and to indicate briefly how they might each provide a unique vantage-point from which to view their familiar canonical counterparts. The texts selected for this exercise are the Apocalypse of Peter, the Ascension of Isaiah and the First Apocalypse of James.

---

[8] The parallels are set out in Andrew Gregory and Christopher Tuckett (eds), *The Reception of the New Testament in the Apostolic Fathers* (Oxford: Oxford University Press, 2005), 152–3. See also Paul Ellingworth, 'Hebrews and 1 Clement: Literary Dependence or Common Tradition?' *BZ* 23 (1979), 262–9.

[9] Origen reports the view that Clement was actually the author of Hebrews (cited by Eusebius, *HE* vi.25.14).

[10] 1 Clement remains unmentioned amid the mass of comparative material cited by Attridge in connection with Hebrews 1 (*Hebrews*, 35–68), although he does examine the parallel in his discussion of the dating of Hebrews (6–8). Lane can see in the 1 Clement passage no more than 'a patchwork of phrases culled from Heb. 1' (*Hebrews 1–8*, 13).

[11] For an attempt to address this issue within the field of early gospel literature, see Francis Watson and Sarah Parkhouse (eds), *Connecting Gospels: Beyond the Canonical/Non-canonical Divide* (Oxford: Oxford University Press, 2018).

Apocalypse of Peter

This text was provisionally included within the Muratorian canon, the oldest extant New Testament canon list,[12] and it was cited as scripture by Clement of Alexandria and as belonging to 'the inspired writings' by Methodius of Olympus.[13] It is preserved in full only in Ethiopic (Ge'ez). A substantial Greek excerpt from what may be a different recension of this work occurs in the Akhmim codex containing the passion-and-resurrection narrative of the Gospel of Peter.[14] The possibility cannot be ruled out that the Greek apocalyptic fragment actually belongs to the Petrine gospel, with the Apocalypse as its source.[15] In any case, it is the Ethiopic version alone that concerns us here.[16]

The Apocalypse may be divided into three sections. The first takes its cue from the eschatological discourse of Matthew 24; the setting on the Mount of Olives makes the intertextual connection explicit (Apoc. Pet. 1–6). The Petrine author initially rewrites and expands material drawn from Matthew as he reports the disciples' questions and Jesus' response (Apoc. Pet. 1–2), but he moves beyond his Matthean exemplar to describe the general resurrection, the destruction of the world through fire, and the last judgement (3–6). A recognizably Matthean parousia is located within this broad eschatological scenario (Apoc. Pet. 6.1; cf. Mt. 24.30, 25.31). In the second section the Petrine Jesus presents a Dante-esque topography of hell, where different locations are provided for the torments appropriate to various categories of sinner following resurrection and judgement (Apoc. Pet. 7–14). Those who have sinned in the body must be punished in the body, with the punishment directed where possible at the body-part associated with the relevant sin: the tongue, the lips, the eyes, the genitals, female breasts or hair. The damned appeal in vain for mercy, to the satisfaction of the righteous as they are wafted up to their heavenly home by angelic hands. The eschatological discourse concluded, Jesus commissions Peter to preach the gospel throughout the world. The third section is marked by a change of scene: the Mount of Olives as the place of instruction gives way to the 'holy mountain' as the place of Jesus' departure (Apoc. Pet. 15–17). Here it becomes clear in retrospect that a

---

[12] On the probable second- or early third-century origin of the Muratorian canon, see J. Verheyden, 'The Canon Muratori: A Matter of Dispute', in J.-M. Auwers and H. J. de Jonge (eds), *The Biblical Canons* (Leuven: Peeters, 2003), 487–556. A case for a fourth-century dating is made by Geoffrey Hahneman, *The Muratorian Fragment and the Development of the Canon* (Oxford: Oxford University Press, 1992).

[13] Texts in Thomas J. Kraus and Tobias Nicklas (eds), *Das Petrusevangelium und die Petrusapokalypse mit deutscher und englischer Übersetzung* (Berlin: de Gruyter, 2004), 89–92, 94–5.

[14] The secondary character of the Greek fragment is demonstrated by Dennis D. Buchholz, *Your Eyes Will Be Opened: A Study of the Greek (Ethiopic) Apocalypse of Peter* (Atlanta: Scholars Press, 1988), 413–24.

[15] A strong case for attribution to the Gospel of Peter was made by M. R. James, 'A New Text of the Apocalypse of Peter III' (*JTS* 12 [1911], 573–83). 577–82

[16] The Ethiopic Apocalypse of Peter is embedded in a pseudo-Clementine text published by S. Grébaut on the basis of a Paris MS., d'Abbadie 51 (*Revue de l'Orient Chrétien* 15 [1910], 198–214, 307–23, 425–39). Dennis Buchholz provides an edition (with English translation) based on a second MS. photographed in 1968 on an island in Lake Tana by E. Hammerschmidt, noting textual variants from d'Abbadie 51 (*Your Eyes*, 157–244). Translations are provided in standard collections of New Testament apocrypha. My chapter-and-verse references follow Buchholz.

post-resurrection setting is envisaged for the entire work. The Matthean rewriting and expansion resumes at this point, but it is the transfiguration story that provides the template for the Petrine ascension, with an appearance from Moses and Elijah, a voice from heaven acclaiming the beloved son, and a cloud that takes Jesus as well as his forerunners on the first stage of the upward journey.

After a brief prologue, the Apocalypse of Peter opens by expanding and adapting Matthew 24.3 (italics indicate Matthean wording, underlining a probable Matthean allusion from elsewhere):

And when he was seated on the Mount of Olives, his own came to him. And we underline{worshipped}, and we begged him and implored him *each of us alone*, saying, *'Tell (us) [ ] what are the signs of your coming and the end of the world*, so that we may know and understand the time of your coming and instruct those who come after us, to whom we preach the message of your gospel and whom we appoint over your church; so that having heard these things they may give heed to them and understand the time of your coming.

Apoc. Pet. 1.1–3[17]

'Each of us alone' represents an Ethiopic interpretation of the Matthean κατ' ἰδίαν,[18] itself a vestige of the Markan scenario in which the four leading disciples are separated out from the others. 'Worshipped' may be a link to the post-resurrection scene in Matthew 28, where it is said of the eleven disciples that 'seeing him they worshipped – but some doubted' (v. 17).[19] Thus in the Petrine apocalypse Jesus immediately warns his disciples against doubting (Apoc. Pet. 1.4). Most significant is the replacement of the initial Matthean enquiry about the timing of the temple's destruction ('When will these things be?', cf. Mt. 24.2) with a much more emphatic request for information about 'the time of your coming'. There is here no repetition of the Matthean Jesus' claim that 'this generation will not pass away until all these things come to pass' (Mt. 24.35). From the standpoint of the Petrine author, that claim has proved false; presumably Jesus was misunderstood. It is now envisaged that the parousia will take place after the departure of the apostles' generation, and information about its timing is urgently needed so that the disciples can pass it on to their successors.

---

[17] 'Signs' (*ta'āmer*), rather than the singular σημεῖον in Matthew 24.3. The plural is also found in the Old Ge'ez version of Matthew (Mt. 24.3eth-A.), and so should not be seen as a deviation from Matthew (contra Buchholz, *Your Eyes*, 269–70). The singular is restored in the later Ge'ez B-text. See Rochus Zuurmond, *Novum Testamentum Aethiopice, Part III: The Gospel of Matthew* (Aethiopistische Forschungen 55, Wiesbaden: Harrassowitz, 2001), 240, 241. For the identification of the Old Ge'ez or A-text and its differentiation from the later B-text, see R. Zuurmond, *Novum Testamentum Aethiopice, The Synoptic Gospels: General Introduction, Edition of the Gospel of Mark* (Stuttgart: Franz Steiner, 1989), 1.37–75. For the early dating of the MSS. containing the A-text, see Judith S. McKenzie and Francis Watson, *The Garima Gospels: Early Illuminated Gospel Books from Ethiopia* (Oxford: Manar Al-Athar Monographs, 2016), 206–9 and *passim*.

[18] *baba bāḥtitana*, cf. Mt. 24.3eth-A, where κατ' ἰδίαν is rendered as *babāḥtitomu* (Zuurmond, *Matthew*, 240). The 'mistranslation' (Buchholz, *Your Eyes*, 268) appears to stem from the old Ge'ez version of Matthew.

[19] So Buchholz, *Your Eyes*, 268, also citing Mt. 20.20.

So when does the Petrine apocalypse think that the parousia will take place? Following conventional warnings about the many who will come claiming to be the Christ, the figure emerges of a single 'deceiver' who is 'not the Christ' that he claims to be and who will persecute the faithful in Israel:

> And when they reject him he will kill [them] with the sword, and there will be many martyrs ... Enoch and Elijah will be sent to teach them that this is the deceiver who is to come into the world, who will perform signs and wonders so as to deceive. And thus those who die at his hand will be martyrs, and they shall be counted among the good and righteous martyrs who pleased God by their lives.
> Apoc. Pet. 2.10, 12–13

It has been plausibly suggested that the reference here is to Bar Kokhba, the messianic leader of the Jewish revolt of 132–35 CE, whose persecution of Christians is attested by Justin Martyr, a contemporary who originated in the area affected by the revolt.[20] If so, the Petrine author is updating the Matthean apocalypse that related to conditions before and after the first Jewish revolt of 66–70 CE, applying it to parallel events in the 130s in the expectation that the parousia would follow shortly. The author has Jesus communicate this expectation by developing the parabolic saying from Matthew 24.32 (cf. also v. 3): 'And you, *learn from the fig-tree its parables. When it produces* buds *and its branches grow tender*, then it will be the end of the world' (Apoc. Pet. 2.1). In Jesus' interpretation of the parable, the sprouting branches are identified with the martyrs among the people of Israel. Here, incidentally, the Ge'ez wording is particularly close to the oldest accessible Ge'ez text of Matthew, disproving the assumption of a translation from Arabic rather than Greek.[21]

If Eusebius and others had failed in their attempt to keep the Apocalypse of Peter out of the New Testament canon, its disagreements with Matthew would have posed an acute problem of harmonization. In the apocalypse as in the gospel, Jesus is seated on the Mount of Olives and answers the disciples' questions about the end of the world. In the apocalypse, however, Jesus is risen; in the gospel, he has not yet been arrested. There is no indication that the risen Jesus of the apocalypse is repeating and elaborating the teaching of the Matthean Jesus: in the apocalypse the Matthean presentation is replaced rather than supplemented, corrected rather than interpreted. Matthew, after all, has Jesus prophesying wrongly about the date of the parousia (Mt. 24.34). This gospel is employed as a source but not as a normative text to which the later author must defer.

---

[20] So Richard Bauckham, 'The Two Fig-Tree Parables in the Apocalypse of Peter' (*JBL* 104 [1985], 269–87), 285–7; D. Buchholz, *Your Eyes*, 408–12. See Justin, *1Apol*. 31.6: καὶ γὰρ ἐν τῷ νῦν γεγενημένῳ Ἰουδαϊκῷ πολέμῳ Βαρχωχέβας ὁ τῆς Ἰουδαίων ἀποστάσεως ἀρχηγέτης Χριστιανοὺς μόνους εἰς τιμωρίας δεινάς εἰ μὴ ἀρνοῖντο Ἰησοῦν τὸν Χριστὸν καὶ βλασφημοῖεν ἐκέλευεν ἀπάγεσθαι.

[21] (1) 'Its parables' (*'amsālihu*), as in Mt. 24.32eth-A, corrected from the Greek to 'its parable' (*mesālēhu*) in Mt 24.32eth-B. (2) Apoc. Pet. 2.1 and Mt 24.32eth-A read *lamlema 'aṣuqihu/-hā* to render ὁ κλάδος αὐτῆς γένηται ἁπαλός. The reading in Mt 24.32eth-B is quite different (Zuurmond, *Matthew*, 246, 247). There is no reason to suppose a transmission from Greek through Coptic and Arabic to Ge'ez, as asserted by C. Detlef G. Müller (*New Testament Apocrypha, Volume Two: Writings Relating to the Apostles; Apocalypses and Related Subjects*, ed. Wilhelm Schneemelcher, Eng. trans. (Louisville: WJK; Cambridge: James Clarke, 1992), 622).

The issues of canonicity that preoccupied Eusebius will have seemed less pressing to an author convinced that at last the parousia was at hand.

The Ascension of Isaiah

Again preserved in full only in Ge'ez, substantial fragments have survived of the original Greek of this work and of Latin, Coptic and Slavonic translations, demonstrating both a relatively stable text and the popularity of this work across a number of language areas.[22] The Ascension of Isaiah is divided into two halves, the first concerned primarily with the prophet's martyrdom under King Manasseh (1.1–5.16), the second with his earlier visionary ascent through the heavens (6.1–10.6) and his proleptic account of the descent, earthly career, and ascension of Christ (10.7–11.35). A Slavonic and a second Latin version cover only the ascent chapters (6–11). The two halves of the Ascension are unified by a long digression within the martyrdom section in which Isaiah's Christological and eschatological revelations are presented as grounds for the satanic hostility that brought about his death (3.13–4.22), and by a conclusion that refers back to the martyrdom (11.36–43).[23]

It was earlier assumed that this is a composite work in which a pre-Christian Jewish account of Isaiah's martyrdom has been interpolated by Christian additions (1.2b–6a, 13b; 2.9; 3.13–4.22) and supplemented by an originally independent Christian account of the prophet's visionary ascent.[24] This complex and unconvincing analysis stems from a failure to grasp the pivotal role of Chapter 1 in relation to the work as a whole. Towards the end of his life, in the twenty-sixth year of his reign, Hezekiah passes on to his son Manasseh his own testament, dating from his fifteenth regnal year (1.2–5a; cf. Is 36.1 +

---

[22] The various witnesses to the Ascension of Isaiah have been edited with Italian translations by Paulo Bettiolo et al. (*Ascensio Isaiae*, Corpus Christianorum Series Apocryphorum 7, Turnhout: Brepols, 1995). There is broad agreement between the complete Ge'ez text (44–129), a Greek fragment of 2.4–4.4 (136–45), fragments from two Coptic versions (154–87), and the Latin fragments of 2.14–3.13 + 7.1–19 (204–9). This Greek, Coptic and Latin material is dated to the fourth to the sixth centuries, and confirms the basic reliability of the full Ge'ez text attested – as is usual with Ethiopic material – in much later manuscripts.

[23] Jonathan Knight argues convincingly that the martyrdom section is unlikely to be Jewish in view of its downgrading of Moses in relation to the prophets (Asc. Isa. 3.7–9; cf. 3.17, 4.21–2); J. Knight, *Disciples of the Beloved One: The Christology, Social Setting and Theological Content of the Ascension of Isaiah*, JSPSupp 18, 1996, 190–5. This downgrading might be compared with Hebrews and Barnabas.

[24] So R. H. Charles, *The Ascension of Isaiah* (London: A&C Black, 1900), xxxvi–xlv. Charles's source-analysis is accepted (with modifications) by M. A. Knibb in J. H. Charlesworth (ed.), *The Old Testament Pseudepigrapha*, 2 vols (London: Darton, Longman, and Todd), 1985, 2.143, 147–9; and by J. M. T. Barton, in H. F. D. Sparks (ed.), *The Apocryphal Old Testament* (Oxford: Oxford University Press, 1984), 779–81. According to Knibb, '[I]t is obvious that chapters 6–11 are Christian in origin, and that chapters 1–5 ... include a good deal of Jewish material' (147). In reality, there is nothing to suggest a Jewish origin as opposed to a Christian one in the narrative of events leading up to Isaiah's martyrdom; the overtly Christian material in Chapters 1–5 need not be seen as interpolated. Nor is there any reason to suppose that the composition of this text extended over a period of 500 years, from the second century BCE to the fourth century CE (143, 149–50). The separate circulation of Chapters 6–11 demonstrates not that Isaiah's vision of the incarnation, earthly life and ascension of Christ was originally independent but that this section of the two-part work was of more interest to some readers than the account of the prophet's martyrdom.

38.1, 9), together with Isaiah's account of his vision, dating from the twentieth year (1.5b–6a). Isaiah, present along with his son Josab, warns the king that Manasseh will be an apostate from the true faith and that he himself will suffer martyrdom under him by being sawn in two (1.6b–10). Thus, from its initial setting at the end of Hezekiah's reign the narrative points in two directions, ahead to the prophet's martyrdom and back to his earlier vision. Although the account of the visionary ascent follows the account of the martyrdom, within the work's sophisticated chronological scheme it precedes it. Since the ascent section culminates in a vision of the descent of Christ, it is appropriate that the prophet's martyrdom should have been narrated earlier.[25]

If the Ascension of Isaiah is a unity, then the clear allusion to it in Hebrews 11 must be to a prior Christian work, not to a Jewish text of the Second Temple Period. As he draws his catalogue of heroes of faith to a close, the author to the Hebrews tells how

> they were stoned, they were sawn in two, they were killed with the sword, they went about in the skins of sheep or goats, they were in want [ὑστερούμενοι], oppressed, ill-treated (of whom the world was not worthy), wandering in desert places and mountains [ἐπὶ ἐριμείαις πλανώμενοι καὶ ὄρεσιν] and caves and holes in the ground.
>
> Heb. 11.37–8

The primary reference in the latter part of this passage is to the response of Isaiah and his fellow-prophets to the growing evils of Manasseh's reign – following the allusion to Isaiah's death ('sawn in two').[26] In a passage extant in Greek, we read how, leaving Bethlehem, Isaiah

> lived *on a mountain in a desert place* [ἐκάθισεν ἐν τῷ ὄρει ἐν τόπῳ ἐρήμῳ]. And Micah the prophet and the aged Ananias and Joel and Habakkuk, and Josab his son, and many of the faithful who believed in the ascension into heaven [τῶν πιστευόντων εἰς οὐρανοὺς ἀναβῆναι] departed and lived *on the mountain*. They were all clothed in <u>sackcloth</u>, and they were all prophets. <u>They had nothing with them but they were destitute</u> [γυμνοὶ ἦσαν], mourning a great mourning over the error of Israel. <u>And they had nothing to eat</u> except plants gathered *from the mountains*...
>
> Asc. Isa. 2.8b–10[27]

---

[25] A 'narrative-critical' account of the unity of the work complements the fundamental critique of older source analyses by Mauro Pesce ('Presupposti per l'utilizzazione storica dell'Ascensione di Isaia. Formazione e tradizione del testo; genere letterario, cosmologia angelica', in M. Pesce (ed.), *Isaia, il Diletto e la chiesa. Visione ed esegesi profetica cristiano-primitiva nell'Ascensione di Isaia. Atti del Convegno di Roma, 9–10 aprile 1981* (Brescia: Paideia, 1983), 13–76). Pesce's argument is accepted by Knight, *Disciples*, 28–32.

[26] Isaiah's unusual death is known to Justin, for whom it is a type of Christ's division of the people of Israel (*Try.* 120.5); to Tertullian, who knows that Isaiah continued to bear witness while being cut in two (*De Patientia* 14; cf. Asc. Isa. 5.14); to Origen, who refers explicitly to the 'apocryphon' in which the story is told (*Ep. ad Afric.* 9; *In Matt.* x.18); and to the author of the Testimony of Truth, who finds here a Christological allegory (NHC IX 40, 21–41, 4). A later Talmudic version of the legend of Isaiah's death may have been influenced indirectly by the (Christian) Ascension of Isaiah (b. Yeb. 48b; cf. Asc. Isa. 3.8–10). None of these passages suggests the existence of a Jewish tradition or text predating the Ascension of Isaiah (contra Knight, *Disciples*, 34).

[27] Italics indicate verbal links; underlinings, closely related content.

A literary relationship between this and the Hebrews passage seems probable, and it is more likely that Hebrews is dependent on the Ascension than that the author of the Ascension has created a narrative out of a Hebrews passage with few clear links to prior scriptural or para-scriptural material.[28] Given the dependence on Hebrews of 1 Clement, the conventional dating of 1 Clement at the end of the first century results in a dating of Hebrews to the 80s, which would make the Ascension of Isaiah earlier still. The first century dating for 1 Clement is unreliable, however, and an early second century date for the Ascension might still allow it to be the oldest of the three works. It is also older than the Epistula Apostolorum (c. 170 CE), which reproduces its account of the descent of Christ through the heavens to take human form (Ep. Ap. 13.1–14.7; cf. Asc. Isa. 10.7–11.16).[29]

In the second half of the Ascension, Isaiah is taken up through the firmament and seven heavens, guided by an angel, and then descends and resumes his bodily life.[30] The prophet's ascent and descent is a mirror image of the descent and ascent of Christ, and the two descents coincide: Christ's descent through the seven heavens is shadowed and observed by Isaiah as he too descends. Christ is characterized as 'the Beloved' or 'the Elect One', a being of transcendent glory who, along with his Father, is the object of unceasing praise that rises from the angelic inhabitants of the seven heavens. Nevertheless, he is to descend incognito, adopting as a disguise the angelic form appropriate to each of the heavens through which he passes. Now there is no praise. When he reaches the third, second and first heaven, he is compelled to give passwords to angelic gatekeepers in order to be permitted to continue on his downward journey:

> And again I saw when he descended into the third heaven that he made his form like that of the angels of the third heaven. And those who kept the gate of the heaven demanded the password, and the Lord gave it to them so that he should not be recognized. And when they saw him they did not praise him or glorify him, for his form was like their form.
>
> Asc. Isa. 10.23–24

The same is true when Christ arrives at the firmament that divides the sky from the first heaven above. Now he enters the hostile sphere of the prince or god of this world, and still he remains unrecognized. At this point the scene changes, and Isaiah finds himself observing two human individuals: Mary, a virgin of the family of David and her

---

[28] Attridge notes that 'sheepskins and goatskins' may allude to Elijah and Elisha (cf. 3 Kgdms 19.13; 4 Kgdms 2.8, 13, 14: μηλωτή), but suggests that the rest of the passage makes no specific allusion though it is 'particularly applicable to the community addressed' (*Hebrews*, 350–1). A reference to Elijah and Elisha is confirmed by 1 Clement 17.1, where it is said of Elijah, Elisha, Ezekiel, and other prophets that they 'walked in the skins of goat and sheep' (ἐν δέρμασιν αἰγείοις καὶ μήλωταῖς περιεπάτησαν). Hebrews' περιῆλθον ἐν μηλωταῖς καὶ ἐν αἰγείοις δέρμασιν probably adapts the Ascension's σάκκον περιβεβλημένοι so as to incorporate an allusion to Elijah. Thus garments of animal skin are substituted for penitential garments of animal hair.

[29] On the dating of Ep. Ap., see Carl Schmidt, *Gespräche Jesu mit seinen Jüngern: Ein katholisch-apostolisches Sendschreiben des 2. Jahrhunderts* (Leipzig: J. C. Hinrich, 1919; repr. Hildesheim: Georg Olms, 1967), 361–402.

[30] For a useful summary, see Jonathan Knight, *The Ascension of Isaiah* (Sheffield: Sheffield Academic Press, 1995), 66–78.

betrothed, Joseph, also of the family of David. Mary is pregnant, but the child is not born naturally but simply materializes outside her body, to her great astonishment; thus she experiences no labour pains and her womb remains intact. The author here seems to draw on the Matthean birth story (Mt. 1.18–25), but the incognito motif is very much his own: the child's identity and origin remain 'hidden from all the heavens and all the archons and every god of this world' (11.16). When he grows up, his miracles evoke envy among the hostile spiritual powers and they secure his crucifixion; but still he remains unrecognized. Alluding perhaps to this passage, Ignatius writes to the Ephesians: 'And hidden from the archon of this world was the virginity of Mary and her giving birth and the Lord's death: three mysteries of a cry, which were accomplished in the silence of God!' (Ignatius, Eph. 19.1)[31] Only at the ascension is the Lord's true identity and glory revealed and acknowledged both by Satan below the firmament and by the good angels above it. How, they ask, could he have passed us unrecognized when he descended?

The Ascension's elaborate narrative of descent and ascent is also present in compressed form in Paul.[32] In the Philippians hymn, Christ is originally 'in the form of God' (Phil. 2.6). As Isaiah notes, 'his glory surpassed that of all, and his glory was great and wonderful' (Asc. Isa. 9.27). Yet, 'he emptied himself, taking the form of a slave, being found in human likeness' (Phil. 2.7). As he descends through the heavens, the glory gradually fades as he adapts his appearance to progressively less glorious environments – until, on our side of the firmament, the glory disappears entirely as the divine Son appears as a human child. The purpose of the incognito is not so much to show solidarity with humans but rather to destroy the power of the archons. If the archons had been aware of the secret divine wisdom, 'they would not have crucified the Lord of glory' (1 Cor. 2.8). Their error is fatal yet understandable, for divine glory had been temporarily set aside so that the Beloved of God might enter hostile territory and appear on earth disguised as a mere human.[33]

The First Apocalypse of James

According to Paul, the risen Christ 'appeared to James, then to all the apostles' (1 Cor. 15.7). He had previously appeared to Cephas, to the twelve, and then to 'more than five hundred' (vv. 5–6). It has been plausibly suggested that Paul here combines two distinct

---

[31] The link with Asc. Isa. is noted by William R. Schoedel, *Ignatius of Antioch* (Hermeneia, Philadelphia: Fortress, 1985), 89–90.

[32] The point could also be illustrated from John. Comparing Asc. Isa. to Pauline texts does not imply acceptance of Jonathan Knight's claim that the Ascension exemplifies the 'growing use of the New Testament material' characteristic of 'post-apostolic Christianity' (*Disciples*, 275). No 'New Testament' existed when Asc. Isa. was composed, and most of the texts included in the later collection are themselves 'post-apostolic'. The dialectical model I assume here is that of shared traditions – in this case, the tradition of a descent-ascent Christology – articulated in texts, and conversely of texts as impacting the ongoing tradition. Unmediated impact of one text on another (as perhaps in the case of Matthew 1, above) is the exception rather than the rule.

[33] On the relation between the widespread motif of the disguised Christ and so-called 'docetism', see my 'Pauline Reception and the Problem of Docetism', forthcoming. Markus Bockmuehl's rejection of the view that the Christ of Philippians 2 was 'in some aspects ... *unlike* human beings' may be justified theologically, but not exegetically (M. Bockmuehl, *Philippians*, BNTC, London: A&C Black, 1997, 137; italics original).

traditions, in one of which Christ appears first to Cephas, in the other to James. The canonical post-resurrection narratives know nothing of an appearance to James, and only in Luke 24.34 is reference made to an appearance to Cephas ('Simon'). James, indeed, is a relatively marginal figure within the New Testament writings, where there is no trace of the extravagant tradition preserved in the Gospel of Thomas in which Jesus speaks of 'James the Just' as his successor and claims that 'heaven and earth came into being for his sake' (Gos. Thom. 12). James is known to Paul and to Josephus simply as the brother of Jesus (Gal. 1.19; *Ant.* xx.200), but the epithet 'the Just' (ὁ δίκαιος) refers to him without reference to Jesus and in recognition of his outstanding piety, and in particular his devotion to prayer. Writing in the mid-second century, Hegesippus reports that James 'was in the habit of entering the temple alone, and was frequently found on his knees begging forgiveness for the people, so that his knees became hard as those of a camel' (Eusebius, *HE* ii.23.6). In Hegesippus's version of the James legend, James is put to death when he publicly acknowledges Jesus as the Christ. He is thrown down from the pinnacle of the temple, and, after surviving the fall, he is stoned before finally being despatched with a blow from a fuller's club (*HE* ii.23.8–18). As he is being stoned, he prays: 'I beg you, Lord God our Father, forgive them, for they know not what they do' (*HE* ii.23.16).

The same prayer concludes an account of the death of James in the First Apocalypse of James, a text that survives in part in Nag Hammadi Codex V and in more complete form in Codex Tchacos, which also contains the Gospel of Judas and two other works.[34] In the Apocalypse there is no fall from the temple or fuller's club. James is put to death by stoning, as in Josephus's presumably accurate report (*Ant.* xx.200; CT 30, 6–26, NHC V 43, 7–44, 8).[35] In this text as in Hegesippus, James is known as 'James the Just' (CT 18, 19–20, NHC V 32, 1–3; *HE* ii.23.4,7) and his death is occasioned by his acknowledgement of Jesus. In the Apocalypse, however, that acknowledgement occurs not at the scene of his martyrdom but in his post-resurrection encounter with Jesus. And the acknowledgement offends not only scribes and Pharisees, as in Hegesippus, but also the deity they serve. James is known as 'the Just' because of his devotion to the just God. In acknowledging the risen Lord, James is liberated from his allegiance to this deity as he recognizes that Jesus is from a divine realm far transcending that of the God of the Jews.

The First Apocalypse of James consists in a two-part dialogue between James and Jesus set on a mountain immediately before and after Jesus' passion. As he awaits Jesus' promised return, James is instructing his own loyal disciples in the practice of piety:

> And Jesus went, he accomplished what was necessary for him. And James heard of his sufferings and he was greatly grieved. And he waited for his coming. (In this alone did he find comfort, in waiting for his coming.) And two days passed, and

---

[34] Texts and German translations in Johanna Brankaer and Hans-Gebhard Bethke, *Codex Tchacos: Texte und Analyse* (TU 161, Berlin & New York: de Gruyter, 2007), 88–129. Lack of access to the Codex Tchacos text impairs Judith Hartenstein's account of 1ApocJas in her impotant monograph on dialogue gospels, *Die zweite Lehre: Erscheinungen des Auferstandenen als Rahmenerzählungen Frühchristlicher Dialoge* (TU 146, Berlin: Akademie Verlag, 2000), 189–214.

[35] In Nag Hammadi Codex V the First Apocalypse is followed by a Second Apocalypse of James, where James survives being thrown from the pinnacle of the temple, dragged along the ground with a stone on his abdomen, and trampled underfoot. He is then made to stand in the hole he has dug himself, and is stoned to death with his arms outstretched in prayer (NHC V 61,12–62,11).

behold, James was ministering on the mountain called Galgelam, where he remained another day with his disciples, who heard him gladly. And they found comfort in him, for they said, 'This is the Second Teacher'. And behold, they dispersed, and James remained alone and prayed much, as was his custom.

CT 16, 26–17, 19; cf. NHC V 30, 11–31, 1[36]

James is 'the Second Teacher' as a replacement for the departed Jesus, whom James himself addresses as 'Rabbi'. James's disciples are content with their new instructor, but for James himself there is an unresolved tension between his teaching role and his longing for Jesus' return to impart the promised knowledge of redemption. When his disciples depart, James turns to the activity for which he is justly celebrated: he engages in prolonged prayer.

As he did so, Jesus suddenly appeared to him, and he ceased praying and began to embrace him, saying, 'Rabbi, I was separated from you. I heard what you endured and I grieved greatly – you know my compassion! This is why I did not want to be with you, so that I might not see this people, who will be condemned, for the things they did are abominable to think of!'

CT 17, 19–18, 4; cf. NHC V 31, 2–14[37]

James' immediate concern is to explain why he had absented himself from the site of Jesus' sufferings: he could not bear to see his own people committing such an appalling sin. Jesus makes light of the matter, however, and quite unexpectedly finds crucial significance in the fact that James stopped praying in order to embrace him:

'James, do not be concerned about the people or myself! ... Take heed to yourself, for the just god is angry, for you were his servant, which is why you received the name "James the Just". See, already you have been freed! You know me and you know yourself, and you abandoned the prayer the just god required, and so you have embraced me and kissed me. Truly I say to you, he has directed his fury against you and his wrath; but this too must take place.'

CT 18, 4–6, 16–19, 6; cf. NHC V 31, 14–18, 31, 29–32, 12[38]

It seems that the instinctive act of ceasing prayer in order to embrace the returning Jesus is profoundly significant, representing nothing less than the abandonment of the Jewish deity James has served so faithfully. The anger of the slighted deity at the loss of a valuable slave is only to be expected. Thus,

James was afraid, and he wept and grieved greatly. And the two of them sat down on a rock. Jesus said, 'James, it is necessary for you to undergo these things, but do not grieve! The weak flesh will receive what is determined for it, but as for you, do

[36] Commentary on this passage in Brankaer and Bethge, *Codex Tchacos*, 203–9.
[37] Commentary on this passage in Brankaer and Bethge, *Codex Tchacos*, 209–11.
[38] Commentary on this passage in Brankaer and Bethge, *Codex Tchacos*, 211–16.

not be afraid and fear nothing!' When James heard these things, he wiped away his tears and was greatly relieved of the grief that was in him.

CT 19, 6–21; cf. NHC V 32, 13–28[39]

Comforted by Jesus, James is now reconciled to the fate that awaits him. His martyrdom will be instigated by the just deity after whom he is named 'the Just', but James is not to fear: for James as for Jesus himself, his death is his victory and his redemption.

The First Apocalypse of James appears to date from the mid-second century, for it shows an awareness of the second Jewish revolt[40] and is quoted by Irenaeus.[41] The pre-Pauline tradition that the risen Lord appeared to James and then to all the disciples is clearly known to the author, for after speaking at length with James it is briefly reported that Jesus went and 'reprimanded the twelve for the unbelief in their heart' (CT 29, 18–20, cf. NHC V 42, 21–23). Like the Hegesippus James legend and the saying preserved in *Gos. Thom.* 12, this text bears witness to the central significance attributed by some early Christian traditions to a figure who is marginal to the writings of the New Testament, with their heavily Pauline orientation.[42] The existence of these James traditions make it impossible to assume that the New Testament collection adequately represents the Christianity of the so-called 'apostolic age'.

The aim of these three case studies has been to demonstrate an obvious yet widely overlooked methodological point: that our understanding of the New Testament texts is enhanced if they are read not just in relation to one another or to prior Jewish or Graeco-Roman materials but within their primary Christian literary environment. Each of the three comparative exercises – juxtaposing the Apocalypse of Peter with the Matthean eschatological discourse, the Ascension of Isaiah with the Pauline Christology of descent and ascent, and the First Apocalypse of James with the pre-Pauline tradition of James as witness to the resurrection – has potential for considerable further development. Yet enough has hopefully been said to demonstrate the methodological point at issue. This comparative approach is justified both by its results and by the historical realities of canon formation. It makes no sense for a historical discipline concerned with Christian origins to concern itself so exclusively with an anthology of twenty-seven early Christian texts that reached something like its present form only in the fourth to fifth centuries, while neglecting the many related texts that the anthology passed over. Early Christian reading practices were rather different. To judge from the mass of extant non-canonical material, there were many who read and valued texts on both sides of the canonical boundary, in spite of episcopal disapproval.

---

[39] Commentary on this passage in Brankaer and Bethge, *Codex Tchacos*, 216–17.
[40] Jesus predicts three wars affecting Jerusalem over several generations (CT 23, 15–19, NHC V 36, 17–19; CT 24, 10–11; CT 25, 1–2). The first war takes place immediately after James' death.
[41] There are verbal correspondences between CT 20, 12–22, 23 (cf. NHC V 33, 16–35, 25) and Irenaeus, *AH* i.21.5. In the Tchacos and Nag Hammadi version, James is receiving instruction from Jesus about post mortem responses to interrogation by the archons; in Irenaeus, the instruction occurs in the general context of the last rites. The correspondences between the Coptic versions and Irenaeus's Latin are so extensive and so close that a direct literary relationship is virtually certain.
[42] James' significance is, however, conceded by Acts. See Richard Bauckham, 'James and the Jerusalem Church', in *The Book of Acts in its First Century Setting, Volume 4: Palestinian Setting* (Grand Rapids: Eerdmans; Exeter: Paternoster, 1995), 415–80.

11

Resemblance and Relation

Comparing the Gospels of Mark, John and Thomas

Simon Gathercole

Introduction

The purpose of this chapter is to compare the Gospels of Mark, John and Thomas, and in so doing to discuss two distinct kinds of comparison. These two kinds of comparison have different goals, namely the identification of 'resemblance' and the identification of 'relation'. This chapter is a fragment of a larger argument to be published in monograph form, which will be a broader comparison of early Christian Gospels including all the canonical Gospels and seven of the most important non-canonical works. There is value in comparing Mark, John and Thomas, however, because a number of scholars have sought to argue for commonalities between Thomas and John, often with the claim that they have more in common with each other than they do with the Synoptics. Hence Mark is included here in this chapter as an example of a Synoptic Gospel.

The line of argument will involve several stages. The first three points are broadly methodological. First, an initial section will attempt to define the terms 'resemblance' and 'relation' and the distinction between them. After this, previous claims of John's relation or resemblance to Thomas will be examined, from which certain features will emerge as important criteria for (significant) resemblance and relation, namely *distinctiveness* and *saliency*. Third, some of the goals which comparison seeks to identify will be explored, with a focus on a neglected result of comparison, namely the identification of absences. The fourth section aims to provide two parallel case studies for the process of relating early Christian Gospels to movements or groups, namely classifying certain Gospels as 'Gnostic' or 'Valentinian'. The final section will examine Mark, John and Thomas for their relations.

The resemblance/relation distinction

A central concern of this chapter is to clarify the distinction between 'resemblance' and 'relation'. The former, resemblance, is something which is commonly sought in comparisons, and depends on the identification of similar features in two or more comparanda. As we will see in some of the examples later, however, the identification of resemblances does not entail a *relation* or proximity: *resemblance* is not a *relation*.[1]

We can illustrate this from the phenomena of the Synoptic Gospels. Most New Testament scholars have at times observed: 'Matthew, Mark and Luke are very similar!' To reach this preliminary observation, comparison has consciously or unconsciously been in operation. The naïve assertion that 'Matthew, Mark and Luke are very similar' is elliptical and incomplete, however.[2] Two further terms are needed. The first requirement is a comparator, which is the 'with respect to' in the comparison, because the Synoptics are not identical. The second requirement is for additional comparanda from which the Synoptics differ: if the Synoptics were the only texts that had ever been written, no one would have been particularly impressed by their similarity.[3] In its full meaningful form, then, our proposition about the Synoptic Gospels would be:

Matthew, Mark and Luke are much more similar to one another,
[COMPARATOR:] with respect to verbal agreement and order,
[ADDED COMPARANDUM:] than any is to John.

Or:

Matthew, Mark and Luke are much more similar to one another,
[COMPARATOR:] with respect to verbal agreement and order,
[ADDED COMPARANDA:] than ancient biographies usually are to one another.[4]

Having introduced the additional comparanda of John and other ancient biographies, as well as clear comparators with respect to which the comparison is undertaken, we are no longer talking naïvely about vague similarity, but in terms of a meaningful comparative resemblance of the Synoptics. In the same way, we might talk about the resemblance between the daylight sky and the folder in front of me with respect to blueness over against other folders. Resemblance is the possession of shared attributes, or properties in common.

So far we have been looking merely at resemblances. However, there is also usually a further unstated implication in the naïve expression 'Matthew, Mark and Luke are very similar', viz. 'Matthew, Mark and Luke are *so* similar to one another *that the*

---

[1] Panayot Butchvarov, *Resemblance and Identity: An Examination of the Problem of Universals* (Bloomington: Indiana University Press, 1966), 133, has shown this in the cognate sphere of the philosophical problem of identity.
[2] Dan J. O'Connor, 'On Resemblance', *Proceedings of the Aristotelian Society* NS 46 (1945–1946), 47–76 (53); Butchvarov, *Resemblance and Identity*, 114–15. The point is also emphasized in Jonathan Z. Smith, *Drudgery Divine: On the Comparison of Early Christianities and the Religions of Late Antiquity* (Chicago: University of Chicago Press, 1990), 33, 99.
[3] Cf. O'Connor, 'On Resemblance', 54 n. 1: 'If our visual field had never contained anything but two shades of blue, we should never come to make the judgment "B(lue)1 resembles B(lue)2". A third term is necessary even as a stimulus to the judgment of similarity.'
[4] This is of course a more complex comparandum than in the former case, because in this case the 'added comparanda' category contains a comparison of its own (that of ancient biographies with each other).

similarity cannot be coincidental.' This consecutive clause, by ruling out coincidence, is what implies a 'relation', and thereby generates the Synoptic Problem: *how did this similarity arise*? On almost any scholarly solution there is a 'real relation' among the Synoptics. It is *not only* that, relative to John, for example, Mark and Matthew and Luke have more verbatim overlap and agreement of order. Simply to observe that Mark and Matthew are closer to each other than each is to John does not in itself entail a relation between Mark and Matthew. To posit *real relations*, or genealogy, is to go considerably beyond observing resemblances, and involves different scholarly procedures.

In short, then, resemblance depends on merely sharing certain properties, like the blue folder in front of me and blue sky above me, although scholars of course tend to be more interested in more complex resemblances involving multiple shared properties. Showing a multiplicity of shared properties between X and Y may show that they are, relatively speaking, more similar to one another than they are to Z. But even then, X and Y are only closer to each other *in respect of properties P^1 and P^2 etc*. If one used a different comparator, Y and Z may be closest to each other.

Relation, by comparison, involves genealogy. This is not necessarily a genealogy of a direct kind, such as parental or grandparental (etc.) ancestry, but can include sibling or cousin (etc.) relations. Mark has a parental relation to Matthew and Luke, but Matthew and Luke are on most accounts also related: on the Farrer hypothesis, both parentally and as siblings; on the two-source hypothesis, as mere siblings. Alternatively, the relation between two works need not be one of literary dependence, but can be the result of their origins in a particular author or group. *Twelfth Night* and *Hamlet*, for example, do not obviously have a direct literary relation *to each other*, but are siblings because they were both generated by Shakespeare. Or again, the *Psalms of Solomon* and *1QS* both count as 'Jewish' because of a similar historical origin. Relation, then, is not just resemblance with the volume turned up, but – unlike resemblance – depends on related historical origins, whether quite specific (Shakespeare, 1599–1600) or quite general (Jewish, second to first century BCE).

Previous claims of John's relation or resemblance to Thomas

A number of scholars have made cases for, or have observed in passing, John's similarities to Thomas.[5] Gregory Riley, for example, has remarked: 'the two Gospels stand in a somewhat similar and parallel position relative to the traditions preserved in the Synoptics. Each expresses its own distinctive and at times opposing theology in part by manipulating this common inheritance, yet the two are much closer to each other in spirit than either is to the Synoptics.'[6] Thomas and John, then, have a *relation*, in that they share knowledge of 'the traditions preserved in the Synoptics', traditions which constitute a 'common inheritance' – an image which already suggests a sibling relation. They are also said to *resemble* one another more than they do the Synoptics,

---

[5] On the whole question, see now Stephan Witetschek, *Thomas und Johannes - Johannes und Thomas: Das Verhältnis der Logien des Thomasevangeliums zum Johannesevangelium* (Freiburg im Breisgau: Herder, 2015).
[6] Gregory J. Riley, *Resurrection Reconsidered* (Minneapolis: Fortress, 1995), 3.

and this claim is fair enough as long as one proceeds to identify the particular way in which this comparison is made: in this context the key phrase is similarity 'in spirit'. This is not a very useful comparator, however, and in the rest of this section we will explore more productive criteria for relation and resemblance.

Davies and the problem of saliency

Stevan Davies has argued that a central feature of the Gospel of Thomas is the text's identification of Jesus with Wisdom.[7] This theme which he sees as crucial in the Gospel of Thomas is also found, Davies contends, in a strong form in John's Gospel. In the latter, this theme is 'of central significance', in contrast to Matthew's 'rather casual' interest in the subject.[8] For Davies, this is not coincidental, but is a result of historical connections, one older and one more immediate. In the former case, their ancestral roots mean that 'the Christology of Thomas shares with that of John a place of origin in the Jewish Wisdom tradition'.[9] As far as the latter, more immediate connection is concerned, the relation is spelled out in Davies' suspicion that 'the *Gospel of Thomas* is a sayings collection from an early stage of the Johannine communities', and that one might 'see in the later Johannine writings a developed and transformed version of Thomasine Christianity'.[10]

Here, then, we have a particular kind of argument for the relative resemblance of John, Thomas and the Synoptics. Indeed, the resemblance is taken to be so striking that a relation should be posited. The argument hinges on the *saliency* of the theme of Wisdom in John and Thomas on the one hand, and its relative lack of importance in Matthew. The saliency of this theme might be questioned, however. For example, while σοφία features in the Synoptic Gospels, Acts, Romans, 1–2 Corinthians, Ephesians, Colossians, James, 2 Peter and Revelation, it never appears in John's Gospel or the Johannine epistles. While the concordance is not an infallible guide to theology, one might have expected some clear reference to the term if the identification of Jesus with Wisdom were of central significance to John. Similarly, in the case of Thomas, we might have expected something more than one (probably disapproving) description of Jesus as 'wise' if he were in Thomas 'fully identified with Wisdom incarnate'.[11] The predication of Jesus by the disciple Matthew as a 'wise philosopher' in *Gos. Thom.* 13 is almost certainly implied to be wrong.[12] In consequence, the argument from the shared saliency of Wisdom in both John and Thomas is rather exposed.[13] As a criterion for relation in principle, however, saliency is of undoubted importance.

---

[7] Stevan Davies, *The Gospel of Thomas and Christian Wisdom* (Oregon House: Bardic Press, 2005), 81–99.
[8] Davies, *The Gospel of Thomas and Christian Wisdom*, 106.
[9] Davies, *The Gospel of Thomas and Christian Wisdom*, 116.
[10] Davies, *The Gospel of Thomas and Christian Wisdom*, 116.
[11] Davies, *The Gospel of Thomas and Christian Wisdom*, 96.
[12] See Simon Gathercole, *The Gospel of Thomas: Introduction, Translation and Commentary* (Leiden: Brill, 2014), 259–66.
[13] By contrast, for most scholars, Wisdom is much more of a theme in Matthew's Gospel, with five passages commonly advanced (rightly or wrongly) as evidence for a Wisdom Christology (Matt. 11.19; 11.25–7; 11.28–30; 23.34–6; 23.37–9). For a survey of scholarship, see Simon Gathercole, *The Preexistent Son: Recovering the Christologies of Matthew, Mark and Luke* (Grand Rapids: Eerdmans, 2006), 193–209.

Dunderberg and the problem of distinctiveness

Dunderberg, citing the remark of Riley quoted earlier, argues for a different kind of resemblance between John and Thomas: 'Differences in literary style aside, John and *Thomas* do share many ideas that make their symbolic worlds look quite similar to each other. John and *Thomas* are, as Riley has correctly pointed out, "much closer to each other in spirit than either is to the Synoptics".'[14]

Dunderberg's focus, then, is not to argue for a relation between John and Thomas, or at least not for a proximate relation.[15] He nevertheless considers that the question of relation is a subject worth investigating: 'The similarities between Thomas and John listed above are abundant enough to raise a question about their mutual relationship.'[16] As it turns out, his book concludes the opposite. He does argue for resemblance, however, specifically as we have seen above in 'their symbolic worlds'.

Dunderberg identifies twelve ideas in common between John and Thomas.[17] In short summary, these are: (§1) Jesus as pre-existent co-creator, (§2) incarnation vs human ignorance, (§3) immortality resulting from Jesus' words, (§4) disciples as elect, (§5) anticipated persecution, (§6) negativity towards 'the world', (§7) light–dark dualism, (§8) realized eschatology, (§9) potential distraction by Scripture, (§10) misunderstanding by 'the Jews', (§11) attitudes to Jewish customs, and (§12) claim to authorship by a disciple. In addition to specifying the overall field of resemblance ('symbolic worlds'), then, Dunderberg provides a polythetic account with numerous individual similarities (§§1–12). Some of these themes are genuinely distinctive similarities (e.g. §§3, 6, 10, 12).

Others, however, are less distinctive. Some are features common to John and Thomas but also to the Synoptics. The idea (§4) that 'discipleship is based upon election' also has a strong presence in the Synoptic Gospels.[18] Similarly, the thought (§5) that 'both gospels anticipate persecution, either spiritual or physical, of Jesus' followers (*Gos. Thom.* 68–69; John 16:1–4)' is probably just as widely attested in the Synoptics as in John, even if one adds Jn 9.22 and 12.42.[19] Additionally, the idea (§7) that 'Both gospels bear witness to a dualism of light and dark (*Gos. Thom.* 24; 61; John 1:5; 8:12; 9:4; 11:9–10; 12:35)' is superficially attractive, until one notes that of the two places in Thomas with the antithesis, one is clearly (and probably both are) inspired by *Synoptic* formulations.[20]

---

[14] Ismo Dunderberg, *Beloved Disciple in Conflict? Revisiting the Gospels of John and Thomas* (Oxford: Oxford University Press, 2006), 6, quoting Riley, *Resurrection Reconsidered*, 3.

[15] In this he is in disagreement with those who see a polemical relationship between John and Thomas, e.g. A. D. DeConick, *Voices of the Mystics: Early Christian Discourse in the Gospels of John and Thomas and Other Ancient Christian Literature* (JSNTSuppS; Sheffield: Sheffield Academic Press, 2001) and Elaine Pagels, *Beyond Belief: The Secret Gospel of Thomas* (New York: Random House, 2003).

[16] Dunderberg, *Beloved Disciple in Conflict*, 8.

[17] Ibid., 6–8.

[18] Dunderberg cites *Gos. Thom.* 49–50; Jn 6.70; 13.18; 15.16, 19. Compared to four references in John, the motif occurs in Matt. x5; Mk x3; Lk. x2. Cf. Mk 13.20/ Matt. 24.22; Mk 13.22/Matt. 24.24; Mk 13.27/Matt. 24.31; Matt. 11.27/Lk. 10.22; Matt. 22.14; Lk. 18.7.

[19] Mk x5; Matt. x8; Lk. x7 (though numbers will depend partly on how the sayings are counted). Markan material: Mk 4.17/ Matt. 13.21; Mk 10.30; Mk 13.9/ Matt. 10.17/ Lk. 21.12; Mk 13.11/ Matt. 10.19–20/ Lk. 21.14; Mk 13.13/ Lk. 21.17. Double tradition: Matt. 10.16/ Lk. 10.3; Matt. 5.10–12/ Lk. 6.22; Single tradition: Matt. 5.44; 10.23; 24.9; Lk. 10.16; 11.49.

[20] Gathercole, *Gospel of Thomas*, 316. *Gos. Thom.* 24.3 is clearly more indebted to Matt. 6.22–23//Lk. 11.34–36 than to, say, Jn 11.9–10. Cf. esp. 24.3b ('If he does not give light, he is darkness') with Matt. 6.23 ('If then the light within you is darkness, how great is that darkness!') or Lk 11.34c ('But when

In some cases the lack of distinctiveness arises because the categories are constructed along too general lines. For example, in the claim that in John and Thomas 'attitudes towards Jewish customs are similar' (§11), 'Jewish customs' is a very broad category. Dunderberg focuses on the external perspective perhaps implied in Jesus' references to 'your law' in John, comparing this to Thomas's criticism of circumcision. These two elements are thus brought together (though not included are Jewish festivals, which might change the picture). Given the breadth of the formulation 'attitudes towards Jewish customs', the Synoptics could easily be described as evincing the same attitude as well, in particular in passages such as Mark 7.1–23/Matthew 15.1–20 or Matthew 23/Luke 11.29–54. Again, given the level of generality, it is not obvious what would prevent the inclusion of letters of Paul such as Galatians or Philippians. Or again (§9), a high level of generality is evident in the claim that both Gospels 'affirm that studying the scriptures may distract one from recognizing Jesus (*Gos. Thom.* 52; John 5:39)', reflecting 'similar attitudes towards the Hebrew Bible'. This could apply to virtually any writing about Christian themes, from 2 Corinthians 3 to *Barchester Towers*. Antonio's quip, 'The devil can cite Scripture for his purpose', is a truism.[21] Importantly, there is a significant difference between John and Thomas on this point: For John 5.46, the Jews reject Jesus *despite* their study of Scripture ('if you believed Moses . . .'), whereas for *Gos. Thom.* 52 distraction from the living one comes *because of* attention to Scripture: speaking of Scripture as testifying to Jesus is actually to neglect him.

Of course, a degree of generalization is by definition always going to be the case in any comparison: 'A comparison is a disciplined exaggeration in the service of knowledge. It lifts out and strongly marks certain features within difference as being of possible intellectual significance, expressed in the rhetoric of their being "like" in some stipulated fashion.'[22] The question, then, is whether in the process of generalizing, the distinctiveness becomes too blunt to be a useful tool and the result is no longer a very distinctive similarity.

Saliency and distinctiveness as criteria for significant similarity

The point here is not to single out Davies and Dunderberg for criticism, but to use their studies as avenues for exploring resemblance and relation. Two important criteria have emerged here, namely saliency and distinctiveness. These are not criteria which need to be used in all comparisons, but they are necessary in identifying significant resemblance and relation.

'Distinctiveness' should be distinguished from trying to find a common feature 'unique' to two works, as in various ways 'uniqueness' is a problematic category.[23] Distinctiveness is

---

they are unhealthy, your body also is full of darkness.') In the Greek text of *Gos. Thom.* 24.3, [φ]ωτ'ε'ινῷ is legible: cf. φωτεινόν in Matt. 6.22 and Lk. 11.34–6 *tris*.) Similarly, though to a lesser extent, *Gos. Thom.* 61.5 ('When he becomes equal, he will be filled with light, but when he becomes divided, he will be filled with darkness') is structurally similar to the pairs of conditional clauses ('If X, then light; if Y, then dark') about being light and being dark in those Synoptic passages.

[21] *The Merchant of Venice* 1.iii.96.
[22] Smith, *Drudgery Divine*, 52.
[23] Smith, *Drudgery Divine*, is in part a polemic against the notion of 'uniqueness', noting that in a sense everything is unique; Sanders objects to use of the term on the grounds that it implies a claim to omniscience. See, e.g., E. P. Sanders, *The Question of Uniqueness in the Teaching of Jesus*. The Ethel M. Wood Lecture, 15 February 1990 (London: University of London, 1990), 6.

important in establishing resemblance, however, because if one identifies too many similarities which are also widely dispersed across other works, the danger is that the similarities end up being trivial. Put positively, it is important that comparanda possess *distinctive* features in common if the scholar is seeking significant resemblance between two works. It is additionally essential that certain other works are adduced as a contrasting backdrop (as Dunderberg introduces the Synoptics) to show that the comparanda are distinctive vis-à-vis another body of literature. This criterion of distinctiveness is equally necessary – though not sufficient – in the construction of a relation.

In identifying similarities among early Christian Gospels, saliency is also a necessary criterion for resemblance, in order to avoid the identification of merely trivial similarities, such as noting that the Gospel of Thomas and the Gospel of Truth both refer to Jesus as 'Son', or that the two Gospels were both written in Greek.[24] If one is looking for resemblance, the criterion of saliency ensures that comparators will be themes which are of considerable significance in the two works. Of course, a different kind of comparison might, for good reason, choose not to use themes of importance in the works themselves: a feminist exegesis might compare two works even if neither thematizes gender, for example. But if one is looking for resemblance or relation, comparison will employ comparators which are salient for the works themselves.

We can relate this to the proposition about the Synoptics noted earlier, viz. that 'Matthew, Mark and Luke are much more similar to one another, with respect to verbal agreement and order, than any is to John'. We can plug in 'salience' and 'distinctiveness' as follows:

Matthew, Mark and Luke are much more similar to one another,
[*SALIENT* COMPARATOR:] with respect to verbal agreement and order,
[ADDED COMPARANDUM*:] than any is to John.
[* Included to illustrate the Synoptics' distinctiveness.]

The point here, then, is that Matthew, Mark and Luke have significant resemblance in their order and wording. This is not a trivial point of comparison but a *salient* one, and any New Testament scholar who speaks of 'Synoptic Gospels' recognizes this. Moreover, there happen not to be other works with such a strong degree of resemblance on this point: they are *distinctive* in this respect. Their resemblance in order and wording is strong, relative to John, which is introduced, in the comparandum above, as a work in other respects very similar to the Synoptics, but on these points rather different. The Synoptics have something which John does not have.

The products of comparison: similarities, differences and absences

Consideration of John as a 'have-not' leads us into an aspect of comparison which is often neglected, namely the identification of absence. This will play an important role

---

[24] On this whole point see Kathryn Pyne Parsons, 'Three Concepts of Clusters', *Philosophy and Phenomenological Research* 33.4 (1973), 514–23 (517).

in the comparison of Mark, John and Thomas at the end of this chapter. We have already seen it in operation: the point of the particular shared similarities between John and Thomas identified by Dunderberg was that they were deemed not to be shared by (i.e. are absent from) the Synoptics. A claim to distinctive similarity relies on at least a degree of absence of the shared feature elsewhere.

As has just been noted, similarity is not the only aspect of comparison. Comparative study needs to be interested both in similarities and in differences. Some versions of the old 'comparative method' have been characterized as only interested in similarity,[25] whereas conversely some postmodern trends resist generalization and the possibility of meaningful resemblance.[26] There is an oft-quoted dictum in theoretical studies of comparative religion that similarities make comparisons possible, while differences make them interesting.[27] This is misleading. Similarities can also be interesting, as Dunderberg's analysis discussed earlier makes clear.

Whether one is more interested in similarity and or in difference is not a result of scholarly necessity but a matter of choice, or even of the scholar's personality. We can probably all think of colleagues who press similarities ('lumpers') and others who stress differences ('splitters'). Emmanuel Le Roy Ladurie divided all historians into truffle hunters, whose snouts are rubbed into the dirt of detail, and parachutists, who survey the terrain from above and see grand patterns etched into the landscape.[28] Or again, one thinks of Isaiah Berlin's division of thinkers into foxes, who attend to particularities, and hedgehogs, who have overarching visions:[29] as the pre-Socratic philosopher Archilochus put it, 'The fox knows many things, but the hedgehog knows one big thing.'[30]

In fact, comparison inevitably requires consideration of both similarity and difference. As Segal has put it, if one is focusing on seeking *similarities*: 'To compare phenomena is necessarily to find differences as well as similarities. Even if one were *seeking* only similarities, one would know that one had found them all only at the point at which no further differences could be converted into similarities.'[31] Conversely, as Segal comments

---

[25] So Jonathan Z. Smith, 'In Comparison a Magic Dwells', in Jonathan Z. Smith, *Imagining Religion: From Babylon to Jonestown* (Chicago: University of Chicago Press, 1982), 19–35 (21), though see the criticisms in Robert A. Segal, 'Classification and Comparison in the Study of Religion: The Work of Jonathan Z. Smith', *JAAR* 73 (2005), 1175–88.

[26] Robert A. Segal, 'In Defense of the Comparative Method', *Numen* 48 (2001), 339–73 (342–3) notes Clifford Geertz in particular as an opponent of generalization.

[27] Fitz John Porter Poole, 'Metaphors and Maps: Towards Comparison in the Anthropology of Religion', *JAAR* 54 (1968), 411–57 (417); William E. Paden, 'Elements of a New Comparativism', *MTSR* 8 (1996), 5–14 (9); Segal, 'Classification and Comparison in the Study of Religion', 1183, quotes Paden critically on this point, rightly rejecting the implication that differences are more interesting. Cf. Wendy Doniger, *The Implied Spider: Politics and Theology in Myth* (New York: Columbia, 2011), 75: 'any discussion of difference must begin from an assumption of sameness', citing Dilthey's comment that 'interpretation would be impossible if expressions of life were completely strange. It would be unnecessary if nothing strange were in them.'

[28] I owe this remark to my colleague James Carleton Paget. Apparently no one now, Ladurie himself having forgotten, knows where or when the illustration was used. See John H. Elliott, *Spain, Europe & the Wider World, 1500–1800* (New Haven: Yale University Press, 2009), xx n. 11.

[29] Isaiah Berlin, *The Hedgehog and the Fox: An Essay on Tolstoy's View of History* (London: Weidenfeld & Nicolson, 1953).

[30] Archilochus, *Frag.* 201: πόλλ' οἶδ' ἀλώπηξ, ἀλλ' ἐχῖνος ἓν μέγα.

[31] Segal, 'In Defense of the Comparative Method', 349–50; cf. also Segal, 'In Defense', 358: 'While the comparative method can be used to find differences as well as similarities, the method itself seeks similarities and finds differences only when the similarities cease.'

elsewhere, if one is focusing on seeking *differences*: 'Differences begin only where similarities end and can therefore be found only by pressing similarities as far as they will go.'[32] Hence the comparative enterprise must attend to both similarity and difference.

A significant part of the identification of differences also lies in observing and explaining *absences*. Several theorists of religion have noted that it is not just the appearance of particular features in religious discourse that can be unexpected, but also the non-appearance of certain elements. Comparison is a key way of identifying such non-appearances. As Wendy Doniger has put it:

> We cannot, to borrow the Zen koan, hear the sound of one hand clapping; we cannot hear sameness. But through the comparative method we can see the blinkers that each culture constructs for its retelling of myths. Comparison makes it possible for us literally to cross-examine cultures, by using a myth from one culture to reveal to us what is *not* in a telling from another culture, to find out the things not 'dreamt of in your philosophy'.[33]

Doniger describes such an absence, following Sherlock Holmes' *The Adventure of Silver Blaze*, as 'the dog that didn't bark', a trope also employed by Jonathan Z. Smith: 'In religious disclosure, the unexpected is not only the surprising occurrence (a burning bush), it may as well be the lack of occurrence of an expected element which, as in the case of Sherlock Holmes, provides a "clue" to which one's thought and attention may be directed.'[34] We can apply this to our cases of Mark, John and Thomas. To focus on points at which Thomas and John are in agreement, then, is in danger not only of fudging similarity (e.g. through a category such as 'realized eschatology'[35]), but also of neglecting aspects which are absent in one work but present or even crucial in the other. It is vital to take into account not only difference, but that extreme kind of difference, i.e. absence, before one comes to any conclusion about a similarity of symbolic worlds.

Case studies of relations and resemblances: Gnostic and Valentinian Gospels

This penultimate section aims to prepare the way for the last, in illustrating how one can talk of relations between or among early Christian Gospels. Real relations can exist

---

[32] Segal, 'Classification and Comparison', 1184.
[33] Doniger, *The Implied Spider*, 36. Cf. Wendy Doniger, *Other Peoples' Myths: The Cave of Echoes* (New York: Macmillan, 1988), 136, in a comparison of the slaughtered Lamb in Christianity and the leonine Hindu shepherd: 'It is easier to understand the role of an animal in one culture if we can see where it does not appear in another, and we can notice the lacuna left by an animal in one culture if we see where it does appear in another. To borrow the Zen koan, we cannot hear the sound of one hand clapping. But through the comparative method we can see the cultural blinkers that each culture constructs for its archetypes. In this way, a look at *their* divine animals makes us see things we never noticed in *our* divine animals – either because in fact those things are not there or because it troubles us to see that they are.'
[34] Jonathan Z. Smith, *Map is Not Territory: Studies in the History of Religions* (Studies in Judaism in Late Antiquity 23; Leiden: Brill, 1978), 301.
[35] Dunderberg, *Beloved Disciple*, 7.

between one Gospel and another, as in the case of the Synoptics noted earlier, or relations can obtain between a Gospel and an identifiable community of people. Furthermore, if two or more works are related to the same community, then those works can be described as having some kind of sibling relation to each other as well. This is not wholly without analogue in New Testament studies, where scholars commonly attribute Paul's epistles to a particular author, and describe Luke and Acts, as siblings, two products of the same person. This is a classification by *relation*, not merely a matter of comparison and relative resemblance. To recap the point made in the first section earlier, one does not conclude that Acts is written by the author of Luke simply because Acts is more like Luke than it is like any of the other Gospels. Conversely, in Pauline studies, to say that the man who wrote the *Hauptbriefe* also wrote Philippians is to claim that no one else in the whole wide world wrote Philippians: it is a positive or absolute claim rather than a comparative one.

Or again, thinking more in terms of groups than individual authors, it is common (rightly or wrongly[36]) to assign both John's Gospel and Epistles to a particular 'community', on the basis of the commonalities in 'vocabulary, idiom, point of view, and worldview'.[37] Here again, it is not just that there are some similarities, but rather that it is thought impossible that these similarities could be produced by two separate groups: the fourth Gospel and the Epistles have a level of agreement, as it were, *contra mundum*.

I want to focus in this section, as most relevant to our task, on how some scholars have connected early Christian Gospels by assigning them to the same 'communities' or 'movements' or 'schools'.

The Valentinian *Gospel of Truth* and *Gospel of Philip*

Einar Thomassen, for example, considers that the Valentinians produced both the *Gospel of Truth* and the *Gospel of Philip*, and it is probably true to say that a good number of scholars would assent to such a view.[38] We can identify the *Gospel of Truth* and the *Gospel of Philip* as Valentinian because there is a pre-existing school from which they emerged.

In the case of the *Gospel of Truth*, we have a testimonium to a Gospel of Truth by Irenaeus, who describes the work as emanating from the school of Valentinus. The manuscripts of the *Gospel of Truth* from Nag Hammadi do not have *subscriptiones* with a title, but the opening words of the work are 'The gospel of truth ...', and opening words can function as titles.[39] Furthermore, the Nag Hammadi text, which in one of the

---

[36] The correctness of this is not the issue here; rather it is that scholars deem it at least a plausible or rational thing to do.
[37] John Painter, 'Johannine Literature: The Gospel and Letters of John', in David C. Aune (ed.), *The Blackwell Companion to the New Testament* (Oxford: Wiley-Blackwell, 2008), 344–72 (344).
[38] Einar Thomassen, *The Spiritual Seed: The 'Church' of the Valentinians* (Leiden: Brill, 2006). Some dispute this, e.g. Hugo Lundhaug, *Images of Rebirth: Cognitive Poetics and Transformational Soteriology in the Gospel of Philip and the Exegesis on the Soul* (Leiden: Brill, 2010), who issues a very helpful warning about the circularity of reading *Philip* as a Valentinian work and therefore discovering it to be one. For earlier discussion, see Einar Thomassen, 'How Valentinian is the Gospel of Philip?', in John D. Turner and Anne McGuire (eds), *The Nag Hammadi Library after Fifty Years: Proceedings of the 1995 Society of Biblical Literature Commemoration* (Leiden: Brill, 1997), 251–79.
[39] See E. Nachmanson, *Der griechische Buchtitel: Einige Beobachtungen* (Darmstadt: Wissenschaftliche Buchgesellschaft, 1969) 37–52, for examples of titles derived from the opening words of works.

manuscripts is well preserved, shares a number of characteristic and even distinctive Valentinian motifs. In terms of literary style, it employs etymology and word-play. Prominent too are theological themes such as the plight of emptiness and deficiency, the solutions to which are the anointing of disciples and the disciple's unification with the 'name' – the name itself being a key theme for Valentinian christology and theology proper.[40] Overall the soteriology is like that of the *Excerpts of Theodotus*.[41] Matter comes about as a result of ignorance, rather than from a perfect, good God or from an evil demiurge such as that of the Gnostic system (on which more later). There are passages which make good sense on the basis of a tripartition of the material, psychic and spiritual. The whole scheme is based on the triunity of protological myth, salvation in history, and ritual, although the *Gospel of Truth* is muted (but not silent) on the last of these. In these respects, while it has its own particularities, the *Gospel of Truth* has a level of agreement with known Valentinian literature that is unlikely to be coincidental.

The *Gospel of Philip* does not have the advantage of a patristic testimonium, but there are strong reasons for assigning the Nag Hammadi *Gospel of Philip* to the Valentinian school.[42] We have the characteristic etymological interest. The demiurge is again merely incompetent, rather than either perfect or evil. We see evidence again of a soteriology expressed as protological myth, salvation in history and ritual; just as the *Gospel of Truth* gave less attention to ritual, the *Gospel of Philip* gives less attention to the myth, but all three are present.[43] The plight consists of being the offspring only of the female, and not of the male, and thus being in a deficient state (*Gos. Phil.* 52.21–4; cf. *Exc. Theod.* 68). Salvation consists in, among other things, the unification of the empirical self with the 'image' above (*Gos. Phil.* 58.10–14), and the union in bridal chamber (cf. *Exc. Theod.* 68, 79).[44] Jesus himself is in need of redemption, which takes place at his baptism (*Gos. Phil.* 70.34–71.3; cf. *Exc. Theod.* 22.6–7; *Tri. Trac.* 124.32–125.11), and this supplies the pattern for the redemption of the elect.

This brief sketch illustrates the grounds in both cases for assigning these Gospels to the Valentinians, on the basis both of a striking level of similarity on central theological topics ('saliency') and the unlikelihood of other groups having penned these works (very strong 'distinctiveness'). Both the *Gospel of Truth* and the *Gospel of Philip* have a relation to the Valentinian movement, which means that each work has a sibling relation to the other.

The Gnostic *Gospel of Judas* and *Gospel of the Egyptians*

Similarly, many would classify the *Gospel of Judas* and the Nag Hammadi *Gospel of the Egyptians* as 'Sethian' or 'Classical Gnostic' in theological outlook. I am taking 'Gnostic'

---

[40] On these see Thomassen, *Spiritual Seed*, 383–5.
[41] Ibid., 154–5, 163–5.
[42] Or rather we do have a reference and a quotation in Epiphanius (*Pan.* 36.13.2), but apparently to a different *Gospel of Philip*.
[43] Cf. Thomassen, 'How Valentinian is the Gospel of Philip?', 254: '*Gos. Phil.* does not deal with protology.' If 'deal with' means 'discuss at length', then, true, but it is mentioned. The primeval sowing of truth (*Gos. Phil.* 55.19–22), and the distortion of it by the archons (54.18–25) could be noted, for example.
[44] Thomassen, 'How Valentinian is the Gospel of Philip?', 254–5.

here in the specific sense which it has both in the neo-Platonist circle of Plotinus and in the earliest of the Fathers (Irenaeus, Hippolytus et al.), where Gnostics and Valentinians and others are distinguished.[45]

In the case of the *Gospel of Judas*, we again have a testimonium, with Irenaeus this time assigning the work to a Gnostic group (*AH* 1.31.1). The supreme being is the 'Great Invisible Spirit' (as in, e.g., the *Apocryphon of John*). Alongside this Spirit, there is Barbelo, from whose aeon Jesus originates. 'Barbelo' is a distinctively Gnostic figure, present in (again) the *Apocryphon of John*, as well as in *Zostrianus* and *Allogenes* which are described by Porphyry as Gnostic works.[46] The demiurge in *Judas*, in contrast to that of the Valentinian literature above, appears very much to be evil. 'Nimrod' a.k.a. 'Yaldabaoth' is introduced as follows: 'And behold, an [angel] appeared out of the cloud with his face pouring forth fire. His appearance was polluted with blood, and his name was "Nimrod", which interpreted means "apostate"' (*Gos. Jud.* 51.12–14). The other demiurge figure, Saklas, is similarly negative.[47] In this respect, they are like the Gnostic creator described as evil by Plotinus.[48] The list of demonic rulers created by Nimrod-Yaldabaoth and Saklas conforms in general, if not in exact detail, to other comparable lists in the *Apocryphon of John*, as well as in a Sethian list.[49] The true seed, i.e. the elect Gnostics, are the generation of Seth, whereas the world is defined as 'corruption' (*Gos. Jud.* 50.13–14) with no prospect of redemption; indeed the text suggests nothing but the destruction of the world (*Gos. Jud.* 55.21–2). This is in keeping with Plotinus's statement that, for the Gnostics, the world reflects the character of its creator, and is therefore also evil.

In the case of the *Gospel of the Egyptians*, many of the same themes appear again. The supreme being is the Great Invisible Spirit; one of the titles this work gives itself is 'The Holy Book of the Great Invisible Spirit'. Alongside this Spirit, again, is Barbelo, and a succession of spirits including Seth and his indestructible seed – the elect generation. Again there is a list of demonic figures which conforms loosely to the lists noted earlier, in the *Apocryphon of John*, and the Sethian list in the Berlin Codex.[50] Others in the dramatis personae of the *Gospel of the Egyptians* are Ephesech/Esephech, Domedon/Doxomedon and the Triple Male Child, who also appear in, for example, *Zostrianus* (as noted earlier, one of the revelations mentioned by Porphyry as 'Gnostic'). These features are unknown in Valentinian literature, while the *Gospel of the Egyptians* and a cluster of other Gnostic texts have frequent reference to them. As in the *Gospel of Judas*, the creator is evil, and indeed is probably identified with 'the devil' (III 61.17). Again, then,

---

[45] See on the whole issue of the distinction M. J. Edwards, 'Gnostics and Valentinians in the Church Fathers', *JTS* 40 (1989), 26–47; M. J. Edwards, 'Neglected Texts in the Study of Gnosticism', *JTS* 41 (1990), 26–50.

[46] Porphyry, *Life of Plotinus*, 16.

[47] He creates those who rule over the underworld (ⲁⲙⲛⲧ[ⲉ], 55.13). Cf. *Gos. Jud.* 55.10–11: 'and all the generations which sinned in my name will serve Saklas', and *Gos. Jud.* 56.12–18: 'Judas, [those who] offer up sacrifice to Saklas ... all, since (almost 3 lines missing) everything which is evil.'

[48] Plotinus, *Enn.* 2.9.

[49] Of the various lists in the *Apocryphon of John*, see e.g. *Ap Jn* II 11.26–34/ IV 18.17–25. For the Sethian list, see the Berlin 'Coptic Book' (P 20915), leaf 128 lines 6–8. Cf. also the Ophite Diagramme in Origen, *Cels.* 6.31.

[50] See previous note.

even though they have their own particular interests, these two works share Gnostic features which are both salient and distinctive. The naming of the supreme levels of deity, for example, as the Great Invisible Spirit and Barbelo, are both salient and distinctive features of the Gnostic myth.

Relations and resemblances

This process of identifying relations is, to be sure, a kind of comparison. In positing a relation of a work to a community, there is comparison involved, and in a sense it is a triadic comparison. But the three terms involved in the comparative process, instead of being three individual works are: <a community>, <the work potentially related to that community> and, finally, <everything else>. When the scholar compares 'vocabulary, idiom, point of view, and worldview'[51] in group *G* and work *W*, and notices an accumulation of distinctive and salient features which cannot be found in <everything else>, then the verdict is reached that the similarities cannot be accidental. This is just the procedure which we have employed in the sketch of the Valentinian and Gnostic Gospels earlier. Of course, as Sanders warns, we do not know '*everything* else', and so identifications of this sort need to remain provisional.[52]

Comparing and relating Mark, John and Thomas

The situation with Mark, John and Thomas is not as different from this as is usually supposed. In what follows I want, first, to describe an early Christian tradition of the (preached) gospel as a reference point, and in particular those people, i.e. the group, who defined themselves in relation to it. The two subsequent stages each involve defining works in relation to this early Christian tradition of what the gospel is, one step offering additional testimony to this tradition, and the next defining the relation of Mark, John and Thomas to it. Hence, the first two steps aim to identify a particular 'group', or perhaps better, 'movement', on analogy to the Gnostics and the Valentinians. The final step seeks to evaluate the respective *relations* of Mark, John and Thomas to this movement.

---

[51] Thus Painter above.
[52] There are also *resemblances* across these Gnostic and Valentinian Gospels. It is not an accident that the category of 'Gnostic' has been used by some to embrace a very wide range of literature, including Valentinian works. The mythological style of the *Gospel of Truth* resembles in certain respects these Gnostic Gospels. In terms of content, there is an unknowable God, which makes the plight of humanity not so much a post-lapsarian moral plight, but at a profound level an intrinsic and epistemological one. 'Gnosis' is no less a feature of the *Gospel of Truth* than it is of the 'Gnostic' works. The world is often pictured not as a creation of the unknowable god, but rather as an unfortunate accident or as the production of an inferior deity. And so on. Such similarities as these have often led to a rather unsophisticated 'lumping' of Valentinian and *sensu stricto* Gnostic works, which has in turn led to an overreaction by some scholars who have wanted to jettison the category of Gnostic altogether. In my judgement, however, there is justification for chastened lumpings of the Gnostic Gospels discussed above (*Egyptians, Judas*) and, in a different category, the Valentinian Gospels of *Truth* and *Philip*.

Paul's account of the apostolic gospel

In 1 Corinthians 15, Paul gives a summary of what he identifies as 'the gospel' and 'of first importance', and the means of salvation:

> Let me tell you, brothers and sisters, of the gospel which I preached to you, which you received, and on which you stand. Through it you are also saved, namely by that message which I preached to you – as long as you hold on to it, and have not believed it in vain. For I passed on to you as of first importance what I also received:
>
> Christ died for our sins according to the Scriptures;
>> he was buried;
>
> he was raised on the third day according to the Scriptures;
>> he appeared to Peter, then to the Twelve.
>
> 1 Cor. 15.1–5

In this formula which Paul cites, we find four essential components in the two principal lines (references to the burial and appearances support the main lines): (a) Jesus as messiah, (b) his saving death and (c) resurrection, both deemed to have taken place (d) according to Scripture. Paul identifies this gospel, moreover, as the apostolic gospel common to all those he lists in 1 Cor. 15.5–8 (Peter, 'the twelve', James, 'the apostles', the 'more than five hundred'): 'Whether, then, it is I or they, this is what we preach' (15.11a), as well as including the Corinthians themselves – 'and this is what you believed' (15.11b). According to Paul, then, this is the common apostolic gospel. The Pauline circle and the other resurrection witnesses noted in 1 Corinthians 15 constitute the group or movement defined, at least in part, by this message. This definition is not just an incidental one, but a definition by a message 'of first importance' which is the basis of their present status before God ('on which you stand') and of their salvation ('through it you are also saved').

The apostolic gospel reflected in Hebrews, 1 Peter and Revelation

There are various ways in which one could defend Paul's claim to this apostolic agreement. The point to be made here is that Paul is not passing off his own eccentricity as common knowledge because we see this message reflected more widely in earliest Christian literature. This section will summarize the evidence in very brief compass from Hebrews, 1 Peter and Revelation, which are substantial enough to include detail about (a) Jesus' messiahship, (b) saving death, (c) resurrection and (d) scriptural attestation.

In Hebrews, Jesus is clearly messiah: the term appears frequently, as do some standard messianic proof-texts.[53] Hebrews clearly refers to Jesus' death as having saving efficacy: he tasted death for all (2.9), breaking the power of death and the devil (2.14–15); as the suffering servant he takes away sins (9.28). His resurrection, sometimes downplayed in Hebrews scholarship, has enjoyed a recent resurgence;[54] in any case,

---

[53] E.g. Psalm 2 in Heb. 1.5a (cf. *Pss. Sol.* 17.23–4), and 2 Samuel 7 in Heb. 1.5b (cf. *Pss. Sol.* 17.4).

[54] David Moffitt, *Atonement and the Logic of Resurrection in the Epistle to the Hebrews* (Leiden: Brill, 2011).

Hebrews 5.7 and 13.20 make fairly unambiguous reference to Jesus rising from the dead (cf. also 7.16). Scripture is woven throughout the epistle. Hebrews of course develops these elements in particular ways, including for example a high-priestly dimension to Jesus' messiahship, and explaining his heavenly offering as part of the process of atonement. The essential elements remain, however, even if they are supplemented.

In 1 Peter, the title 'Christ' is extremely frequent, and messianic expectation in the OT prophets a theme in 1 Peter 1.11. The substitutionary and exemplary death of Jesus is emphasized in 1 Pet. 2.21-5 and 3.18. The resurrection of Jesus is the basis of Christian rebirth and hope (1.3) and what makes baptism effective (3.21). Again, Scripture permeates the letter, with Isaiah 53 particularly prominent in Chapter 2.

Similarly, for Revelation, the snapshot in the prefatory Rev. 1.5-6 refers to

> Jesus Christ, who is the faithful witness, the firstborn from the dead, and the ruler of the kings of the earth. To him who loves us and has freed us from our sins by his blood, and has made us to be a kingdom and priests to serve his God and Father – to him be glory and power for ever and ever! '*Look, he is coming with the clouds*' (Dan. 7.13) and '*every eye will see him, even those who pierced him*' and all peoples on earth '*will mourn because of him*' (Zech. 12.10). So shall it be! Amen.

Here already in this introductory statement we have the 'Christ', saving death, resurrection, and messianic proof-texts referring to his death and future vindication. As we saw with Hebrews, Revelation also has some distinctive interpretations of these themes, but these themes are recognizably intact.

These non-Pauline New Testament works therefore all give emphasis to the features which Paul stresses as the key components of the gospel. They thereby corroborate his testimony that the gospel summarized in 1 Corinthians 15 is not his private message but one shared more widely. Such a claim by Paul is, by its very nature, not amenable to mathematical proof, but we have strong support for his claim in Hebrews, 1 Peter and Revelation. Hence the authors of these works form part of the movement defined by these theological themes.[55]

The apostolic gospel and Mark, John and Thomas

We have established, then, that there is a movement or group in earliest Christianity which is defined, in part, but significantly, by belief in and proclamation of Jesus' messiahship, his saving death and resurrection, and the fulfilment of Scripture in these events. The next stage of the argument is now no longer corroboration of that but evaluation of whether and to what extent Mark and/or John and/or Thomas belong to that movement.

---

[55] Even if Paul were mistaken about the agreement of the other parties in 1 Corinthians 15.5-8, we would have a group consisting of Paul and the authors of Hebrews, 1 Peter and Revelation.

Mark

Mark clearly views Jesus as the Messiah, a point flagged in the opening verse (Mk 1.1), confessed by Peter at the mid-point of the Gospel (8.29), and also confessed by Jesus at his trial (14.61–2). The title is clearly a salient one for Mark, then, appearing as it does at the very beginning and then at a pivotal position in the middle. As some scholars have pointed out, the particular type of Messiah that Mark sees in Jesus is the 'son of God' variety, probably already in the opening verse, but also in the baptism, the demonic confession, the transfiguration, the parable of the tenants, and in Jesus' affirmative answer to the High Priest's question about whether he was 'the messiah-the-Son-of-the-Blessed-One'.[56] Messianism in Mark is, as elsewhere, very much a scriptural discourse. Mark shares with a number of other messianic depictions (qualified) appeal to Davidic descent (Mk 10.47–8; 12.35–7; cf., e.g., *Pss. Sol.* 17), the usage of Daniel 7 (cf. *4 Ezra* 12), as well as interest in the less common alignment of the messiah with Zechariah 13.7 (cf. CD-B 9.7–9).

Mark also develops this messiahship especially with reference to its connection to the suffering and vindication of the Son of Man, and in contrast to the other canonical Gospels, Mark has a quite schematic usage of the title. The passion predictions initially state the bare fact of the necessity of Jesus' death, without explaining it (Mk 8.31, 9.31, 10.33–4). Eventually this death is described as salvific: it is a 'ransom for many' and a life 'poured out for many' (10.45; 14.22–4). Alongside Jesus' death, his resurrection is also forecast (Mk 8.31; 9.31; 10.33–4), and the resurrection is as necessary as the cross, with the 'must' (δεῖ) governing both (8.31). As necessities, then, they are clearly salient events for Mark. The resurrection is a pivotal event, apparently, after which the disciples are permitted to broadcast Jesus' glorious heavenly identity (9.9). Although not narrated, the resurrection is clearly announced: 'He has risen! He is not here' (16.6). The absence of resurrection appearances in Mark does not in any way dent the presence of the event in the Gospel: we should not judge Mark retrospectively by the standards of the later evangelists. Already in Mark, the stone has been rolled away, the women do not see Jesus in the empty tomb; or rather, the tomb is not empty but is occupied by an angelic figure who announces the resurrection, and declares that Jesus is currently on his way to Galilee.

Both Jesus' death and resurrection are in fulfilment of Scripture: the rejection of the stone and its exaltation to 'cornerstone' status alike are seen as presaged in Psalm 118 (Mk 12.10). The passion narrative contains numerous Scriptural references: Psalm 22 is particularly important both for the division of Jesus' clothes (Ps. 22.10/Mk 15.24) and the cry of dereliction (Ps 22.1/2; Mk 15.34).

Mark clearly sees all four of these themes as salient. Potentially the least important to Mark is the resurrection, and yet it is (as we have seen) a *necessity*, and still the conclusion to the work as far as we can tell. It is probably partly because of the greater attention to the resurrection in Matthew, Luke and John that we consider Mark's resurrection narrative skimpy. As far as distinctiveness is concerned, some might say

---

[56] On this, see Matthew Novenson, *The Grammar of Messianism: An Ancient Jewish Political Idiom and Its Users* (Oxford: Oxford University Press, 2016), 83, 90; Joel Marcus, 'Are You the Messiah-Son-of-God?', *NovT* 31 (1989), 125–41.

that Mark is not especially eccentric as far as these particular themes are concerned. Within the field of early Christian Gospels, however, there is a great number of works which take a different view of what constitutes the 'good news', and of these four themes. Mark can therefore be said to belong to the movement described in 1 Corinthians 15.1–11, and to which the authors of Hebrews, 1 Peter and Revelation also belong.

John

Demonstrating the messiahship of Jesus is the express purpose of John's Gospel (Jn 20.30–1): 'Jesus performed many other signs in the presence of his disciples, which are not recorded in this book. But these are written that you may believe that Jesus is the Messiah, the Son of God, and that by believing you may have life in his name.' The juxtaposition of 'messiah' there with 'son of God' indicates the main direction of John's Christology, although son of God is not exactly synonymous with its sense in Mark. Despite John's interest in 'higher' matters, such as divinity, pre-existence and incarnation, the messiahship of Jesus is never out of view for long, the term featuring twenty-one times in as many chapters in the Gospel, of which two are of the transliteration Μεσσίας. It is a thematized topic of discussion, both in the question of whether John the Baptist is messiah (1.20, 25) and the debate in John 7 over Jesus' qualifications for the office. In the latter passage, John is possibly ambivalent towards the category of son of David, which is not mentioned elsewhere in the Gospel, while 'son of man' is of considerable significance.

The demonstration of Jesus' identity takes place through a series of 'signs', and supremely in his death and resurrection, which – even if they are not signs – overlap in function.[57] The death of Jesus deals with sins, as is initially suggested in John 1.29; at this point it is not clear how the lamb of God will take away the sin of the world, but this unfolds in the rest of the Gospel. His death is also more broadly salvific beyond the removal of sin. John employs a great variety of images to convey the saving effects of Jesus' death: it is the gift of his flesh for the life of the world (6.51), the shepherd laying down his life for the sheep (10.10–11), the death of one person to avoid the loss of the whole nation (11.49–51), the kernel of wheat dying so that it can produce many seeds (12.24) and the elevation which draws everyone to him (12.30–5).[58] The resurrection on the third day, sometimes sidelined as a theme in John's Gospel, has recently been the subject of a collection of essays pursuing the various strands of its significance.[59] In contrast to Mark, John devotes considerable space to the resurrection appearances already in Chapter 20, and Chapter 21 only reinforces their import. Indeed, the resurrection is a theme of Jesus' teaching even before his death (Jn 2.19; 10.17–18; 16.16–22).

As with Mark, both the death of Jesus and this resurrection are fulfilments of Scripture.[60] Only one passage explicitly links the resurrection with Scripture (20.9),

---

[57] C. Kingsley Barrett, *The Gospel according to St John*. Second Edition (London: SPCK, 1978), 78, comments that they are not signs because they are the truth to which the signs point.
[58] Similarly Donald A. Carson, *The Gospel according to John* (Grand Rapids: Eerdmans, 1991), 97.
[59] Craig R. Koester and Reimund Bieringer (eds), *The Resurrection of Jesus in the Gospel of John* (Tübingen: Mohr Siebeck, 2008).
[60] For Jesus' death in John as a fulfilment of Scripture, see, e.g., Jn 3.14; 19.24, 28, 36–7.

although if the 'lifting-up' motif includes the resurrection and exaltation, then the passages about the raising of the serpent (Num. 21.9) and the exaltation of the servant (Isa. 52.13) alluded to by John will include reference to the resurrection as well (Jn 3.14–15; 12.30–6). Again, the passion narrative makes considerable appeal to the scriptural forecasting of individual elements of Jesus' suffering on the cross: the division of the clothes (Ps. 21.19 LXX; Jn 19.25), Jesus' thirst (Ps. 63.1; 69.21; Jn 19.28) and the presentation of the vinegar (Ps. 69.21; Jn 19.30). John's mode of scriptural citation differs considerably in style from that of Mark, however.[61]

Although John's Gospel as a whole is different in a number of ways from Mark, John also assigns these four themes considerable saliency. Eliciting belief in Jesus' messiahship is the specific aim of the book, and Scripture permeates the Gospel – indeed, *cannot* be set aside (οὐ δύναται λυθῆναι ἡ γραφή, Jn 10.35). The saving death and resurrection constitute not only the very long climax of the Gospel (98 verses in all), but in addition to their narration their significance is mentioned repeatedly throughout the Gospel. The same point made about Mark applies in the case of the distinctiveness of these themes: to some John might seem to be within the mainstream of early Christian theology as far as these four points are concerned, but from the point of view of other early Christian Gospels it is not so ordinary. Like Mark, then, John's Gospel is a product of the broad movement delineated earlier.

Thomas

Noticeably, Thomas does not fit into the same pattern. There is no reference to Jesus as Messiah, despite the appearance of other titles such as 'Son' and 'living one'. The death of Jesus is a feature, but only as exemplary: 'Whoever does not hate his brothers and sisters, and take his cross like me, will not be worthy of me' (*Gos. Thom.* 55.2). The resurrection does not play a role, indeed it is not necessary (perhaps even not possible) to imagine Jesus being raised in Thomas. One of the few scholars who comments on the idea remarks, probably correctly, that Jesus' death only brought his physical appearance to an end; he is eternally immortal, and in that sense 'the living Jesus' (*Gos. Thom.* prologue).[62] Far from desiring to demonstrate Jesus as fulfilling Scripture, the only point made about Scripture is its deadness (*Gos. Thom.* 52).[63] As Watson has put it, Thomas 'appears to sever the link with the scriptures, contrasting the living Jesus

---

[61] See Richard B. Hays, *Echoes of Scripture in the Gospels* (Waco: Baylor University Press, 2016), especially the concluding chapter.

[62] Enno E. Popkes, 'Die Umdeutung des Todes Jesu im koptischen Thomasevangelium', in J. Frey and J. Schröter (eds), *Deutungen des Todes Jesu im Neuen Testament* (WUNT 181; Tübingen: Mohr Siebeck, 2005), 513–43 (542): 'In diesem neuen Gesamtkontext beendet der Tod Jesu nur dessen körperliche Existenz.' Cf. Popkes, 'Umdeutung', 533: 'Für das Thomasevangelium ist Jesus vielmehr *per se* der Lebendige'; Stephen J. Patterson, 'A View from Across the Euphrates', *HTR* 104 (2011), 411–31 (419): 'In Thomas the 'living Jesus' is the *immortal* Jesus who brings to others the secret of immortality.' Charles H. Hedrick, *Unlocking the Secrets of the Gospel according to Thomas: A Radical Faith for a New Age* (Eugene: Cascade, 2010), 19, leaves open the possibility of a reference to the risen Jesus in 'living Jesus'. Uwe-Karsten Plisch, *The Gospel of Thomas: Original Text with Commentary* (New York: American Bible Society, 2010), 37–9, is almost certainly correct to reject it.

[63] See Gathercole, *Gospel of Thomas*, 414–16.

with the twenty-four dead prophets in Israel'.[64] In this instance, then, we cannot add Thomas to the library of that school of thought to which Paul, Hebrews, 1 Peter and Revelation – and Mark and John – belonged. To echo the discussion of Jonathan Z. Smith and Wendy Doniger earlier, when we come to the Gospel of Thomas, there are too many dogs which do not bark.

Interim conclusion: the relations of Mark, John and Thomas

Of course, in certain senses – especially in literary terms – Thomas is related to Mark and John.[65] Thomas differs considerably from Mark and John in its theology, however. John and Mark can be considered as part of a theological movement which preserved the apostolic gospel described earlier in a way which Thomas cannot. Mark and John clearly emerge from such a school of thought, or probably more accurately, from the cluster of the various groups with this shared set of beliefs. We can draw an analogy between this cluster and the Valentinian 'church', which despite its geographical spread, diverse teachers and even schism, can nevertheless be described as *'un phénomène religieux possédant un certain degré de cohésion sociale et de continuité historique'*.[66] This Valentinian movement is the broad movement from which the *Gospel of Truth* and the *Gospel of Philip* emerged. Again, Edwards captures the unity-in-diversity of the Gnostics in describing them as a 'congeries of obscure and related sects'.[67] This congeries produced the *Gospel of the Egyptians* and the *Gospel of Judas*. Mark and John similarly emerged as siblings from a diverse but still theologically defined association of Christian circles, just as did the Gospels of *Truth* and *Philip* from the more or less closely associated Valentinian groups, and as did the Gospels of the *Egyptians* and *Judas* from the Gnostics. The question of how one is to label the group marked by the theology shared by Mark and John is too complex to grapple with here: neither the ancient label *magna ecclesia* nor the modern 'proto-orthodoxy' has garnered widespread agreement.[68]

Thomas belongs neither to this 'apostolic' or 'proto-orthodox' school, nor to the Valentinians or Gnostics. Nevertheless, scholars have sought sometimes to assign Thomas to a different school. Leaving aside the generalizing descriptions of Thomas in earlier scholarship as 'Gnostic' in the broad, ill-defined sense, the Gospel has been

---

[64] Francis Watson, *Gospel Writing* (Grand Rapids: Eerdmans, 2013), 608.
[65] In the first place, they all belong in the field of early Christian Gospels. Moreover, because Thomas is also influenced by Matthew and Luke to some degree, it is thereby indirectly influenced by Mark. See Mark Goodacre, *Thomas and the Gospels* (Grand Rapids: Eerdmans, 2012); Simon Gathercole, *The Composition of the Gospel of Thomas: Original Language and Sources* (Cambridge: Cambridge University Press, 2012). (More direct influence on Thomas from Mark, independent of Matthew and Luke, is in the nature of the case more difficult to identify.) In terms of broader literary character, then, and in its Synoptic relations, it has a *literary* relation to Mark. John, by contrast does not have the same kind of literary relation that Thomas and the Synoptics have: while John almost certainly (in my view at least) has some knowledge of one or more of the Synoptic Gospels, its literary relation is not the same as that between Thomas and the Synoptics.
[66] Einar Thomassen, 'L'histoire du valentinisme et le Traité Tripartite', in *École pratique des hautes études, Section des sciences religieuses. Annuaire 1994–1995. Tome 103*, 301–3 (301). Cf. Thomassen, *Spiritual Seed*, 504, with reference to 'schism' there.
[67] Edwards, 'Gnostics and Valentinians', 34.
[68] Respectively, e.g. Origen, *Cels*. 5.59; D. Brakke, *The Gnostics: Myth, Ritual and Diversity in Early Christianity* (Cambridge, MA: Harvard University Press, 2010), 10, with reservations.

described variously as Manichaean, Valentinian, Encratite and – as we saw in the discussion of Davies earlier – proto-Johannine. The patristic designation of Thomas as Manichaean can be set aside on chronological grounds, as Mani was not born until after our first testimonium to the Gospel of Thomas.[69] The characterization as Valentinian depends on pressing certain similarities with the *Gospel of Truth*, but which are not necessarily Valentinian distinctives.[70] Again, Thomas has some general similarities with Encratite views, but more specific proposals, such as a relation between Thomas and Tatian, are extremely precarious.[71] Indeed, one of the difficulties in analysing Thomas is that, although it appears to have been used by various groups (e.g. Naassenes, Manichees), it is very hard to assign its origin to a particular group. The mode of Thomas's theological expression, both in the absence of narrative and in its often unspecific theologoumena, means that it is very malleable. At the present state of scholarship, it is not possible to identify a specific group or movement which produced it.

Conclusion

The goal of this essay has been to clarify the distinction between two different goals of comparison, namely comparing for resemblance and comparing for relation. In certain respects they overlap, as both can be triadic, although the kinds of terms at the three points of the triangle are different when one goes beyond merely exploring similarities and differences to seeking the relation of a work to a group. In the case of comparing Mark, John and Thomas with an eye to resemblances, there is some scope for seeing points at which John and Thomas are more similar to one another against Mark (and the Synoptics more widely), although the case for an overall resemblance between John and Thomas that is greater than each has to Mark is not proven. Indeed, 'overall resemblance' is a false category, because constructions of resemblances are just that: constructions.

In describing *relations* (as opposed to resemblances), however, historians hope to escape the relativism of our postmodern condition and seek to describe realities. Anyone who thinks this a Rankean mirage should ask themselves whether they think Paul wrote/dictated Romans or Hebrews. To answer that Paul wrote Romans is to stake a claim to a relation; conversely to answer that Paul did not write Hebrews is to claim a non-relation. When the four central theologoumena of the earliest Christian kerygma in 1 Cor. 15.3–5 are seen as salient and distinctive characteristics of an early Christian movement, Mark and John clearly have a relation to this movement, and therefore a sibling relation to each other. The Gospel of Thomas on the other hand, while it has certain *resemblances* to the canonical Gospels considered here, does not have the same kind of *relation* to this early Christian movement as do Mark and John.

---

[69] For Manichaean authorship, the earliest statements are Cyril of Jerusalem, *Catechesis* 4.36 and 6.31 (c. 348 CE). For these and other texts, with discussion, see Gathercole, *Gospel of Thomas*, 35–61; Simon Gathercole, 'Named Testimonia to the *Gospel of Thomas*: An Expanded Inventory and Analysis', *HTR* 105.1 (2012), 53–89.

[70] See Bertil Gärtner, *The Theology of the Gospel According to Thomas* (New York: Harper & Brothers, 1961), 272, as an advocate of this view.

[71] E.g. in Nicholas Perrin, *Thomas and Tatian: The Relationship between the Gospel of Thomas and the Diatessaron* (Atlanta: Society of Biblical Literature, 2002).

Bibliography

Adams, Edward. "First-Century Models for Paul's Churches: Selected Scholarly Developments since Meeks." In *After the First Urban Christians: The Social-Scientific Study of Pauline Communities Twenty-Five Years Later*. Edited by Todd D. Still and David G. Horrell. London: T&T Clark, 2009. p. 60–78.
Arendt, Hannah. *Eichmann in Jerusalem: A Report on the Banality of Evil*. London: Penguin Books, 2006.
Attridge, Harold W. *Hebrews*. Hermeneia, Philadelphia: Fortress Press, 1989.
Bakhtin, M. *Speech Genres and Other Late Essays*. Austin: University of Texas Press, 1986.
Bakhtin, M. 'Toward a Methodology for the Human Sciences'. In *Speech Genres and Other Late Essays*, edited by C. Emerson and M. Holquist, translated by V. W. McGee, 159–72. Austin: University of Texas Press, 1986.
Barclay, John M. G. *Flavius Josephus: Translation and Commentary Volume 10: Against Apion*. Leiden: Brill, 2007.
Barclay, John M. G. 'Constructing a Dialogue: *4 Ezra* and Paul on the Mercy of God'. In *Anthropologie und Ethik im Frühjudentum und im Neuen Testament*, edited by M. Konradt and E. Schläpfer, 3–22. Tübingen: Mohr Siebeck, 2014.
Barclay, John M. G. *Paul and the Gift*. Grand Rapids: Eerdmans, 2015.
Barr, James. *The Semantics of Biblical Language*. Oxford: Oxford University Press, 1961.
Barrett, C. Kingsley. *The Gospel according to St John*. 2nd edn. London: SPCK, 1978.
Barth, Karl. *Church Dogmatics*. 4 vols. Edinburgh: T&T Clark, 1936–7.
Bauckham, Richard. 'The Two Fig-Tree Parables in the Apocalypse of Peter'. *JBL* 104 (1985): 269–87.
Bauckham, Richard. 'James and the Jerusalem Church'. In *The Book of Acts in its First Century Setting, Volume 4: Palestinian Setting* (p. 415–80). Grand Rapids: Eerdmans; Exeter: Paternoster, 1995.
Bayer, Oswald. 'Hermeneutical Theology'. *Scottish Journal of Theology* 56.2 (2003): 131–47.
Bayer, Oswald. *Freedom in Response*. Oxford: Oxford University Press, 2007.
Bayer, Oswald. *A Contemporary in Dissent: Johann Georg Hamann as a Radical Enlightener*, translated by R. A. Harrisville and M. C. Mattes. Grand Rapids: Eerdmans, 2012.
Bayer, Oswald. 'God as Author: On the Theological Foundations of Hamann's Authorial Poetics'. In *Hamann and the Tradition*, edited by L. M. Anderson, 163–75. Evanston: Northwestern University Press, 2012.
Berlin, Isaiah. *The Hedgehog and the Fox: An Essay on Tolstoy's View of History*. London: Weidenfeld & Nicolson, 1953.
Betz, J. R. 'Hamann before Kierkegaard: A Systematic Theological Oversight'. *Pro Ecclesia* 16.3 (2007): 299–333.
Betz, J. R. *After Enlightenment: The Post-Secular Vision of J. G. Hamann*. Oxford: Wiley-Blackwell, 2012.
Black, Max. *Models and Metaphors: Studies in Language and Philosophy*. Ithaca: Cornell University Press, 1962.
Blumhofer, Christopher. *The Gospel of John and the Future of Israel*. SNTSMS; Cambridge: Cambridge University Press, 2019.

Bockmuehl, Markus. *Philippians*, Black's New Testament Commentary. London: A&C Black, 1997.

Bockmuehl, Markus. *Ancient Apocryphal Gospels*. Louisville: WJK, 2017.

Boswell, John. *Christianity, Social Tolerance, and Homosexuality: Gay People in Western Europe from the Beginning of the Christian Era to the Fourteenth Century*. Chicago: University of Chicago Press, 1980.

Brakke, David. *The Gnostics: Myth, Ritual and Diversity in Early Christianity*. Cambridge, MA: Harvard University Press, 2010.

Brankaer, Johanna, and Hans-Gebhard Bethke. *Codex Tchacos: Texte und Analyse*. TU 161, Berlin: de Gruyter, 2007.

Braudel, F. 'History and the Social Sciences'. In *Economy and Society in Early Modern Europe*, edited by P. Burke, 11–42. New York: Harper & Row, 1972.

Braun, Herbert. *An die Hebräer* (HNT). Tübingen: J. C. B. Mohr, 1984.

Brooten, Bernadette J. *Love Between Women: Early Christian Responses to Female Homoeroticism*. Chicago: University of Chicago Press, 1996.

Brown, Peter. 'Paganism: What We Owe the Christians'. *New York Review of Books*, 7 April 2011.

Brown, Peter. 'Reply to Ramsay MacMullen'. *New York Review of Books*, 9 June 2011.

Bruce, F. F. *The Epistle to the Hebrews*, New International Commentary on the New Testament. Grand Rapids: Eerdmans, 1964.

Buchholz, Dennis D. *Your Eyes Will Be Opened: A Study of the Greek (Ethiopic) Apocalypse of Peter*. Society of Biblical Literature Dissertation Series. Atlanta: Society of Biblical Literature, 1988.

Butchvarov, Panayot. *Resemblance and Identity: An Examination of the Problem of Universals*. Bloomington: Indiana University Press, 1966.

Carson, Donald A. *The Gospel According to John*. Grand Rapids: Eerdmans, 1991.

Cavanaugh, William T. *The Myth of Religious Violence*. New York: Oxford University Press, 2009.

Charles, R. H. *The Ascension of Isaiah*. London: A&C Black, 1900.

Charlesworth, J. H., ed. *The Old Testament Pseudepigrapha*. 2 vols. London: Darton, Longman, and Todd, 1985.

Clark, Elizabeth A. 'From Patristics to Early Christian Studies'. In *The Oxford Handbook of Early Christian Studies*, edited by Susan Ashbrook Harvey and David G. Hunter, p. 7–41. New York: Oxford University Press, 2008.

Cochran, Elizabeth Agnew. 'Bricolage and the Purity of Traditions: Engaging the Stoics for Contemporary Christian Ethics'. *Journal of Religious Ethics* 40 (2012): 720–9.

Cockerill, Gareth Lee. *The Epistle to the Hebrews* (NICNT). Grand Rapids: Eerdmans, 2012.

Davies, Stevan. *The Gospel of Thomas and Christian Wisdom*. Oregon House: Bardic Press, 2005.

DeConick, A. D. *Voices of the Mystics: Early Christian Discourse in the Gospels of John and Thomas and Other Ancient Christian Literature*. JSNTSuppS; Sheffield: Sheffield Academic Press, 2001.

den Dulk, Matthijs. *Between Jews and Heretics: Refiguring Justin Martyr's Dialogue with Trypho*. London: Routledge, 2018.

Detienne, Marcel. *Comparing the Incomparable*. Translated by Janet Lloyd. Stanford: Stanford University Press, 2008.

Diamond, Cora. 'The Difficulty of Reality and the Difficulty of Philosophy'. *Partial Answers: Journal of Literature and the History of Ideas* 1 (2003): 1–26.

Doniger, Wendy. *Other Peoples' Myths: The Cave of Echoes*. New York: Macmillan, 1988.
Doniger, Wendy. *The Implied Spider: Politics and Theology in Myth*. New York: Columbia, 2011.
Dunderberg, Ismo. *Beloved Disciple in Conflict? Revisiting the Gospels of John and Thomas*. Oxford: Oxford University Press, 2006.
Edwards, M. J. 'Gnostics and Valentinians in the Church Fathers'. *The Journal of Theological Studies* 40 (1989): 26–47.
Edwards, M. J. 'Neglected Texts in the Study of Gnosticism'. *The Journal of Theological Studies* 41 (1990): 26–50.
Ellingworth, Paul. 'Hebrews and 1 Clement: Literary Dependence or Common Tradition?' *Biblische Zeitschrift* 23 (1979): 262–9.
Ellingworth, Paul. *The Epistle to the Hebrews* (The New International Greek Testament Commentary). Grand Rapids: Eerdmans, 1993.
Elliott, John H. *Spain, Europe & the Wider World, 1500–1800*. New Haven: Yale University Press, 2009.
Engberg-Pedersen, Troels, ed. *Paul in His Hellenistic Context*. Edinburgh: T&T Clark, 1994.
Engberg-Pedersen, Troels, ed. *Paul and the Stoics*. Edinburgh: T&T Clark, 2000.
Engberg-Pedersen, Troels, ed. 'Self-Sufficiency and Power: Divine and Human Agency in Epictetus and Paul'. In *Divine and Human Agency in Paul and His Cultural Environment*, edited by John M. G. Barclay and S. J. Gathercole, 117–139. London: T&T Clark, 2008.
Englehardt, H. Tristan. *The Foundations of Bioethics*. 2nd edn. New York: Oxford University Press, 1996.
Fitzgerald, John T., T. H. Olbricht, and L. M. White, ed. *Friendship, Flattery, and Frankness of Speech: Studies in the New Testament World*. Leiden: Brill, 1996.
Fitzgerald, John T., T. H. Olbricht, and L. M. White, ed. *Greco-Roman Perspectives on Friendship*. Atlanta: Scholars Press, 1997.
Fitzgerald, John T., T. H. Olbricht, and L. M. White, ed. *Early Christianity and Classical Culture: Comparative Studies in Honour of Abraham J. Malherbe*. Atlanta: Soc. of Biblical Literature, 2003.
Fürst, Alfons, Therese Fuhrer, Folker Siegert and Peter Walter. *Der apokryphe Briefwechsel zwischen Seneca und Paulus – Zusammen mit dem Brief des Mordechai an Alexander und dem Brief des Annaeus Seneca über Hochmut und Götterbilder*. SAPERE 11, Tübingen: Mohr Siebeck, 2006.
Gadamer, Hans-Georg. *Wahrheit und Methode: Grundüzge einer philosophischen Hermeneutik, Gesammelte Werke* 1. Tübingen: J. C. B. Mohr, 1990.
Gärtner, Bertil. *The Theology of the Gospel According to Thomas*. New York: Harper & Brothers, 1961.
Garver, Eugene. *For the Sake of Argument: Practical Reasoning, Character, and the Ethics of Belief*. Chicago: University of Chicago Press, 2004.
Gathercole, Simon. *Where is Boasting? Early Jewish Soteriology and Paul's Response in Romans 1–5*. Grand Rapids: Eerdmans, 2002.
Gathercole, Simon. *The Preexistent Son: Recovering the Christologies of Matthew, Mark and Luke*. Grand Rapids: Eerdmans, 2006.
Gathercole, Simon. *The Composition of the Gospel of Thomas: Original Language and Sources*. Cambridge: Cambridge University Press, 2012.
Gathercole, Simon. 'Named Testimonia to the *Gospel of Thomas*: An Expanded Inventory and Analysis'. *Harvard Theological Review* 105.1 (2012): 53–89.

Gathercole, Simon. *The Gospel of Thomas: Introduction, Translation and Commentary*. Leiden: Brill, 2014.
Goodacre, Mark. *Thomas and the Gospels*. Grand Rapids: Eerdmans, 2012.
Grässer, Erich. *An die Hebräer (Hebr 1–6)*, EKKNT XVII/1. Zurich/Neukirchen-Vluyn: Neukirchener, 1990.
Gregory, Andrew, and Christopher Tuckett, ed. *The Reception of the New Testament in the Apostolic Fathers*. Oxford: Oxford University Press, 2005.
Griffith-Dickson, G. 'God, I, and Thou: Hamann and the Personalist Tradition'. In *Hamann and the Tradition*, edited by L. M. Anderson, 56. Evanston: Northwestern University Press, 2012.
Griffith-Dickson, G. *Johann Georg Hamann's Relational Metacriticim*. Berlin: de Gruyter, 1995.
Griffiths, Paul. *Problems of Religious Diversity*. Oxford: Blackwell, 2001.
Gruen, Erich S. *Rethinking the Other in Antiquity*. Princeton: Princeton University Press, 2011.
Habermas, Jürgen. *Knowledge and Human Interests*. Cambridge: Polity Press, 1987.
Habermas, Jürgen. *Theory and Practice*. 4th edn. London: Heinemann, 1974.
Habermas, Jürgen. "Zu Gadamer's *Wahrheit und Methode.*" In *Hermeneutik and Ideologiekritik*. Edited by Karl-Otto Apel. Frankfurt am Main: Suhrkamp, 1971. p. 45–56.
Hadot, Pierre. *Plotinus or The Simplicity of Vision*. Chicago: University of Chicago Press, 1994.
Hadot, Pierre. *Philosophy as a Way of Life*. New York: Blackwell, 1995.
Hadot, Pierre. *The Inner Citadel*. Cambridge: Harvard University Press, 1998.
Hadot, Pierre. *What is Ancient Philosophy?* Cambridge, MA: Harvard University Press, 2002.
Hadot, Pierre. *The Veil of Isis: An Essay on the History of the Idea of Nature*, translated by Michael Chase. Cambridge, MA: Belknap, 2008.
Hahneman, Geoffrey. *The Muratorian Fragment and the Development of the Canon*. Oxford: Oxford University Press, 1992.
Halperin, David M. *One Hundred Years of Homosexuality: and Other Essays on Greek Love*. New York: Routledge, 1990.
Hamann, J. G. *Briefwechsel*, edited by W. Ziesemer and A. Henkel. 8 vols. Wiesbaden/Frankfurt: Insel, 1751–88.
Hamann, J. G. *Sämtliche Werken*, edited by J. Nadler. 6 vols. Vienna: Verlag Herder, 1949–57.
Hamann, J. G. *Writings on Philosophy and Language*. Edited by K. Haynes. Cambridge: Cambridge University Press, 2007.
Hartenstein, Judith. *Die zweite Lehre: Erscheinungen des Auferstandenen als Rahmenerzählungen Frühchristlicher Dialoge*. Berlin: Akademie Verlag, 2000.
Hauerwas, Stanley. 'Bearing Reality: A Christian Meditation'. *Journal of the Society of Christian Ethics* 33 (2013): 3–20.
Hays, Richard B. *Echoes of Scripture in the Gospels*. Waco: Baylor University Press, 2016.
Hays, Richard B. *The Moral Vision of the New Testament*. San Francisco: Harper, 1996.
Hedrick, Charles H. *Unlocking the Secrets of the Gospel according to Thomas: A Radical Faith for a New Age*. Eugene: Cascade, 2010.
Hester, Lee, and Jim Cheney. 'Truth and Native American Epistemology'. *Social Epistemology* 15 (2001): 319–34.
Hoffman, V. *Johann Georg Hamanns Philologie: Hamanns Philologie zwischen enzyklopädischer Mikrologie und Hermeneutik*. Stuttgart: Verlag W. Kohlkammer, 1972.
Hollis, Martin, and Steven Lukes, eds. *Rationality and Relativism*. Cambridge, MA: MIT Press, 1972.

Hübner, H. *Die Weisheit Salomons*. Göttingen: Vandenhoeck and Ruprecht, 1999.
Hughes, Aaron. *Comparison: A Critical Primer*. Sheffield: Equinox, 2017.
Hurtado, Larry W. *Destroyer of the Gods: Early Christian Distinctiveness in the Roman World*. Waco: Baylor University Press, 2016.
Hurtado, Larry W. *Lord Jesus Christ: Devotion to Jesus in Earliest Christianity*. Grand Rapids: Eerdmans, 2003.
Inwood, Brad, ed. *The Cambridge Companion to the Stoics*. Cambridge: Cambridge University Press, 2006.
James, M. R. 'A New Text of the Apocalypse of Peter III'. *The Journal of Theological Studies* 12 (1911): 573–83.
James, William. *The Varieties of Religious Experience: A Study in Human Nature*. New York: Mentor, 1958.
Kierkegaard, Søren. *Sickness unto Death*. New York: Doubleday, 1954.
King, Karen L. 'Which Early Christianity?' In *The Oxford Handbook of Early Christian Studies*, edited by Susan Ashbrook Harvey and David G. Hunter, p. 66–86. New York: Oxford University Press, 2008.
Knight, Jonathan. *The Ascension of Isaiah*. Sheffield: Sheffield Academic Press, 1995.
Knight, Jonathan. *Disciples of the Beloved One: The Christology, Social Setting and Theological Content of the Ascension of Isaiah*. JSPSupp 18, 1996.
Koester, Craig R. *Hebrews* (Anchor Bible Commentary vol. 36). New York: Doubleday, 2001.
Koester, Craig R., and Reimund Bieringer, eds. *The Resurrection of Jesus in the Gospel of John*. Tübingen: Mohr Siebeck, 2008.
Konstan, David. *Friendship in the Classical World*. Cambridge: Cambridge University Press, 1997.
Kraus, Thomas J., and Tobias Nicklas, eds. *Das Petrusevangelium und die Petrusapokalypse mit deutscher und englischer Übersetzung*. Berlin: de Gruyter, 2004.
Lane, William L. *Hebrews 1–8*. WBC 47a. Dallas: Word, 1991.
Larcher, C. *Le Livre de la Sagesse, ou La Sagesse de Salomon*. Paris: Gabalda, 1983.
Lincoln, Bruce. *Gods and Demons, Priests and Scholars: Critical Explorations in the History of Religions*. Chicago: University of Chicago Press, 2012.
Linebaugh, Jonathan A. *God, Grace, and Righteousness in Wisdom of Solomon and Paul's Letter to the Romans: Texts in Conversation*. Leiden: Brill, 2013.
Linebaugh, Jonathan A. 'Righteousness Revealed: The Death of Christ as the Definition of the Righteousness of God in Romans 3: 21–6'. In *Paul and the Apocalyptic Imagination*, edited by B. C. Blackwell, J. K. Goodrich, and J. Maston, 219–38. Minneapolis: Fortress Press, 2016.
Linebaugh, Jonathan A. 'Not the End: The History and Hope of the Unfailing Word in Romans 9–11'. In *God and Israel: Providence and Purpose in Romans 9–11*, edited by T. D. Still, 149–72. Waco: Baylor University Press, 2017.
Lundhaug, Hugo. *Images of Rebirth: Cognitive Poetics and Transformational Soteriology in the Gospel of Philip and the Exegesis on the Soul*. Leiden: Brill, 2010.
MacIntyre, Alasdair. 'Epistemological Crises, Dramatic Narrative, and the Philosophy of Science'. *The Monist* 60.4 (1977): 453–72.
MacIntyre, Alasdair. *Three Rival Traditions of Moral Enquiry: Encyclopaedia, Genealogy, and Tradition*. Notre Dame: University of Notre Dame Press, 1990.
MacIntyre, Alasdair. *Edith Stein: A Philosophical Prologue 1913–1922*. New York: Rowman & Littlefield, 2006.
MacIntyre, Alasdair. *After Virtue*. 3rd edn. South Bend: University of Notre Dame Press, 2009.
MacMullen, Ramsay. 'The Tenacity of Paganism'. *New York Review of Books*, 9 June 2011.

Mannheim, Karl. *Ideology and Utopia* (New York, n.d.; reprint).
Marcus, Joel. 'Are You the Messiah-Son-of-God?' *Novum Testamentum* 31 (1989): 125–41.
Marshall, Bruce. 'Christ and Israel: An Unsolved Problem in Catholic Theology'. In *The Call of Abraham: Essays on the Election of Israel in Honor of Jon D. Levenson*, edited by Gary A. Anderson and Joel S. Kaminsky, 330–50. Notre Dame: University of Notre Dame Press, 2013.
Martin, Dale B. *Biblical Truths: The Meaning of Scripture in the Twenty-First Century*. New Haven: Yale University Press, 2017.
Martin, Dale B. *The Corinthian Body*. New Haven: Yale University Press, 1995.
Martin, Dale B. *Inventing Superstition from the Hippocratics to the Christians*. Cambridge, MA: Harvard University Press, 2004.
Martin, Dale B. *Pedagogy of the Bible: An Analysis and Proposal*. Louisville: Westminster John Knox, 2008.
Martin, Dale B. *Sex and the Single Savior: Gender and Sexuality in Biblical Interpretation*. Louisville: Westminster John Knox, 2006.
Mason, Steve. *Josephus and the New Testament*. Peabody, MA: Hendrickson, 2003.
McKenzie, Judith S., and Francis Watson. *The Garima Gospels: Early Illuminated Gospel Books from Ethiopia*. Oxford: Manar Al-Athar Monographs, 2016.
Meeks, Wayne A. *The First Urban Christians: The Social World of the Apostle Paul*. New Haven: Yale University Press, 1983.
Meier, John P. *A Marginal Jew: Rethinking the Historical Jesus*. 4 vols. ABRL. New York: Doubleday, 1991.
Michaelis, J. D. *Beurtheilung der Mittel, welche man anwendet, die ausgestorbene Hebräische Spache zu verstehen*. Göttingen, 1757.
Mitchell, Margaret M. *Paul, the Corinthians, and the Birth of Christian Hermeneutics*. Cambridge: Cambridge University Press, 2010.
Mitchell, Margaret M. *Paul and the Emergence of Christian Textuality: Early Christian Literary Culture in Context* (Collected Essays, volume 1) Wissenschaftliche Untersuchungen zum Neuen Testament 393, Tübingen: Mohr Siebeck, 2017.
Moffitt, David. *Atonement and the Logic of Resurrection in the Epistle to the Hebrews*. Leiden: Brill, 2011.
Müller, C. Detlef G. *New Testament Apocrypha, Volume Two: Writings Relating to the Apostles; Apocalypses and Related Subjects*, edited by Wilhelm Schneemelcher, translated by Louisville: WJK; Cambridge: James Clarke, 1992.
Nachmanson, E. *Der griechische Buchtitel: Einige Beobachtungen*. Darmstadt: Wissenschaftliche Buchgesellschaft, 1969.
Nongbri, Brent. *Before Religion: A History of a Modern Concept*. New Haven: Yale University Press, 2013.
Novenson, Matthew. *The Grammar of Messianism: An Ancient Jewish Political Idiom and Its Users*. Oxford: Oxford University Press, 2016.
Nussbaum, Martha C. *Therapy of Desire: Therapy and Practice in Hellenistic Ethics*. Princeton: Princeton University Press, 1994.
Osborn, Eric. *Clement of Alexandria*. Cambridge: Cambridge University Press, 2008.
Paden, William E. 'Elements of a New Comparativism'. *Method & Theory in the Study of Religion* 8 (1996): 5–14.
Pagels, Elaine. *Beyond Belief: The Secret Gospel of Thomas*. New York: Random House, 2003.
Painter, John. 'Johannine Literature: The Gospel and Letters of John'. In *The Blackwell Companion to the New Testament*, edited by David C. Aune, 344–72. Oxford: Wiley-Blackwell, 2008.

Parsons, Kathryn Pyne. 'Three Concepts of Clusters'. *Philosophy and Phenomenological Research* 33.4 (1973): 514–23.
Patterson, Stephen J. 'A View from Across the Euphrates'. *Harvard Theological Review* 104 (2011): 411–31.
Patton, Kimberley. 'Juggling Torches: Why We Still Need Comparative Religion'. In *A Magic Still Dwells: Comparative Religion in the Postmodern Age*, edited by Kimberley C. Patton and Benjamin C. Ray, 153–71. Berkeley: University of California Press, 2000.
Patton, Kimberly C., and Benjamin C. Ray, eds. *A Magic Still Dwells: Comparative Religion in the Postmodern Age*. Berkeley: University of California Press, 2000.
Perrin, Nicholas. *Thomas and Tatian: The Relationship between the Gospel of Thomas and the Diatessaron*. Atlanta: Society of Biblical Literature, 2002.
Pervo, Richard I. *Dating Acts: Between the Evangelists and the Apologists*. Santa Rosa, CA: Polebridge Press, 2006.
Plisch, Uwe-Karsten. *The Gospel of Thomas: Original Text with Commentary*. New York: American Bible Society, 2010.
Poole, Fitz J. P. 'Metaphors and Maps: Towards Comparison in the Anthropology of Religion'. *Journal of the American Academy of Religion* 54 (1986): 414–15.
Rebank, James. *The Shepherd's Life: Modern Dispatches from an Ancient Landscape*. New York: Flatiron Books, 2015.
Richlin, Amy. 'Not Before Homosexuality: The Materiality of the *Cinaedus* and the Roman Law Against Love Between Men'. *Journal of the History of Sexuality* 3 (1993): 523–73.
Ricoeur, Paul. 'Erzählung, Metapher und Interpretationstheorie'. *Zeitschrift für Theologie und Kirche* 84 (1987): 232–53.
Ricoeur, Paul. *Oneself as Another*. Chicago: University of Chicago, 1995.
Riley, Gregory J. *Resurrection Reconsidered*. Minneapolis: Fortress, 1995.
Rowe, C. Kavin. *World Upside Down: Reading Acts in the Graeco-Roman Age*. New York: Oxford University Press, 2009.
Rowe, C. Kavin. 'The Grammar of Life: The Areopagus Speech and Pagan Tradition'. *New Testament Studies* 57 (2011): 31–50.
Rowe, C. Kavin. *One True Life: The Stoics and Early Christians as Rival Traditions*. New Haven: Yale University Press, 2016.
Salmond, Anne. *The Tears of Rangi: Experiments across Worlds*. Auckland: Auckland University Press, 2017.
Sanders, E. P. *Paul and Palestinian Judaism: A Comparison of Patterns of Religion*. Minneapolis: Fortress Press, 1977.
Sanders, E. P. 'The Question of Uniqueness in the Teaching of Jesus'. The Ethel M. Wood Lecture, University of London, London, 15 February 1990.
Schmidt, Carl. *Gespräche Jesu mit seinen Jüngern: Ein katholisch-apostolisches Sendschreiben des 2. Jahrhunderts*. Leipzig: J. C. Hinrich, 1919; repr. Hildesheim: Georg Olms, 1967.
Schoedel, William R. *Ignatius of Antioch*. Philadelphia: Hermeneia-Fortress, 1985.
Segal, Robert A. 'In Defense of the Comparative Method'. *Numen* 48 (2001): 339–73.
Segal, Robert A. 'Classification and Comparison in the Study of Religion: The Work of Jonathan Z. Smith'. *Journal of the American Academy of Religion* 73, no. 4 (2005): 1175–88.
Smith, Jonathan Z. *Map Is Not Territory: Studies in the History of Religions (Studies in Judaism in Late Antiquity 23)*. Leiden: Brill, 1978.
Smith, Jonathan Z. *Imagining Religion: From Babylon to Jonestown*. Chicago: University of Chicago Press, 1982.

Smith, Jonathan Z. 'What a Difference a Difference Makes'. In *To See Ourselves as Others See Us: Christians, Jews, 'Others' in Late Antiquity*, edited by Jacob Neusner and Ernest Frerichs, Chico: Scholars Press, 1985.

Smith, Jonathan Z. *Drudgery Divine: On the Comparison of Early Christianities and the Religions of Late Antiquity*. Chicago: University of Chicago Press, 1990.

Smith, Jonathan Z. 'The "End" of Comparison: Redescription and Rectification'. In *A Magic Still Dwells: Comparative Religion in the Postmodern Age*, edited by Kimberley C. Patton and Benjamin C. Ray, 237–41. Berkeley: University of California Press, 2000.

Sokolowski, Robert. *Phenomenology of the Human Person*. Cambridge: Cambridge University Press, 2008.

Stout, Jeffrey. 'Commitments and Traditions in the Study of Religious Ethics'. *Journal of Religious Ethics* 25 (1997): 23–56.

Stout, Jeffrey. *Ethics after Babel: The Languages of Morals and Their Discontents*. 2nd edn. Princeton: Princeton University Press, 2001.

Stout, Jeffrey. *Democracy as Tradition*. Princeton: Princeton University Press, 2004.

Stout, Jeffrey. *Blessed are the Organized: Grassroots Democracy in America*. Princeton: Princeton University Press, 2010.

Swancutt, Diana M. 'Paraenesis in Light of Protrepsis: Troubling the Typical Dichotomy'. In *Early Christian Paraenesis in Context* (Beihefte zur Zeitschrift für die neutestamentliche Wissenschaft), vol. 125, edited by James Starr and Troels Engberg-Pedersen, 113–53. Berlin: de Gruyter, 2004.

Taylor, Charles. *Sources of the Self: The Making of Modern Identity*. Cambridge, MA: Harvard University Press, 1989.

Taylor, Charles. 'Explanation and Practical Reason,' and Nussbaum's reply in Martha Nussbaum and Amartya Sen, eds. *The Quality of Life*. New York: Oxford University Press, 1993.

Taylor, Charles. 'Understanding the Other: A Gadamerian View of Conceptual Schemes'. In *Dilemmas and Connections*, Cambridge, MA: Belknap Press of Harvard University Press, 2011.

Thom, Johan Carl. *Cleanthes* Hymn to Zeus: *Text, Translation and Commentary*. STAC 33; Tübingen: Mohr Siebeck, 2006.

Thomassen, Einar. 'L'histoire du valentinisme et le Traité Tripartite', in *École pratique des hautes études, Section des sciences religieuses. Annuaire* 1994–1995. Tome 103, 301–3 (301).

Thomassen, Einar. 'How Valentinian Is the Gospel of Philip?' In *The Nag Hammadi Library after Fifty Years: Proceedings of the 1995 Society of Biblical Literature Commemoration*, edited by John D. Turner and Anne McGuire, 251–79. Leiden: Brill, 1997.

Thomassen, Einar. *The Spiritual Seed: The 'Church' of the Valentinians*. Leiden: Brill, 2006.

Verheyden, J. 'The Canon Muratori: A Matter of Dispute'. In *The Biblical Canons*, edited by J.-M. Auwers and H. J. de Jonge, 487–556. Leuven: Peeters, 2003.

Viveiros de Castro, Eduardo. 'Perspectival Anthropology and the Method of Controlled Equivocation'. *Tipiti: Journal for the Society for the Anthropology of Lowland South America* 2 (2004): 3–22.

Watson, Francis. *Paul and the Hermeneutics of Faith*. London: T&T Clark, 2004.

Watson, Francis. *Gospel Writing*. Grand Rapids: Eerdmans, 2013.

Watson, Francis, and Sarah Parkhouse, eds. *Connecting Gospels: Beyond the Canonical/Non-Canonical Divide*. Oxford: Oxford University Press, 2018.

Weckman, G. 'Questions of Judgment in Comparative Religious Studies'. In *Comparing Religions*, edited by Thomas A. Idinopulos, B. C. Wilson and J. C. Hanges, 17–25. Leiden: Brill, 2018.

Westerholm, Stephen. *Perspectives Old and New: The 'Lutheran' Paul and His Critics*. Grand Rapids: Eerdmans, 2004.
Williams, Bernard. *Ethics and the Limits of Philosophy*. London: Fontana Press/Collins, 1985.
Williams, Bernard. 'Life as Narrative'. *European Journal of Philosophy* 17 (2007): 305–14.
Wilson, Bryan R., ed. *Rationality*. Oxford: Blackwell, 1970.
Winston, D. *The Wisdom of Solomon* (Anchor Bible Commentary vol. 43). Garden City: Doubleday, 1979.
Witetschek, Stephan. *Thomas und Johannes – Johannes und Thomas: Das Verhältnis der Logien des Thomasevangeliums zum Johannesevangelium*. Freiburg im Breisgau: Herder, 2015.
Wittgenstein, Ludwig. *The Blue and Brown Books*. New York: Harper & Row, 1958.
Wittgenstein, Ludwig. *Culture and Value*. London: Wiley-Blackwell, 1995.
Wittgenstein, Ludwig. *Philosophical Investigations*, edited by P. M. S. Hacker and Joachim Schulte, translated by G. E. M. Anscombe, P. M. S. Hacker and Joachim Schulte. 4th rev. edn. Oxford: Wiley Blackwell, 2010.
Zuurmond, Rochus. *Novum Testamentum Aethiopice, Part III: The Gospel of Matthew*. Aethiopistische Forschungen 55, Wiesbaden: Harrassowitz, 2001.

Index of Modern Authors

Adams, Edward 58–60
Arendt, Hannah 149 n.37
Attridge, Harold 161 n.6, 162 n.10, 168 n.28

Bahktin, Mikhail 144, 149–50
Barclay, John M.G. 6, 37 n.50, 94 n.55, 136, 151 n.49
Barr, James 128
Barrett, C.K. 189 n.57
Barth, Karl 37 n.50, 137 n.36, 156
Bayer, Oswald 146 n.15, 147, 152 n.53
Berlin, Isaiah 180
Betz, Hans Dieter 122
Betz, J.R. 146 n.17, 157 n.66
Black, Max 64
Blumhofer, Christopher 138 n.38
Bockmuehl, Markus 160 n.2, 169 n.33
Boswell, John 65 n.8
Brakke, David 191 n.68
Brankaer, Johanna 170 n.34, 171 n.36–8, 172 n.39
Braudel, Fernand 18
Braun, Herbert 161 n.6,
Brooten, Bernadette J. 65 n.8
Brown, Peter 85
Bruce, F.F. 160 n.1
Buchholz, Dennis 163 n.14, 16, 164 n.17–19, 165 n.20
Butchvarov, Panayot 174 n.1–2

Carson, Donald A. 189 n.58
de Castro, Eduardo Viveiros 10 n.4, 21 n.41
Cavanaugh, William T. 38 n.54
Charles, R.H. 166 n.24
Charlesworth, J.H. 166 n.24
Cheney, Jim 25 n.7, 28, 30 n.27
Clark, Elizabeth A. 84 n.17
Cochran, Elizabeth Agnew 26 n.12
Cockerill, Gareth Lee 161 n.6

Davies, Stevan 176, 178, 192
DeConick, A.D. 177 n.15
Detienne, Marcel 93–4
Diamond, Cora 23, 34
Doniger, Wendy 180 n.27, 181, 191
den Dulk, Matthijs 120 n.147
Dunderberg, Ismo 177–81

Edwards, M.J. 184 n.45
Ehrman, Bart D. 80 n.3
Elliott, John H. 180 n.28
Ellingworth, Paul 160 n.1, 162 n.8
Engberg-Pedersen, Troels 5–6, 18 n.31, 71, 87–90, 97 n.15, 114–15, 117, 122, 128 n.6, 130, 135 n.30, 136 n.31, 141 n.44, 151 n.49
Englehardt, H. Tristan 136 n.33

Fitzgerald, John T. 1 n.1, 38 n.52, 41–2
Fürst, Alfons 23 n.3

Gadamer, Hans-Georg 5, 33, 36 n.46, 43–4, 46–8, 144, 147
Gärtner, Bertil 192 n.70
Garver, Eugene 37, 38 n.55
Gathercole, Simon 6–7, 13 n.12, 151 n.49, 155 n.62
Goodacre, Mark 191 n.65
Grässer, Erich 161 n.6
Gregory, Andrew 162 n.8
Griffith-Dickson, Gwen 144–5, 146 n.13, 15, 147–9, 151 n.49
Griffiths, Paul 35 n.42
Gruen, E.S. 10 n.5

Habermas, Jürgen 5, 47–9, 53, 152 n.52
Hadot, Pierre 112 n.111, 130–1
Hahneman, Geoffrey 163 n.12
Halperin, David M. 65 n.7
Hamann, J.G. 5, 7, 125, 143–53, 157
Hartenstein, Judith 170 n.34

Hartley, L.P. 41 n.1
Hauerwas, Stanley 34 n.40
Hays, Richard B. 154–5, 190 n.61
Hedrick, Charles H. 190 n.62
Hester, Lee 25 n.7, 28, 30 n.27
Hoffman, Volker 151
Hollis, Martin 48 n.17
Hübner, Hans 153 n.59
Hughes, Aaron 16 n.27, 20 n.36, 92
Hurtado, Larry 80–5, 92–4

James, M.R. 163 n.15
James, William 82

Kierkegaard, Søren 34 n.42, 51–2, 111, 126–8, 135, 139–40, 146 n.17, 157 n.66
King, Karen L. 84 n.17
Knight, Jonathan 166 n.23, 167 n.25–6, 168 n.30, 169 n.32
Konstan, David 38 n.52

Lane, William 161 n.7, 162 n.10
Lincoln, Bruce 109 n.87, 110 n.91, 94
Linebaugh, Jonathan A. 5–7, 125
Long, A.A. 199 n.146
Lukes, Steven 48 n.17

MacIntyre, Alasdair 5, 24–6, 28, 31, 34–5, 46–54, 69, 86–91, 111–15, 117, 124, 128 n.6, 133–7
MacMullen, Ramsay 85
Malherbe, Abraham 1 n.1, 41 n.2, 44 n.4, 56–7, 61, 87–8, 114–15, 117, 122, 136 n.34
Mannheim, Karl 76–7
Marcus, Joel 19 n.34, 188 n.56
Marshall, Bruce 138 n.39
Martin, Dale 4 n.10, 7, 58 n.44, 85 n.18, 128 n.6, 129, 132 n.20
Mason, Steve 161 n.5
McKenzie, Judith S. 164 n.17
Meeks, Wayne 57–61, 89, 99 n.26
Meier, John P. 160 n.3
Michaelis, Johann David 143–6, 148, 151
Mitchell, Margaret M. 7, 19 n.34, 38 n.44, 90, 125 n.2, 126 n.4, 127–31, 133 n.23, 134 n.27, 136–9, 141 n.44
Moffitt, David 185 n.54

Nongbri, Brent 73
Novenson, Matthew 6–7, 33 n.34, 127, 128 n.6, 135 n.29
Nussbaum, Martha 39 n.57, 111, 130

O'Connor, Dan J. 174 n.2–3
Osborn, Eric 99 n.26

Paden, W.E. 2 n.4, 15 n.24, 180 n.27
Pagels, Elaine 177 n.15
Painter, John 182, 185
Parsons, Kathryn Pyne 179 n.24
Patterson, Stephen J. 190 n.62
Patton, Kimberly C. 2 n.3, 3 n.7, 13 n.14 & 16, 15 n.24, 16 n.28, 20 n.37, 110 n.95
Perrin, Nicholas 192 n.71
Pervo, Richard I. 161 n.5
Pesce, Mauro 167 n.25
Plisch, Uwe-Karson 190 n.62
Poole, Fitz J.P. 2 n.3, 3, 13–15, 17, 56, 64, 151 n.46, 152

Ray, Benjamin C. 2 n.3, 3 n.7, 13 n.14 & 16, 15 n.24, 16 n.28, 20 n.37, 110 n.95
Rebanks, James 28 n.18
Richlin, Amy 65 n.8
Ricoeur, Paul 128, 129 n.10, 144, 147
Riley, Gregory J. 175
Rowe, C. Kavin 5–7, 14 n.19, 15, 21 n.39, 46–7, 49, 51–4, 66–72, 76–7, 80, 85–94, 95 n.1, 100 n.29, 111–24, 149

Salmond, Anne 21 n.40
Sanders, E.P. 18–19, 45, 151, 178 n.23
Sandmel, Samuel 1 n.1
Schmidt, Carl 168 n.29
Schoedel, William R. 169 n.31
Segal, Robert A. 2 n.3, 16 n.26, 180–1
Sokolowski, Robert 141
Smith, Jonathan Z. 1–4, 9, 12–13, 16 n.26, 17, 26, 33 n.35, 40 n.59, 55–6, 58–61, 63–6, 68, 72, 76–7, 81, 84, 93–4, 96, 110, 150–2, 174 n.2, 178 n.22–3, 180 n.25, 181, 191
Steiner, George 129 n.9
Stout, Jeffrey 29, 33 n.34, 38 n.54, 69, 86 n.26, 87, 88 n.32, 111, 135, 136 n.34
Swancutt, Diana 97 n.15, 99 n.26

Index of Modern Authors

Taylor, Charles 36, 39 n.57, 111, 137 n.36, 141 n.46
Thomassen, Einar 182–3, 191
Tuckett, Christopher 162 n.8

Verheyden, Joseph 163 n.12
Vollenweider, Samuel 60 n.52

Watson, Francis 7, 13 n.12, 132 n.20, 156, 190
Weckman, George 17 n.29

Westerholm, Stephen 151 n.48
White, L.M. 1 n.1, 41–2
Williams, Bernard 27–9, 45 n.6, 52, 54 n.32, 130 n.16, 136, 141
Wilson, Bryan R. 48 n.17
Winston, David 153 n.59
Witetschek, Stephan 175 n.5
Wittgenstein, Ludwig 5, 27 n.15, 39, 47, 49, 70–1, 94, 125, 128, 132–3

Zuurmond, Rochus 164 n.17–18, 165 n.21

Index of Subjects

anachronism 7, 63, 71–6

comparative religion 1–2, 6, 16, 18, 180
comparisons
    challenges 2–4, 18, 23–8, 34, 36–7, 92–3, 129–31, 159–62, 175–8
    definition/conceptualization 9, 43, 63, 66, 79, 140–1, 150–2
    examples 95–7, 98–108, 153–8, 159, 163–72, 181–91
    principles 1, 10–16, 37–40, 43–5 64, 66, 92–4, 109–10, 178–9
    types 55–61, 144, 160–2, 173–5
cosmopolitanism 116, 139

difference 3–4, 9, 13, 16, 22, 23, 28–9, 36, 40 n.59, 42, 44, 55–6, 60–1, 63, 65, 70–1, 92–3, 109–10, 150, 152, 159, 178–81
distinctiveness 4, 7, 81–4, 173, 177–9, 188, 190

encyclopaedism 88–90

friendship 6, 23–4, 35, 37–9, 144–5, 151

historical criticism 44–5
humanities 5, 33–5, 86 n.26, 93, 139–40

incommensurability 5, 15, 29, 31, 35, 47, 51–2, 69, 118–19 n.46, 122, 126–8, 132

non-compossibility 130–1, 138 n.38

parallelism 1, 56–7, 60–1
patience 35, 38–40
purity 27, 63, 71, 76

relational Hermeneutics 7, 144–9
resemblance/Relation Distinction 173–82

saliency 173, 176, 178–9
similarity 2–4, 13, 22, 27–9, 51, 55–7, 65–7, 92–3, 109–10, 126, 144, 150, 152, 159–60, 174–6, 178–81
Stoics 23, 34 n.39, 53, 60, 67–72, 83–4, 86–8, 90–1, 102, 115–16, 118–20, 129, 137–8

www.ingramcontent.com/pod-product-compliance
Lightning Source LLC
Chambersburg PA
CBHW052042300426
44117CB00012B/1939